German Workbook

by Wendy Foster

German Workbook For Dummies®

Published by: **John Wiley & Sons, Inc.,** 111 River Street, Hoboken, NJ 07030-5774, www.wiley.com

Copyright © 2023 by John Wiley & Sons, Inc., Hoboken, New Jersey

Published simultaneously in Canada

For general information on our other products and services, please contact our Customer Care Department within the U.S. at 877-762-2974, outside the U.S. at 317-572-3993, or fax 317-572-4002. For technical support, please visit https://hub.wiley.com/community/support/dummies.

Wiley publishes in a variety of print and electronic formats and by print-on-demand. Some material included with standard print versions of this book may not be included in e-books or in print-on-demand. If this book refers to media such as a CD or DVD that is not included in the version you purchased, you may download this material at http://booksupport.wiley.com. For more information about Wiley products, visit www.wiley.com.

ISBN: 978-1-119-98667-6 (pbk); 978-1-119-98668-3 (ebk); 978-1-119-98669-0 (ebk)

SKY10065298_011824

Contents at a Glance

Table of Contents

Introduction

You may have had *German Workbook For Dummies* delivered to your doorstep, or you were opening birthday presents, and . . . surprise! No matter how you came across this book, acquiring more German helps you in a myriad of ways. You cannot help noticing that globalization is taking place at an ever-increasing pace. German is spoken by more members of the European Union than any other language, and Germany plays a leading economic role in the European Union. You may be a businessperson, adventurer, or avid language learner; it doesn't matter. At some point in your life, you're bound to come in contact with German. So get a head start and be ready to communicate, travel, and — most of all — have some fun **auf Deutsch** (*in German*).

Using this book builds your confidence in no time. Well, okay, you do need some free hours here and there, but the time you do spend using this book will pay off down the road. Consider what you can gain from *German Workbook For Dummies* as the equivalent of having invested a huge chunk of money, time, and effort at the local health club to become super-fit for a trek across the Alps. The obvious difference is that you have to plunk out only a small chunk of change, plus some time and effort, to reap personal and professional gain.

About This Book

German Workbook For Dummies is your key to success in becoming confident using German. In this book, you get basic skills, straight talk, the nitty-gritty, and enough detail to see you successfully through any major and minor roadblocks to communicating in German.

You'll find this book very user-friendly because you can go through it in any order you choose, zeroing in on your priorities. You can skim or, better, skip the grammar you don't need. Use the book to find answers to specific questions you may have on a topic that comes up while you're acquiring useful language. All the chapters have ample practice exercises following the grammar explanations so you can check whether you've grasped the material. Flip to the end of the chapter, and you'll find the answer key for the exercises, with explanations pertinent to problematic usage. Without even realizing it, you'll find your German vocabulary expanding as you cruise through the book. The example sentences and exercises use practical, everyday German that let you flex your vocabulary muscles as you complete the tasks. Most important, as you go through this book, **Viel Spaß!** (*Have a lot of fun!*)

Conventions Used in This Book

To make your progress go as smoothly as possible, I use some conventions in this book that can help you spot essential elements in the text and exercises:

>> I boldface the essential elements in verb tables, which may be information such as verb endings or irregular conjugations. Elsewhere, I boldface German words and example sentences.

>> I italicize English translations that accompany German words and sentences. I also italicize English terms that I immediately follow with a definition.

>> The answer key at the end of each chapter has not only the solutions to the practice exercises (in bold), but also italicized English translations. Answers have explanations when I feel it's important to clarify why the answer given is the correct one.

>> Before each group of practice exercises, I provide an example exercise in Q&A format to show you how to complete the task. The example (Q.) is followed by the answer (A.) and an explanation for that answer, as needed.

Foolish Assumptions

In writing *German Workbook For Dummies*, I made the following assumptions about you, dear reader:

>> Your goal is to build your knowledge of German so that you feel comfortable with communicating in the language. (Alternatively, you want to dream in German.)

>> You're willing to jump into German at the deep end and start swimming, even if you need some water wings at first. Or perhaps you're already acquainted with some basics of German grammar and want to get going full steam ahead.

>> You don't want to be burdened by long-winded explanations of unnecessary grammatical terms; neither do you care to hold a scholarly discussion in German about Goethe's *Faust*. You just want to you express yourself in clear and reasonably accurate German.

>> You're enthusiastic about having some fun while honing your German skills because the last thing you want from this book is to be reminded of boring school days, when success meant figuring out how to (a) sleep and learn at the same time, (b) skip class and not be missed, and/or (c) wrap the teacher around your little finger so that no matter what you did, you still got good grades.

If any of these statements describes you, you're ready to get started using this book. **Willkommen!** *(Welcome!)*

How This Book Is Organized

This book is divided into six parts. The first four parts are divided into several chapters each, containing explanations, tables, and exercises. In the last two parts, you find practical learning tips and the appendix with charts, tables, and a mini dictionary. Here's the preview.

Part 1: The Basic Building Blocks of German

In this part, you find out how to introduce yourself and start a simple conversation. You acquaint yourself with the world of nouns and verbs, numbers and dates, word order and more fundamentals. See the mysteries of gender and case unveiled. Part 1 also contains a practical guide to increasing your word power exponentially. You become familiar with techniques that help you retrieve newly acquired vocabulary and expressions.

Part 2: Focusing on the Present

Here you get the tools needed to construct sentences in the present tense. I give you ample practice combining nouns and pronouns with verbs. I include info on asking and answering questions, as well as agreeing and disagreeing. This part also shows you the seven modal verbs that help you be polite, ask for help, and talk about what you can do, want to do, would like to do, should do, or must do.

Part 3: Adding Flair to Your Conversations

You want to sound like a native, right? This part helps you find out how to express yourself using two-part verbs and reflexive verbs. It also delves into the finer points of expressing yourself using adjectives of description. The chapters here show you how to put adjectives and adverbs to work for you by making comparisons, show how to connect shorter ideas with conjunctions, and touch on using prepositions.

Part 4: Talking about the Past and the Future

In this part, you practice expressing yourself using past and future verbs. You become familiar with the difference between the conversational past and the simple (narrative) past, and you see how to choose the correct verb form to express yourself in the future.

Part 5: The Part of Tens

Here you find my top ten easy and useful tips for optimizing your German (in other words, how to make your German the best it can be). I close things out with a list of pitfalls to avoid.

Part 6: Appendixes

The three appendixes provide an assortment of references to help you communicate success-fully in German. The first appendix includes verb tables for conjugating verbs. The second and third appendixes are the mini-dictionaries, which allow you to find the meaning of a German word you don't understand or the German equivalent of an English word.

Icons Used in This Book

Consider these icons to be key points as you take the journey through this book. You find them in the margins throughout. The icons include the following:

Helpful hints like these would've made it a whole lot easier for me to feel more comfortable using German when I was first living in Bavaria, stumbling along in my shaky German.

The Warning icon points out hidden dangers you may encounter as you journey through the deep forest of tangled words, slippery sentence structure, and the like.

This icon alerts you to key information that's worth revisiting. You want to stash this info in your mind because you'll end up using it again and again.

Pay attention to these key points. By noticing similarities and differences between German and English, you see patterns that show you how to assemble German into meaningful statements.

This icon marks the core learning tool in this book: a set of exercises designed for you to check your progress. Grab a pencil and get started.

Beyond the Book

In addition to what you're reading right now, this book comes with a free, access-anywhere Cheat Sheet containing some must-have basic vocabulary and an overview of German gram-mar. To get this Cheat Sheet, simply go to www.dummies.com and type **German Workbook For Dummies Cheat Sheet** in the search box.

1

The Basic Building Blocks of German

IN THIS PART . . .

Meet and greet people

Start a conversation

Get introduced to basic grammar principles

Deal with numbers

Build vocabulary efficiently

Use bilingual dictionaries effectively

Chapter **1**

Laying the Foundations of German

When you set out to learn another language, you want to find out how to get along in everyday situations, such as greeting people in a socially acceptable manner. In other words, if there's a difference between addressing someone you know and a complete stranger, you'd want to know about it. You also want to be able to feel confident in understanding and using some key components, such as numbers, time, dates, and whatnot.

In this chapter, I get you started on the crucial building blocks of German. You get going on some basic communication skills, such as finding out how to say hello in a formal manner and in a casual way. Along with numbers, I provide you days of the week, months of the year, and seasons, all of which will enable you to strike up a conversation in a German-speaking environment. **Los geht's!** (*Let's get started!*)

Saying Hello and Goodbye

In German-speaking countries, the cultural norm is that adults often greet one another with a handshake. In a formal situation or when you're introduced to someone, you're expected to shake hands. However, in a (post) COVID world, you might need to observe the body language of those around you before extending your hand. Also, know that in Europe, people tend to stand closer together than they do in English-speaking cultures.

Table 1-1   Saying Hello and Goodbye

Expression	Usage	English
Guten Morgen	standard/formal	*Good morning*
Guten Tag	standard/formal	*Good day/Hello*
Hallo/Hi	familiar (with friends)	*Hello/Hi*
Guten Abend	standard/formal	*Good evening*
Auf Wiedersehen	standard/formal	*Goodbye*
Tschüss/Ciao	familiar (with friends)	*Bye/Bye*
Gute Nacht	standard/formal	*Good night (at bedtime)*
Bis bald/Bis dann	familiar (with friends)	*See you soon/'Til then*
Mach's gut	familiar (with friends)	*Take care*

Table 1-1 shows German expressions for saying hello and goodbye, notes on usage, and the English equivalents. In this table, I include the term *standard* together with *formal* to express both everyday and formal situations, in contrast to *familiar* situations.

Some regional expressions are

>> **Grüß Gott,** a standard greeting in southern Germany and Austria, meaning *Good day* or *Hello*. **Grüß dich** is the familiar regional counterpart, similar to *Hi* or *Hi there*.

>> **Grüezi,** a standard greeting in Switzerland, as a way of saying *Good day* or *Hello*.

>> **Servus,** a familiar way to say both *Hi* and *Bye* in southern Germany and Austria.

TIP

Addressing people in a familiar tone when it isn't appropriate can turn German speakers off — fast. Language and culture are bonded with superglue, so avoid pasting your culture onto the German-speaking world. You show respect for others by observing their way of life.

PRACTICE

In the following exercise, you find yourself in some German-speaking situations. Write the appropriate German response for the situation. The example shows you how to proceed. You'll find the solutions to the exercises in the answer key at the end of every chapter.

Q. The shopkeeper in a store greets you with **Guten Tag**. Your response is

_____

A. Guten Tag.

1   You greet your Austrian neighbors with the customary expression of that region. You say _____.

2   You're staying with a host family in Germany. Before going to your room for the night, you say _____.

3   The next morning, you greet your host family with _____.

4. You say goodbye to your German friends like this: (more than one option)
   _____.

5. With the same German friends, you want to add something like *See you then*, so you say
   _____.

6. When you depart your hotel, you say _____.

Introducing yourself and others

The next step after saying **Guten Tag** *(good day/hello)* is introducing yourself. Depending on the situation, you may want to shake hands as you introduce yourself. Look at the following exchange between **Herr Hahn** *(Mr. Hahn)* and **Frau Maier** *(Ms. Maier)* at an international conference. They introduce themselves with full names, an indication of a formal situation.

> **Guten Tag. Ich heiße Gisela Maier.** *(Hello. My name is Gisela Maier.)* **Und Sie, wie heißen Sie?** *(And you, what is your name?)*
>
> **Guten Tag. Ich heiße Josef Hahn.** *(Hello. My name is Josef Hahn.)*
>
> **Freut mich.** *(Nice to meet you.)*
>
> **Mich auch.** *(Nice to meet you too.)*

To introduce another colleague (or friend or partner), you may start with

> **Das ist . . .** *(This is . . .)*

and add the person's name.

After initial introductions, what's next? It's **Wie geht es Ihnen?** *(How are you?)*, of course. The following day of the conference, the same two colleagues, Herr Hahn and Frau Maier, greet each other at the breakfast buffet. They may or may not address each other with first names or Herr/Frau with last names, depending on the company culture and social norms in place. Look at their conversation:

> **Guten Morgen, Gisela (Frau Maier). Wie geht es Ihnen?** *(Good morning, Gisela [Frau Maier]. How are you?)*
>
> **Guten Morgen, Josef (Herr Hahn). Gut, danke. Und Ihnen?** *(Good morning, Josef [Herr Hahn]. Fine, thanks. And you?)*
>
> **Danke, sehr gut/ganz gut.** *(Thanks, I'm very/really good.)*

PRACTICE

In this exercise, write the German equivalent to the English prompt in the space provided. Check out the previous sections for help. The practice exercise gets you on track. You may use your own name(s) in place of the names shown in parentheses. As usual, you find the solutions to the exercises in the answer key at the end of the chapter.

Q. Good evening, (Maria). _____

A. **Guten Abend, (Sabina).**

(7) Nice to meet you. _____

(8) Nice to meet you too. _____

(9) This is my colleague (*mein Kollege [male]* (Tobias)/*meine Kollegin [female]*(Renate). _____

(10) How are you, (Helena)? _____

(11) Thanks, I'm very good. _____

(12) Good morning. My name is (Hartmut Schmidt). _____

(13) And you? _____

Keeping the conversational ball rolling

After initial introductions and pleasantries, you want to keep the lines of communication open. Asking questions is a terrific way to give yourself some listening practice. You may not understand all the answers, so try **Wie bitte?** (*Sorry, what?*) to politely nudge the other person to repeat what they just said. Or if that attempt fails, try **Langsamer, bitte.** (*More slowly, please.*) The following phrases help you keep the conversation flowing:

>> **Woher kommen Sie?** (*Where are you from?*)

>> **Ich komme aus (Hamburg).** (*I'm from [Hamburg].*)

>> **Und Sie?** (*And you?*)

>> **Wo wohnen Sie?** (*Where do you live?*)

>> **Ich wohne in (Sigmaringen).** (*I live in [Sigmaringen].*)

>> **Und Sie?** (*And you?*)

>> **Wie finden Sie das Hotel/das Essen/Berlin/die Konferenz?**(*What do you think of the hotel/ the food/Berlin/the conference?*)

>> **Exzellent/hervorragend/sehr gut/nicht sehr gut/es geht.** (*Excellent/outstanding/very good/not very good/so, so.*)

A practically universal topic is, of course, **das Wetter** (*the weather*). You can ask: **Wie ist das Wetter?** (*What's the weather like?*) Some replies you may hear are

>> **Es ist schön/sonnig/windig/wolkig/neblig.** (*It's beautiful/sunny/windy/cloudy/foggy.*)

>> **Es ist kalt/kühl/warm/heiß.** (*It's cold/cool/warm/hot.*)

>> **Es regnet/es schneit.** (*It's raining/it's snowing.*) (Literally: *it rains/it snows.*)

To get a forecast, you can add a future time period such as **morgen/heute Abend/am Wochenende** (*tomorrow/this evening/on the weekend*) to your question, as in this example: **Wie ist das Wetter morgen?** (*What's the weather going to be like tomorrow?*) You may hear the following responses:

>> **Schön, aber kühl.** (*Beautiful, but cool.*)

>> **Morgen ist es sonnig und sehr warm.** (*Tomorrow, it's going to be sunny and very warm.*)

>> **Morgen regnet es.** (*Tomorrow, it's going to rain.*)(Literally: *Tomorrow, it rains.*)

PRACTICE

Let's see whether you can respond in German to someone who is speaking to you. This exercise has elements from all the previous sections in this chapter. For some exercises, in which several responses are appropriate, you may use your own imagination. Check out the previous sections for help.

Q. Wie heißen Sie?_____

A. Ich heiße (Jonathan Summer).

14 Gute Nacht. _____

15 Wo wohnen Sie? _____

16 Wie geht es Ihnen? _____

17 Wie ist das Wetter in Kanada im Winter (*in the winter*)? _____

18 Woher kommen Sie? _____

19 Auf Wiedersehen. _____

20 Wie ist das Wetter? _____

21 Grüß Gott (*in southern Germany and Austria*) _____

22 Freut mich. _____

23 Wie finden Sie Ihr Deutsch (*your German*)? _____

Figuring Out How Subject Pronouns Fit with Verbs

Before you understand how to form complete sentences, you need a firm grasp of the subject pronouns. These pronouns stand in for long-winded nouns and pop up everywhere in any language, and they play a key role in helping you get your verbs in shape. In this book, you always see them in tables that conjugate verbs, so get them down pat before you start work on the verbs that accompany them.

You use subject pronouns — **ich** (*I*), **du** (*you*), **er** (*he*), **sie** (*she*), **es** (*it*), and so on — to express who or what is carrying out the action or idea of the verb. Pronouns refer to the noun without naming it, which means that they can serve as placeholders so you don't have to sound redundant by repeating the noun. (For more discussion on pronouns, check out chapters 2 and 3.) To use subject pronouns, you need to know which *person* (first, second, or third) and *number* (singular or plural) the pronoun represents, as with **ich** (*I*) = first person, singular. To connect the correct subject pronoun to a verb, you need to know which conjugated verb form to use.

Table 1-2 shows you the breakdown of subject pronouns in German and English. Notice that singular is on the left, plural is on the right, and the pronoun **Sie** (*you*) is at the bottom. I use the same setup throughout the verb tables in this book.

Table 1-2   Subject Pronouns

Person	Singular	Plural
First	**ich** (*I*)	**wir** (*we*)
Second (familiar)	**du** (*you*)	**ihr** (*you*)
Third	**er** (*he, it*)	**sie** (*they*)
	sie (*she, it*)	
	es (*it*)	
Second (formal)	**Sie** (*you*, both singular and plural)	

Think of the subject pronouns as *persona* because they *impersonate* the subject that they represent. You characterize them by their grammatical *person* (based on who's speaking and listening), *number* (singular or plural), and sometimes *formality* (which I discuss in the next section). Here's a closer look at the three persons:

>> **First person:** The one(s) speaking: **ich** (*I*) or **wir** (*we*).

>> **Second person:** The one(s) spoken *to*: **du, ihr, Sie**. All three mean *you* in English; **du** is the singular, familiar form, which you'd use with a friend; **ihr** is the plural, familiar form, which you'd use with a group of friends; and **Sie** is the formal form, whether singular or plural, which you'd use with the chancellor of Germany and everyone else you're not on a first-name basis with.

   Note: "*Y'all*" as used in the American South is the equivalent of **ihr**.

>> **Third person:** Who or what is spoken *about*: **er** (*he, it*), **sie** (*she, it*), or **es** (*it*); **sie** (*they*). If you're talking about an inanimate object (*it*), the choice of **er, sie,** or **es** depends on the gender of the noun; see Chapter 2 for details.

Making sure "you" dress properly for the occasion: The formality of du/ihr and Sie

Ideally, if you're hobnobbing with some business moguls, the mayor, and a throng of socialites at the charity benefit of the year, you're on your best behavior. On the other hand, most people do and say whatever they feel like while hanging out with their buddies at a backyard barbecue on a Saturday afternoon. That formality/informality factor is what you need to keep in mind when you address people in German, because there are three ways to say *you*: **du, ihr**, and **Sie**.

Use **Sie**, which is always capitalized, to speak to one or more people with whom you have a more distant, formal relationship. It's appropriate

>> When you aren't sure whether **du/ihr** or **Sie** is correct

>> When you're not yet on a first-name basis with someone (using Herr Kuhnagel or Frau Zitzelsberger instead of Sigmund or Hildegard, for example)

>> When you're talking to adults you don't know well

>> In business or at your place of work

>> In public situations to a person in uniform (police officer, airport official, and other such people)

Use **du** when you talk to one person (or animal) in an informal way, and use **ihr**, the plural version of **du**, to address more than one person (or animal) informally. An informal pronoun is appropriate

>> For addressing children and teens younger than 16 or so

>> For talking to a close friend or relative

>> When a German speaker invites you to use **du**

>> When you talk to pets

You may hear **du** among close working colleagues, students, members of a sports team, or people hiking in the mountains, but unless someone asks you, **"Wollen wir uns dutzen?"** *(Shall we say du to each other?)*, try to stick with **Sie**.

TIP

Be careful with recent crossover scenarios at the workplace: people addressing one another with **Sie** although they use first names: **Heinz, haben Sie meine E-mail gelesen?** *(Heinz, have you read my e-mail?)*. If you use last names (Frau Dinkelhuber and Herr Sternhagel), using **Sie** is best.

Distinguishing among sie, sie, and Sie

I have a threesome tangle to help you unravel, and then you'll be on your way to success with subject pronouns. Look back at Table 1-2, and you'll find the Three Musketeers — **sie** *(she)*, **sie** *(they)*, and **Sie** *(you)* — lurking in their separate boxes. Seeing them in what looks like random places may seem to be daunting, but a few clues can help you sort them out.

First, you know the meanings by their context. The conjugated verb and capitalization also help reveal the meaning. Here's what to watch out for:

>> **Conjugation:** When **sie** means *she*, its verb form is distinct; in the present tense, the conjugated verb usually ends in **-t**. When **sie/Sie** means *they* or *you*, the present-tense verb ends in **-en**.

>> **Capitalization:** The *they* and *you* forms of **sie/Sie** have identical conjugations, but only the *you* version, which is formal, is capitalized.

The following examples show how you figure out which one to use when:

>> **Wo wohnt sie?** *(Where does she live?)* The verb is in third-person singular form.

>> **Wo wohnen sie?** *(Where do they live?)* The verb is in third-person plural form, and **sie** isn't capitalized.

>> **Wo wohnen Sie?** *(Where do you live?)* The verb is in second-person plural form (which is identical to the third-person plural form), and **Sie** is capitalized.

PRACTICE

In the following situations, decide which subject pronoun you would use (**ich, du, er, sie, es, wir, ihr, sie,** or **Sie**), and write it in the space provided. Refer to Table 1-2 on subject pronouns.

Q. Someone talking about his father uses _____

A. er

24 Friends talking to each other use (plural form) _____.

25 You're talking about your friends, so you use _____.

26 An adult meeting another adult for the first time uses _____.

27 When you talk about yourself, you use _____.

28 An adult talking to three children ages 8, 11, and 14 uses _____.

29 You're talking to an animal, so you use _____.

30 A man talking about his wife uses _____.

31 When you talk about your cousin and yourself, you use _____.

32 You're talking about your colleagues, so you use _____.

33 A teenage customer talking to a sales assistant uses _____.

34 When you talk to someone on a ski lift in Switzerland, you use _____.

35 A military comrade talking to another comrade uses _____.

Using gender-neutral pronouns

In some German-speaking academic and progressive circles, gender-neutral pronouns are being used among intersex, trans and nonbinary individuals. For the English *they,* some German speakers use **they** as well as **dey**. The pronoun **xier** has also grown in popularity. A replacement for **er/sie** (*he/she*) is **z/zet.**

Doing the Numbers

In German-speaking countries, I love seeing **die Bedienung** (*the server*) in street cafés walking around with a bulging black leather change purse either tucked in the back of the pants (the male version) or attached at the waist in front, neatly camouflaged under a starched white apron (the female version). When you say **die Rechnung, bitte** or its more informal version, **Zahlen, bitte** (*the check, please*), they have a crafty way of whipping it out of hiding and opening it wide, ready for action. The next part is my favorite: watching the seasoned **Kellner/Kellnerin** (*waiter/waitress*) take a quick look, add up the tab without pen and paper, and blurt out, **"Das macht siebenundvierzig Euro"** (*That'll be forty-seven euros*). That's the moment of reckoning: How good are you at understanding numbers in German?

Forming and using German **Zahlen** (*numbers*) isn't difficult. In fact, barring a few exceptions — notably the one I call the cart before the horse — most numbers follow a logical pattern. Feeling confident around numbers without any hesitation means you're ready to feed the waiter's portable cash wallet. You can likewise understand which **Bahnsteig** (*track*) the train is leaving from (and at what time) and jump on the correct train when there's been a last-minute track change. This section covers cardinal and ordinal numbers as well as a few other number situations so you can use numbers in German without any problems.

Counting off with cardinal numbers

Cardinal numbers have nothing to do with religious numbers colored red or a songbird that can sing numbers. These numbers are just plain, unadulterated numbers like 25, 654, or 300,000. In this section, you get a list of cardinal numbers, details on differences, and practice using these numbers.

Table 1-3 shows numbers 1–29. Notice a couple of points about numbers 21 and up:

>> They're written as one word: **einundzwanzig** (21), **zweiundzwanzig** (22).

>> They follow the cart-before-the-horse rule — that is, you say the ones digit before the tens digit, linking the words with **und**: for example, **vierundzwanzig** (*24*; Literally: *four and twenty*). Does that remind you of the "four and twenty blackbirds" from the nursery rhyme "Sing a Song of Sixpence"?

Table 1-4 shows representative numbers spanning 30–999. Double-digit numbers follow the same pattern as 20–29 do in Table 1-3: **einunddreißig** (31; literally: *one and thirty*), **zweiund-dreißig** (32; literally: *two and thirty*), and the like. Numbers with more digits likewise flip the ones and tens digits: You'd read 384, for example, as **dreihundertvierundachtzig,** which literally means *three hundred four and eighty.*

Table 1-3 Cardinal Numbers 1–29

Numbers 0–9	Numbers 10–19	Numbers 20–29
0 **null**	10 **zehn**	20 **zwanzig**
1 **eins**	11 **elf**	21 **einundzwanzig**
2 **zwei**	12 **zwölf**	22 **zweiundzwanzig**
3 **drei**	13 **dreizehn**	23 **dreiundzwanzig**
4 **vier**	14 **vierzehn**	24 **vierundzwanzig**
5 **fünf**	15 **fünfzehn**	25 **fünfundzwanzig**
6 **sechs**	16 **sechzehn**	26 **sechsundzwanzig**
7 **sieben**	17 **siebzehn**	27 **siebenundzwanzig**
8 **acht**	18 **achtzehn**	28 **achtundzwanzig**
9 **neun**	19 **neunzehn**	29 **neunundzwanzig**

Table 1-4 Cardinal Numbers 30–999

Numbers 30–100	Numbers 101–114	Numbers 220–999
30 **dreißig**	101 **hunderteins**	220 **zweihundertzwanzig**
40 **vierzig**	102 **hundertzwei**	348 **dreihundertachtundvierzig**
50 **fünfzig**	103 **hundertdrei**	452 **vierhundertzweiundfünfzig**
60 **sechzig**	104 **hundertvier**	573 **fünfhundertdreiundsiebzig**
70 **siebzig**	111 **hundertelf**	641 **sechshunderteinundvierzig**
80 **achtzig**	112 **hundertzwölf**	767 **siebenhundertsiebnundsechzig**
90 **neunzig**	113 **hundertdreizehn**	850 **achthundertfünfzig**
100 **hundert**	114 **hundertvierzehn**	999 **neunhundertneunundneunzig**

Especially in spoken German, you can use **einhundert** (*one hundred*) instead of **hundert** (*hundred*) to make the number clearer to the listener. Also, when people quote numbers over the phone, you might hear **"zwo"** instead of **"zwei."** This practice serves to clearly distinguish **"zwei"** from **"drei"** and thus avoids mishearing certain numbers.

In the German-speaking world, as well as in many other parts of the world, you write the number 7 with a small horizontal line through the downward stroke. Why? It's simply a way to distinguish between 7 and 1.

For numbers higher than 999, look at Table 1-5. Notice that the decimal point in German numbers represents the comma in English.

In English, you use a comma to indicate thousands and a period to show decimals. German (and many other languages) does the reverse: It uses a *period* (**Punkt**) for indicating thousands, and the *comma* (**Komma**) works as a decimal point.

Table 1-5   Numbers over 999

English Numerals	German Numerals	Numbers Written in German
1,000	**1.000**	**tausend or ein tausend**
1,000,000	**1.000.000**	**Million or eine Million**
1,650,000	**1.650.000**	**eine Million sechshundertfünfzigtausend**
2,000,000	**2.000.000**	**zwei Millionen**
1,000,000,000	**1.000.000.000**	**eine Milliarde**
2,000,000,000	**2.000.000.000**	**zwei Milliarden**

PRACTICE

You're hearing numbers on the phone, and you have to write them down. Write each number in numerical form the German way, remembering that the comma and decimal point are switched in German.

Q. zweiundneunzig _____

A. 92

(36) siebenundvierzig _____

(37) achthundertdreiundsiebzig _____

(38) eintausenddreihunderteinundsiebzig _____

(39) vierzehn Komma fünf _____

(40) zwanzigtausendzweihundertneunundsechzig _____

(41) siebzehntausendneunhundertachtunddreißig _____

(42) vierundachtzigtausendzweihundertsieben _____

Getting in line with ordinal numbers

Ordinal numbers are the kinds of numbers that show what order things come in. (Was that a *duh* moment for you?) You need ordinal numbers when you're talking about **das Datum** (*the date*), **die Feiertage** (*the holidays*), **die Stockwerke in einem Hotel** (*the floors in a hotel*), and stuff like that.

The general rule for forming ordinal numbers is to add **-te** to the numbers 1 through 19 and then **-ste** to the numbers 20 and above, as in this example: **Der dritte Oktober ist der Tag der Deutschen Einheit** (*The third of October is German Unity Day*).

This rule has three exceptions: **erste** (*first*); **dritte** (*third*); and **siebte** (*seventh*). Here's an example: **Reinhold Messner war der erste Mensch, der Mount Everest ohne Sauerstoffmaske bestieg.** (*Reinhold Messner was the first person to climb Mount Everest without an oxygen mask.*)

Table 1-6   Ordinal Numbers

Ordinals as Numerals	Ordinals as Words	On the (First . . .)
1st	**der erste** (*the first*)	**am ersten** (*on the first*)
2nd	**der zweite** (*the second*)	**am zweiten** (*on the second*)
3rd	**der dritte** (*the third*)	**am dritten** (*on the third*)
4th	**der vierte** (*the fourth*)	**am vierten** (*on the fourth*)
5th	**der fünfte** (*the fifth*)	**am fünften** (*on the fifth*)
6th	**der sechste** (*the sixth*)	**am sechsten** (*on the sixth*)
7th	**der siebte** (*the seventh*)	**am siebten** (*on the seventh*)
18th	**der achtzehnte** (*the eighteenth*)	**am achtzehnten** (*on the eighteenth*)
22nd	**der zweiundzwanzigste** (*the twenty-second*)	**am zweiundzwanzigsten** (*on the twenty-second*)

Here are two other adjectives you need to know when putting things in order: **letzte** (*last*) and **nächste** (*next*). You can use them to refer to a sequence of numbers, people, things, or the like:

>> **Könnten Sie bitte die letzte Nummer wiederholen?** (*Could you repeat the last number, please?*)

>> **Wann fährt der nächste Zug nach Bremen?** (*When does the next train leave for Bremen?*)

To write dates as numerals, write the digit followed by a period: **Der 1. Mai ist ein Feiertag in Deutschland** (*May 1 is a holiday in Germany*). If you say the same sentence, it's **Der erste Mai ist ein Feiertag in Deutschland**.

Look at the examples of ordinal numbers in Table 1-6. The first column shows the ordinal numbers as digits, the second column shows the same ordinal numbers as words, and the third column shows how to say *on the* (*fifth floor, sixth of December*, and so on).

When you combine an ordinal number with a noun, it conforms to the gender of the noun (**der**=masculine/**die**=feminine/**das**=neuter), as in the examples: **der siebte Stock** (*the seventh floor*), **die zweite Woche** (*the second week*), or **das erste Mal** (*the first time*). (For more info on gender, check out Chapter 3.)

Was Ist das Datum?: Expressing Dates

To make sure you know how to express dates correctly, you need to know how to correctly use **die Tage der Woche** (*the days of the week*), **die Jahreszeiten** (*the seasons*), and **die Monate** (*the months*). That way, you can clearly and correctly ask and answer **Was ist das Datum?** (*What is the date?*).

All weekdays in German are masculine. This becomes important when they are combined with an adjective (For more info on forming sentences with adjectives, go to Chapter 10). Normally, however, they are used without an article just as in English.

Die Tage der Woche (*the days of the week*), their short forms used in calendars, and some pertinent notes are as follows:

>> **Montag (Mo)** (*Monday*)

>> **Dienstag (Di)** (*Tuesday*)

>> **Mittwoch (Mi)** (*Wednesday*)

>> **Donnerstag (Do)** (*Thursday*)

>> **Freitag (Fr)** (*Friday*)

>> **Samstag (Sa)** (*Saturday;* used in most of Germany, as well as Austria and German-speaking Switzerland) or **Sonnabend (Sa)** (*Saturday;* used in eastern and northern Germany)

>> **Sonntag (So)** (*Sunday*)

In German–speaking countries, calendars begin with **Montag**.

Sometimes, you want to be more casual in your references to days and use words like *tomorrow* and *this morning* rather than the specific name of the day. The following list helps you refer to specific days without saying them by name:

>> **heute** (today)

>> **gestern** (yesterday)

>> **vorgestern** (the day before yesterday)

>> **morgen** (tomorrow)

>> **übermorgen** (the day after tomorrow)

When you want to talk about a slice of the day, such as *morning* or *afternoon*, you have several options, as you see in the following list:

>> **der Morgen** (*morning* [includes all the morning hours])

>> **der Vormittag** (*morning* [starting from around 9 a.m. to noon])

>> **der Mittag** (*midday* [around noon])

>> **der Nachmittag** (*afternoon*)

>> **der Abend** (*evening*)

>> **die Nacht** (*night*)

To be more specific in talking about a part of a specific day, you can combine words from the previous two lists like this:

>> **heute Morgen** *(this morning)* (Literally: today in the morning)

>> **morgen Nachmittag** *(tomorrow afternoon)*

>> **gestern Abend** *(yesterday evening/last night)*

You also need to have a firm grasp of the German terms for seasons and months because they're major parts of dates. (The last thing you want to do is invite someone to your July barbecue and tell them that it's in the winter.) The following outlines **die Jahreszeiten** *(the seasons)*:

>> **der Frühling** or **das Frühjahr** *(the spring)*; you can use either term interchangeably in German-speaking regions

>> **der Sommer** *(the summer)*

>> **der Herbst** *(the autumn)*

>> **der Winter** *(the winter)*

The following list lays out **die Monate** *(the months)* of the year:

>> **Januar** *(January)* or **Jenner** *(January;* often used in Austria)

>> **Februar** *(February)*

>> **März** *(March)*

>> **April** *(April)*

>> **Mai** *(May)*

>> **Juni** *(June;* some German speakers say **Juno** to distinguish it, acoustically speaking, from **Juli**)

>> **Juli** *(July;* some German speakers pronounce it as *"you lie"* instead of *"you lee"* to avoid confusion with *Juni*)

>> **August** *(August)*

>> **September** *(September)*

>> **Oktober** *(October)*

>> **November** *(November)*

>> **Dezember** *(December)*

Dates are written in day–month–year order in German (and in the other European languages as well). You need the periods in dates in German, just as you need to write the date in English with a slash between the month, day, and year.

PRACTICE

Fill in the missing information in the following exercise. For help, refer to the previous lists of German numbers and expressions for days and dates. You find some hints in parentheses. The first example gets you started.

Q. Der Winter beginnt im _____.

A. Der Winter beginnt im Dezember. (*Winter begins in December.*)

43 Heute ist Freitag. Morgen ist _____.

44 Die Blätter (*leaves*) fallen im_____.

45 April, _____, Juni, _____. (Complete the sequence.)

46 Der erste Januar ist ein_____ in vielen Ländern. (*holiday* is the missing word.)

47 Morgen ist der erste Oktober. Was ist heute? _____. (Write the date in words.)

48 Vorgestern war (*was*) Sonntag. Was ist heute? _____.

49 Der Tag der Deutschen Einheit (*German Unity Day*) is am _____. (*October 3rd*) Write the date in words.)

50 Februar hat _____ Tage. (Write the number as a word.) (except in leap years, of course)

51 Im deutschen Kalender, der erste Tag der Woche ist _____.

52 Dienstag, _____ Donnerstag _____. (Complete the sequence.)

53 Der letzte Tag im Jahr ist der _____. (Write the date in words.)

54 Heute ist der siebte August. Morgen ist _____.

55 Wie viele (*How many*) Monate haben einunddreißig Tage? _____.

56 In den USA, "Labor Day" ist am _____ im _____. (*first Monday [in] September*)

On the Clock: Expressing Time

You're in **Interlaken (in der Schweiz)** (*Interlaken, Switzerland*), and you want to know what time it is. You have four choices: Look at your **Handy** (*cellphone*); look at the nearest clock tower (most are absolutely stunning; many have four clocks, one for each side) to find out how accurate the Swiss are in keeping time (very!); buy a Rolex for 1,399 Swiss francs (no euros in

Switzerland); or practice understanding German clock time by asking someone on the street, **Wie viel Uhr ist es?** *(What time is it?).* You're just about guaranteed to hear the precise time.

In conversational German, you use the system comparable to English, in which **nach** *(past)* refers to times past the hour up until half past. **Vor** *(to)* refers to the times from half past to the next hour.

REMEMBER

In English, you use *half* (German **halb**) to refer to half past the hour. In German, however, you name the next hour. **Halb acht** (Literally: *Half eight*) means *half past seven*, or 7:30.(Think of it as *half of the way to eight.*)

For official time, such as train or plane schedules (and frequently in everyday German), you use the 24-hour system, reading the numbers as you'd read a digital clock. In other words, for 1 p.m. and later, you add 12; 2 p.m. + 12, therefore, is **14 Uhr: Unser Zug fährt um 14.45** (pronounced **vierzehn Uhr fünfundvierzig**) *(Our train leaves at 2:45 p.m.).* Table 1-7 shows the German time expressions and their English equivalents.

The numerical method of telling time may be the easiest. German traditionally uses a period where English uses a colon. Note that when you read the time, you say **Uhr** *(o'clock)* where the period appears. Alternatively, you can leave it out, just as you can leave out the o'clock in English. Here's an example: **Um wie viel Uhr kommst du? Um sechs oder um sieben?** *(What time are you coming? At six or at seven?)*

PRACTICE

Follow the instructions for stating the times shown in parentheses. You may need to change from words to numerals or vice versa or write the time a different way. For help check out the example.

Table 1-7   Expressing Time

German (conversational language)	English equivalent	German (official time)	English Equivalent
drei (Uhr)	three (o'clock)	drei (Uhr)	three (o'clock)
zehn (Minuten) nach drei	ten (minutes) past three	drei Uhr zehn	three ten
Viertel nach drei	quarter past three	drei Uhr fünfzehn	three fifteen
halb vier	half past three	drei Uhr dreißig	three thirty
Viertel vor vier	quarter to four	drei Uhr fünfundvierzig	three forty-five
zehn vor vier	ten to four	drei Uhr fünfzig	three fifty
vier (Uhr)	four (o'clock)	vier (Uhr)	four (o'clock)

Q. *What time does the flight land?* Write the time as digits.

Der Flug 629 landet um _____. (einundzwanzig Uhr fünfundzwanzig)

A. **Der Flug 629 landet um 21.25 Uhr.** *(Flight 629 lands at 9:25 p.m.)*

 What time do the shops close? Write the time as digits.

Die Geschäfte schließen schon um _____. (achtzehn Uhr)

58 Someone tells you the time. Write the time shown in parentheses a different way (in words).

Es ist _____. (sieben Uhr fünfundvierzig)

59 At the train station, you hear when your train is leaving. Write the time as words the way you would hear it announced:

Der Zug fährt um _____. (20.05)

60 What is another way to state the time (in words) in German? **Es ist drei Uhr fünfzehn.**

Es ist _____.

61 You call your German friend to say when you are arriving tomorrow. Write the time as words the way you would say the time on the phone (two alternatives here).

Morgen kommen wir um _____. (10.30 Uhr)

62 *We're playing tennis at 2:45 p.m.* Write the time in words.

Wir spielen um _____Tennis.

63 *We went to bed late last night.* Write the time shown in parentheses as digits.

Gestern Abend sind wir um _____ ins Bett gegangen. (halb zwei)

Answers to "Laying the Foundations of German" Practice Questions

1. You greet your Austrian neighbors with **Grüß Gott.**

2. Before going to your room at your host family for the night, you say **Gute Nacht.**

3. The next morning, you greet your host family with **Guten Morgen.**

4. You say goodbye to your German friends with **Tschüss./Ciao.**

5. With the same German friends, you add something like *See you then*: **Bis bald./Bis dann.**

6. When you depart your hotel, you say **Auf Wiedersehen.**

7. *Nice to meet you.* **Freut mich.**

8. *Nice to meet you too.* **Mich auch.**

9. *This is my colleague. . . . .* **Das ist mein Kollege (John)/meine Kollegin (Kathy).**

10. *How are you, ...?* **Wie geht es Ihnen, (Sarah)?**

11. *Thanks, I'm very good.* **Danke, sehr gut/ganz gut.**

12. *Good morning. My name is . . . .* **Guten Morgen. Ich heiße (Jack Sprat).**

13. *And you?* **Und Ihnen?**

14. **Gute Nacht. Gute Nacht.** (*Good night.*)

15. **Wo wohnen Sie? Ich wohne in LA.** (*Where do you live? I live in LA.*)

16. **Wie geht es Ihnen? Gut, danke.** (*How are you? Fine, thanks.*)

17. **Wie ist das Wetter in Kanada im Winter? Es ist sehr kalt.** (*What's the weather like in Canada in the winter? It's very cold.*)

18. **Woher kommen Sie? Ich komme aus Boston.** (*Where are you from? I'm from Boston.*)

19. **Auf Wiedersehen. Auf Wiedersehen.** (*Good bye.*)

20. **Wie ist das Wetter? Es ist sonnig und heiß.** (*How's the weather? It's sunny and hot.*)

21. **Grüß Gott. Grüß Gott.** (*Hello.*) (greeting in southern Germany and Austria)

22. **Freut mich. Mich auch.** (*Nice to meet you. Nice to meet you too.*)

23. **Wie finden Sie Ihr Deutsch? Es ist sehr gut.** (*What do you think of your German? It's very good.*)

24. Friends talking to each other use (plural form) **ihr.** *Talking to* is your key for second person, and *friends* is your key for the informal, plural form.

(25) You're talking about your friends, so you use **sie**. *Talking about* tells you that you need third person, and *friends* is your key for plural form.

(26) An adult meeting another adult for the first time uses **Sie**. You show respect and formality with **Sie**.

(27) When you talk about yourself, you use **ich**.

(28) An adult talking to three children ages 8, 11, and 14 uses **ihr**.

(29) You're talking to an animal, so you use **du**.

(30) A man talking about his wife uses **sie**. He says *she*, so you need **sie**, the third-person singular form.

(31) When you talk about your cousin and yourself, you use **wir**.

(32) You're talking about your colleagues, so you use **sie**. Here, **sie** stands for *they*.

(33) A teenage customer talking to a sales assistant uses **Sie**. The teen's age doesn't matter; saying **Sie** is polite and respectful. An adult would also use **Sie**.

(34) When you talk to someone on a ski lift in Switzerland, you use **Sie**. Start out with **Sie**; you're always safe. Maybe you'll hear the person using **du**, however. Or you may hear something like **"Sollen wir uns dutzen?"** (*Shall we say du to one another?*) That's your opportunity to answer **"Gern!"** ("*Yes, I'd like to!*" or "*Gladly!*").

(35) A military comrade talking to another comrade uses **du**. Especially in times of stress, people working side by side need each other's support, and familiarity and closeness are indicated by **du**.

(36) **siebenundvierzig: 47**

(37) **achthundertdreiundsiebzig: 873**

(38) **eintausenddreihunderteinundsiebzig: 1.371**

(39) **vierzehn Komma fünf: 14,5**

(40) **zwanzigtausendzweihundertneunundsechzig: 20.269**

(41) **siebzehntausendneunhundertachtunddreißig: 17.938**

(42) **vierundachtzigtausendzweihundertsieben: 84.207**

(43) **Heute ist Freitag. Morgen ist Sonnabend/Samstag.** (*Today is Friday. Tomorrow is Saturday.*)

(44) **Die Blätter fallen im Herbst.** (*The leaves fall in the fall.*)

(45) **April, Mai, Juni, Juli.** (*April, May, June, July*)

(46) **Der erste Januar ist ein Feiertag in vielen Ländern.** (*The first of January is a holiday in many countries.*)

47. **Morgen ist der erste Oktober. Was ist heute? Heute ist der dreißigste September.** (*Tomorrow is the first of October. What is today? Today is the thirtieth of September.*)

48. **Vorgestern war Sonntag. Was ist heute? Heute ist Dienstag.** (*The day before yesterday was Sunday. What is today? Today is Tuesday.*)

49. **Der Tag der Deutschen Einheit ist am dritten Oktober.** (*German Unity Day is on October 3.*)

50. **Februar hat achtundzwanzig Tage.** (*February has twenty-eight days.*)

51. **Im deutschen Kalender ist der erste Tag der Woche Montag.** (*In the German calendar, the first day of the week is Monday.*)

52. **Dienstag, Mittwoch, Donnerstag Freitag.** (*Tuesday, Wednesday, Thursday, Friday.*)

53. **Der letzte Tag im Jahr ist der einunddreißigste Dezember.** (*The last day of the year is the thirty-first of December.*)

54. **Heute ist der siebte August. Morgen ist der achte August.** (*Today is the seventh of August. Tomorrow is the eighth of August.*)

55. **Wie viele Monate haben einunddreißig Tage? Sieben Monate.** (*How many months have thirty-one days? Seven months.*)

56. **In den USA ist "Labor Day" am ersten Montag im September.** (*In the USA, Labor Day is on the first Monday in September.*)

57. **Die Geschäfte schließen schon um 18.00 Uhr.** (*The shops already close at 6 p.m.*)

58. **Es ist Viertel vor acht. (sieben Uhr fünfundvierzig)** (*It's quarter to eight.*) (*seven forty-five*)

59. **Der Zug fährt um zwanzig Uhr fünf.** (*The train leaves at eight-oh-five p.m.*)

60. **Es ist drei Uhr fünfzehn. Es ist Viertel nach drei.** (*It's three-fifteen. It's quarter past three.*)

61. **Morgen kommen wir um halb elf/zehn Uhr dreißig.** (*Tomorrow, we're coming at half-past ten/ten-thirty.*)

62. **Wir spielen um Viertel vor drei Tennis.** (*We're playing tennis at 2:45 p.m.*)

63. **Gestern Abend sind wir um 1.30 Uhr ins Bett gegangen.** (*We went to bed at 1:30 a.m. last night.*)

Chapter **2**

Assembling the Basic Tools for German Sentences

You need some basic grammar tools to help you assemble your thoughts into winning sentences. In this chapter, I explain the roles of the grammar tools — such as your trusty cases, clauses, and cognates — to help you boost your confidence in German. Next, you need to find some parts to build a sentence: parts of speech such as a noun, or (better) a couple of nouns, a verb, an adjective or two, and a maybe a preposition. These spare parts — er, words — are easy to find in a big dictionary. At the end of this chapter, I give you pointers on how to navigate a bilingual dictionary.

Throughout *German Workbook For Dummies*, you encounter the terms I describe in this chapter. I use these terms to explain grammar, vocabulary, and the idiosyncrasies of building sentences in German. If you're not familiar with such terms, getting the hang of the exercises in later chapters will take longer. Lingering here before jumping ahead can save you time in the future. At the very least, scan the headings and tables in this chapter; when you see a term that you're fuzzy about, stop and have a look.

If English is your native language, chances are that you don't need to bother with deciding whether the words you're using are verbs, nouns, or adjectives, because you know how to fit words together. The path to success in German is a different story. You're prone to run into roadblocks caused by not knowing which word to use, how to use it, or where to place it in a sentence. This chapter removes the barriers to your progress with German.

Grasping German Grammar Terms

To get a firm grasp on German grammar, you need to make sure you can keep track of the many terms you'll encounter. This section clears up any fuzzy ideas you may have about the names for tools of German grammar, such as *gender, case,* and *tense.* (I use terms for parts of speech in this section, but I give a fuller explanation of nouns, verbs, adjectives, and so on in a separate section of this chapter.)

Conjugating verbs and understanding tenses

Verbs are the words of action, and a verb that isn't yet part of a sentence is an *infinitive* or is *in infinitive form.* This is the verb as it's listed in a dictionary entry, as in **wohnen** (*to live*). In English, *to* indicates that the word is in infinitive form; the German equivalent is the **-en** ending of the verb.

When you *conjugate* a verb, you change the verb form so that it fits in your sentence to convey information such as which subject is doing the action and when something happens. Conjugation involves breaking the verb into its usable parts. Look at the conjugation of the verb *to live: I live, you live, he/she/it lives, we live, you live, they live.* English has only two spellings of *live* (with and without *s*). The same conjugation in German — **ich wohne, du wohnst, er/sie/es wohnt wir wohnen, ihr wohnt, sie wohnen, Sie wohnen** — reveals four verb endings, which are **-e, -st, -t,** and **-en.**

Verbs are conjugated in different *tenses,* which describe time. The three main descriptions of time are past, present, and future. Here's a briefing on the tenses I cover in this book, with the relevant verbs underlined:

>> **Present tense:** This tense describes an action that's happening now, habitual actions, or general facts. Look at the following sentence, which uses the verb **wohnen** (*to live*) in the present tense: **Ich wohne in den U.S.A.** You can translate it as *I live in the USA* or *I'm living in the USA.* (See Chapter 5 for details on the present.)

>> **Present perfect (conversational past):** In German, the present perfect describes something that happened in the past, whether that something is finished or unfinished. The verb is used in conversational German. **Ich habe in den USA gewohnt** can mean *I have lived in the USA* or *I lived in the USA.* (See Chapter 14.)

>> **Simple past (narrative past):** The simple past serves to narrate a series of connected events in the past. It is frequently used in formal writing, for example, in literature and newspaper articles. News broadcasts also use it. **Ich wohnte in den USA** means *I lived in the USA.* (See Chapter 15.)

>> **Future:** The future, obviously, describes events that haven't yet occurred. **Ich werde in den USA wohnen** means *I will live in the USA* or *I'm going to live in the USA.* German makes much less use of the future tense than English does, often opting for the simple present instead. (Check out Chapter 16.)

English uses continuous (progressive) tenses — verbs with a form of *to be* and *-ing*, as in *am living, was living,* or *have been living* — to describe a temporary or ongoing action. But because German has no continuous forms, you can simply use the basic German tenses — **ich wohne**, for example — for the continuous form in English. German also uses other tenses slightly differently from English.

DIFFERENCES

In the following exercise, the verb is indicated in bold, and the verb you see in parentheses is the infinitive form together with its English equivalent. Decide which verb tense it is and write your answer in the space provided (refer to the bold, underlined verbs in this section for help). Then translate the verb. The example shows the English translation of the complete sentence. You find the complete translations to the exercises in the answer key at the end of every chapter.

PRACTICE

Q. Ich **kaufte** ein neues Auto. (**kaufen** [*to buy*])

A. Ich kaufte ein neues Auto. (*I bought a new car.*) Simple past, *bought*. The -te ending signals the simple past tense.

 1 Ich **werde** ins Restaurant **gehen**. (**gehen** [*to go*])

_____

 2 Ich **reise** oft nach Zürich. (**reisen** [*to travel*])

_____

 3 Ich **habe** ein Glas Wein **getrunken**. (**trinken** [*to drink*])

_____

 4 Ich **werde** nach Rom **fliegen**. (**fliegen** [*to fly*])

_____

 5 Ich **habe** einen Salat **gegessen**. (**essen** [*to eat*])

_____

 6 Ich **lernte** Spanisch in der Schule. (**lernen** [*to learn*])

_____

7 Ich **habe** den Film **gesehen**. (**sehen** [*to see*])

_____

 8 Ich **fahre** morgen nach Chemnitz. (**fahren** [*to drive/go*])

_____

9 Ich **spiele** Gitarre. (**spielen** [*to play*])

_____

10 Ich **studierte** Mathematik an der Universität. (**studieren** [*to study*])

_____

Getting gender, number, and case

The trio of gender, number, and case are closely linked to help you make sense of single words and to connect them into sentences. You need to know how to use gender, number, and case to express your ideas in language people will understand. Check out the following explanations:

>> **Gender:** The times may be a changin', but grammatically speaking, English speakers tend to think in terms of two genders, masculine and feminine. The same goes for Mitzie, Fido, and all other household pets. But do stones and water have a gender? In German, yes, indeed! Every noun has a gender; the triumvirate **der** (*masculine*), **die** (*feminine*), and **das** (*neuter*) are the choices. All three are the gender-specific versions of the English word *the*. (If this were a soccer game, the German team would've already won by a margin of 2.)

WARNING

When looking at German, don't confuse gender. Gender has to do with the word itself, not the meaning of the word. There's nothing particularly masculine about a table, for example, but Germans call it **der Tisch**. The same is true of a wall, which doesn't seem to be particularly feminine, but Germans call it **die Wand**.

>> **Number:** Number refers to singular and plural, such as *one potato, two potatoes, three potatoes*. German plurals are more intricate than English plurals. In fact, German offers five major types of plural endings. Some plurals compare with the irregular English plurals, such as *man* and *men* (**der Mann, die Männer**). (Check out Chapter 3 for more on making nouns plural.)

>> **Case:** There are four cases in German: nominative, accusative, dative, and genitive. But what does case mean? Cases help tell you what role the word plays in the sentence; they have to do with the difference between *I* and *me* or *she* and *her*. Cases deal with the significance of the *to* in *give it to me* or the apostrophe *s* in *dog's Frisbee*.

German case endings are numerous, and they show the relationship between the words that have those cases. English uses case far less often. (Chapter 3 has more info on case.)

Understanding word order

German word order plays a key role in forming a sentence. When you're positioning words in a German sentence, keep a few major points in mind:

>> The most common word order in simple sentences looks like English word order:

1. Subject in first position: **Meine Wohnung** (*My apartment*)

2. Verb in second position: **hat** (*has*)

3. Other information follows: **einen großen Balkon** (*a large balcony*)

Put the pieces all together, and you have **Meine Wohnung hat einen großen Balkon.**

» Yes/no questions have inverted word order. Flip the conjugated verb with the subject: **Hat deine Wohnung einen Balkon**? (*Does your apartment have a balcony?*)

» More complex sentences, such as those that have two verb parts, require more understanding of where to position the verbs in a sentence. In various sections of this book, you find out more about correct word order.

Describing words, parts of words, and word groupings

REMEMBER

You need to know several terms that describe words that you put together to convey meaning — *sentence, clause, phrase,* and so on. The following list shows the most important key words I use in this book:

» **Phrase:** A group of words without a subject or a verb; most often used to describe a prepositional phrase, such as **in dem Haus** (*in the house*), **für die Familie** (*for the family*), and **mit mir** (*with me*)

» **Clause:** A group of related words that has subject and a verb, such as **wir arbeiten** . . . (*we're working . . .*) or **meine Mutter weiß. . .** (*my mother knows. . .*)

» **Sentence:** A group of words that represents a complete thought and has a complete sentence structure: subject, verb, and punctuation, such as **Ich fliege nach Japan.** (*I'm flying to Japan.*), **Gehen wir!** (*Let's go!*), and **Woher kommen Sie?** (*Where are you from?*)

» **Prefix:** A word beginning that alters the word's meaning, such as **un** (*un-*) + freundlich (*friendly*) = **un**freundlich (*unfriendly*) or **inter** (*inter-*) + aktiv (*active*) = **inter**aktiv (*interactive*)

» **Suffix:** A word ending that alters the word's meaning, such as (der) Kapital + **ismus** = Kapital**ismus** (*capital + ism = capitalism*) or (der) Wind + **ig** = wind**ig** (*wind + y = windy*)

» **Cognates:** Words that have the same meaning and the same (or nearly the same) spelling in two languages, such as **das Ende** (*the end*), **der Hammer** (*the hammer*), and **die Melodie** (*the melody*)

Note: Technically, *cognates* are two words that come from a common ancestor.

PRACTICE

Write the name of the term that describes the word(s) in the exercises.

Q. in der Nacht _____

A. in der Nacht (*in the night*) phrase

 der Safe _____

5 Ich schwimme oft im Sommer. _____

6 die Vorarbeit _____

7 er kommt . . . _____

8 mit meiner Familie _____

9 national _____

10 für meinen Vater _____

11 intolerant _____

12 wunderbar _____

Identifying Parts of Speech

To build a sentence, you need to figure out which words to use and how to put them together. To do this, you figure out what you want to say, identify the parts of speech you need to express your ideas, and then decide which words you want to use. Word order in a German sentence can depend on the parts of speech that you're using. In Table 2-1, I explain what these terms mean.

Table 2-1   Parts of Speech

Name	Definition	Examples	Notes
Noun	A person, place, animal, thing, quality, concept, and so on	**Dracula** **Hotel California** **Känguru**h (*kangaroo*) **Liebe** (*love*)	In German, nouns are always capitalized. (See Chapter 3.)
Pronoun	A word that replaces or stands in for a noun	**er** (*he*) **sie** (*she* **uns** (*us*)	German has far more pronoun variations; the four cases influence pronoun endings. (See Chapter 3.)
Article	A word that indicates the gender of a noun	**der/die/das** (*the*) **ein/eine/ein** (*a/an*)	German has three genders, so it uses three different articles for *the* — der/die/das — and *a/an* — ein/eine/ein. (See Chapter 3.)
Verb	A word that shows action or a state of being	**denken** (*to think*) **haben** (*to have*) **reisen** (*to travel*)	Verbs are conjugated according to person (I, you, he, and so on), tense (present, past, and future), and mood (for example, the difference between *it is* and *it would be*).
Adjective	A word that modifies or describes a noun or a pronoun	**schön** (*beautiful*) **praktisch** (*practical*) **interessant** (*interesting*)	Adjectives may or may not have case endings. (See chapters 10 and 11.)
Adverb	A word that modifies or describes a verb, an adjective, or another adverb	**schnell** (*fast, quickly*) **sehr** (*very*) **schrecklich** (*terribly*)	In German, adjectives and adverbs can be the same word. (See Chapter 11.)

Name	Definition	Examples	Notes
Conjunction	A word that connects other words or sentence parts	**und** (*and*), **aber** (*but*) **weil** (*because*)	In German, some conjunctions affect the word order of the sentence. (See Chapter 12.)
Preposition	A word that shows a relationship between its object (a noun or pronoun) and another word in a sentence	**mit (mir)** (*with [me]*), **ohne (mich)** (*without[me]*), **während (des Tages)** (*during [the day]*)	In German, a preposition uses case (dative, accusative, or genitive) to show the relationship to its object. (See Chapter 13.)

PRACTICE

In the sentences that follow, identify the part of speech in boldface, and write it next to the sentence. Then try your hand at writing the sentence in English. The clues and word translations in parentheses help you with both tasks.

Q. Wo **sind** meine Schlüssel?

A. Wo **sind** meine Schlüssel? verb. The verb is **sind**, and it's in second position, as is typical in German word order. *Where are my keys?*

 Sie sind auf dem Tisch. (This is the answer to the question above.)

_____

 Es gibt viele **exotische** Tiere (*animals*) im Zoo.

_____

 Ich mag (*like*) die Pinguine, **aber** die Elefanten sind noch interessanter.

_____

 Im Zoo sind **die** Tiere nicht glücklich (*not happy*). _____

_____

 Der Garten ist **sehr schön**. (two parts of speech)

_____

 Kommen Sie **mit** uns?

_____

 Wie heißt das schwarze **Pferd**?

_____

 Es **heißt** Black Beauty. (This is the answer to the question above.)

_____

21 Fahre bitte nicht so **schnell**! (something you might say to your friend who thinks they're a race-car driver)

Finding Meaning through Context

One essential tool for making sense of a foreign language is to consciously look for meaning through the context of the words. You probably do the same thing in your own language. Imagine you're reading a text that's not in your field of expertise. You instinctively look at any headings; scan the text; and get more clues from any illustrations, charts, or tables. When you're looking at a text in German, you can meet the challenge by employing the techniques you already use in your native language.

TIP

To understand what a whole sentence means, see how the words fit together. Identify the verb or verbs and a noun or pronoun, and that's the meat of your sentence. Check out how the other words are related to the subject and verb; look for a prepositional phrase or a conjunction, for example. (See the preceding section "Identifying Parts of Speech.") In short, use all the tools at your disposal to understand German sentences.

PRACTICE

What do you know about the city of **München** (Munich)? Do the following exercise, which combines the tools and parts explained in the previous sections of this chapter. Each sentence has one word missing. Decide which word of the four choices is the correct one and write your answer in the space. When you finish, go to the answer key to check your answers and get some info on Munich.

Q. Viele Leute _____, dass München "die heimliche Hauptstadt Deutschlands" ist.

   a) behaupten   b) Sonne   c) der   d) vorwärts

A. Viele Leute a) behaupten, dass München die heimliche Hauptstadt Deutschlands ist. (*Many people claim that Munich is "the secret capital of Germany."*) The verb **behaupten** is in second position in the clause; next comes a second clause that is set apart by a comma.

22 Es gibt (*There are*) _____ Bezeichnungen (*names*) für München.

   a) der   b) Personen   c) zwei   d) das

23 Die Einwohner (*the inhabitants*) sagen, München ist "die Weltstadt mit Herz," _____ "das Millionendorf."

   a) in   b) arbeiten   c) oder   d) interessant

24 In der Tat _____ die Stadt voller Überraschungen (*surprises*).

   a) von   b) ist   c) in   d) können

25 Jedes Jahr wird das grösste (*largest*) Volksfest der Welt in München _____.

   a) eine   b) Stein   c) schön   d) gefeiert

26 Millionen Touristen kommen zum Oktoberfest, aber _____ Leute (*people*) kommen zu spät. Warum?

    a) manche   **b) haben**   **c) nicht**   **d) grün**

27 Leider (*Unfortunately*) geht _____ Oktoberfest am ersten Sonntag im Oktober zu Ende.

    a) nur   **b) in**   **c) das**   **d) von**

Using a Bilingual Dictionary

Horses are only as good for riding as their training is, and dictionaries are only as useful for finding words as their owners' knowledge of how to use a dictionary. Except for the phrases "breaking in a horse" and "breaking in a book," that's about it for parallels (unless, of course, you want to speak German to your horse).

A bilingual dictionary is a challenge at first; take on the challenge and read the information at the front of the dictionary on how to use the dictionary. The symbols and abbreviations are your key to successful scouting for the right word or expression. This section helps you sort out this handy tool.

Making the right choice

When choosing a bilingual dictionary, your first task is selecting the right dictionary. First and foremost are the size and quality. Don't scrimp here. Take your bathroom scales to a serious bookstore, weigh all the German/English bilingual dictionaries, and pick the two heaviest ones. Okay, just kidding. These days, you're most likely doing your shopping online. Not to worry. You still want to start by comparing two or, better, three dictionary entries of a word. My suggestion is to start with a frequently used verb such as **machen**. The following shortened dictionary entry for the verb **machen** shows you how a good dictionary organizes the information on the first two lines:

> ≫ **machen 1** *vt* (**a**) to do; (*herstellen, zubereiten*) to make. **was ~ Sie (beruflich)**? what do you do for a living?; **gut, wird gemacht** right, I'll get that done *or* will be done (*coll*).

You may notice two abbreviations and a symbol in this entry:

> ≫ The abbreviation *vt* stands for *transitive verb,* which is a verb that can take a direct object. The verb **haben** (*to have*) is one example; in the sentence **ich habe Zeit** (*I have time*), **Zeit** is the direct object. Other verbs have the abbreviation *vi,* which stands for an *intransitive verb* which is a verb without a direct object. **Reisen** (*to travel*) has no direct object; for example, **wir reisen oft** (*We travel often*) indicates frequency of travel. **Oft** is not an object of the verb.

> ≫ The second abbreviation, *coll,* stands for *colloquial.* Expressions or words marked by this abbreviation are used in informal conversation.

> ≫ The ~ symbol represents the *headword* (the first word) **machen**. The complete expression is **Was machen Sie (beruflich)?**

TIP Start your dictionary comparison task by following these steps:

1. **Look at how comprehensive the entries are.**

   Check for commonly used phrases such as **was machst du denn da**? (*what in the world are you doing here?*), **mach schneller!** (*hurry up!*), **das macht nichts** (*it doesn't matter/ never mind*), **das macht (24€)** (*that is/comes to [24€]*), **mach schon!** (*get a move on!*) or **mach's gut** (*take care*) and compare their translations for detail and content. You should be able to find complete sentences and phrases using **machen**. Comprehensive dictionaries should offer alternative words in German (at least for frequently used verbs such as **machen**), along with possible translations. After **machen**, for example, you may find **herstellen** (*to produce, manufacture*) or **zubereiten** (*to prepare*), as in the example entry.

2. **Ask yourself which dictionary is more user-friendly.**

   In other words, does the dictionary provide plenty of helpful abbreviations to help you understand the entries? Do you see clearly marked sections under the headword **machen**? They should be marked by numbers and letters in bold; in the example entry, you find **1** and **(a)**. Some quality dictionaries indent the numbered sections to make them even easier to locate. You can see whether there's a phonetic pronunciation for tricky words. Also, check whether the dictionary makes ample use of symbols like *coll* to indicate usage of the word.

   Apart from the abbreviations that show parts of speech [*adj* (adjective) or *adv* (adverb)], gender [*m, f, nt* (masculine, feminine, neuter)], number, case, and so on, you find many more details in any large, quality dictionary. A (very) short list of such abbreviated terms should include *fig* (figurative), *coll* (colloquial), *abbr* (abbreviation), *lit* (literal), *esp* (especially), *sl* (slang), *Tech* (technology), *Psych* (psychology), *Prov* (proverb), *Jur* (law), *spec* (specialist term), *Aus* (Austrian usage), *Sw* (Swiss usage), and many more.

TIP Make your choice wisely and start enjoying your new **Wörterbuch** (*dictionary*). And if you consider yourself as a visual learner, check out a German picture dictionary too. Some of those dictionaries have useful phrases in addition to pictures with labels.

If you prefer a web-based dictionary, and you're not sure how to make a good selection, follow the same criteria. Select a couple of reputable dictionary publishers, go to their online dictionaries, and find out how extensive and (ideally, accurate) they are. If you're not familiar with dictionary publishers, go to https://www.google.de and check out the dictionaries listed under **deutsch-englisches wörterbuch**. Do a thorough web search to find what's available and compare the sources you find. A great advantage of using an online dictionary is being able to hear the pronunciation of a word or a phrase.

When you compare free online dictionaries, consider the quality of the entries shown. You might not choose an online dictionary that has an entry for **machen** (*to do sth*) with the following (in my humble opinion, strange) example sentence: **Hast du die Kartoffeln/Türen/ Badezimmer gemacht?** (*Have you done the potatoes/doors/bathroom?*) A better choice might be a dictionary that has an example sentence like this: **Was machst du heute Abend?** (*What are you doing this evening?*) You may also want to be careful about assuming that online translation tools and apps are always accurate.

Performing a word search

Maybe you didn't buy a paper dictionary because you found a nifty online alternative that matches your criteria for accuracy and user-friendliness. That's all right. No matter whether you're using a hard copy or an online dictionary, you still have to know how to find the right word.

TIP

Familiarize yourself with the symbols and abbreviations used by looking up a few nouns, verbs, adjectives, and so on. See whether you understand them in the context of the dictionary entry. Instead of trying to memorize the meaning of all the abbreviations, make a photocopy of the list, and keep it as a bookmark in your dictionary. Better, laminate it. That way, you can use it as a mouse pad, a table mat, or whatever. Then you can cross-check definitions to get more information on words you're looking up.

When you look up a word that has several definitions, read beyond the first or second entry line, and try to decide which one suits your needs. Think about context and decide which word fits best into the rest of the sentence. Here are some factors other than meaning that may affect your word choice:

>> **Nouns:** Think of gender and number as the vital statistics of a noun.

Gender is indicated by *m, f,* and *nt* (for *masculine, feminine,* and *neuter*) in some dictionaries.

Number is indicated with the plural ending form for that noun. There are five main groups of noun endings. A common ending is **-en**; some other nouns add **-n** or **-s**. With some nouns, you see the genitive case ending indicated for that noun in addition to the plural ending.

>> **Verbs:** Verbs also have vital statistics you need to know.

A verb is *transitive* or *intransitive* (symbols like *vt* and *vi*). A transitive verb takes a direct object; an intransitive verb doesn't.

A transitive verb may have a separable prefix (*vt sep*) or an inseparable prefix (*vt insep*). If the prefix is separable, it usually gets booted to the end of the sentence when the verb is conjugated.

Some verbs are reflexive (*vr*), meaning that they require a reflexive pronoun.

The simple past form and the past participle are also indicated (in some dictionaries with *pret* and ptp, respectively).

>> **Prepositions:** Prepositions in German dictionary entries show which case they have: accusative (*prep + acc*), dative (*prep + dat*), or genitive (*prep + gen*). Some prepositions have more than one case, and most prepositions have more than one meaning.

>> **Pronouns:** Pronouns include personal pronouns (*pers pron*), such as **ich** (*I*); demonstrative pronouns (*dem pron*), such as **denen** (*them*); relative pronouns (*rel pron*), such as **das** (*that*); and reflexive pronouns (*reflexive pron*), such as **mich** (*myself*). See Chapter 3 for details on pronoun types.

TIP

Adjectives and adverbs may be the same word in German. Memorize both, and you have two words for the effort of looking up one.

PRACTICE

Look at three excerpts from the dictionary entry for **Reise** (*trip, journey*), and answer the questions about the words and abbreviations. Refer to the previous information to help you.

>> **Reise** *f* -**n** trip, journey; *(Schiffs~)* voyage; **eine ~ machen** to go on a trip; **er ist viel auf ~n** he does a lot of traveling; **gute ~!** bon voyage!, have a good trip!

>> **reisen** *vi aux sein* to travel; **viel gereist sein** to be well-traveled.

>> **Reise-:** ~**pass** *m* passport: ~ **pläne** *pl* travel plans; ~**prospekt** *m*: travel brochure; ~ **route** *f* route, itinerary; ~**verkehr** *m* holiday traffic; ~**versicherung** *f* travel insurance: ~ **ziel** *nt* destination.

Key for abbreviations: *m* = masculine, *f* = feminine, *nt* = neuter, *pl* = plural, *vi* = intransitive verb, *aux sein* = the auxiliary verb used is **sein**

Q. In the first entry for **Reise**, what does the abbreviation *f* stand for? What does -**n** mean?

A. The *f* means that *Reise* has a feminine gender (**die Reise**), and -**n** shows the plural ending, for example, **zwei Reisen** (*two trips*).

 28 In the first entry, what is the German word for *voyage*? Is it one or two words?

_____

 29 In the first entry, how do you say *Have a good trip!* in German?

_____

30 Look at the second entry. What do the abbreviations *vi aux sein* mean?

_____

31 Look at the second entry. How would you construct the following in German?: *They are well-traveled.*

_____

32 In the third entry, the headword (first one, in bold) has a hyphen at the end of the word like this: **Reise-:** What does the hyphen mean?

_____

33 In the third entry, what's the word for *destination*, and which gender is it?

_____

Answers to "Assembling the Basic Tools for German Sentences" Practice Questions

(1) Ich **werde** ins Restaurant **gehen**. (*I'm going to go to the restaurant.*) **Future, will go/am going to go**. Either translation is appropriate; **am going to go** sounds more natural here because it expresses an intention. **Werde** plus the verb at the end signals the future tense.

(2) Ich **reise** oft nach Zürich. (*I often travel to Zürich.*) **Present, travel**. The ending **-e** signals the present tense.

(3) Ich **habe** ein Glas Wein **getrunken**. (*I drank/have drunk a glass of wine.*) **Present perfect, drank/have drunk**. **Habe** plus the participle at the end of the sentence signals present perfect tense.

(4) Ich **werde** nach Rom **fliegen**. (*I'm going to fly to Rome.*) **Future, will fly/am going to fly**. Either translation is appropriate; *am going to fly* sounds more natural here because it expresses an intention. **Werde** plus the verb at the end signals the future tense.

(5) Ich **habe** einen Salat **gegessen**. (*I ate/have eaten a salad.*) **Present perfect, ate/have eaten**. **Habe** plus the participle at the end of the sentence signals present perfect tense.

(6) Ich **lernte** Spanisch in der Schule. (*I learned Spanish in school.*) **Simple past, studied**. The **-te** ending signals the simple past tense.

(7) Ich **habe** den Film **gesehen**. (*I have seen/saw the film.*) **Present perfect, have seen/saw**. **Habe** plus the participle at the end of the sentence signals present perfect tense.

(8) Ich **fahre** morgen nach Chemnitz. (*Tomorrow I'm driving to Chemnitz.*) **Present, am driving**. The ending **-e** signals the present tense. German has no continuous forms.

(9) Ich **spiele** Gitarre. (*I play the guitar.*) **Present, play**. The ending **-e** signals the present tense.

(10) Ich **studierte** Mathematik an der Universität. (*I studied math at the university.*) **Simple past, studied**. The **-te** ending signals the simple past tense.

(11) der Safe (*the safe/vault*) **cognate**

(12) **Ich schwimme oft im Sommer.** (*I often swim in the summer.*) **sentence**

(13) **die Vorarbeit** (*the preliminary work*) **prefix**

(14) **er kommt . . .** (*he's coming...*) **clause**

(15) **mit meiner Familie** (*with my family*) **phrase**

(16) **national** (*national*) **cognate**

(17) **für meinen Vater** (*for my father*) **phrase**

(18) **intolerant** (*intolerant*) **prefix;** the whole word is a **cognate**

(19) **wunderbar** (*wonderful*) **suffix**

20. **pronoun; They're on the table. Sie** is a pronoun. The usual German word order is subject + verb. Here, the subject is a pronoun.

21. **adjective; There are a lot of exotic animals in the zoo. Exotische** describes the plural noun **Tiere**. The suffix ending **-isch** is often comparable to the suffix *-ic* or *-ical* in English.

22. **conjunction; I like the penguins, but the elephants are more interesting.** The two sentence parts are joined by the conjunction **aber** (*but*).

23. **definite, plural article; In the zoo, the animals aren't happy. Die** is the plural article in nominative case, indicating that **Tiere** is plural.

24. **adverb, adjective; The garden is very beautiful. Sehr** is an adverb that modifies the adjective **schön**.

25. **preposition; Are you coming with us? Mit** is a preposition. The prepositional phrase is **mit uns** (*with us*).

26. **noun; What's the black horse called? Pferd** is a noun with neuter gender: **das Pferd.**

27. **verb; It's called Black Beauty. Heißt** is a verb; its infinitive form is **heißen.** It's in the second position in the sentence after the subject **es.**

28. **adverb; Please don't drive so fast! Schnell** is an adverb in this sentence because it describes how the person is driving (**fahre**), and *driving* is the verb.

29. c. **zwei**; Es gibt **zwei** Bezeichnungen für München. (*There are two [other] names [monikers] for Munich.*)

30. c. **oder**; Die Einwohner sagen, München ist "die Weltstadt mit Herz," **oder** "das Millionendorf." (*The inhabitants say [that] Munich is the "friendly city" or "the village with a million inhabitants."*) Literally, the **Weltstadt mit Herz** is the *world city with a heart.*

31. b. **ist**; In der Tat **ist** die Stadt voller Überraschungen. (*Indeed, the city is full of surprises.*) Many tourists aren't aware of another celebration of beer known as **das Starkbierfest** (*strong beer festival*). The Munich carnival season is also very lively, with people taking to the streets to celebrate Mardi Gras.

32. d. **gefeiert**; Jedes Jahr wird das grösste Volksfest der Welt in München **gefeiert.** (*Every year, the largest folk festival in the world is celebrated in Munich.*)

33. a. **manche**; Millionen Touristen kommen zum Oktoberfest, aber **manche** Leute kommen zu spät. Warum? (*Millions of tourists come to the Oktoberfest, but some people come too late. Why?*)

34. c. **das**; Leider geht **das** Oktoberfest am ersten Sonntag im Oktober zu Ende. (*Unfortunately, the Oktoberfest ends on the first Sunday in October.*) It's actually better to get there before the Oktoberfest begins if you don't like crowds and just want to see the enormous venue. You may even be able to drink a beer with the workers constructing the tents. **Prost!** (*Cheers!*)

35. The German word for *voyage* is **Schiffsreise.** It is one word. The symbol ~ is shown directly after **Schiffs,** like this: **Schiffs~.** This indicates that it's a compound word.

(36) **Gute Reise!** is the equivalent of: *Have a good trip!*

(37) The abbreviation *vi* indicates that the verb **reisen** is an *intransitive verb,* one that has no direct object. The abbreviation *aux sein* means that **reisen** uses the auxiliary verb **sein** *(to be)*. The majority of verbs use the auxiliary verb **haben** *(to have).*

(38) **Sie sind viel gereist** *(They are well-traveled)* is formed by using the conjugated form **sind** *(are)* of the verb **sein.** The sentence has the most common word order of subject + verb + other information: **Sie + sind + viel gereist.**

(39) The hyphen at the end of the word like this: **Reise-** indicates that the following entries are combined to form words such as **Reisepass** (passport) or **Reisepläne** (travel plans).

(40) **Reiseziel** is the word for *destination,* and it's neuter: **das Reiseziel.**

Chapter **3**

Sorting Out Word Gender and Case

Most words in a German sentence take their cues from the nouns (or their esteemed representatives, the pronouns). When studying German, you really don't know a new noun unless you know its characteristics, which include gender. So for each new noun you come across, you need to accept its gender as a part of the word and commit it to memory. To use nouns and pronouns (as well as adjectives and prepositions) in a German sentence, you need to know how they fit together; this is the role of case. Case and gender are closely linked, and I consider them to be pieces of a puzzle in making German sentences. Case and gender may look complicated at first, but as soon as you start fitting the pieces in, the picture becomes clearer. In this chapter, you get the lowdown on how gender and case work hand in hand to form various endings for the members of two large families of words: the article family and the pronoun family.

Rounding Up Grammatical Genders

Not everything with gender lives and breathes. Listen to people talk about inanimate objects, and you may hear them use "he" or "she" when referring to the faithful bicycle they cherish, the old sailboat, or the rickety pickup that starts only on Wednesdays and Fridays. Like these other things you may have a love–hate relationship with, German words have gender.

REMEMBER

In German grammar, *gender* is the classification of a noun or a pronoun into one of three categories: masculine, feminine, or neuter. These genders often have nothing to do with the meaning of the word; they're simply an identity bracelet. Note that *gender* refers to the word, not whatever the word represents. You need to know a word's gender because it can dictate the spelling of other words in the sentence.

How can you get a grasp of gender so that you can form a word correctly? Each time you come across a new noun, be firm with yourself; find out its gender and how to form its plural form. With a little time, you can master the concept. This section helps you identify a word's gender, form plural nouns (and note the effects on gender), eye indefinite articles, and identify when not to use articles.

Identifying German genders and figuring out which one to use

In English, you mark a noun as one of three genders: male (masculine), female (feminine), or inanimate/neither (neuter). The descriptions *male, female,* and *inanimate* refer to living beings and things. The words in parentheses — *masculine, feminine,* and *neuter* — refer to grammatical distinction, which is how German describes *noun gender.*

Gender distinction in English is *natural,* which means that you need to know only whether the noun refers to a female being, a male being, or an inanimate object (neither male nor female). You can refer to the nouns as *he, she,* or *it.* And the articles you use — such as *the, a,* and *an* — don't tell you anything about gender at all.

DIFFERENCES

In German, you likewise have three genders, but gender distinction isn't natural, as it is in English. It's like a marker that refers to the word, not its meaning. The three markers for *the* (singular) in German are **der** (*masculine*), **die** (*feminine*), and **das** (*neuter*). Look at the words for eating utensils, which cover all three bases: **der Löffel** (*the spoon*), **die Gabel** (*the fork*), and **das Messer** (*the knife*). Why should a spoon be masculine, a fork feminine, or a knife neuter? Do you see any logical pattern here? I don't. Much of gender designation in German is unnatural, which means that there's no silver bullet to help you remember the gender of a word. German dictionary entries identify nouns as **der, die,** or **das.** (Have a look at Chapter 2 for more information on using a dictionary.)

All of the three gender markers — the definite articles **der, die,** and **das** — mean *the.* Look at the three following German sentences:

>> **Kannst du das Mädchen da drüben sehen? Es ist sehr groß.** (*Can you see the girl over there? She's really tall.*) *The girl* in German is **das Mädchen,** a neuter-gender noun, as are all nouns ending in **-chen.** The ending indicates that a person or thing is small or young. You refer to the girl as **es,** which means *it.* (This example is simply a grammatical reference. It's not an affront to you girls out there!)

>> **Der neue Deutschlehrer ist Herr Mangold. Ich glaube, er kommt aus Bremen.** (*The new German teacher is Herr Mangold. I think he comes from Bremen.*) You refer, grammatically speaking, to **Herr Mangold** as **er** (*he*). In most (but not all) cases in German, male beings are **der** nouns, and female beings are **die** nouns.

>> **Hast du die tolle Gitarre im Schaufenster gesehen? Sie hat zwölf Seiten.** (*Have you seen the cool guitar in the shop window? It has 12 strings.*) Strange but true: Grammatically speaking, a guitar is feminine, so you refer to it as **sie** (*she*). Most nouns ending in **-e** are feminine nouns, although some plural nouns end in -e as well.

So how do you know exactly how to form/use genders correctly in German? First, remember that gender is an integral part of each noun; it's like a piece of the noun's identity. When you see a new noun, you have several ways to find out its gender. A dictionary can help, and some of the following noun-gender categories can help you make a reasonable guess.

REMEMBER

Some categories of nouns are consistently masculine, feminine, or neuter. Noun gender usually follows the gender of people, for example, as in **der Onkel** (*the uncle*) and **die Schwester** (*the sister*). Most often, the noun groups have to do with the ending of the noun. Tables 3-1 and 3-2 list some fairly reliable groups. (Note, however, that exceptions exist.)

Table 3-1   Common Genders by Noun Ending (or Beginning)

Usually Masculine (der)	Usually Feminine (die)	Usually Neuter (das)
-ant		
-er (especially when referring to male people/jobs)	**-ade, -age, -anz, -enz, -ette, -ine, -ion, -tur** (if foreign/borrowed from another language)	**-chen**
-ich	**-e**	**-ium**
-ismus	**-ei**	**-lein**
-ist	**-heit**	**-ment** (if foreign/borrowed from another language)
-ling		
-ner	**-ie**	**-o**
	-ik	**-tum** or **-um**
	-in (when referring to female people/occupations)	starting with **Ge-** (for collective nouns)
	-keit	
	-schaft	
	-ität	
	-ung	

Table 3-2   Common Noun Genders by Subject

Usually Masculine (der)	Usually Feminine (die)	Usually Neuter (das)
Days, months, and seasons: **der Freitag** (*Friday*)	Many flowers: **die Rose** (*the rose*)	Colors (adjectives) used as nouns: **grün** (*green*), **das Grün** (*the green*)
Map locations: **der Süd(en)** (*the south*)	Many trees: **die Eiche** (*the oak*)	Geographic place names: **das Europa** (*Europe*)
Names of cars: **der Audi** (*the Audi*)		Infinitives used as nouns (gerunds): **schwimmen** (*to swim*), **das Schwimmen** (*swimming*)
Nationalities and words showing citizenship: **der Amerikaner** (*the American[masculine]*)		Young people and animals: **das Baby** (*the baby*)
Occupations: **der Arzt** (*the doctor*)		

Note: The **-er** ending of words such as **der Amerikaner** applies to the masculine form; later you will learn the feminine equivalent which adds an extra **-in** to the already existing masculine **-er** form.

REMEMBER

Compound nouns (nouns with two or more nouns in one word) always have the gender of the last noun: **die Polizei** (*the police*) + **der Hund** (*the dog*) = **der Polizeihund** (*the police dog/K9*).

Corralling plurals

When you want to make a noun plural in English, all you usually need to do is add *-s* or *-es*. But you have five ways to form plural nouns in German. Before you throw your hands up in dismay, think about how English varies from the one standard form of making plurals with *-s* or *-es*. Think of *mouse/mice, tooth/teeth, child/children, shelf/shelves, phenomenon/phenomena, man/men,* and *country/countries.* Better yet, you can form the plural of some words in two ways. Think about *hoof/hoofs/hooves.* See what I mean? Many English plurals are also a matter of memorization. So in both languages, you have a variety of plural endings and/or changes in the noun.

Here's the good news: You don't have to worry much about gender in plural definite articles in German because **die** (*the* in plural form) is all you need.

REMEMBER

The article **die** corresponds to all three singular definite article forms: **der** (*the*, masculine), **die** (*the*, feminine), and **das** (*the*, neuter).

Table 3-3 shows you the five main ways of forming plural nouns in German. There's no hard-and-fast method of knowing which plural ending you need, but you can recognize some patterns as you expand your vocabulary. At any rate, you need to place high priority on knowing plural forms. Look at some patterns for forming plural nouns (and keep in mind that exceptions may exist):

>> Feminine nouns with (feminine) suffixes **-heit, -keit,** and **-ung** usually have an **-en** plural ending: **die Möglichkeit** (*the possibility*) ⇨ **die Möglichkeiten** (*possibilities*).

>> Singular nouns ending in **-er** may not have any ending in plural: **das Fenster** (*the window*) ⇨ **die Fenster** (*the windows*).

>> Many nouns have an umlaut in the plural form, including many one-syllable words: der **Kuss** (*the kiss*) ⇨ **die Küsse** (*the kisses*); der **Traum** (*the dream*) ⇨ **die Träume** (*the dreams*).

>> Some German nouns are used only in the plural or in the singular: **die Ferien** (*the [often: school] vacation*) is always plural; **die Milch** (*the milk*) is always singular.

Table 3-3   The Five German Plural Groups

Change Needed	English Singular and Plural	German Singular	German Plural
Add **-s**	the office(s)	**das Büro**	**die Büros**
	the café(s)	**das Café**	**die Cafés**
	the boss(es)	**der Chef**	**die Chefs**
	the email(s)	**die E-Mail**	**die E-Mails**
	the cellphone(s)	**das Handy**	**die Handys**
	the hotel(s)	**das Hotel**	**die Hotels**
No change, or add umlaut (¨)	the knife, knives	**das Messer**	**die Messer**
	the window(s)	**das Fenster**	**die Fenster**
	the garden(s)	**der Garten**	**die Gärten**
	the girl(s)	**das Mädchen**	**die Mädchen**
	the mother(s)	**die Mutter**	**die Mütter**
	the father(s)	**der Vater**	**die Väter**
Add **-e** or umlaut (¨) + **-e**	the train station(s)	**der Bahnhof**	**die Bahnhöfe**
	the friend(s) (singular is male)	**der Freund**	**die Freunde**
	the problem(s)	**das Problem**	**die Probleme**
	the city/cities	**die Stadt**	**die Städte**
	the chair(s)	**der Stuhl**	**die Stühle**
	the train(s)	**der Zug**	**die Züge**
Add **-er** or umlaut (¨) + **-er**	the book(s)	**das Buch**	**die Bücher**
	the bicycle(s)	**das Fahrrad**	**die Fahrräder**
	the house(s)	**das Haus**	**die Häuser**
	the child/children	**das Kind**	**die Kinder**
	the castle(s)	**das Schloss**	**die Schlösser**
Add **-n**, **-en**, or **-nen**	the bed(s)	**das Bett**	**die Betten**
	the file(s)	**die Datei**	**die Dateien**
	the idea(s)	**die Idee**	**die Ideen**
	the boy(s)	**der Junge**	**die Jungen**
	the sister(s)	**die Schwester**	**die Schwestern**
	the student(s) (female)	**die Studentin**	**die Studentinnen**
	the newspaper(s)	**die Zeitung**	**die Zeitungen**

PRACTICE

In the following exercise, you need to decide why I group the words together. Choose one of the following:

>> All words have the same gender; if so, what is the gender?

>> All words have the same plural form; if so, what is the plural ending?

>> All words in the group are related somehow, such as all are names of flowers.

>> There are two (or three) reasons why the words are grouped.

Q. Autor, Direktor, Motor, Radiator _____

A. Three reasons: All are masculine gender (**der**); all form the plural with (**-en**), and all are cognates or near cognates with English: **Der Autor** (*the author*), **der Direktor** (*the director*), and so on.

1. Fabrik, Logik, Politik, Statistik, Technik _____

2. Audi, BMW, Ford, Mercedes, Porsche _____

3. Leben, Lernen, Schwimmen, Skifahren, Wissen _____

4. Bäckerei, Bücherei, Konditorei, Metzgerei _____

5. Flöte, Klarinette, Piano, Saxophon, Trompete _____

6. Argument, Dokument, Experiment, Instrument, Moment _____

7. Aktion, Diskussion, Information, Region, Religion _____

8. Baby, Hündchen, Kalb, Kätzchen _____

9. Gabel, Löffel, Messer, Teller _____

10. Blume, Farbe, Hose, Katze, Lampe, Straße, Torte _____

11. Auto, Büro, Piano, Radio _____

Here are some bonus questions:

12. Der Polizist is the policeman. How do you form the female counterpart?

_____

13. Der Architekt is the male architect, What is the female counterpart? What are the plural forms for male architects and female architects?

_____

14. What are the plural forms of these singular nouns?

der Kuss _____

der Fluss _____

die Nuss _____

15. Make a compound word from these two words. das Tier (*the animal*) + der Arzt (the doctor) What is the English word? What is the gender of the compound word?

_____

Lassoing indefinite articles

Just as English has two indefinite articles — *a* and *an* — that you use with singular nouns, German has two indefinite articles (in the nominative case): **ein** for masculine and neuter-gender words and **eine** for feminine-gender words. An indefinite article has many of the same uses in both languages. You use it before a singular noun that's countable the first time it's mentioned — **Ein Mann geht um die Ecke** (*A man is walking around the corner*) — or when a singular countable noun represents a class of things — **Ein Elefant vergisst nie** (*An elephant never forgets*). You can also use **ein/eine** with a *predicate noun* (a noun that complements the subject): **Angela Merkel war eine geschickte <u>Bundeskanzlerin</u>** (*Angela Merkel was a skillful <u>chancellor</u>*).

Another similarity with English is that there's no plural form of the German indefinite article **ein/eine**. (Also, depending on how you're describing something plural, you may not need to use the plural definite article.) Look at the following generalized statement, which requires no article: **In Zermatt sind Autos verboten** (*Cars are forbidden in Zermatt [Switzerland]*).

The following minitable shows you the definite articles and the corresponding indefinite articles (nominative case only shown here):

Gender/Number	Definite (the)	Indefinite (a/an)
Masculine	der	ein
Feminine	die	eine
Neuter	das	ein
Plural	die	(no plural form)

Missing articles

In a few instances in German, you don't use an article in the sentence. First, you don't use the indefinite article when you mention someone's profession, nationality, or religion. Look at three examples:

>> **Mein Onkel war General bei der Bundeswehr.** (*My uncle was [a] general in the army.*)

>> **Sind Sie Australier oder Neuseeländer?** (*Are you [an] Australian or [a] New Zealander?*) Nationalities are nouns in German.

>> **Ich glaube, sie ist Lutheranerin.** (*I think she's [a] Lutheran.*) Members of a religious affiliation (or an affiliation such as a political party) are nouns in German.

Second, just as in English, you don't use the definite article in generalized statements using plural nouns in German. But you do use the plural definite article when you're not making a generalization: **Die Bäume haben keine Blätter** (*The trees have no leaves*).

Third, names of countries have genders in German, most often **das**, or *neuter* (refer to Chapter 1), but you generally don't include the definite article, such as in **Viele berühmte Komponisten sind aus Deutschland oder Österreich** (*Many famous composers are from Germany or Austria*).

A small number of exceptions exist, however:

>> **Die Schweiz gehört nicht zur Europäischen Union.** (*Switzerland doesn't belong to the European Union.*) Note **die**, the feminine definite article.

>> **Die Vereinigten Staaten sind die größte Volkswirtschaft der Welt.** (*The United States has the largest economy in the world.*) Note **die**, the plural definite article.

PRACTICE

Fill in the missing German words as indicated by the English in parentheses. You can find the German for these English words in previous sections, including tables 3-2 and 3-3. Refer to the earlier tables for help in deciding whether you need **der, die, das, ein, eine,** or no article, and for help selecting the correct endings for plurals. *Note:* All examples are in nominative case.

Q. _____ (*a window*) **im Wohnzimmer ist kaputt.**

A. **Ein Fenster im Wohnzimmer ist kaputt.** (*A window in the living room is broken.*)

16   _____ (*the chairs*) **sind nicht bequem** (*comfortable*).

17   **Ist er** _____ (*an American*)?

18   **Siehst du?** _____ (*the baby*) **spielt mit dem Hund.**

19   **Das ist** _____ (*a*) **gute** _____ (*idea*).

20   **Wo ist** _____ (*the castle*)?

21   **Können** _____ (*the boys*) **gut Fußball spielen?**

22   **Ist Herr Elster** _____ (*a doctor*)?

23   **Haben** _____ (*the two female students*) **einen Nebenjob** (*part-time job*)?

24   _____ (*the hotels*) **in der Stadtmitte sind laut.**

25   **Ist das** _____ (*a problem*) **für Sie?**

26   **Achtung!** _____ (*the knife*) **ist sehr scharf!**

27   **Wie heißt** _____ (*the girl*)?

28   **Mein Vater** _____ (*Australian*).

29   _____ (*laptops*) **sind heutzutage** (*these days*) **relativ billig** (*inexpensive*).

Calling All Cases: The Roles That Nouns and Pronouns Play

Cases indicate the role or function of nouns and pronouns in the sentence. English and German both have cases, as do most languages. Cases allow you to know the function of these words and how they connect with other words in a sentence. This section identifies the four German cases and how they're used, as well as how English and German cases compare.

Identifying the four cases

REMEMBER

German has four cases, and you need to know the ins and outs of them because they're the reason why nouns, pronouns, articles, and adjectives go through changes in spelling, the way a chameleon changes its color. Here are the four cases:

>> **Nominative case (nom.):** This case is for the subject of the sentence. The subject is a person or thing acting like the baseball player, Ortiz, who's at bat and hits the ball. In a sentence, it's who or what carries out the action. In **Ortiz schlägt den Ball** (*Ortiz hits the ball*), Ortiz is the subject.

You use the nominative case for *predicate nouns* as well; these nouns (or noun phrases) express more about the subject, such as a description or an identification. In *he's a remarkable baseball player*, both the subject (*he*) and the predicate noun phrase (*a remarkable baseball player*) are in the nominative case.

>> **Accusative case (acc.):** This case is for the direct object of the sentence. The direct object is a bit similar to the batter's ball; the subject is acting on it. In **Ein Zuschauer fängt den Ball** (*A spectator catches the ball*), the ball is the direct object.

Note: Prepositions also use the accusative case for the words they connect. (See Chapter 13 for more on prepositions.)

>> **Dative case (dat.):** This case is for the indirect object of the sentence. The *indirect object* receives the direct object; it's like the person the spectator gives the ball to. In **Der Zuschauer gibt seinem Sohn den Ball** (*The spectator gives his son the ball*), **seinem Sohn** (*his son*) is the indirect object, so it's in the dative case. In both German and English, you generally use the verb **geben** (*to give*) the same way; you *give* (the verb) something (**den Ball**, accusative case) to someone (**seinem Sohn**, dative case).

Note: Prepositions also use the dative case for the words they link with. (Again, see Chapter 13 for more on prepositions.)

>> **Genitive case (gen.):** This case shows possession. A person or thing can be the possessor, or owner. In **Die Mutter des Sohns jubelt** (*The mother of the son cheers*), the son "belongs to" his cheering mother; *des Sohns* is in the genitive case.

Note: Prepositions also use the genitive case for the words they link with. (See Chapter 13.)

Word endings alter slightly according to the case. These changes are necessary to identify what you want to express in a German sentence. (You find case-ending tables in Appendix B in the online content for *German Workbook for Dummies.* These tables come in extremely handy when you want to find the correct word and its word ending.)

Both English and German use the nominative case — the same case you use for subjects — when you have a predicate noun as the object of a sentence. A *predicate noun* is a person, thing, or a concept that you place on equal footing with the subject. These nouns state more about the subject. For English and German, the verb **sein** (*to be*) is the prime example of a verb that's followed by the predicate nominative. German also uses the predicate nominative with the verbs, **heißen** (*to be named, called*), **werden** (*to become*), and in a few cases **bleiben** (*to stay, remain*). (In English, people often call these verbs *linking verbs*.) Here's an example: **Mein Zahnarzt ist auch der Zahnarzt meiner Eltern** (*My dentist is also my parent's dentist*). **Mein Zahnarzt** and **der Zahnarzt** are both nominative case. (Isn't it fun to think of the literal translation of *dentist*? It's *tooth doctor*.)

Table 3-4 shows how the definite articles **der**, **die**, **das**, and **die** change in both gender and case. You see the four cases and the three genders, plus the plural form of the definite article *the*.

Table 3-4   German Words That Mean The

Case	Masculine	Feminine	Neuter	Plural
Nominative (subjects, predicate nouns)	der	die	das	die
Accusative (direct objects)	den	die	das	die
Dative (indirect objects)	dem	der	dem	den
Genitive (owned objects)	des	der	des	der

You have a grand total of six definite articles in German and one lonely word, *the*, in English. Practice makes perfect, so set your standards high for mastering the definite article in German. Try your hand at the following exercises.

Put in the missing German definite articles. Use Table 3-4 for help in deciding whether you need **der, die, das, den, dem,** or **des.** The grammar information in parentheses offers you help in doing the exercises. You see these abbreviations: *m.* = masculine, *f.* = feminine, *n.* = neuter, *pl.* = plural, *nom.* = nominative, *acc.* = accusative, *dat.* = dative, and *gen.* = genitive. These abbreviations refer to the noun that directly precedes them.

Q. _____ **Mannschaft** (*f., nom.*) **spielt sehr gut Fußball.**

A. **Die Mannschaft spielt sehr gut Fußball.** (*The team plays soccer very well.*)

30 Lesen Sie _____ Zeitung online (*f., acc.*)?

31 Ich möchte (*would like*) _____ Auto (*n., acc.*) kaufen.

32 Sehen Sie _____ Vogel? (*m., acc.*)

33 _____ Konzert (*n., nom.*) findet in der Olympiahalle statt.

34 Das ist _____ Freund (*m., nom.*) meiner Schwester.

35 Ich gebe _____ Pferd (*n., dat.*) eine Karotte.

36 _____ Leute (*pl., nom.*) sind sehr freundlich.

37 Ich finde _____ Stadt (*f., acc.*) wunderbar.

38 Der Hut _____ Frau (*f., gen.*) ist fantastisch.

39 _____ Kinder (*pl., nom.*) lernen sehr viel in der Schule.

40 _____ Essen (*n., nom.*) schmeckt sehr gut.

41 Kennst du _____ Mädchen (*n., acc.*)?

Putting Pronouns in Place

What's the big deal about pronouns — *you, me, it, them, this, that,* and more? First of all, these plentiful, useful, and essential critters are lurking in various corners of many sentences. Second, they're great for replacing or referring to nouns elsewhere in a sentence. Third, like articles in German, they need to change spelling/endings according to the role they're playing in a sentence (case) and the noun for which they may be doing the pinch-hitting.

This section discusses the personal pronouns. (For information on demonstrative and relative pronouns, go to the online case tables found in Appendix B of *German Workbook for Dummies*.) (See Chapter 9 for details on reflexive pronouns.) In German, all these pronouns are more affected by the gender/case patterns than they are in English, so I put them in tables for your reference. I arrange such tables in order of frequency of use: nominative, accusative, dative, and genitive.

REMEMBER

One more group of pronouns, called the possessive pronouns — **mein** (*my*), **dein** (*your*), **unser** (*our*), and so on — are technically classified as adjectives; they have endings that resemble those of descriptive adjectives such as *interesting, tiny,* or *pink.* (See Chapter 10 for more details on possessive adjectives/pronouns.)

Using personal pronouns

The personal-pronoun family comes in very handy in all kinds of situations when you want to talk (or write) about people, including yourself, without repeating names all the time. You use the nominative case very frequently in almost any language. Practically every sentence needs a subject, after all, and German is no exception. (See "Identifying the four cases" earlier in this chapter for more on cases.)

TIP

Try to memorize the personal pronouns as soon as possible and be sure that you know all three cases (no genitive here). With German personal pronouns, the biggest difference is that you have to distinguish among three ways to formulate how to say *you* to your counterpart: **du, ihr,** and **Sie.** Other personal pronouns, such as **ich** and **mich** (*I* and *me*) or **wir** and **uns** (*we* and *us*), bear a closer resemblance to English.

REMEMBER The genitive case isn't represented among the personal pronouns because it indicates possession. The personal pronoun **mich** (*me*) can represent only a person, not something they possess.

Check out Table 3-5 for the personal pronouns. Notice that *you* and *it* don't change, and the accusative (for direct objects) and dative (for indirect objects) pronouns are identical in English. I've added the distinguishing factors for the three forms **du, ihr,** and **Sie** in abbreviated form: singular = *s.*, plural = *pl.*, informal = *inf.*, formal = *form.*

Table 3-5 German Personal Pronouns

Nominative (nom.)	Accusative (acc.)	Dative (dat.)
ich (I)	**mich** (*me*)	**mir** (*me*)
du (*you*) (*s., inf.*)	**dich** (*you*)	**dir** (*you*)
er (*he*)	**ihn** (*him*)	**ihm** (*him*)
sie (*she*)	**sie** (*her*)	**ihr** (*her*)
es (*it*)	**es** (*it*)	**ihm** (*it*)
wir (*we*)	**uns** (*us*)	**uns** (*us*)
ihr (*you*) (*pl., inf.*)	**euch** (*you*)	**euch** (*you*)
sie (*they*)	**sie** (*them*)	**ihnen** (*them*)
Sie (*you*) (*s. or pl., form.*)	**Sie** (*you*)	**Ihnen** (*you*)

PRACTICE You have this exercise with the personal pronoun left out, followed by what you need to insert in parentheses (the pronoun in English/the case/directives for *you*, if that's the word needed). Refer liberally to Table 3-5.

Q. Wohnen _____ in der Nähe? (*you/nom./s., form.*)

A. Wohnen Sie in der Nähe? (*Do you live nearby?*)

42 Ich glaube, _____ arbeitet zu viel. (*you/nom./pl., inf.*)

43 Nein, _____ arbeiten nicht genug. (*we/nom.*)

44 Spielst _____ gern Karten? (*you/nom. /s., inf.*)

45 Ja, _____ spiele gern Poker. (*I/nom.*)

46 Kennst du _____ ? (*her/acc.*)

47 Ich gehe ohne _____ in die Stadt. (*you/acc./pl., inf.*)

48 Wirklich? Ich dachte, du gehst mit _____ . (*us/dat.*)

49 Der neue Chef? Ich finde _____ sehr kompetent. (*him/acc.*)

50 Mein Bruder braucht _____. (*me/acc.*)

51 Du sollst (*should*) mit _____ ausgehen. (*her/dat.*)

52 Aber ich möchte (*would like*) mit _____ ausgehen. (*you/dat./s., inf.*)

53 Könnte ich bitte mit _____ fahren? (*you/dat./s., form.*)

Answers to "Sorting Out Word Gender and Case" Practice Questions

1. **Fabrik, Logik, Politik, Statistik, Technik.** All are feminine (die). Only **die Statistik** has a plural form: die Statistiken.

2. **Audi, BMW, Ford, Mercedes, Porsche.** There are three reasons (almost). All are masculine nouns (der). All are cars, obviously, and even though Ford isn't a German automobile, Fords have been built in Germany since 1925.

3. **Leben, Lernen, Schwimmen, Skifahren, Wissen.** There are three reasons. All have the same gender (**das**) and no plural use. All are derived from the infinitive verb form: **das Leben** ([*the*] *life/living*), **das Lernen** (*learning*), **das Schwimmen** (*swimming*), **das Skifahren** (*skiing*), and **das Wissen** (*knowledge*).

4. **Bäckerei, Bücherei, Konditorei, Metzgerei.** There are three reasons (almost). They all have the same gender (**die**) and the same plural (**-en**). Almost all are shops that sell a particular item. **die Bäckerei** (*the bakery*), **die Bücherei** (*the library*), **die Konditorei** (*the pastry shop*), and **die Metzgerei** (*the butcher shop*). **Die Buchhandlung** (*the bookstore*) sells books.

5. **Flöte, Klarinette, Piano, Saxophon, Trompete.** There are two reasons. All are instruments; all are near cognates with English. **die Flöte** (*the flute*), **die Klarinette** (*the clarinet*), **das Piano** (*the piano*), **das Saxophon** (*the saxophone*), and **die Trompete** (*the trumpet*).

6. **Argument, Dokument, Experiment, Instrument, Moment.** There are two reasons. All have the same plural (**-e**), and all are cognates, but unlike the first four, which are neuter-gender, (**das**), **Moment** is **der Moment**.

7. **Aktion, Diskussion, Information, Region, Religion.** There are three reasons. All are feminine (**die**) gender, all have a (**-en**) plural ending, and all are cognates in English.

8. **Baby, Hündchen, Kalb, Kätzchen.** There are two reasons. All are (**das**) nouns, and all are young animals. Plurals are different: **die Babys** (*the babies*), **die Hündchen** (*the puppy dogs*), **die Kälber** (*the calves*), and **die Kätzchen** (*the kittens*).

9. **Gabel, Löffel, Messer, Teller.** All are items needed for eating: **die Gabel** (*the fork*), **der Löffel** (*the spoon*), **das Messer** (*the knife*), and **der Teller** (*the plate*). None has a change in plural except **die Gabeln** (plural).

10. **Farbe, Hose, Katze, Lampe, Straße, Torte.** There are two reasons. All are feminine (**die**) gender, and all have (**-n**) plurals: **Blume** (*flower*), **Farbe** (*color/paint*), **Hose** (*pants*), **Katze** (*cat*), **Lampe** (*lamp*), **Straße** (*street/road*), and **Torte** (*pie*). Note: **Die Hose** is singular, meaning a pair of pants: **Meine Hose ist sehr alt** (*My pants are very old.* Literally: *My pant is very old*).

11. **Auto, Büro, Piano, Radio.** There are two reasons. All are neuter-gender (**das**), and all have (**-s**) plurals: **das Auto** (*the car*), **Büro** (*the office*), **Piano** (*the piano*), and **Radio** (*the radio*).

12. **Der Polizist** (*the policeman*), **die Polizistin** (*the policewoman*).

13. **Der Architekt, die Architekten** (*the male architect[s]*); **die Architektin, die Architektinnen** (*the female architect[s]*).

14. **Der Kuss, die Küsse** (*the kiss[es]*), **der Fluss, die Flüsse** (*the river[s]*), **die Nuss, die Nüsse** (*the nut[s]*).

15) **Der Tierarzt** (*the veterinarian*). Remember that compound nouns always have the gender of the last noun.

16) **Die Stühle sind nicht bequem.** (*The chairs aren't comfortable.*)

17) **Ist er Amerikaner?** (*Is he an American?*)

18) **Siehst du? Das Baby spielt mit dem Hund.** (*Do you see? The baby is playing with the dog.*)

19) **Das ist eine gute Idee.** (*That's a good idea.*)

20) **Wo ist das Schloss?** (*Where is the castle?*)

21) **Können die Jungen gut Fußball spielen?** (*Can the boys play soccer well?*)

22) **Ist Herr Elster Arzt?** (*Is Herr Elster is a doctor?*)

23) **Haben die zwei Studentinnen einen Nebenjob?** (*Do the two students have a part-time/side job*)

24) **Die Hotels in der Stadtmitte sind laut.** (*The hotels in the city center are loud.*)

25) **Ist das ein Problem für Sie?** (*Is that a problem for you?*)

26) **Achtung! Das Messer ist sehr scharf!** (*Watch out! The knife is very sharp!*)

27) **Wie heißt das Mädchen?** (*What's the girl's name?*)

28) **Mein Vater ist Australier.** (*My father is [an] Australian.*)

29) **Laptops sind heutzutage relativ billig.** (*Laptops are relatively inexpensive these days.*)

30) **Lesen Sie die Zeitung online?** (*Are you reading/do you read the newspaper online?*)

31) **Ich möchte das Auto kaufen.** (*I'd like to buy the car.*)

32) **Sehen Sie den Vogel?** (*Do you see the bird?*)

33) **Das Konzert findet in der Olympiahalle statt.** (*The concert is taking place in the Olympiahalle.*)

34) **Das ist der Freund meiner Schwester.** (*That's my sister's friend.*)

35) **Ich gebe dem Pferd eine Karotte.** (*I'm giving/going to give the horse a carrot.*)

36) **Die Leute sind sehr freundlich.** (*The people are very friendly.*)

37) **Ich finde die Stadt wunderbar.** (*I think the city is wonderful.*)

38) **Der Hut der Frau ist fantastisch.** (*The woman's hat is fantastic.*)

39) **Die Kinder lernen sehr viel in der Schule.** (*The children learn/are learning a lot in school.*)

40) **Das Essen schmeckt sehr gut.** (*The food tastes really good.*)

41) **Kennst du das Mädchen?** (*Do you know the girl?*)

(42) **Ich glaube, ihr arbeitet zu viel.** (*I think you work too much.*)

(43) **Nein, wir arbeiten nicht genug.** (*No, we don't work enough.*)

(44) **Spielst du gern Karten?** (*Do you like to play cards?*)

(45) **Ja, ich spiele gern Poker.** (*Yes, I like to play poker.*)

(46) **Kennst du sie?** (*Do you know her?*)

(47) **Ich gehe ohne euch in die Stadt.** (*I'm going downtown without you.*)

(48) **Wirklich? Ich dachte, du gehst mit uns.** (*Really? I thought you were going with us.*)

(49) **Der neue Chef? Ich finde ihn sehr kompetent.** (*The new boss? I think he's very capable.*)

(50) **Mein Bruder braucht mich.** (*My brother needs me.*)

(51) **Du sollst mit ihr ausgehen.** (*You should go out with her.*)

(52) **Aber ich möchte mit dir ausgehen.** (*But I want to go out with you.*)

(53) **Könnte ich bitte mit Ihnen fahren?** (*Could I go/travel with you, please?*)

Chapter **4**

Building Your Word Power

U nless you want to confine your conversations to things like *The girl is pretty, I'm hungry,* and *Do you speak English?*, you probably want to develop your German vocabulary. Luckily, paying attention to how words are related to each other can boost your word power exponentially. As you discover how words are formed, you can categorize and store them in logical groups, such as word families, word categories, opposites, prefixes, and suffixes. You can also practice identifying *cognates* (words with a common source that mean the same thing in two languages), *near cognates* (words with a common source that mean nearly the same in two languages), and *false friends* (words that look the same but mean something different in two languages).

Even when you encounter a word you don't know, if you can identify something about that word, you may be able to figure out its meaning. The word **das Reisefieber**, for example, has two easily recognizable parts: **Reise** (*travel*) and **Fieber** (*fever*); together, they approximate the idea of excitement about traveling. This chapter takes a look at word structures specific to the German language, providing great opportunities for interesting word storage, among them compound nouns and picture language.

Working with Word Combinations

Word combinations are the kinds of words that have two or more parts, some of which may be separate words combined into one; others may be combinations of a prefix together with a noun, adjective, or verb. You find them frequently in both English and German, and in the case of German nouns, they sometimes look daunting from the standpoint of sheer length. When you're familiar with one or more parts of the word, however, you can often piece the others together.

REMEMBER Your key to increasing your vocabulary beyond the basics is getting the hang of recognizing the separate parts that fit together to form word combinations. Before you know it, you'll be feeling comfortable with the likes of words like **das Erntedankfest** *(Thanksgiving)* without thinking twice because you're able to figure out what the separate parts mean: **(die) Ernte** = *harvest, crop*, **(der) Dank** = *thanks* (the verb **danken** = *to thank*), and **(das) Fest** = *festival, celebration*. Each word element is useful as a separate word, so you're getting three words for the price — er, effort of one.

Spotting compound nouns

At times, German looks like a language made up of complicated, extremely long words. In fact, some people say that it not only sounds heavy and ponderous, but also looks heavy and ponderous. Most of these culprit words, called *compound words,* are really quite innocuous. After all, they're nothing more than a few smaller words strung together. German is rife with compound words that may or may not be two or more separate words in English. **Der Geschäftsmann** *(the businessman)* and **die Geschäftsfrau** *(the businesswoman)* are one word in both languages, but **der Kugelschreiber** *(the ballpoint pen)* is two words in English.

Recognizing the parts of compound words is a great way to increase your vocabulary threefold, sometimes more, depending on how many words combine to form a single word. When you break a long word into its parts, you can generally make a very accurate guess about what the compound means.

REMEMBER A *compound noun* is a combination of two or more words, usually both nouns. Some compound nouns are the exact equivalent of two words in English. **Das Fotoalbum** *(photo album),* for example, is a combination of **das Foto** *(photo)* + **das Album** *(album).* Others have a slightly different meaning compared with their usage as separate words. **Der Ruhetag** *(closing day)* is **die Ruhe** *(quiet, calm)* + **der Tag** *(day);* "**Montag Ruhetag**" could be a sign outside a restaurant indicating that it's closed on Monday.

My favorites among the compound nouns are what I call *picture word*s; they describe the meaning of the word in visual language that differs from the descriptions in English. I deal with picture words in the next section of this chapter.

REMEMBER There are a small number of changes in spelling in some compound words. The most common added letter you find is **s**; it appears in the middle of die **Arbeitszeit** *(the working hours),* a combination of **die Arbeit** *(the work)* and **die Zeit** *(the time.* In the word **der Orangensaft** *(the orange juice),* the **n** added in the middle indicates the plural of **die Orange** (**die Orangen**). Sometimes, a letter or two is dropped: **Das Fernsehprogramm** *(the TV program)* is composed of **der**

Fernseher or **das Fernsehen** (both mean *TV*) with the last two letters dropped (**-en** or **-er**) plus **das Programm.**

Compound nouns always take the gender of the last word in the combination. **Die Sportabteilung** (*sports department in a department store*) is feminine because the last word in the combination **der Sport** (*sport[s]*) + **die Abteilung** (*department*) is feminine.

Here are some more examples of how gender is determined:

>> **Wo sind meine Tennisschuhe?** (*Where are my tennis shoes?*) **Die Tennisschuhe** = **das Tennis** (*tennis*) + **die Schuhe** (*shoes*).

>> **Sie sind im Wohnzimmer.** (*They're in the living room.*) **Das Wohnzimmer** = **wohnen** (*to live*) + **das Zimmer** (*room*).

>> **Was ist deine Lieblingsspeise?** (*What's your favorite food?*) **Die Lieblingsspeise** = **Lieblings** (*favorite,* combined with other words) + **die Speise** (*food*).

>> **Ich liebe Himbeereis.** (*I love raspberry ice cream.*) **Das Himbeereis** = **die Himbeere** (*raspberry*) + **das Eis** (*ice cream*).

There's no easy test to determine whether a word is in fact a compound noun. Just look at the word, try to see where it breaks down, figure out what the parts mean, and put it back together again, making a reasonable stab at the meaning of that compound word. You may recognize one part as the noun form of a verb you know, or you may see a prefix that you're familiar with. The context of the word in a sentence is usually a good means of making an educated guess. And good dictionaries are your best bet if you're still stumped.

Combine the words from the word bank with the words in the exercise to form compound nouns in the exercise. Include the definite article. Some words undergo a slight change. Then write the English definition of the word next to the compound noun.

Q. der Rock _____.
_____.

A. **das Rockkonzert** (*the rock concert*). The definite article is **das** because **das Konzert** is the last word in the combination.

das Konzert	das Eis	die Stadt	die Tasche
der Knödel	das Spiel	das Essen	die Zeit
das Zimmer	der Kasten	das Brot	

1 der Käse _____ (Hint: The Earl of . . . may have invented them.)
Literally, it means *cheese bread*.

2 Haupt _____ (Hint: Berlin is an example of one.)

3 die Erdbeere _____ (Hint: It's a cool treat on a hot day.)

4 der Brief _____ (Hint: You find letters in it.)

5 der Schlaf _____ (Hint: It's the place you go to at the end of your day.)

6 der Computer _____

7 das Jahr _____ (Hint: There are four every year. Add **-es** between the two words.)

8 die Kartoffel _____. (Hint: It's a southern German/Austrian specialty often served with **Schweinebraten** [*roast pork*].)

9 die Hand _____

10 der Mittag _____

Describing picture compound nouns

With most compound nouns, you can easily get the general idea of what they mean by putting the meanings of the two (or more) parts together to form one meaning. With picture compound words, however, meaning isn't exactly obvious at first glance. These nouns may be only single words in English or English words that appear to be descriptive, making it a challenge to figure out their meaning.

>> **das Haus** (*house*) + **die Schuhe** (*shoes*) = **die Hausschuhe** (*slippers,* shoes you wear in the house)

TIP

The key to understanding the meaning of a picture compound word is using your imagination to think figuratively if the literal meaning doesn't make sense. Alternatively, try thinking (way) outside the box. Take the word **der Zahnstein,** which is made up of two reasonably common nouns: **Zahn** (*tooth*) and **Stein** (*stone*). So what in the world is a *tooth stone*? You may first conjure a picture of a stone that looks like a tooth. Good idea; close, but no dice. Now imagine what it would look like to have stones, or stonelike material, attached to a tooth. Does that sound like a possible description of *tartar*? That's it! **Zahnstein** is the reason the dental hygienist is always reprimanding you!

PRACTICE

Read the hints in the following exercise; each hint is for the picture compound noun that follows. Try to translate each element of the compound noun separately; then guess the meaning of the compound word.

Q. (*I need it when using a needle and thread.*) der Fingerhut _____ + _____ = _____.

A. *finger + hat = thimble*

11 (*I use them in the winter.*) die Handschuhe _____ + _____ = _____.

12 (*I use it on rainy days.*) der Regenschirm _____ + _____ = _____.

13. (*A black-and-white animal*) das Stinktier _____ +
_____ = _____ .

14. (*I can't get it out of my head.*) der Ohrwurm _____ +
_____ = _____ .

15. (*I read newsworthy articles in it.*) die Zeitschrift _____ +
_____ = _____ .

16. (*I wear it when I go to bed.*) der Schlafanzug _____ +
_____ = _____ .

Checking out verb combinations

Nouns aren't the only ones that can combine to form long words; verbs are guilty of the same habit. Figuring out the meaning of a verb combination is just as easy when you can break down the parts, which may be prefixes, prepositions, or verbs that combine with another verb.

TIP

How do you figure out the meaning of the verb? You need to break the verb into its parts, try to figure out what each part means, and put it back together again. The following tips can help:

>> **Try to recognize the discrete parts of the verb.** Look for prefixes or prepositions at the beginning of the word.

>> **Find out what these prefixes or prepositions mean if you don't know already.** (Chapter 8 deals with separable- and inseparable-prefix verbs, Chapter 13 handles prepositions, and Chapter 9 includes a section on verbs and prepositions.)

>> **Some prefixes or prepositions have equivalents in English.** Take the example of **vor**: It usually means *before,* and as far as pronunciation goes, it resembles the prefix *fore-* in words such as *foreshadow* and *foresight.* With others, you may need to find out what they mean: **Zusammen** *(together)* doesn't resemble English, but it has the same number of syllables, so that may be a method of remembering its meaning.

Take the verb **regenerieren**. Break it down into **re-** + **gener-** + **-ieren**. The prefix **re-** has the same meaning in English *(to repeat an action),* and **-ieren** is a variation on the regular infinitive verb ending **-en**; it often means *-ate* or *-ify* in English. Putting the word together, you can make a correct guess that **regenerieren** means *to regenerate.*

>> **Ich möchte zum Hotel zurückgehen.** *(I'd like to go back to the hotel.)* The prefix **zurück** means *back* or *return,* and the verb **gehen** is *to go* or *walk.*

>> **Die Familie ist zum Erntedankfest zusammengekommen.** *(The family gathered together for Thanksgiving.)* The verb **zusammenkommen** is in present perfect tense; the prefix **zusammen** means *together,* and **kommen** means *to come.*

Furthermore, many nouns are derived from the verb combinations. Most have different endings. Look at these examples:

>> The verb is **fortsetzen** (to continue); the noun is **die Fortsetzung** (continuation, sequel).

>> The verb is **vorfahren** (to drive up; the noun is **die Vorfahrt** (right of way).

PRACTICE

Match the English definitions of the verbs with the given German verb. Look at the prefix/preposition/verb tables in Chapter 8 first or try to make an educated guess. Refer to the English word bank. If you want to challenge yourself more, cover the list — now! Then write the English definition without looking.

Q. zusammenbrechen _____

A. to collapse, break down

to collapse, break down	to complete	to plan	to spend [money]
to leave, take off	to arrive	to be fond of	to assemble
to collaborate			

17 ankommen _____

18 abfahren _____

19 vorhaben _____

20 vollenden _____

21 mitarbeiten _____

22 ausgeben _____

23 zusammensetzen _____

24 liebhaben _____

Grasping Word Families and Word Categories

Memory works best when your brain can make lots of connections, so grouping German words in word families and word fields can help you remember vocab for the long term. This is good news, because enhancing your vocabulary dramatically increases the ways you can express yourself.

TIP

Explore a frequently used verb and find out some other useful words and expressions related to it. Use a good German–English dictionary as a reference. (See Chapter 2 for information on using a bilingual dictionary.) You often find related words and expressions under more than one *headword* (main dictionary entry), especially if it's a frequently used verb. Record new vocabulary in groups, using the headword for reference. Below the headword **leben** (to live), for example, you find the expression **Hier läßt es sich gut leben** (*It's a good life here*). The previous headword is **das Leben** ([the] *life*) with the expression **So ist das Leben** (*That's life*). Following **leben** is **lebendig** (*alive, lively*), with the expression **eine lebendige Diskussion** (*a lively discussion*). Another headword, **Lebens-**, combines to form several compound words, such as **die Lebensbedingungen** (*living conditions*), **die Lebenserfahrung** (*life experience*), and **die Lebenshaltungskosten** (plural in German) (*cost of living*).

This section discusses how you can use word families and word categories to your advantage to strengthen your German vocabulary.

Working with word families

Picture a family seated around a bountiful table for **das Erntedankfest** (*Thanksgiving*). Replace the family members with words, put the family elder(s) at the head of the table, and there you have it: a word family. It's made up of words that have the same root or origin. Some word families are very numerous, including ten or more nouns (descendants of the elders), a verb (family elder), adjectives, and maybe even an adverb, all of which are related. Some word families have an extended family — cousin words that have the same root but are words combined from other families.

DIFFERENCES

Nouns and verbs in an English word family may be exactly the same or slightly different: *to heat* and *the heat, to live* and *the life*. German follows suit, but it puts an infinitive ending (**-en**) on verbs, as in **arbeiten** and **die Arbeit**. Some English and German words have *suffixes* — endings tacked on to words. English adjective endings include *-able, -y*, and *-al*, as in *likeable, windy*, and *critical*. Some German adjective endings are **-lich, -ig**, and **-isch**, as in **lieblich** (*delightful*, or *sweet* as in wine), **windig** (*windy*), and **kritisch** (*critical*). (See Chapter 10 for more on adjectives.)

Consider the verb **arbeiten** (*to work*). It's pretty much the same as the noun **die Arbeit** (*the work*). Other words in the same family include **der Arbeiter** (*the worker*) and **die Arbeiterin** (*the female worker*). The extended family includes word combinations like **die Arbeiterschaft** (*the workforce*, **der Arbeitsablauf** (*the workflow*), and **arbeitswütig** (*workaholic* — an adjective in German).

PRACTICE

Match the English definitions in the word bank with the German words in the exercise. Some hints are indicated in parentheses; adj. is the abbreviation for adjective. The root (family elder) is **arbeiten** (*to work*).

Q. das Arbeitsamt _____

A. the employment office; **das Amt** means *the (public) office.*

the employment office	labor saving	the employer
the attitude to work	the employee	the working class
the place of work, workstation	the workroom	the unemployment compensation
jobless		

25   die Arbeiterklasse _____

26   der Arbeitgeber (**geben** = *to give*) _____

27 das Arbeitslosengeld (**Geld** = *money*) _____

28 arbeitsparend (adj.) (**Geld sparen** = *to save money*)_____

29 arbeitslos (adj.) (suffix **-los** = *-less, without*) _____

30 der Arbeitnehmer (**nehmen** = *to take*) _____

31 der Arbeitsplatz _____

32 die Arbeitsmoral _____

33 der Arbeitsraum _____

PRACTICE

Write each English translation from the word bank next to its German equivalent. Some hints are indicated in parentheses; adj. is the abbreviation for adjective. The root is **fahren** (*to drive, go*).

Q. die Fahrbahn (*of traffic on a highway*) _____

A. the lane

the lane	the direction of traffic	the exit
driver's license	the ticket	the driving instructor
negligent, reckless	the passenger	the entrance
the schedule		

34 die Fahrkarte _____

35 die Einfahrt (*here: entrance to a highway*) _____

36 der Fahrgast (**der Gast** = *the guest*) _____

37 die Fahrtrichtung _____

38 der Führerschein or die Fahrerlaubnis (**erlauben** = *to allow, permit*) _____

39 fahrlässig (adj.) (*It's dangerous to be near someone driving like this.*)_____

40 der Fahrlehrer _____

41 der Fahrplan _____

42 die Ausfahrt (*here: from a highway*) _____

Picture that!: Working with word categories

To record new vocabulary in categories, use the techniques that work best with that category. Sketch your home office, for example, and label it in as much detail as you can. Are you planning on going skiing or hiking in the Alps? Draw a mountain scene, and label it. You won't need to use any English translations. (Even if your rendition of a chairlift looks like planks hanging on a rope, *you* know what it is.) The categories are practically limitless, and they can include your interests in German.

The key to successful word storage is choosing the best means of organizing words. By organizing the words well, you usually don't need to translate them into English. You're on the road to thinking in German. Select meaningful categories that correspond to any interests you have, personal or professional, sports or hobbies, intellectual or mundane — the sky's the limit. When you're motivated by such topics, you're bound to find it extremely easy and fun to find and store words in your area of interest.

TIP

Here are some great ways to store new words:

>> **List related words in an order that's meaningful to you.** You might write shopping lists, grouped by vegetables, snacks, or proteins, or list fruits and vegetables by color. Or tell a story. Write words (verbs are always useful) or sentences describing your morning routine in order.

>> **Write words in a way that reflects their meaning.** You might write color words in German in the colors they represent. Use emojis to show feelings. You could write **Er ist sehr traurig** + 😢 (crying emoji). Presto — no English translation needed. Well, if you do need it: *He's very sad.*

>> **Flashcards are great — if you write them yourself.** Instead of German on one side and English on the other, be creative: Write a question on one side and the answer on the other: **Was möchten Sie trinken?/Ich hätte gerne ein helles (Bier).** *(What would you like to drink?/I'll have a lager beer.)* No need to use English. Or write opposite adjectives and put them in a phrase: **ein interessanter Dokumentarfilm/ein langweiliger Dokumentarfilm** *(an interesting documentary film/a boring documentary film)*. If you must resort to German/English, use color coding to help you, such as red for feminine nouns, blue for masculine nouns, and green for neuter nouns. Be sure to include the gender of the noun and its plural form. Always read out loud as you review the flashcards.

>> **Develop a "word fan" showing the spectrum of words in a range of description.** For verbs of speed, start with **kriechen** *(to crawl)* and move on up to **laufen** *(to run)*. Other categories of words that work well arranged in this fashion are adverbs of frequency (arranged from **niemals** *[never]* to **immer** *[always]*) and a range of emotions starting with **deprimiert** *(depressed)* and ending with **entzückt** *(delighted)*.

>> **Describe how to do simple tasks or routines.** This description could be making coffee, hanging a picture on the wall, or getting ready to go to work. Use as many verbs as possible.

>> **Label words describing locations where they belong on a picture or a map.** To remember prepositions such as *over, under, beside,* and *in front of,* draw a picture of a living room, and write the word **über** *(above)* over the coffee table. Or draw an object, such as a cat under the table, and write a sentence like **Die Katze ist unter dem Tisch** *(The cat's under the*

table). Use a street map and a starting point on it for labeling **links** *(left)*, **rechts** *(right*, **an der Kreuzung** *(at the intersection)*, and so on.

» **Make a word web or chart to show how ideas relate.** If you're listing words related to air travel, write the word **der Flughafen** *(the airport)* in the middle. Then add several branches for word groups like **die Abfertigung** *(check-in)*, **die Sicherheitskontrolle** *(security check)*, **im Flugzeug** *(in the airplane)*, and so on.

» **Draw a bird's-eye view of die Nachbarschaft** *(neighborhood)* **or die Stadtmitte** *(the city center)*, **and label places.** Sketch a dollhouse and label the rooms and furniture, or choose a single room, such as **die Küche** *(the kitchen)* or **das Wohnzimmer** *(the living room)*. Make a diagram of your family tree. Draw a person, and label all the parts of the body. For every noun you write, remember to include the articles **der/die/das** and the plural form.

» **For individual words within a group, draw a picture of that word, and incorporate the word into the picture.** Nouns, adjectives, and even verbs lend themselves well to this storage method. Take **der Berg** *(the mountain)*. Draw the outline of a mountain and fill it with the word **der Berg**. Draw adjectives to resemble what they mean: Write **gross** and **klein** *(large* and *small)* using huge letters and tiny letters. Picture-compound nouns are great fun to draw. With **der Leckerbissen** *(the treat;* literally: *tasty + bite)*, draw someone who is licking their lips or whose mouth is watering, add a plus sign (+), and draw some teeth biting something you love to eat.

PRACTICE

Using the word bank of colors, write **die Farben** *(the colors)* in the exercise. You need to use some colors more than once. Why is this exercise so simple? Instead of translating German to English, you place colors in some context, eliminating translation.

Q. Wenn du alt bist, werden deine Haare _____ oder _____.

A. grau/weiß *(When you're old, your hair will turn gray or white.)*

grau	blau	braun	gelb	gold	grün
lila	orange	rosa	rot	schwarz	weiß

43 Ich trinke_____ -nsaft zum Frühstück.

44 Drei Augenfarben sind (**Augen** = *eyes*) _____, _____ und _____.

45 Flamingos sind _____.

46 Die deutsche Flagge ist _____, _____ und _____.

47 Pflaumen *(plums)* und Auberginen *(eggplants)* sind _____.

48 Die Sonne ist _____, das Gras ist _____ und der Himmel *(sky)* ist _____.

Streamlining Word Storage

In reading and listening to German, you're likely to find a surprisingly large number of words that are comparable in the two languages (words that have the same common source and mean the same thing); they're called *cognates*. Their cousins are the *near cognates*: words that have a common source, mean nearly the same in two languages, and may be spelled somewhat differently. Then you run across the *false friends*, which have a surprisingly different meaning in the other language, even though they look the same.

Half the battle of vocabulary acquisition is knowing how a word fits into a larger group and, of course, how to use it. Imagine a chest of many drawers marked *cognates*, *near cognates*, and *false friends*. As you open the drawers of this section one by one, you find hands-on opportunities to increase your awareness of storing words in ways that enable you to retrieve them easily.

Recognizing cognates and near cognates

Cognates and near cognates are words with a common source that mean the same or nearly the same thing in two languages. In the case of German and English, many words have the same roots, although some have undergone spelling changes over time. Aside from **der Arm, die Hand, der Kindergarten, das Knie, der Rucksack, die Wanderlust, der Zeitgeist,** and other such classics, you can discover a plethora of others, many of which you can group by the similarity of their structure. As you recognize the similarities, place the words accurately in their groups. Some minor spelling changes are easy to recognize. The letter *c* in English is usually **k** in German, *sh* in English is **sch** in German, and so on.

TIP

Here's a small sampling of characteristics that signal English/German cognates:

>> Nouns ending in **-er** often denote a person who works at the job the word describes. Someone who designs is a designer, which is a cognate (**der Designer**).

Nouns ending in **-or** build a similar group of cognates: **der Professor**.

>> Adjectives ending in **-al** are often cognates: **liberal**.

>> Verbs ending in **-ieren** are often near cognates: **reparieren** = *to repair*.

>> French words used in English and German are sometimes cognates: **das Portrait**.

>> German words used in English aren't exactly cognates because they're the same word, but why not make use of this precious resource? **der Ersatz** = *the alternative, replacement*.

Here are some verbs ending in **-ieren** that are near cognates: **denunzieren** (denounce), **existieren** (exist), **fotografieren** (photograph), **frustrieren** (frustrate), **reformieren** (reform), **regulieren** (regulate), and **simulieren** (simulate).

Arrange the following words from the word bank in groups according to five characteristics for categorizing cognates described in this section: nouns ending in **-er**, nouns ending in **-or** adjectives ending in **-al**, French words, and German words. To challenge you, the words that belong to the three categories with endings (**-er, -or,** and **-al**) are written without the ending. Add the ending to the word after the hyphen and list the word in the correct category.

PRACTICE

Q. Nouns ending in -er

A. der Jogger

der Jogg-	norm-	das Café	der Reakt-
kitschig	form-	der Priest-	der Direkt-
das Restaurant	der Design-	gemütlich	diagon-
der Report-	optim-	der Chauffeur	der Profess-
der Fisch-	das Dekolleté	der Poltergeist	liber-
das Portrait	der Ventilat-	kaputt	die Angst
der Radiat-			

49 Nouns ending in -**er**

   der Jogger

   ††††† _____ ††††† _____ ††††† _____ ††††† _____

50 Nouns ending in -**or**

   ††††† _____ ††††† _____ ††††† _____ ††††† _____ ††††† _____

51 Adjectives ending in -**al**

   ††††† _____ ††††† _____ ††††† _____ ††††† _____ ††††† _____

52 French words

   ††††† _____ ††††† _____ ††††† _____ ††††† _____ ††††† _____

53 German words

   ††††† _____ ††††† _____ ††††† _____ ††††† _____ ††††† _____

False friends: Bad buddies

The following can easily happen: You start getting chummy with some words that are the same in both languages. You're borrowing English words left and right, plopping them into German phrases with great success. Along comes a word in German that looks like an English word, so you decide to use it. It's your new German colleague's birthday, so you buy a little present, walk up, and say "**Ein Gift für Sie.**" You've just offered them some poison! (Yes, it's a unique gift, but did you have to blurt it out and ruin the surprise?) That's right: **Das Gift** means *poison*. The word for *present* is **das Geschenk.**

WARNING

If you assume that you can blithely use a word you read in German without being sure what it actually means, watch out! German is rife with potential bloopers, called *false friends* or *false cognates,* such as **das Gift.** Conversely, German has borrowed words from English, using them differently. A cellphone, for example, is called **ein Handy** in German. When cellphones were new, some German speakers swore up and down that *handy* was the correct expression in English as well. Without a handy bilingual dictionary, leave any questionable words out of your active vocabulary for the time being. Better safe than sorry.

Take a look at some words that can lead to mixups: **Das ist das Albert Einstein Gymnasium**. "Strange — was Einstein a star basketball player too?" you think as the tour guide points out a large building that looks an awful lot like a school. That's because **das Gymnasium** is *high school* in German. Here's another one: **Das ist ein grosses** *(large)* **Bad**. Does this mean, a big bad somebody, such as big bad John? Well, that's one way to remember what it means; **das Bad** is a *bathroom, john, loo, head*, or whatever you want to call it.

TIP

To remember some tricky false friends, draw a picture of what the word means and label it, show what the word means by incorporating the word into the picture itself, or make the letters of the word take the shape of an object. You may be visualizing something slightly bizarre, and that's the fun part, which will probably help you remember the word more readily. **Der Herd** *(stove, range)* may work if, in your mind's eye, you see a bunch of stoves with horns out on the range in Texas. (*Note:* **Die Herde** means *the herd*, as in a *group of cows*. It's a different entry in the dictionary, however, because it has a different meaning, spelling, and gender.)

PRACTICE

The following 12 German words embedded in sentences have a different meaning from their English lookalikes. Read the word in the context of the sentence, look at the English definitions in the word bank, and write the definition that logically fits.

Q. Ich arbeite am Samstag, <u>also</u> schlafe ich am Sonntag. _____

A. **so, therefore, thus** (*I'm working on Saturday, so I'll sleep on Sunday.*)

so, therefore, thus	daily special	vintage car	friendly, likeable
consistent, logical	good, well behaved	condom	sensitive
prescription	advice	soon	dung
perhaps, possibly			

54 Ich komme **bald** — warte nur fünf Minuten. _____

55 Diese Kinder sind **brav**. Sie gehorchen *(obey)* ihren Eltern. _____

56 **Ein Präservativ** hilft gegen Schwangerschaften *(pregnancies)*. _____

57 Du bist sehr logisch und **konsequent** — bravo. _____

58 Was ist **das Menü** heute im Restaurant? _____

59 Ich habe **Mist** unter meinen Schuhen. Es stinkt! _____

60 Kommen Sie? Ich weiß nicht — **eventuell**. _____

61 Er geht zum Arzt *(doctor)*; er braucht **ein Rezept**. _____

62 Was soll ich tun? Ich brauche **einen Rat**. _____

63 Sie hat viele Freunde; sie ist sehr **sympathisch**. _____

Answers to "Building Your Word Power" Practice Questions

1. **das Käsebrot** (*cheese sandwich*). Literally, it means *cheese bread*.

2. **die Hauptstadt** (*capital city*). Literally, it means *main city*.

3. **das Erdbeereis** (*strawberry ice cream*). The last **-e** from **Erdbeere** is dropped for pronunciation purposes.

4. **der Briefkasten** (*mailbox*).

5. **das Schlafzimmer** (*bedroom*). The verb **schlafen** drops the -en infinitive ending.

6. **das Computerspiel** (*computer game*).

7. **die Jahreszeit** (*season*).

8. **der Kartoffelknödel** (*potato dumpling*).

9. **die Handtasche** (*handbag*).

10. **das** Mittagessen (*lunch*). Literally, it means *noon meal*.

11. **die Handschuhe**: *hand + shoes = gloves*.

12. **der Regenschirm**: *rain + shield = umbrella*.

13. **das Stinktier**: *stink + animal = skunk*.

14. **der Ohrwurm**: *ear + worm = catchy tune*.

15. **die Zeitschrift**: *time + script/text = magazine*.

16. **der Schlafanzug**: *sleep + suit = pajamas*.

17. **ankommen**: *to arrive*.

18. **abfahren**: *to leave*.

19. **vorhaben**: *to plan*.

20. **vollenden**: *to complete*.

21. **mitarbeiten**: *to collaborate*.

22. **ausgeben**: *to spend (money)*.

23. **zusammensetzen**: *to assemble*.

24. **liebhaben**: *to be fond of* (also **lieben**, *to love*).

(25) **die Arbeiterklasse**: *the working class.*

(26) **der Arbeitgeber**: *the employer.*

(27) **das Arbeitslosengeld**: *the unemployment compensation.*

(28) **arbeitsparend**: *labor-saving.*

(29) **arbeitslos**: *jobless.*

(30) **der Arbeitnehmer**: *the employee.*

(31) **der Arbeitsplatz**: *the place of work, workstation.*

(32) **die Arbeitsmoral**: *the attitude toward work.*

(33) **der Arbeitsraum**: *the workroom.*

(34) **die Fahrkarte**: *the ticket.*

(35) **die Einfahrt**: *the entrance.*

(36) **der Fahrgast**: *the passenger.*

(37) **die Fahrtrichtung**: *the direction of traffic.*

(38) **der Führerschein, die Fahrerlaubnis**: *driver's license.*

(39) **fahrlässig**: *negligent, reckless. (lässig* can also mean *casual.)*

(40) **der Fahrlehrer**: *the driving instructor.*

(41) **der Fahrplan**: *the schedule.*

(42) **die Ausfahrt**: *the exit.*

(43) **Ich trinke Orangensaft zum Frühstück.** *(I drink orange juice for breakfast.)*

(44) **Drei Augenfarben sind grün, blau und braun.** *(Three eye colors are green, blue, and brown.)*

(45) **Flamingos sind rosa.** *(Flamingos are pink.)*

(46) **Die deutsche Flagge ist schwarz, rot, und gold.** *(The German flag is black, red, and gold.)*

(47) **Pflaumen und Auberginen sind lila.** *(Plums and eggplants are purple.)*

(48) **Die Sonne ist gelb, das Gras ist grün und der Himmel ist blau.** *(The sun is yellow, the grass is green, and the sky is blue.)*

(49) Nouns ending in **-er**: **der Jogger, der Designer, der Fischer, der Priester, der Reporter.**

(50) Nouns ending in **-or**: **der Direktor, der Professor, der Radiator, der Reaktor, der Ventilator.**

(51) Adjectives ending in **-al**: **diagonal, formal, liberal, normal, optimal.**

(52) French words: **das Café, der Chauffeur, das Decolleté, das Portrait, das Restaurant.**

(53) German words: **die Angst, gemütlich, kaputt, kitschig, der Poltergeist.**

(54) **bald**: *soon. (I'm coming soon, wait just five minutes.)*

(55) **brav**: *good, well-behaved. (These children are well-behaved. They obey their parents.)*

(56) **Ein Präservativ:** *condom. (A condom helps against pregnancies.)*

(57) **konsequent**: *consistent, logical. (You're very logical and consistent.)*

(58) **das Menü:** *daily special. (What's the daily special in this restaurant today?)*

(59) **Mist**: *dung. (I've got dung under my shoes. It stinks!)*

(60) **eventuell:** *perhaps, possibly. (Are you coming? I don't know.)*

(61) **ein Rezept:** *prescription. (He's going to the doctor; he needs a prescription.)*

(62) **einen Rat:** *advice. (What should I do? I need advice.)*

(63) **sympathisch:** *friendly, likeable. (She has many friends; she's very friendly.)*

2
Focusing on the Present

Chapter **5**

Grasping the Present Tense

Y ou're driving down the road when you see a small herd of cows. Some *are grazing*, others *are chewing* their cud. Okay, so they*'re drooling* too, but even so, it gets you on to thoughts about milk, and the idea *hits* you: You*'re going to get* some ice cream. You say to yourself, "I think I*'ll go* to Jan and Berry's because I really *do owe* myself a treat. After all, I*'ve been working* hard, and —" you *wake up* and *realize* you*'ve been dreaming* for the past five minutes. Darn!

Believe it or not, this isn't a plug for ice cream. It is, however, a superb example of how streamlined German can be, because you can put all the verbs in the preceding paragraph (marked in italics) in the present tense in German. This multitalented player stands in for the plain old simple present tense (*gets, wake up*), the present continuous (*are driving, are chewing*), an emphatic form (*do owe*), some futures (*are going to get, will go*), and even references to actions that started in the past (*have been working, have been dreaming*). **Das hört sich gut an, oder?** *(That sounds good, doesn't it?)* (For more information on the terminology of verb tenses, see Chapter 2.)

And all along, you thought I was going to start with something along the lines of "First things first: The *present tense* is the verb form you use to talk about the present. Period." Well, that's true for sure, but there's more to it. In this chapter, you see how to conjugate regular and irregular verbs. You also see how surprisingly versatile the present tense is in German.

Getting Your Verbs in Shape: Present-Tense Conjugations

I love to talk — about myself, family, friends, job, and what's going on in my life. Talking (and writing) about all these things and more in German is usually a matter of knowing how to construct a verb in the present tense with the help of a noun (subject) and a few other elements. Most German verbs are *regular*, meaning that they follow a standard pattern of conjugation. Think of conjugation as activating a verb from its sleepy infinitive form found in dusty dictionaries (**leben, lachen, lieben**) and its English equivalent with that pesky *to* (*to live, to laugh, to love*) into a form that's compatible with the subject.

This section shows you how to put verbs through their paces by conjugating them and combining them with nouns, pronouns, and other grammar goodies so you can start using German with confidence.

Agreeing with the regulars

Regular verbs don't have any change in their basic form, which I call the *stem*. You conjugate a verb by taking the stem — which is almost always the result of lobbing off **-en** from the infinitive form of the verb (the not-yet conjugated form) — and adding the right ending to the verb. In the present tense, English has only the ending *-s* or no ending at all (*I live, you live, he lives*), whereas German has four endings (**-e, -st, -t,** and **-en**).

To conjugate a regular verb in the present tense, just drop the **-en** from the infinitive and add the appropriate ending to the stem. The endings are **-e, -st, -t, -en, -t, -en,** and **-en.** (Note that **-t** gets used twice and **-en** three times.) The following verb table shows how to conjugate the verb **kommen** *(to come)*. I've simply added the present-tense endings, marked in bold, to the stem **komm-.** (Make sure that you know the meanings of the subject pronouns by checking Table 1-1 in Chapter 1.)

kommen (to come)

ich komm**e**	wir komm**en**
du komm**st**	ihr komm**t**
er/sie/es komm**t**	sie komm**en**

Sie komm**en**.

Here's **kommen** in action:

> » **Er kommt aus Irland.** (*He comes from Ireland.*)

If the verb stem ends in **-d** or **-t**, place **e** in front of the verb endings **-st** and **-t** to make the verb easier to pronounce. The following table shows how you conjugate a regular verb like **arbeiten** *(to work)* in the present tense. The endings are marked in bold in the table. The stem **arbeit-** ends in **-t**, so you add an **e** before the verb endings for the second- and third-person singular (**du arbeitest, er/sie/es arbeitet**) and the second-person plural familiar form (**ihr arbeitet**).

arbeiten (to work)

ich arbeite	wir arbeiten
du arbeitest	ihr arbeitet
er/sie/es arbeitet	sie arbeiten

Sie arbeiten.

And here's **arbeiten** in action:

>> **Du arbeitest sehr schnell.** *(You work very fast.)*

REMEMBER

Both English and German sometimes insert extra vowels to make a verb easier to pronounce. Just try saying *she teachs* as one syllable: it's not easy. English adds an *e* before the *-s* so *teaches* expands to two syllables; the listener can then recognize that the speaker is using the third-person singular. German adds **-est** and **-et** to du **arbeit-** and **er/sie/es arbeit-** for the same reason: pronunciation. Adding the **e** lets speakers pronounce **arbeitet** with three syllables.

With a few verbs that don't have an **-en** infinitive ending, notably **wandern** *(to hike)* and **tun** *(to do)*, drop **-n** from the infinitive and add only **-n** (not **-en**) to

>> The first-person plural form: **wir wandern** *(we hike)* and **wir tun** *(we do)*

The third-person plural form: **sie wandern** *(they hike)* and **sie tun** *(they do)*

>> The formal second-person singular and plural form: **Sie wandern** *(you hike)* and **Sie tun** *(you do)*

The following table lists other common regular German verbs. You can use the regular conjugation on all of them:

arbeiten *(to work)*	**kosten** *(to cost)*
besuchen *(to visit)*	**lachen** *(to laugh)*
bringen *(to bring)*	**leben** *(to live)*
finden *(to find, have an opinion)*	**lernen** *(to learn)*
gehen *(to go, walk)*	**machen** *(to make, do)*
heißen *(to be called, named)*	**machen** *(to make, do)*
hören *(to hear)*	**reisen** *(to travel)*
finden *(to find, have an opinion)*	**sagen** *(to say)*
gehen *(to go, walk)*	**schmecken** *(to taste)*
heißen *(to be called, named)*	**schreiben** *(to write)*
kaufen *(to buy)*	**schwimmen** *(to swim)*
kennen *(to know [a person])*	**singen** *(to sing)*
kochen *(to cook)*	**spielen** *(to play [a game, cards])*
kommen *(to come)*	**trinken** *(to drink)*
kaufen *(to buy)*	**wandern** *(to hike, wander)*
kochen *(to cook)*	**wohnen** *(to live [reside])*

PRACTICE

In the following exercise, decide which verb conjugation to insert in the space provided. The English verb is at the end of the phrase, and the personal pronoun provides the clue for the German ending. If you don't see the personal pronoun, think which one would replace the noun(s) or name(s) that you do see and conjugate as you would for that pronoun.

Q. Was _____ ihr? (*to play*)

A. Was spielt ihr? (*What are you playing?*)

1. Sabina und Moritz _____ nach Australien. (*to travel*)

2. Das Handy (*cellphone*) _____ sehr viel Geld. (*to cost*)

3. Meine Großmutter und ich _____ beide Monika. (*to be named, called*)

4. _____ du oft E-Mails? (*to write*)

5. Ich _____ sehr gern in den Bergen. (*to hike*)

6. Wo _____ Sie? (*to live*)

7. Manfred _____ heute Abend spät nach Hause. (*to come*)

8. _____ ihr den Mann da drüben? (*to know*)

9. Ja, mein Mann _____ mit ihm. (*to work*)

10. Wohin _____ Sie? (*to go*)

11. Heute _____ Florian und Maria ein Auto. (*to buy*)

12. Ich _____ Deutsch sehr leicht zu lernen. (*to find, have the opinion*)

Conjugating verbs with spelling changes

The verbs in this section are more or less regular, but their stems undergo a few small changes in spelling. Luckily — or unluckily, depending on how you see it — many of the spelling-change verbs are frequently used, so perhaps you can acquire them by osmosis! You may notice that some of the verbs here are *cognates* — words that come from a common ancestor and are often similar in meaning and spelling. **Fallen** and *to fall*, for example, are the same, taking into account the German infinitive ending **-en**. Also, **helfen** and *to help* closely resemble each other. (Check out Chapter 4 for more information about cognates.).

These verbs with spelling changes are technically classified as verbs with stem-vowel changes because — you guessed it — the vowel(s) in the stem changes when you conjugate the verb. (The *stem* is the part of the infinitive left after you slice off the **-en** ending. **Sprechen** [*to speak*] is the infinitive, and **sprech-** is the stem.)

The stem-vowel changes take place in the **du** and **er/sie/es** forms (and, in one verb type, the **ich** form). When dealing with these types of verbs, you encounter the following changes:

» a ⇨ ä; au ⇨ äu (very small group including **laufen** *[to run]*)

» e ⇨ i

» e ⇨ ie

» e ⇨ i (**nehmen**); also, consonant change **hm** to **mm** (see the **nehmen** verb table)

» I ⇨ ei (**wissen**); also, **ich** and **er/sie/es** forms have no endings (see the **wissen** verb table)

The next five tables show each of these stem-vowel changes, along with the additional changes in **nehmen** *(to take)* and **wissen** *(to know as a fact)* groups. In these tables, only the stem-vowel changing verb forms are in bold.

fahren *(to drive):* **a ⇨ ä**

ich fahre	wir fahr**en**
du **fährst**	ihr fahr**t**
er/sie/es **fährt**	sie fahr**en**

Sie fahr**en**.

Take **fahren** for a drive:

» **Du fährst sehr vorsichtig.** *(You drive very carefully.)*

Other **a ⇨ ä** verbs include the following:

backen *(to bake)*	**laufen** *(to run)*
fallen *(to fall)*	**schlafen** *(to sleep)*
gefallen *(to like, enjoy)*	**tragen** *(to carry, wear)*
halten *(to stop, think about)*	**waschen** *(to wash)*

sprechen *(to speak):* **e ⇨ i**

ich sprech**e**	wir sprech**en**
du sprich**st**	ihr sprech**t**
er/sie/es sprich**t**	sie sprech**en**

Sie sprech**en**.

Let **sprechen** speak its mind:

» **Adrienne spricht fließend Englisch, Deutsch, und Französisch.** *(Adrienne speaks fluent English, German, and French.)*

Here are some other **e ⇨ i** verbs:

>> **essen** *(to eat)*

>> **geben** *(to give)*

>> **helfen** *(to help)*

>> **vergessen** *(to forget)*

lesen *(to read)*: **e ⇨ ie**

ich les**e**	wir les**en**
du lies**t**	ihr les**t**
er/sie/es lies**t**	sie les**en**
Sie les**en**.	

Read all about **lesen**:

>> **Das Kind liest schon Romane.** *(The child already reads novels.)*

Sehen *(to see)* is also an **e ⇨ ie** verb:

nehmen *(to take)*: **e ⇨ i, hm ⇨ mm**

ich nehm**e**	wir nehm**en**
du nimm**st**	ihr nehm**t**
er/sie/es nimm**t**	sie nehm**en**
Sie nehm**en**.	

Take your time to find out about **nehmen**:

>> **Du nimmst zu viele Kekse!** *(You're taking too many cookies!)*

wissen *(to know as a fact)*: **I ⇨ ei**

ich weiß	wir wiss**en**
du weiß**t**	ihr wiss**t**
er/sie/es weiß	sie wiss**en**
Sie wiss**en**.	

I know you want to know about **wissen**:

>> **Weißt du, wer das ist?** *(Do you know who that is?)*

When you use **wissen** to refer to information in the sentence, you use a comma to separate the two sentence parts.

PRACTICE

Try your hand at mastering the fine art of stem-vowel changes. In the following exercise, decide which verb conjugation to insert into the space provided. Keep in mind that the stem-vowel changes take place in the **du** and **er/sie/es** (second-person singular familiar and third-person singular). You may have to make a few other changes, so make sure to refer to the preceding tables.

Q. _____ du eine Jacke zum Abendessen? (*to wear*)

A. **Trägst du eine Jacke zum Abendessen?** (*Are you wearing a jacket to dinner?*)

13 Helena _____ am schnellsten (*the fastest*). (*to run*)

14 Ich _____ sehr schlecht ohne meine Brille (*eyeglasses*). (*to see*)

15 Mein Vater _____ mir viel Geld. (*to give*)

16 Was _____ ihr zum Frühstück? (*to eat*)

17 Meistens _____ die Kinder nur bis 6.00 Uhr. (*to sleep*)

18 Wohin _____ du am Wochenende? (*to drive*)

19 Ludwig _____ Deutsch mit einem schwäbischen Akzent. (*to speak*)

PRACTICE

The following conversation between Karen and Jenny uses both regular verbs and verbs with stem-vowel changes. In the exercise, choose the correct form of the verb in parentheses and put it in the space provided. Refer to the preceding tables to check your answers before turning to the answer key.

Q. Jenny: **Was_____ du heute Nachmittag (*afternoon*)? (macht/machst)**

A. Jenny: **Was machst du heute Nachmittag** (*What are you doing this afternoon*)?

20 Karen: Ich _____ Peter mit seinem kaputten Fahrrad (*bicycle*). (helfe/hilft)

21 Jenny: *Cool!* Du _____ ihm sehr oft, stimmt's? (*right?*) (hilft/hilfst)

22 Karen: Ja, ja. Er _____, ich _____ ihm gern. Ich habe eine Idee. (weiß/weißt) (helfe/hilft)

23 Karen:_____ wir heute Abend ins neue Restaurant in Schwabing. (geht/gehen)

24 Jenny: Wie _____ das Restaurant? (heißt/heissen)

25 Karen: Ich _____ es nicht, aber die Adresse ist Haimhauserstraße 27. (wissen/weiß)

26 Jenny: Gut, dann _____ wir um 19 Uhr dorthin (*there*). (gehen/geht)

Later, at the restaurant . . .

27 Der Kellner (*server*) _____ mit der Speisekarte (*menu*). (kommen/kommt)

28 Jenny: Was _____ du, Karen? (esst/isst)

29 Karen: Ich _____ den Schweinebraten (*roast pork*). (nimmt/nehme)

30 Jenny: Ich auch. _____ du ein Bier dazu (*with that*)? (trinke/trinkst)

Karen: Ja, sicher.

They are nearing the end of the meal . . .

31 Karen: Mmm. Der Schweinebraten _____ gut. (schmecken/schmeckt)

32 Jenny: Ja, sehr gut. _____ wir noch ein Bier? (trinkst/trinken)

33 Karen: Nein. Morgen _____ Peter und ich nach Tegernsee und _____ in den Bergen. Kommst du mit? (fahren/fährt) (wandere/wandern)

34 Jenny: Leider nicht (*Unfortunately not*). Morgen _____ ich in die Stadt und _____ ein neues Handy. (gehst/gehe) (kaufe/kaufen)

35 Karen: Dann _____ wir etwas zusammen (*together*) am kommenden Wochenende. (macht/machen)

Conjugating the irregulars haben and sein: To have and to be

These two common verbs are irregular. Just as in English, you come across them as full-fledged, free-standing, autonomous verbs and as auxiliary (helping) verbs. (For more on auxiliary verbs, see Chapter 7.) The auxiliary verb function of **haben** and **sein** is to work with other verbs in a frequently used verb tense: the **present perfect**, which I discuss in Chapter 14. For now, I simply show you what **haben** and **sein** look like in the present tense and explain how the English and German uses of these verbs compare.

Haben: Let me have it

Look at the conjugation of **haben** in the present tense. Notice that the verb actually has only two irregular verb forms: **du hast** and **er/sie/es hat**. The rest follow the regular verb conjugation pattern of taking the stem (in this case, **hab-**) and adding the usual ending.

haben (*to have*)

ich hab**e**	wir hab**en**
du ha**st**	ihr hab**t**
er/sie/es ha**t**	sie hab**en**
Sie hab**en**.	

Here's **haben** in action:

> **≫ Sie hat eine grosse Familie.** *(She has a large family.)*

German, like English, has many expressions that involve the verb *to have*. Many of them are the same in German and in English: **Zeit haben** *(to have time)*. Others aren't. English, for example, has two ways to express that something is absolutely necessary, *must* and *have to*. German has only one, **müssen** *(must)*: **Ich muß anfangen** *(I have to start)*. In other cases, German uses the verb **haben** when English has a different construction:

> **≫ Expressing likes with haben and the adverb gern: Gern** means *gladly, with pleasure* when you use it alone. When expressing likes, **gern** is usually placed at the end of the sentence: **Hast du klassische Musik gern?** *(Do you like classical music?)* You find more on this expression in Chapter 7.

> **≫ Talking about your birthday:** You say **Ich habe am achten Oktober Geburtstag** *(My birthday is on the eighth of October).*

> **≫ With expressions that describe a physical condition, an emotional condition, or a state of being:** Five common expressions are
>
> * **Angst haben** *(to be afraid)*
> * **Durst haben** *(to be thirsty)*
> * **Glück haben** *(to be lucky, fortunate)*
> * **Hunger haben** *(to be hungry)*
> * **Recht haben** *(to be right)*

PRACTICE

Try these exercises using the verb **haben**. First, write the sentence in German. You have the elements you need to form the sentence (or question) separated by a slash (/). Combine the parts, making sure to use the right conjugated form of **haben**. Second, try to write the same sentence in English. If you find this task difficult, look at the answer key at the end of this chapter.

Q. Haben/du/einen Hund?

A. Hast du einen Hund? *(Do you have a dog?)*

36 Nein, ich/haben/eine Katze.

37 Haben/du/Durst?

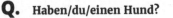

38 Nein, ich/haben/Hunger.

_____

39 Wann/haben/du/Geburtstag?

_____

40 Ich/haben/Geburtstag am 11. Dezember.

_____

41 Wann/haben/ihr/Zeit?

_____

42 Am Freitag/haben/wir/Zeit.

_____

43 Haben/Max und Moritz/ein Auto?

_____

44 Nein, sie/haben/kein Auto.

_____

45 Haben/Sie/Rockmusik gern?

_____

46 Nein, aber (but) ich/haben/Jazz sehr gern.

_____

47 Wer (who)/haben/viel Glück?

_____

48 Franz/haben/viel Glück.

_____

49 Wie viele Kinder/haben/Anne?

_____

50 Anne/haben/vier Kinder.

_____

51 Viele Menschen/haben/Angst vor Spinnen (spiders).

_____

52 Ein Polizist/haben/immer Recht.

_____

Sein: To be or not to be

Look at the conjugation of **sein** *(to be)* in the present tense. Notice that all the verb forms are irregular, although **wir sind, sie sind,** and **Sie sind** are identical. Regular verb conjugations in the present tense also have the same endings for **wir, sie, and Sie** pronouns. For comparison, consider the regular verb **gehen** *(to go, walk)*: **wir gehen, sie gehen,** and **Sie gehen.**

sein *(to be)*

ich bin	wir sind
du bist	ihr seid
er/sie/es ist	sie sind

Sie sind.

Putting **sein** through its paces:

> » **Sind Sie Herr Schumpich?** *(Are you Mr. Schumpich?)*

The verb **sein** is a true workhorse in German. Not only does it tell you what is and what isn't, but you also use it to form the present perfect — although **haben** is the main auxiliary verb for that task. (For more information on the present perfect tense, see Chapter 14.)

German and English use the verb **sein** (to be) in similar ways (What's your boss like? Is it time yet? Who's that? Is it quiet? Are you ready? No, we're not. Am I too old? How much is that? What's up? Where are we? Isn't she funny? Where are you? I'm lost.). Here's how you can use **sein:**

> » **With an adjective:** This way is the most common:
>
> - **Du bist sehr lustig.** *(You're very funny.)*
>
> - **Mein Sohn ist nicht musikalisch.** *(My son is not musical.)*
>
> Some expressions in German use the verb **sein** with an adjective plus a noun or pronoun in the dative case. (For more information on cases, refer to Chapter 3.) A couple of common expressions are
>
> - **Mir ist kalt/warm.** *(I'm cold/warm.)* **Mir** is the dative case of the pronoun **ich.**
>
> - **Ihm ist schlecht/übel.** *(He's feeling sick/sick to his stomach.)* **Ihm** is the dative case of the pronoun **er.**
>
> » **With an adverb:**
>
> - **Wir sind morgen nicht hier.** *(We're not here tomorrow.)*
>
> - **Sie ist dort.** *(She's there.)*
>
> » **With nouns:**
>
> - **Sind Sie Kanadier?** *(Are you a Canadian?)*
>
> - **Ich bin Bauingenieur.** *(I'm a civil engineer.)*
>
> » German leaves out the article **ein** *(a)* for professions.

REMEMBER

A few expressions using **sein** are expressed slightly differently from their English equivalents:

>> **Wie ist ihre Handynummer/Adresse?/Wie ist ihr Name?** *(What's your cellphone number/ address?/What's your name? Literally, **wie** means how.)* Chapter 6 deals with questions.

>> **Hier ist Frau Becker.** *(I'm Mrs. Becker. — to identify yourself on the phone)*

>> **Ihr seid hier richtig**. *(You're in the right place.)*

Try these exercises using the verb **sein**. First, write the sentence in German. You have the elements needed to form the sentence (or question) separated by a slash (/). Combine the parts, making sure you use the right conjugated form of **sein**. Then try to write the same sentence in English.

Q. **Unser Haus/sein/nicht sehr groß.**

A. **Unser Haus ist nicht sehr groß.** *(Our house isn't very large.)*

53 Wie alt/sein/die Kinder?

_____

54 Uns/sein/kalt.

_____

55 Du/sein/sehr tolerant.

_____

56 Meine Schwester/sein/athletisch.

_____

57 Sein/ich/hier richtig?

_____

58 Wie/sein/ihre Adresse?

_____

59 Sein/ihm/übel?

_____

60 Mein Vater/sein/zu Hause.

_____

61 Wo/sein/wir?

_____

62 Wie alt/sein/du?

_____

63 Frau Hugendubel/sein/keine Professorin.

_____

64 Sein/Sie/Amerikaner?

_____

Using the Very Versatile Present Tense

When you want to gain confidence in any language, you work on polishing your verb skills so you feel competent using the present, the past, and the future tenses. In German, grasping the present tense opens the door to several ways of expressing yourself. Knowing how versatile the present tense is in German means that you economize with this handy verb tense.

When you want to talk about something in German, first figure out whether you can use the present tense. In virtually all situations in which you use present tense in English, you use present tense in German. In addition, you have a lot of opportunities in German to use the present tense when you have to use other verb tenses in English. It certainly makes your life easier to know these various situations!

The primary difference in usage is that English has a continuous verb form, and German doesn't. English uses the present continuous (_Our guests are staying until Sunday_) to indicate that an action is happening now, and it uses the present tense for habitual actions or facts without expressing whether the action is going on at the time (_My brother lives on a lake_). Because German doesn't verbally express such time distinctions, the listener can interpret sentences such as **Was denkst du?** in two ways: _What are you thinking?/What's on your mind?_ or _What do you think?/What's your opinion?_

Look at Table 5-1 for three ways to translate one German sentence into English.

Table 5-1   English Present-Tense Translations for German Present Tense

German Present Tense	Possible English Translations	Intended Idea
Jörg spielt sehr gut Basketball.	_Jörg plays basketball very well._	Stating a general fact, common knowledge (simple present)
Jörg spielt sehr gut Basketball.	_Jörg is playing basketball very well._	Happening now, today, this week, and so on (present continuous)
Jörg spielt sehr gut Basketball.	_Jörg does play basketball very well._	Showing emphasis, or to contradict someone's opinion (simple present with auxiliary do)

Hold on — there's more to come on the versatility of the simple present tense in German. You even use it to talk about future plans, predictions, spontaneous decisions made at the time of speaking, and for activities that started in the past and are still going on. Table 5-2 shows how German uses the present tense for talking about the future and the past.

Table 5-2   Future and Present Perfect Tense Translations for German Present

German Present Tense	English Tenses	Intended Idea
Wir treffen uns um acht Uhr, oder?	*We're meeting/going to meet at eight o'clock, aren't we?*	Stating a plan or intention
Vielleicht regnet es morgen.	*Maybe it'll rain tomorrow.*	Predicting or speculating
Warte mal, ich helfe dir. (colloquial)	*Wait a sec, I'll help you.*	Making a spontaneous decision at the time of speaking, such as offering help or promising
Sie arbeitet seit 20 Jahren bei der Firma.	*She's been working at the company for 20 years.*	Expressing an action that started in the past and is still going on

PRACTICE

The following German sentences are all in the simple present. Write the English equivalent sentence. Before you start, look at the previous section, "Using the Very Versatile Present Tense," and Tables 5-1 and 5-2. The context (in English) will also help you.

Q. You look at the dark clouds above, and you say: **Es regnet bald** (*soon.*)

A. *(It's going to rain/will rain soon.)*

65 At the soccer stadium, someone next to you says **Heute spielen sie nicht sehr gut**.

_____

66 You want to offer help to someone with their bags. You say **Ich helfe Ihnen**.

_____

67 You ask your friend what she's doing on the weekend. You say **Was machst du am Wochenende?**

_____

68 Your friend answers **Ich besuche meine Freundin in Hamburg.**

_____

69 Someone wants to know how long you've been learning German. They ask **Seit wie lange lernen Sie Deutsch?**

_____

70 You reply: **Ich lerne Deutsch seit einem Jahr.**

_____

In a hotel where you're staying someone asks you **Wie lange bleiben Sie hier?**

_____

 You answer **Ich bleibe bis Sonntag.**

_____

Answers to "Grasping the Present Tense" Practice Questions

1. **Sabina und Moritz reisen nach Australien.** (*Sabina and Moritz are traveling to Australia.*)

2. **Das Handy kostet sehr viel Geld.** (*The cellphone costs a lot of money.*)

3. **Meine Großmutter und ich heißen beide Monika.** (*My grandmother and I are both named Monika.*)

4. **Schreibst du oft E-Mails?** (*Do you often write emails?*)

5. **Ich wandere sehr gern in den Bergen.** (*I really like to hike in the mountains.*)

6. **Wo wohnen Sie?** (*Where do you live?*)

7. **Manfred kommt heute Abend spät nach Hause.** (*Manfred is coming home late this evening.*)

8. **Kennt ihr den Mann da drüben?** (*Do you know the man over there?*)

9. **Ja, mein Mann arbeitet mit ihm.** (*Yes, my husband works with him.*)

10. **Wohin gehen Sie?** (*Where are you going?*)

11. **Heute kaufen Florian und Maria ein Auto.** (*Florian and Maria are buying a car today.*)

12. **Ich finde Deutsch sehr leicht zu lernen.** (*I find it very easy to learn German/I think it's very easy to learn German.*)

13. **Helena läuft am schnellsten.** (*Helena runs the fastest.*)

14. **Ich sehe sehr schlecht ohne meine Brille.** (*I see very poorly without my glasses.*)

15. **Mein Vater gibt mir viel Geld.** (*My father gives/is giving me a lot of money.*)

16. **Was esst ihr zum Frühstück?** (*What do you eat/are you eating for breakfast?*)

17. **Meistens schlafen die Kinder nur bis 6.00 Uhr.** (*The children usually sleep only until 6 a.m.*)

18. **Wohin fährst du am Wochenende?** (*Where are you driving to/going on the weekend?*)

19. **Ludwig spricht Deutsch mit einem schwäbischen Akzent.** (*Ludwig speaks German with a Swabian accent.*) Swabia is a region in southwest Germany where the inhabitants have a distinctive accent, somewhat similar to Swiss German.

20. Karen: **Ich helfe Peter mit seinem kaputten Fahrrad.** (*I'm helping Peter with his broken-down bicycle.*)

21. Jenny: *Cool!* **Du hilfst ihm sehr oft, stimmt's?** (*Cool! You help him very often, right/don't you?*)

22. Karen: **Ja, ja. Er weiß, ich helfe ihm gern. Ich habe eine Idee.** (*Yeah, yeah. He knows I like to help him. I have an idea.*)

23 Karen: **Gehen wir heute Abend ins neue Restaurant in Schwabing.** (*Let's go to the new restaurant in Schwabing.*)

24 Jenny: **Wie heißt das Restaurant?** (*What's the name of the restaurant?*)

25 Karen: **Ich weiß es nicht, aber die Adresse ist Haimhauserstraße 27.** (*I don't know, but the address is Haimhauserstraße 27.*)

26 Jenny: **Gut, dann gehen wir um 19 Uhr dorthin.** (*Good, then let's go there at 7pm.*)

Later, at the restaurant . . .

27 **Der Kellner kommt mit der Speisekarte.** (*The server comes with the menu.*)

28 Jenny: **Was isst du, Karen?** (*What are you going to eat/have, Karen?*)

29 Karen: **Ich nehme den Schweinebraten.** (*I'll take/have the roast pork.*)

30 Jenny: **Ich auch. Trinkst du ein Bier dazu?** (*Are you having a beer/going to drink a beer with that?*)

Karen: **Ja, sicher.**

They are nearing the end of the meal . . .

31 Karen: **Mmm. Der Schweinebraten schmeckt gut.** (*Mmm. The roast pork tastes good.*)

32 Jenny: **Ja, sehr gut. Trinken wir noch ein Bier?** (*Yes, really good. Shall we drink another beer?*)

33 Karen: **Nein. Morgen fahren Peter und ich nach Tegernsee und wandern in den Bergen. Kommst du mit?** (*No. Tomorrow, Peter and are driving/going to drive to Tegernsee, and we are hiking/going hiking in the mountains. Do you want to come along?*)

34 Jenny: **Leider nicht. Morgen gehe ich in die Stadt und kaufe ein neues Handy.** (*Unfortunately not. Tomorrow, I'm going into the city and buying a new cellphone.*)

35 Karen: **Dann machen wir am kommenden Wochenende etwas zusammen.** (*Then let's do something together next weekend.*)

36 **Nein, ich habe eine Katze.** (*No, I have a cat.*)

37 **Hast du Durst?** (*Are you thirsty?*)

38 **Nein, ich habe Hunger.** (*No, I'm hungry.*)

39 **Wann hast du Geburtstag?** (*When is your birthday?*)

40 **Ich habe am 11. Dezember Geburtstag.** (*My birthday is on December 11.*)

41 **Wann habt ihr Zeit?** (*When do you have time?*)

42 **Am Freitag haben wir Zeit.** (*We have time on Friday.*)

43 **Haben Max und Moritz ein Auto?** (*Do Max and Moritz have a car?*)

44 **Nein, sie haben kein Auto.** (*No, they don't have a car.*)

45 **Haben Sie Rockmusik gern?** (*Do you like rock music?*)

46. **Nein, aber ich habe Jazz sehr gern.** (*No, but I really like jazz.*)

47. **Wer hat viel Glück?** (*Who has a lot of luck?*)

48. **Franz hat viel Glück.** (*Franz has a lot of luck.*)

49. **Wie viele Kinder hat Anne?** (*How many children does Anne have?*)

50. **Anne hat vier Kinder.** (*Anne has four children.*)

51. **Viele Menschen haben Angst vor Spinnen.** (*Many people are afraid of spiders.*)

52. **Ein Polizist hat immer Recht.** (*A policeman is always right.*)

53. **Wie alt sind die Kinder?** (*How old are the children?*)

54. **Uns ist kalt.** (*We're cold.*) **Uns** is the dative-case pronoun; it's like saying *to us it's cold.*

55. **Du bist sehr tolerant.** (*You're very tolerant.*)

56. **Meine Schwester ist athletisch.** (*My sister is athletic.*)

57. **Bin ich hier richtig?** (*Am I in the right place?*)

58. **Wie ist ihre Adresse?** (*What is your address?*)

59. **Ist ihm übel?** (*Is he feeling sick/sick to his stomach?*) **Ihm** is the dative case of the pronoun **er**; it's like saying *to him* or *to his stomach (he)* is sick.

60. **Mein Vater ist zu Hause.** (*My father is at home.*)

61. **Wo sind wir?** (*Where are we?*)

62. **Wie alt bist du?** (*How old are you?*)

63. **Frau Hugendubel ist keine Professorin.** (*Ms/Mrs. Hugendubel isn't a professor.*)

64. **Sind Sie Amerikaner?** (*Are you an American?*)

65. **Heute spielen sie nicht sehr gut.** (*They aren't playing very well today.*)

66. **Ich helfe Ihnen.** (*I'll help you.*)

67. **Was machst du am Wochenende?** (*What are you doing on the weekend?*)

68. **Ich besuche meine Freundin in Hamburg.** (*I'm visiting/going to visit my girlfriend in Hamburg.*)

69. **Seit wie lange lernen Sie Deutsch?** (*How long have you been learning German?*)

70. **Ich lerne seit einem Jahr Deutsch.** (*I've been learning German for a year.*)

71. **Wie lange bleiben Sie hier?** (*How long are you staying here?*)

72. **Ich bleibe bis Sonntag.** (*I'm staying until Sunday.*)

Chapter **6**

Asking and Answering Intelligently; Giving Orders

Asking questions puts you in the conversational driver's seat. You use questions to initiate dialogues, find out what you need to know, and clarify information you're not sure about. When you're communicating in a new language, you may find that your counterpart is speaking so fast that you can barely understand the first word, let alone the barrage that follows. So you ask the person to slow down: **Langsamer, bitte** (*Slower, please*). This isn't bad for a start, but you're still in the back seat, and your goal is to get behind the wheel. How you achieve that goal is simple: You start by implementing effective question techniques. As for answering questions, you certainly need to use **ja** (*yes*) and **nein** (*no*). **Verstehen Sie, was ich meine?** (*Do you understand what I mean?*)

This chapter gets you up to speed on formulating questions and answers, along with a range of positive and negative responses to show agreement and disagreement. I break down the differences in usage between **nicht** and **kein,** which are the two ways of negating information in German. In addition, this chapter gives you tools for understanding and using the imperative. You use the imperative form for giving commands, giving instruction, persuading people, and offering encouragement. At the end of each section, you can go for a test drive (not on the Nürburgring Grand Prix racetrack, **leider** [*unfortunately*]) and see how skillful you are at asking and answering intelligently. Read on.

Inverting Word Order for Yes/No Questions

German word order is easy to follow when you form a question that merits a yes or no answer. You simply flip the subject and the conjugated (main) verb: The verb is in first place, and the subject is in second place (where the verb usually goes in statements). English is more complicated because you usually use the auxiliary (helping) verb *to do* or *to be* together with the main verb; in English, only the auxiliary verb goes in first place. Take a look at the German and its translations:

>> **Leben Sie in einer Großstadt?** *(Do you live in a large city?)*

>> **Bleibt sie hier?** *(Is she staying here?)*

>> **Ist es kalt bei Ihnen im Winter?** *(Is it cold where you live in the winter?)*

The German present tense encompasses two English verb tenses (and more). The present continuous doesn't exist in German, so in the second question here, you use the present. (See Chapter 5 for more on the present tense.)

PRACTICE

Am Bahnhof *(at the train station)*: Imagine that you're in **München** *(Munich)*, and you're planning an **Ausflug** *(outing, excursion)* to Berlin. You decide to take the train, so you go to the window marked **Reiseauskunft** *(travel information)*. In this exercise, you see a list of questions followed by a dialogue. Write the questions in the spaces provided. Read everything before you start to fill in the questions so that you get the gist of the conversation.

>> **Haben Sie viel Gepäck dabei?** *(Do you have much luggage with you?)*

>> **Fährt ein Zug am Nachmittag?** *(Is there a train leaving in the afternoon?)*

>> **Kann ich Ihnen helfen?** *(Can I help you?)*

>> **Ist das Ticket 1. Klasse sehr teuer?** *(Is the first-class ticket very expensive?)*

>> **Gibt es ein gutes Hotel am Bahnhof in Berlin?** *(Is there a good hotel at the train station in Berlin?)*

>> **Wollen Sie ein Ticket 1. Klasse oder 2. Klasse nehmen?** *(Do you want a first- or second-class ticket?)*

>> **Fahren Sie innerhalb Deutschlands?** *(Are you traveling within Germany?)*

>> **Ist der Transport für das Fahrrad sehr teuer?** *(Is it very expensive to transport the bicycle?)*

>> **Kann ich aber ein Fahrrad mitnehmen?** *(Can I take a bicycle with me?)*

>> **Reisen Sie nach Berlin hin und zurück?** *(Are you going round-trip to Berlin?)*

Q. **Bahnhofsangestellter** *(train station clerk)*: **Grüß Gott.**

_____?

Reisender *(traveler)*: **Ja, ich brauche eine Auskunft. Kann ich hier Tickets kaufen?**

A. **Grüß Gott. Kann ich ihnen helfen?** *(Hello. Can I help you?)*

R: Ja, ich brauche eine Auskunft. Kann ich hier Tickets kaufen? *(Yes. I need some information. Can I buy tickets here?)*

1 B: Ja.

_____?

R: Ja. Ich möchte nach Berlin fahren.

2 B

_____?

3 R: Ich weiß nicht. *(I don't know.)*

_____?

4 B: Nein, es kostet nur *(only)* 45€ mehr *(more)*

_____?

R: Ja, genau *(exactly)*.

5 B:

_____?

6 R: Nein, nur eine Tasche *(bag)*.

_____?

B: Sicher, kein *(no)* Problem.

7 R:

_____?

B: Nun, Sie müssen 20€ für das Fahrrad bezahlen *(pay)*.

8 R:

_____?

B: Ja, Sie können um 13.30 Uhr oder um 15.15 Uhr abfahren *(leave)*.

9 R: Gut, dann nehme *(take)* ich den Zug um 13.30 Uhr.

_____?

B: Ja, es gibt mehrere *(several)* Hotels.

R: Sehr freundlich, vielen Dank für ihre Auskunft.

Gathering Information with Question Words: Who, What, Why, and More

When kids reach the age of asking "why," it's marvelous at first, but after weeks of nonstop questioning, you may wonder whether they're practicing for a career in some government spy agency. Asking *why* is a kid's way of engaging an adult in conversation just as much as it is a way of gathering information. As you progress in German, you need question words (interrogative pronouns) such as *who, what, where,* and *when* to gather specific information, but you can also use the kid's tactic of asking **wer** *(who)*, **was** *(what)*, **warum** *(why)*, and so on as a tool for engaging people in conversation. Doing so is a useful tactic because it gives you more control of the direction of the discussion.

TIP

The inverted word order for yes/no questions (see the preceding section) is the same for information-gathering questions except that the question word (or phrase) comes first. Thus, the word order for info-gathering questions is question word(s) + verb + subject, such as **Warum ist der Himmel blau?** *(Why is the sky blue?)* or **Wann fahren wir nach Hause?** *(When are we driving home?)*.

Table 6-1 lists 12 German question words and phrases, the English equivalents in alphabetical order, and example questions in English with the German equivalents.

WARNING

Welcher/welche/welches *(which)* is an interrogative pronoun with three versions to correspond with the three noun genders **der/die/das**: **welcher Zug** *(which train)*, **welche Frau** *(which woman)*, **welches Auto** *(which car)*. You need to remember that it has adjective endings — in other words, the case endings of the noun it's describing. Consider **Mit welchem Bus soll ich fahren?** *(Which bus should I take? Literally: With which bus should I drive/travel?)*. The preposition **mit** uses the dative case, and **der Bus** is masculine, so **mit welchem Bus** uses the masculine dative singular form of **welch-** in the prepositional phrase.

Wer *(who)* is an interrogative pronoun that has three other forms. **Wer** is the nominative case, **wen** *(whom, who)* is accusative, **wem** *(who)* is dative, and **wessen** *(whose)* is genitive.

Table 6-1   Question Words and Example Questions

Question Word	Example Sentence	Translation
wie *(how)*	**Wie heißen Sie?**	*What is your name?*
wie viele *(how many)*	**Wie viele Personen arbeiten in Ihrer Firma?**	*How many people work in your company?*
wie viel *(how much)*	**Wie viel kostet die Karte?**	*How much is the ticket?*
was *(what)*	**Was machen wir nach der Pause?**	*What are we doing after the break?*
was für *(what kind of)*	**Was für ein Auto fahren Sie?**	*What kind of car do you drive?*
wann *(when)*	**Wann beginnt das Konzert?**	*When does the concert begin?*
wo *(where)*	**Wo wohnen Sie?**	*Where do you live?*
woher *(where . . . from)*	**Woher kommen Sie?**	*Where are you from?*
wohin *(where . . . [to])*	**Wohin fährt der Bus?**	*Where does the bus go (to)?*
welcher/welche/ welches *(which)*	**Welche Straßenbahn soll ich nehmen? (die Straßenbahn)**	*Which tram should I take?*
wer (nominative) *(who)*, **wen** (accusative) *(whom, who)*, **wem** (dative) *(who)*, **wessen** (genitive)*(whose)*	**Wer ist Ihr Chef?**	*Who is your boss?*
warum *(why)*	**Warum hält der Zug jetzt (an)?**	*Why is the train stopping now?*

PRACTICE

In the following dialogue, Julian is interested in language courses for his company. He telephones Angelika, the coordinator at Interface Sprachenschule, who answers his questions. Put the appropriate question words from Table 6-1 in the spaces.

Q. _____Buch benutzen Sie in Ihrer Sprachenschule? (das Buch)

A. <u>Welches</u> Buch benutzen Sie in Ihrer Sprachenschule? *(Which book do you use in your language school?)*

Angelika: Interface Sprachenschule, guten Morgen!

 Julian: Guten Morgen, Julian Stromberger von der Firma Nordstern.

A: Kann ich Ihnen helfen?

J: Ja, wir möchten einen Sprachkurs *(language course)* für Spanisch machen.

A: Kein Problem, sehr gerne.

J: _____ kostet so ein Sprachkurs?

11 A: _____ Personen machen den Kurs?

J: Wir sind vier Personen.

A: Dann kostet der Kurs 500€ pro Person.

12 J: _____ Stunden (*hours*) sind es?

A: Es sind 40 Stunden.

13 J: _____ ist es so teuer (*expensive*)?

A: Weil (*because*) es nur vier Personen sind.

14 J: _____ ist der Unterricht (*class*)?

A: Der Unterricht kann in Ihrer Firma sein.

J: Oh, in Ordnung, einverstanden.

15 A: _____ soll die Lehrerin (*[female] teacher*) fahren?

J: Sie muß nach Starnberg fahren.

A: Einverstanden (*Oh, all right/That's agreed*).

16 J: _____ macht den Unterricht?

A: Eine junge Lehrerin.

17 J: _____ heißt die Lehrerin?

A: Sie heiflt Cristina.

18 J: _____ kommt sie?

A: Sie kommt aus Santiago de Chile.

19 J: _____ können wir anfangen (*begin*)?

A: Sie können nächste Woche am Montag anfangen.

J: Ah, gut, vielen Dank. Auf Wiederhören (*Goodbye [on the phone]*).

A: Danke für Ihren Anruf. Auf Wiederhören.

The interrogative pronoun **wer** (*who*) has three other forms. **Wer** is the nominative case, **wen** (*whom, who*) is accusative, **wem** (*who*) is dative, and **wessen** (*whose*) is genitive. To formulate questions by using **wer** and its three other iterations, you need to understand the role that case plays when you want to ask questions using **wer**. The most frequently used of the foursome is **wer**. (For more information on cases, go to Chapter 3.) Table 6-2 shows the four forms of **wer**, their usage, example questions in German, and the English equivalents. The following abbreviations appear in the table: nom. (nominative), acc. (accusative), dat. (dative), and gen. (genitive).

Table 6-2   The Four Cases of Wer and Example Questions

Wer/Case/Usage	Example Sentence	Translation
wer / nom. / subject	**Wer kommt morgen?**	*Who's coming tomorrow?*
wen / acc. /direct object	**Wen magst du?**	*Who do you like?*
wem / dat. / indirect object	**Wem gehört das?**	*Who does this belong to?*
wessen / gen. / possession	**Wessen Fahrrad ist das?**	*Whose bicycle is that?*

When you look at these four pairs of questions and answers, you see how case plays a role in **wer** questions:

>> **Wer kommt morgen?** *(Who's coming tomorrow?)*

>> **Ilse kommt morgen.** *(Ilse is coming tomorrow.)* The answer to the question is **Ilse**. She is the subject of the sentence, **Ilse kommt morgen. Wer** is the question word asking about the subject.

>> **Wen magst du?** *(Who do you like?)*

>> **Ich mag ihn.** *(I like him.)* The answer to the question is **ihn.** *He* is the object of the person's affection. The verb **mögen** *(to like)* is a verb that uses the accusative case. The pronoun **ihn** is the accusative form of **er** *(he).*

>> **Wem gehört das?** *(Who does that belong to?)*

>> **Es gehört meiner Freundin.** *(It belongs to my girlfriend.)* The answer to the question is **meiner Freundin.** The verb **gehören** *(to belong to)* is a verb that uses the dative case, so **meiner** is the feminine dative form of **mein** *(my).*

>> **Wessen Buch ist das?** *(Whose book is that?)*

>> **Das ist mein Buch.** *(It's my book.)* The answer to the question is **mein Buch.** With **wessen,** you're asking who possesses something.

In the following exercise, decide which interrogative pronoun fits into the question. You find hints in parentheses to help you determine whether to use **wer, wen, wem,** or **wessen.**

PRACTICE

Q. _____ **hat sie geheiratet?** (**Heiraten** *[to marry]* uses the accusative case.)

A. <u>**Wen**</u> **hat sie geheiratet?** *(Who did she marry?)*

20 _____ **ist deine Schwester?** (The question is about the subject.)

21 _____ **rufen Sie an?** (Use the accusative case here to indicate the direct object.)

22 **Mit** _____ **spricht der Johanna?** (**Mit** *[with]* is a preposition that uses the dative case.)

23 _____ **kann mir helfen?** (Hint: The answer could be **Ich kann . . .**)

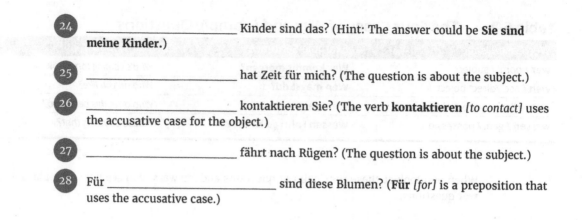

24. _____ Kinder sind das? (Hint: The answer could be **Sie sind meine Kinder.**)

25. _____ hat Zeit für mich? (The question is about the subject.)

26. _____ kontaktieren Sie? (The verb **kontaktieren** [to contact] uses the accusative case for the object.)

27. _____ fährt nach Rügen? (The question is about the subject.)

28. Für _____ sind diese Blumen? (**Für** [for] is a preposition that uses the accusative case.)

Checking Information: Tag! You're It, Aren't You?

When you're talking to someone, and you want to check some information, you may say something like this, expecting the listener to agree with you: *The mall opens at 10, doesn't it?* The same tactic is handy when you're not sure whether the other person is actually listening to you or is more engrossed in the game on TV.

As you delve into the depths of the German language, you can easily wonder at how much more complicated German grammar seems than English grammar. Then you stumble upon the realm of tag questions, and you can giggle at how simple it is to play tag in German. A tag question is simply what you tack onto the end of a statement to make it a question. In English, the tag depends on the subject and verb in the statement. The possibilities are practically endless in English: *isn't she?, do you?, can't you?, wasn't it?, were you?, wouldn't it?, are you?*, and so on. The German equivalent is far simpler.

TIP

To form a tag question in German, just add **stimmt's?** (literally: *correct?*) or **richtig?** (literally: *right?*) Both expressions serve the same function as the long list of tag-question equivalents in English: to shake out a sign of agreement, disagreement, or even just a grunt of acknowledgement from the listener. In addition, you may hear **nicht wahr?** (literally: *not true?*) or less common is **nicht?** (literally: *not?*) to the end of the sentence. You can use tag questions interchangeably. They aren't grammatically linked to the first part of the sentence, as they are in English, so you may use them any time you want to elicit a response from someone as a means of checking your information, to show agreement or disagreement, and so on.

>> **Sie fahren morgen nach Düsseldorf, stimmt's?** *(You're going/driving to Düsseldorf tomorrow, aren't you?)*

>> **Der Film war nicht besonders interessant, nicht wahr?** *(The movie wasn't especially good, was it?)*

One very common tag in colloquial German is **oder?** (literally: *or?*). You hear it in casual conversation, so you want to avoid using it when speaking with people you address with **Sie**.

PRACTICE

In this exercise, you're checking some information. Add your choice of the four standard German tags — **nicht wahr, nicht, stimmt's,** and **richtig** — to the end of the statement. In a situation between friends, you may use **oder**.

Q. Sie wohnen in Graz, _____?

A. Sie wohnen in Graz, **nicht wahr?** (*You live in Graz, don't you?*)

29 Der Mann da drüben heißt Herr Storch, _____?

30 Du bleibst noch eine Nacht, _____?

31 Hier regnet es oft im Frühling, _____?

32 Sie sind morgen im Büro, _____?

33 Du hast Informatik studiert, _____?

Using the Imperative: Do It!

When you want to give someone orders to do something, you can use the *imperative form*, also called the *command form*. But you can also use the imperative form in other situations, such as giving instructions, offering encouragement, making suggestions, and persuading people. This section gives you the lowdown on the imperative.

Giving orders

When you're telling someone to do something, you use the imperative. You want to ensure that you use the correct verb form and punctuation so that the person you're talking to understands (which still doesn't mean that they'll do what you say!). Keep reading to see how to use the imperative correctly.

Verb forms

DIFFERENCES

English has one verb form for the imperative (*stop* here please, *get* me a pen please, *go* home, *watch* out!). You may be talking to one person, several people, a bus driver, a friend, or your neighbor's dog. On the other hand, German has three forms, depending on whom you're addressing. They correspond to the three German pronouns that represent *you*: **Sie, ihr,** and **du.** Table 6-3 shows examples of these three imperative forms and explains how to form the verbs. I mention the few exceptions right after the table.

Table 6-3   The Three German Imperative Forms of You

German Pronoun	Translation	German Example Sentence	Translation	How to Form the Verb
Sie	*you* (formal, singular or plural)	**Zeigen Sie mir, bitte! (zeigen)**	*Please show me.*	Same as present-tense **Sie** form
ihr	*you* (informal, plural)	**Öffnet bitte die Fenster! (öffnen)**	*Please open the windows.*	Same as present- tense **ihr** form (but **ihr** is dropped)
du	*you* (informal, singular)	**Fahre vorsichtig! (fahren)**	*Drive carefully.*	Stem of a verb + **-e** (the stem of **fahren** is **fahr-**)

Note: In addition to the three imperative forms using **Sie, ihr** and **du**, when you want to express something like *Let's go!* or *Let's eat!*, you use the **wir** form, which is generally referred to as an imperative. Here's an example: **Fahren wir!** (*Let's go!*)

Normally, the **du** imperative form is straightforward: verb stem + **-e** (as in **geh** + **-e** = **gehe** [*go*]). Here are the three **du** imperative exceptions:

>> In informal German, the **-e** is often dropped: **pass auf** *(watch out)*

>> In verbs with a stem ending in **-d** or **-t**, you often don't drop the **-e**: **arbeite** *(work)*

>> If the verb has a stem-vowel change, the imperative has this vowel change and doesn't have **-e** at the end of the verb: **essen = iss** *(eat)*. (See Chapter 5 for verbs with stem-vowel changes.)

The verb **sein** *(to be)* is irregular (of course!) in the imperative:

>> **Sie** form: **seien Sie**

>> **ihr** form: **seid**

>> **du** form: **sei**

Punctuation

REMEMBER

When you write a command in German, put an exclamation mark at the end of the phrase. It isn't intended to make the command sound like a do-or-die situation; it's simply a grammatical element of the imperative form, just as a question mark belongs at the end of a question.

The liberal use of exclamation marks on German signage as a means of signaling warning can be a bit overwhelming at first. **Rasen nicht betreten!** (*Don't walk on the grass*) may seem threatening, but don't let it give you the impression that you'll go straight to jail if you dare to place even one toe on the grass. The format of **Rasen nicht betreten!** is not the standard imperative; it's the infinitive form of the verb that you see more often on signs, and it often takes the form of a prohibition with **nicht** preceding the infinitive. Along with **nicht** on signage, you see **kein** (*no, not*) and other words that show strong prohibition, which include **verboten** (*forbidden/prohibited*), **Gefahr** (*danger*), and **Vorsicht** (*caution/beware/Look out!*).

PRACTICE

In the following exercise, you're traveling around Germany, and you come across a several signs that appear to be warning that something is forbidden. But what is it that you should or shouldn't do? The word bank has eight German warnings with a few hints in parentheses. Write the German expressions that match the English equivalents in the spaces provided.

>> **Betreten der Baustelle verboten!** *(sign outside a construction site)*

>> **Kein öffentlicher Durchgang!**

>> **Bitte nicht füttern!** *(sign in a zoo)*

>> **Vorsicht bissiger Hund!** *(where a snarling dog is poking its head through a fence)*

>> **Alkoholkonsum verboten!**

>> **Waldbrandgefahr!** *(in a forest)*

>> **Ballspielen verboten!**

>> **Ausfahrt freihalten!**

>> **Unbefugten ist der Zutritt verboten!** *(trespassers . . .)*

Q. No public walkway

_____

A. **Kein öffentlicher Durchgang!**

34 No ball playing allowed

_____

35 No trespassing

_____

36 Beware of dog

_____

37 No alcoholic beverages allowed

_____

38 Construction site: Do not enter

_____

39 Sign with Smokey the Bear: Only YOU can prevent forest fires!

_____

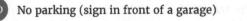

40 No parking (sign in front of a garage)

_____

41 Do not feed the animals

_____

Requests and suggestions: Looking at question-command hybrids

In some cases, the imperative walks the fine line between asking and telling someone to do something. Both have inverted word order with the verb first, followed by the subject. Look at the question **Können Sie das bitte machen?** (*Could you do that, please?*). You're asking someone to do something, so you generally formulate your request more politely by using a helping verb such as **können** (*could*). In addition, you end the request in a rising voice. By contrast, when you want to tell someone to do something in more direct but polite language, you make a request such as **Machen Sie das, bitte** (*Please do that*). Your voice falls at the end.

>> **Können Sie mir bitte helfen?** (*Could you help me, please?*) The question form, **können**, and **bitte** indicate a request that you're asking someone (politely) to do something. When you say it, your voice rises at the end.

>> **Helfen Sie mir, bitte.** (*Please help me/Give me a hand, please.*) The imperative form is a request in more direct language, but **bitte** makes it sound polite.

Another use of the imperative is for making suggestions. When referring to **wir** (*we*) as the people who may follow the suggestion, the German looks like this: **Fahren wir Fahrrad** (*Let's go bicycling*). It's the **wir** verb form with inverted word order.

PRACTICE

For each infinitive, provide the imperative verb forms for **Sie, ihr,** and **du.** Use all the preceding information to help you form the three different imperative forms. Because these are commands, they all need the exclamation mark.

Q. **schneller arbeiten** (*to work faster*)

A. Sie: **Arbeiten Sie schneller!** ihr: **Arbeitet schneller!** du: **Arbeite schneller!**

42 langsam essen (*to eat slowly*)

Sie: _____   ihr: _____   du: _____

43 vorsichtig fahren (*to drive carefully*)

Sie: _____   ihr: _____   du: _____

44 nicht gehen *(to not walk)*

Sie: _____   ihr: _____   du: _____

45 lesen *(to read)*

Sie: _____   ihr: _____   du: _____

46 machen *(to make, do)*

Sie: _____   ihr: _____   du: _____

Responding with No: The Difference between Kein and Nicht

Saying no in German is plain and simple: **nein.** But when you want to negate an action, or an object or person, you have two ways to express *not* (or *not any*): **kein** and **nicht.** Getting them straight is a matter of knowing what they negate in a sentence. The word order of these negations is important to know, as is how to form the endings of **kein.** (**Nicht** doesn't change.) In this section, I take you through the steps of when and how to use **nicht** and **kein.**

Negating with nicht

The nuts and bolts of **nicht** are straightforward as far as its form is concerned. **Nicht** is all you need to know (unlike **kein,** which has case and gender endings; see the next section). **Nicht** generally negates a verb: **nicht einladen** *(not to invite),* **nicht fahren** *(not to drive, travel),* and **nicht feiern** *(not to celebrate).* It can also negate an adjective, as in **nicht interessant** *(not interesting),* or an adverb, as in **nicht pünktlich** *(not on time).* What you do need to figure out is how to position **nicht** in a sentence. Because **nicht** is an adverb, it negates the action of the verb or modifies an adjective or an adverb, and it's generally next to these parts of speech, as in these examples:

>> **Sie fliegen nicht nach London.** *(They're not flying to London.)* **Nicht** directly follows the verb in this sentence, negating the idea that they're flying.

>> **Martin spricht nicht gut Deutsch.** *(Martin doesn't speak good German.)* In this sentence, **nicht** tells you that Martin's ability to speak German isn't good, so **nicht** immediately follows the verb.

>> **Gestern kamen wir nicht pünktlich zum Termin.** *(Yesterday we didn't get to our appointment on time.)* **Nicht** links with the adverb **pünktlich** *(on time),* and you place it before **pünktlich.**

>> **Das Buch ist nicht interessant.** *(The book isn't interesting.)* The negation connects the verb **ist** *(is)* and the adjective **interessant** *(interesting);* **nicht** modifies **interessant,** so you place it in front of the adjective.

Placement is the more complex part of **nicht,** and although **nicht** is generally next to what it modifies, it can be tricky determining whether it comes before or after the thing it is modifying. Most of the time, however, if you're not perfect with word order, you'll still be understandable in spoken or written German. Table 6-4 explains some guidelines for using **nicht,** which should help you sort out where to put this valuable chess piece.

In this exercise, your task is to figure out the word order of the reply to the question. Read the question and then write the reply in the correct word order, using Table 6-4 to see where to place **nicht** in the sentence. All the replies in this exercise begin with **nein,** followed by a comma. When all else fails, sneak a look at the answer key to get started.

PRACTICE

Table 6-4 Guidelines for Positioning Nicht

Position of Nicht	Example Sentence	Translation
After a conjugated verb	Maria fährt **nicht** nach Kiel.	*Maria isn't driving to Kiel.*
After a conjugated verb and preceding a separable prefix	Felix und Gretl sehen **nicht** fern. (Fernsehen is a separable-prefix verb.)	*Felix and Gretl aren't watching TV.*
After most specific adverbs of time	Ich war gestern **nicht** zu Hause. (**Gestern** is the specific adverb of time.)	*I wasn't at home yesterday.*
After the direct object	Ich kenne diesen Mann **nicht.** (**Diesen Mann** is the direct object.)	*I don't know that man.*
Before most adjectives	Das Hotel ist **nicht** gemütlich. (**Gemütlich** is the adjective.)	*The hotel isn't cozy.*
Before most adverbs, except for specific adverbs of time	Ihr lauft **nicht** schnell. (**Schnell** is the adverb.)	*You don't run fast.*
Before infinitives connected to a verb	Ich gehe **nich**t einkaufen. (**Einkaufen** is the infinitive.)	*I'm not going shopping.*
Before most prepositional phrases	Dieser Käse kommt **nicht** aus Frankreich. (**Aus Frankreich** is the prepositional phrase.)	*This cheese isn't from France.*
Before the combinations of parts in a sentence	Matthias geht **nicht** sehr oft in die Bibliothek. (The two parts here are **sehr oft** and **in die Bibliothek**.)	*Matthias doesn't go to the library very often.*

Q. Gehst du heute Abend ins Kino?

Nein,/ich/Kino/gehe/heute/nicht/ins/Abend

A. Gehst du heute Abend ins Kino? *(Are you going to the cinema this evening?)*

Nein, ich gehe heute Abend <u>nicht</u> ins Kino. *(No, I'm not going to the cinema this evening.)*

 Ist das dein Haus?

Nein,/Haus/das/mein/nicht/ist _____

48 Kommen Sie am Mittwoch zu uns?

Nein,/nicht/am Mittwoch/wir kommen/zu Ihnen. _____

49 Gehen Sie jetzt Golf spielen?

Nein,/spielen/Golf/nicht/ich gehe. _____

50 Trinken Sie den Orangensaft nicht?

Nein,/ihn/nicht/trinke/ich. _____

51 Liegt Duisburg in einer schönen Gegend *(pretty area)*?

Nein,/liegt/nicht/einer/in/schönen Gegend/Duisburg. _____

52 Geht ihr heute Nachmittag schwimmen?

Nein,/nicht/heute Nachmittag/wir gehen/schwimmen. _____

Negating with kein

Kein *(no, not, not any)* functions as an adjective; it describes nouns by expressing negation such as **kein Kuchen** *(no cake)*, **keine Zeit** *(no time)*, **kein Brot** *(no bread)*, and so on. Before you can jump in and start adding **kein** to your sentences, however, you need to know the gender and case of the noun you're negating. Look at the following sentence: **Kein Kuchen schmeckt so gut wie ein deutscher Apfelkuchen** *(No cake tastes as good as a German apple cake)*. **Kein Kuchen** is the subject of the sentence, so it's in nominative case, and **Kuchen** is masculine (**der**). **Kein** is the singular masculine form of **kein** in nominative case. (See Chapter 3 for more on gender and case.)

REMEMBER When you look at **kein**, you can see the indefinite article **ein** *(a, an)*. Good news again on the grammar front: The indefinite article **ein** and other very commonly used words are often referred to as **ein-** words because they follow the same pattern in case and gender endings. In the nominative case, **ein** and **kein** are the masculine and neuter forms, and **eine** and **keine** are the feminine and plural forms.

You need to remember only one set of endings for the following words:

>> **ein** *(a, an)*, the indefinite article

>> **kein** *(no, not, not any)*, the adjective that negates a noun

>> **mein, dein, sein, ihr, unser, eurer, ihr, Ihr** *(my, your, his, her, our, your, their, your)*, the possessive adjectives

Table 6-5 shows how to remember the endings for **kein**, with the case and gender endings in bold. (Chapter 3 provides background information on case and gender.) Masculine and neuter are grouped together, and feminine and plural are in one column. This table is also valid for **ein-** words except **ein** itself, which has no plural form.

Table 6-5   Endings of Kein

Case	Masculine(masc.) / Neuter(n.)	Feminine(fem.) / Plural(pl.)
Nominative (nom.)	kein	keine
Accusative (acc.)	keinen (masc.), kein (n.)	keine
Dative (dat.)	keinem	keiner (fem.), keinen (pl.)
Genitive (gen.)	keines	keiner

TIP

Notice that masculine and neuter endings are almost all the same for **kein** and **ein-** words; the accusative is the only one that differs. You can also remember feminine and plural together, keeping in mind that the dative is the only one that isn't the same for the two genders. Look at the example sentences with **kein** in the four cases, followed by the English equivalent and the grammar note explaining the gender:

>> **Nominative case: Keine Menschen leben auf der Insel.** *(No people live on the island.)* **Menschen** (plural) is the subject of the sentence, so **keine Menschen** is nominative plural.

>> **Accusative case: Nach dem grossen Abendessen hatte ich keinen Hunger.** *(I wasn't hungry after the big dinner.)* Literally, *ich hatte keinen Hunger* means *I had no hunger*. **Der Hunger** (masculine) changes to the accusative singular **keinen Hunger** because it's the object of the sentence.

>> **Dative case: In keinem alten Auto gibt es GPS.** *(There's no GPS in any old car[s].)* Literally, **in keinem alten Auto gibt es GPS** means *in no old car is there GPS*. The prepositional phrase **in keinem alten Auto** is in dative case; therefore, **das Auto** becomes **keinem (alten) Auto.**

>> **Genitive case: Während keiner Nacht in der letzten Woche habe ich gut geschlafen.** *(I didn't sleep well [during] any night last week.)* Literally, **während keiner Nacht in der letzten Woche habe ich gut geschlafen** means *during no night in the past week did I sleep well.* **Während** *(during)* is a genitive preposition and **die Nacht** is feminine singular. (Chapter 13 shows you details on prepositions.) You need the genitive case ending **-er** for **kein.**

TIP

When you're reading German, use the examples you see to understand the grammar involved. Train yourself to take a step back and think carefully about which word endings you're dealing with in a sentence. The pieces of the grammar puzzle begin to fit into place when you recognize which gender and case you're looking at.

PRACTICE

The purpose of the next exercise is to put the correct ending on **kein.** The notes in parentheses indicate noun gender and which case to use. Refer to Table 6-5 for help. Here's the situation: Daniel is writing a list of grievances in his good-riddance **Brief** *(letter)* to Susanne, who has run off with Jonas.

Q. Dieser Brief ist _____ Liebesbrief (masc., nom.) von mir.

A. Dieser Brief ist <u>kein</u> Liebesbrief von mir. *(This letter is no love letter from me.)*

Liebe Susanne,

53 Du bist _____ Frau (fem., nom.) für mich. Warum?

54 Du hast _____ Interesse (n., acc.) mehr an mir.

55 Ich habe mit _____ anderen Frau (fem., dat. preposition **mit**) geflirtet.

56 Du hast _____ Grund, (masc., acc.) mit Jonas zu flirten.

57 Er schenkt dir _____ Blumen (pl., acc.) wie ich es immer tue.

58 Er hat _____ Auto (n., acc.), . . .

59 und er hat _____ Arbeit (fem., acc.).

60 Ich sage dir, Jonas ist _____ Mann (masc., nom.) für dich.

61 Vielleicht *(maybe)* magst du mich nicht, weil *(because)* ich _____ Haare (pl., acc.) habe . . .

62 und auch *(also)* _____ Muskeln (pl., acc.) wie Arnold Schwarzenegger.

63 Was kann ich dazu sagen? Du bist auch _____ Schönheit (fem., nom.) wie Heidi Klum.

64 Ich kenne _____ Frau (fem., acc.), die so dumm ist wie du. Leb wohl.

Daniel

PRACTICE

In this exercise, you decide which negation to use, **kein** or **nicht.** The two choices are shown in parentheses. *Note:* The correct form of **kein** is provided, so you can relax because you have a 50 percent chance of getting the answer right.

Q. Das ist _____ schwierig, oder? (keiner/nicht)

A. Das ist <u>nicht</u> schwierig, oder? *(This isn't difficult, is it?)*

65 Sie haben _____ Ahnung *(idea).* (nicht/keine)

66 Sie fliegt morgen _____ nach Paris. (nicht/kein)

67 Trinken Sie _____ Kaffee? (nicht/keinen)

68 Er liebt sie _____. (keine/nicht)

69 Warum fährt Ulla _____ mit uns? (kein/nicht)

70 Ich habe _____ Lust. (keine/nicht)

71 Ist das _____ kompliziert? (nicht/keinen)

72 Wir haben den Film _____ gesehen. (nicht/keine)

73 Meine Schwester hat _____ Kinder. (keine/nicht)

Answers to "Asking and Answering Intelligently: Giving Orders" Practice Questions

1 B: **Ja. Fahren Sie innerhalb Deutschlands?** *(Yes. Are you traveling within Germany?)*

R: **Ja. Ich möchte nach Berlin fahren.** *(Yes. I'd like to go to Berlin.)*

2 B: **Wollen Sie ein Ticket 1. Klasse oder 2. Klasse nehmen?** *(Do you want a first- or second-class ticket?)*

3 R: **Ich weiß nicht. Ist das Ticket 1. Klasse sehr teuer?** *(I don't know. Is the first-class ticket very expensive?)*

4 B: **Nein, es kostet nur 45€ mehr. Reisen Sie nach Berlin hin und zurück?** *(No, it's only 45€ more. Are you going round-trip to Berlin?)*

R: **Ja, genau.** *(Yes, exactly.)*

5 B: **Haben Sie viel Gepäck dabei?** *(Do you have much luggage with you?)* For an extra fee, you may have your luggage picked up at your home and delivered to your destination.

6 R: **Nein, nur eine Tasche. Kann ich aber ein Fahrrad mitnehmen?** *(No, only one bag. But can I take a bicycle with me?)*

B: **Sicher, kein Problem.** *(Of course. No problem.)* You can also rent bicycles from many train stations.

7 R: **Ist der Transport für das Fahrrad sehr teuer?** *(Is it very expensive to transport the bicycle?)*

B: **Nun, Sie müssen 20€ für das Rad bezahlen.** *(Well, you have to pay 20€ for the bicycle.)*

8 R: **Fährt ein Zug am Nachmittag?** *(Is there a train leaving in the afternoon?)*

B: **Ja, Sie können um 13.30 Uhr oder um 15.15 Uhr abfahren.** *(Yes. You can leave at 1:30 p.m. or 3:15 p.m.)* The 24-hour clock time system is easy to calculate by adding 12 to p.m. times.

9 R: **Gut, dann nehme ich den Zug um 13.30 Uhr. Gibt es ein gutes Hotel am Bahnhof in Berlin?** *(Good, then I'll take the train at 1:30 p.m. Is there a good hotel at the train station in Berlin?)*

B: **Ja, es gibt mehrere Hotels.** *(Yes, there are several hotels.)*

R: **Sehr freundlich, vielen Dank für Ihre Auskunft.** *(That's very kind of you. Thank you for your information.)*

10 A: **Interface Sprachenschule, guten Morgen!** *(Interface Language School. Good morning.)*

J: **Guten Morgen, Julian Stromberger von der Firma Nordstern.** *(Good morning. This is Julian Stromberger from Nordstern Company.)* *Note:* In German business situations, and even in private telephone calls, people answer the phone and identify themselves by their last name, but there's a trend to give the whole name.

A: **Kann ich Ihnen helfen?** *(Can I help you?)*

J: **Ja, wir möchten einen Sprachkurs für Spanisch machen.** *(Yes. We'd like to do a Spanish-language course.)*

A: **Kein Problem, sehr gerne.** *(No problem. That's fine.)*

J: **Wie viel kostet so ein Sprachkurs?** *(How much does such a language course cost?)*

(11) A: **Wie viele Personen machen den Kurs?** *(How many people are taking the course?)*

J: **Wir sind vier Personen.** *(There are four of us. Literally: We are four people.)*

A: **Dann kostet der Kurs 500€ pro Person.** *(Then it costs 500€ per person.)*

(12) J: **Wie viele Stunden sind es?** *(How many hours is it?)*

A: **Es sind 40 Stunden.** *(It's 40 hours.)*

(13) J: **Warum ist es so teuer?** *(Why is it so expensive?)*

A: **Weil es nur vier Personen sind.** *(Because there are only four people.)* The conjunction **weil** requires that the verb be placed at the end of the phrase.

(14) J: **Wo ist der Unterricht?** *(Where is the class?)*

A: **Der Unterricht kann in Ihrer Firma sein.** *(The class can take place at your company.)*

J: **Oh, in Ordnung, einverstanden.** *(Oh, all right. That's agreed.)* Another translation for **einverstanden** is *very well.*

(15) A: **Wohin soll die Lehrerin fahren?** *(Where should the teacher go?)*

J: **Sie muß nach Starnberg fahren.** *(She'll need to go to Starnberg.)* **Müssen** means *must,* but it carries a stronger connotation in English than in German.

A: **Einverstanden.** *(Very well.)* Another translation for **einverstanden** is *agreed* or *that's agreed.*

(16) J: **Wer macht den Unterricht?** *(Who is teaching the class?)*

A: **Eine junge Lehrerin.** *(A young teacher.)*

(17) J: **Wie heißt die Lehrerin?** *(What is the teacher's name?)* The fixed expression you use to ask someone's name, **wie heißen Sie?**, literally means *how are you called?*

A: **Sie heißt Cristina.** *(Her name is Cristina.)*

(18) J: **Woher kommt sie?** *(Where is she from?)*

A: **Sie kommt aus Santiago de Chile.** *(She's from Santiago de Chile.)*

(19) J: **Wann können wir anfangen?** *(When can we begin?)*

A: **Sie können nächste Woche am Montag anfangen.** *(You can start on Monday next week.)*

J: **Ah, gut, vielen Dank. Auf Wiederhören.** *(Oh, great, thank you very much. Goodbye.)* In telephone language, you say, literally speaking, *hear you later.*

A: **Danke für Ihren Anruf. Auf Wiederhören.** *(Thank you for your call. Goodbye.)*

(20) **Wer ist deine Schwester?** *(Who is your sister?)*

(21) **Wen rufen Sie an?** *(Who are you calling?)*

(22) **Mit wem spricht der Johanna?** *(Who is Johanna talking to?)*

(23) **Wer kann mir helfen?** *(Who can help me?)*

(24) **Wessen Kinder sind das?** *(Whose children are they?)*

(25) **Wer hat Zeit für mich?** *(Who has time for me?)*

(26) **Wen kontaktieren Sie?** *(Who do you contact/are you contacting?)*

(27) **Wer fährt nach Rügen?** (Who is driving/going to Rügen?) Rügen is a picturesque island in the Baltic Sea.

(28) **Für wen sind diese Blumen?** *(Who are these flowers for?)*

(29) **Der Mann da drüben heißt Herr Storch, nicht wahr?** *(The man over there is Herr Storch, isn't he?)* This sounds like a business situation, or at least formal situation, because the man is described with his last name, so you definitely should use the "official" tags.

(30) **Du bleibst noch eine Nacht, oder?** *(You're staying another night, aren't you?)* If you're talking with a good friend, using **du**, you can use **oder**.

(31) **Hier regnet es oft im Frühling, stimmt's?** *(It often rains here, doesn't it?)*

(32) **Sie sind morgen im Büro, richtig?** *(You'll be in the office tomorrow, won't you?)*

(33) **Du hast Informatik studiert, oder?** *(You studied computer science, didn't you?)*

(34) **Ballspielen verboten!** *(No ball playing allowed)*

(35) **Unbefugten ist der Zutritt verboten!** *(No trespassing)*

(36) **Vorsicht bissiger Hund!** *(Beware of [vicious] dog)*

(37) **Alkoholkonsum verboten!** *(No alcoholic beverages allowed)*

(38) **Betreten der Baustelle verboten!** *(Construction site: Do not enter)*

(39) **Waldbrandgefahr!** *(Forest-fire danger)*

(40) **Ausfahrt freihalten!** *(No parking)* Literally: *Keep exit free.*

(41) **Bitte nicht füttern!** *(Do not feed the animals)*

(42) **Sie: Essen Sie langsam! ihr: Esst langsam! du: Iss langsam!** (stem vowel-change verb in **du** and **er/sie/es** present tense)

(43) **Sie: Fahren Sie vorsichtig! ihr: Fahrt vorsichtig! du: Fahr vorsichtig!**

(44) **Sie: Gehen Sie nicht! ihr: Geht nicht! du: Geh nicht!**

(45) **Sie: Lesen Sie! ihr: Lest! du: Lies!** (stem vowel-change verb in **du** and **er/sie/es** present tense)

(46) **Sie: Machen Sie! ihr: Macht! du: Mach!**

(47) **Ist das dein Haus?** *(Is that your house?)*

Nein, das ist nicht mein Haus. *(No, it isn't my house.)* **Nicht** follows the verb.

(48) **Kommen Sie am Mittwoch zu uns?** *(Are you coming to see us on Wednesday?)*

Nein, am Mittwoch kommen wir nicht zu Ihnen. *(No, we're not coming on Wednesday to see you.)* **Nicht** precedes the prepositional phrase **zu Ihnen**.

(49) **Gehen Sie jetzt Golf spielen?** *(Are you going to play golf now?)*

Nein, ich gehe nicht Golf spielen. *(No, I'm not going to play golf.)* **Nicht** precedes the infinitive expression **Golf spielen**.

(50) **Trinken Sie den Orangensaft nicht?** *(Aren't you going to drink the orange juice?)*

Nein, ich trinke ihn nicht. *(No, I'm not going to drink it.)* **Nicht** follows the direct object **ihn**.

(51) **Liegt Duisburg in einer schönen Gegend?** *(Is Duisburg in a pretty area?)*

Nein, Duisburg liegt nicht in einer schönen Gegend. *(No, Duisburg isn't in a pretty area.)* **Nicht** precedes the prepositional phrase **in einer schönen Gegend.**

(52) **Geht ihr heute Nachmittag schwimmen?** *(Are you going swimming this afternoon?)*

Nein, wir gehen heute Nachmittag nicht schwimmen. *(No, we're not going swimming this afternoon.)* **Nicht** precedes the infinitive **schwimmen.**

Liebe Susanne,

(53) **Du bist keine Frau für mich. Warum?** *(You're not the woman for me. Why?)*

(54) **Du hast kein Interesse mehr an mir.** *(You have no more interest in me.)*

(55) **Ich habe mit keiner anderen Frau geflirtet.** *(I didn't flirt with any other woman.)*

(56) **Du hast keinen Grund mit Jonas zu flirten.** *(You have no reason to flirt with Jonas.)*

(57) **Er schenkt dir keine Blumen wie ich es immer tue.** *(He doesn't give you flowers like I always do.)*

(58) **Er hat kein Auto, . . .** (*He doesn't have a car . . .*)

(59) **und er hat keine Arbeit.** (*and he has no work.*)

(60) **Ich sage dir, Jonas ist kein Mann für dich.** (*I'm telling you, Jonas is not the man for you.*)

(61) **Vielleicht magst du mich nicht, weil ich keine Haare habe . . .** (*Maybe you don't like me because I don't have any hair . . .*)

(62) **und auch keine Muskeln wie Arnold Schwarzenegger.** (*and also no muscles like Arnold Schwarzenegger.*)

(63) **Was kann ich dazu sagen? Du bist auch keine Schönheit wie Heidi Klum.** (*What else can I say? You are no beauty queen like Heidi Klum.*)

(64) **Ich kenne keine Frau, die so dumm ist wie du. Leb wohl.** (*I don't know any woman who is as dumb as you. Farewell.*)

Daniel

(65) **Sie haben keine Ahnung** (*You have no idea.*)

(66) **Sie fliegt morgen nicht nach Paris.** (*She's not flying to Paris tomorrow.*)

(67) **Trinken Sie keinen Kaffee?** (*Don't you drink coffee?/ Aren't you drinking any coffee?*)

(68) **Er liebt sie nicht.** (*He doesn't love her.*)

(69) **Warum fährt Ulla nicht mit uns?** (*Why isn't Ulla going/driving with us?*)

(70) **Ich habe keine Lust.** (*I don't feel like it.*)

(71) **Ist das nicht kompliziert?** (*Isn't that complicated?*)

(72) **Wir haben den Film nicht gesehen.** (*We haven't seen/didn't see the movie.*)

(73) **Meine Schwester hat keine Kinder.** (*My sister doesn't have any children.*)

Chapter **7**

In the Mood: Combining Verbs with Modal Auxiliaries

I hope you're in a good mood as you start on this chapter about modal auxiliary verbs. I'm talking about attitude with a capital *A* in the next few pages. In grammar mumbo jumbo, *modals* are auxiliary (helping) verbs that indicate an attitude about the main verb, even though they don't directly alter the main verb's action.

This motley band of modal verbs helps set the mood of the sentence. They can be quite influential at times in their mood-altering abilities — and all without illegal substances. *Mood* is grammarspeak for how something is expressed in a sentence: The mood of a verb indicates a wide range of, yes, *moods*, such as probability, impossibility, certainty, doubt, or even just plain old facts, without all the **Schnickschnack** (*bells and whistles*).

If you're asking yourself whether you can get by without using modals, the answer is plain and simple. Nope — not unless you're willing to put up with being misunderstood in daily situations in which the modals should make your intended thought clear to the listener. In this chapter, you find out what the seven modal verbs are, together with their equivalents in English, and you discover the importance of modal verbs in everyday situations. You get the present-tense conjugation of these verbs and the particulars on important characteristics of these verbs. Then you put all the information together and try your hand at the exercises at the end of each verb section.

The 4-1-1 on Modal Verbs

Modal verbs modify the main verb in the sentence. Here's how they work: You take a plain old verb or phrase like *eat, sleep, walk, plant a garden, play tennis, learn how to play chess,* or *do nothing.* Then you think about your attitude toward these activities, and you decide that you want to say I <u>like to</u> eat, I <u>must</u> *sleep more,* I <u>would like to</u> *walk every day,* I <u>should</u> *plant a garden,* I <u>can</u> *play tennis well,* I <u>want to</u> *learn how to play chess,* or I <u>may</u> *do nothing.* The underlined modal verbs offer you a wide range of ways to express your attitude toward actions such as *eat, sleep, play,* and *learn.*

This section gives you a quick overview of what modal verbs are and how they work. The rest of this chapter focuses on the seven specific modal verbs.

Identifying modals: Assistants with attitude

Modals are your ticket to conveying your attitude or how you feel about an action. They usually accompany another verb and appear (conjugated) in the second position of a sentence. The verb they assist generally appears as an infinitive at the end of the clause.

Table 7-1 shows the German modal verbs in infinitive form and the English translation, followed by a statement using the modal verb. Look at the various ways of modifying the statement **Ich lerne Deutsch** (*I learn German*) with the modal verbs. Notice that the conjugated form of the modal verb is in second position in the sentence, and the infinitive form of the main verb gets booted to the end.

All these verbs have regular verb endings in their plural forms (**wir, ihr, sie,** and **Sie**). Most of them also have irregular verb changes, some of which you can see in the examples in Table 7-1. As you go through **Die Glorreichen Sieben** (*The Magnificent Seven* — modal verbs, that is) in this chapter, you see the irregular verb endings of these verbs in the present tense.

Table 7-1   German Modal Verbs

German Modal Verb	Translation	Example	English Equivalent
dürfen	*may, to be allowed to*	Ich **darf** Deutsch lernen.	*I may/am allowed to learn German.*
können	*can, to be able to*	Ich **kann** Deutsch lernen.	*I can/am able to learn German.*
mögen	*to like to*	Ich **mag** Deutsch lernen.	*I like to learn German.*
möchten	*would like to*	Ich **möchte** Deutsch lernen.	*I would like to learn German.*
müssen	*must, to have to*	Ich **muss** Deutsch lernen.	*I must/have to learn German.*
sollen	*should, to be*	Ich **soll** Deutsch lernen.	*I'm supposed to learn German/I should learn German.*
wollen	*to want to*	Ich **will** Deutsch lernen.	*I want to learn German.*

DIFFERENCES

In English, you typically have two verbs in a sentence that has a modal verb; the second one is described as the *main verb*. In German, however, the modal verb may be the only verb. The one true rogue is the verb **mögen**, which frequently stands alone; to a lesser extent, so is its sidekick, **möchten**. (Check out the sections "I Like That: Mögen, the Likeable Verb" and "What Would You Like?: Möchten, the Preference Verb" for more information on these two.)

Understanding word order and modals

In terms of word order for modals, German uses pretty much the same order as for other verbs that require an auxiliary verb to complete the meaning of the main verb. The present perfect and the future tenses also use a secondary, auxiliary verb to complete the main verb's meaning. With these verb types (and tenses), you conjugate the auxiliary verb, put it in second position in the sentence, and generally put the main verb in its infinitive form at the end of the clause or phrase. (See Chapter 14 for present-perfect verbs and Chapter 16 for future-tense verbs and their word order.)

Take a look at the examples in Table 7-1. The conjugated, active verb is in second position in the sentence; it directly follows the subject or other elements, such as a reference to time or a prepositional phrase. When you need more than one verb, the others go to the very end of the sentence.

REMEMBER

Questions follow a slightly different word order (inverted word order) if they're the type of questions that can be answered with yes, no, or maybe. See Chapter 6 for more on forming questions.

May I?: Dürfen, the Permission Verb

Some people feel rules and customs crimp their personal style, but such guidelines give people an idea of what they can expect from one another. The rules of the road allow you to do something (or not); you may proceed with caution at a yield sign, but you're not allowed to cross the double yellow line. And being polite by asking permission — May I use your bathroom? May I have another cookie? — is certainly not limited to little boys and girls. Adults in all parts of the world know that asking for and granting permission is part of the code of polite interaction.

TIP

You use the modal verb **dürfen** to ask for and grant permission. Look at the conjugation of **dürfen**. It's irregular in the singular forms: **ich, du,** and **er/sie/es.** In the following minitable, the irregular forms are bold, and the regular forms show the endings in bold.

dürfen (may, to be allowed to, to be permitted to)

ich **darf**	wir dürf**en**
du **darfst**	ihr dürf**t**
er/sie/es **darf**	sie dürf**en**
Sie dürf**en**	

Here's **dürfen** in action:

>> **Sie dürfen dort nicht parken.** (*You're not allowed to park there.*)

German uses **dürfen** in a wide variety of everyday situations. Table 7-2 lists four commonly used idiomatic expressions with **dürfen,** followed by an example sentence in German and the English equivalent. You frequently hear these expressions in polite exchanges between people who don't know each other well.

Generally speaking, German and English use **dürfen** (*may, to be allowed to, to be permitted to*) in very similar ways: to ask for permission, to grant permission, and to state that something is (or isn't) permitted or allowed.

DIFFERENCES

German sometimes uses the impersonal form **man** (*it, one, you*) with **dürfen**. In English, you use the passive construction (*parking/passing/stopping isn't allowed here*), or you simply say *no parking/passing/stopping* (*allowed here*).

DIFFERENCES

English uses *may* to express possibility, whereas **dürfen** doesn't have this meaning. Instead, you'd use **vielleicht** (*maybe/perhaps*) to express possibility or chance. You can translate **Vielleicht komme ich spät nach Hause**, for example, as *I may come home late*. But *Perhaps I'll come home late* is closer to the word-for-word translation, even though German doesn't use future tense in the example sentence. (For more information on present tense, see Chapter 5.)

Watch out for false friends (which I discuss in Chapter 4). The modal verb **müssen** looks somewhat similar to the English *must*, which is the correct meaning in English, but you express *must not* in German with **nicht dürfen: Sie dürfen hier nicht rauchen** (*You must not/are not allowed to smoke here*).

Table 7-2   Uses of Dürfen In Polite Conversation

Situation	Example	English Equivalent
To ask whether a customer needs assistance	**Was darf es sein?**	*May I help you?*
To signal someone to do a favor such as opening the door	**Darf ich Sie bitten?**	*May I trouble you?*
To say that you'd like to introduce two people	**Darf ich Ihnen Frau Feuerstein vorstellen?**	*May I introduce you to Mrs. Feuerstein?*
To explain that something isn't allowed	**Das Obst dürfen Sie nicht anfassen**	*You may not/must not touch the fruit.*

PRACTICE

Try your hand at the situations in these exercises. Put the correct form of **dürfen** into the sentence. The example gets you started.

Q. Ihr Chef (*boss*) sagt: Sie _____ morgen frei haben.

A. Ihr Chef sagt: Sie <u>dürfen</u> morgen frei haben. (*You may have the day off tomorrow.*)

① Uwe hat eine Allergie gegen Nüsse. Er _____ Erdnussbutter (*peanut butter*) nicht essen.

2 Gabi ist in einem Biergarten. Sie fragt: _____ ich hier sitzen?

3 Dieser Fluß (*river*) ist sehr schmutzig (*dirty*). Sie _____ hier nicht schwimmen.

4 Ich bin erst 17. Ich _____ noch nicht wählen (*vote*).

5 Die Bedienung (server) sagt: Was _____ es sein?

You Can Do It!: Können, the Ability Verb

Can you run a marathon barefoot? Do you know how to play chess (and win) against a computer? Are you able to make a 5-course dinner for 12 guests without batting an eye? No matter what your hidden talents may be, if you have a healthy ego, chances are that you enjoy talking about yourself. Know-how, ability, and can-do attitude are all expressed with the verb **können**.

As one of the seven players in the modal verb dugout, **können** (*can, to be able to, to know how to*) is a true champ. In general, German and English use **können** in similar ways. The verb goes up to bat whenever you need to express that

>> You can or can't do something: **Kannst du Tennis/Tischtennis/Volleyball/Schach/Poker spielen?** (*Can you play tennis/table tennis/volleyball/chess/poker?*)

>> You know or don't know how to do something: **Er kann Geige/Klavier/Keyboards/Gitarre/Klarinette/Saxophon spielen.** (*He knows how to play the violin/piano/keyboards/guitar/clarinet/saxophone.*) In German, you don't use the definite article **der, die, das** [*the*] to talk about playing an instrument.

>> You're able to do something: **Ich kann bis Mittag schlafen.** (*I'm able to/can sleep until noon.*)

>> You want to request or offer help in a polite but direct way: **Können Sie mir sagen, wo der Bahnhof/die Straßenbahnhaltestelle/das Hotel Blaue Gans/das Kunstmuseum ist?** (*Can you tell me where the train station/the streetcar stop/the Hotel Blaue Gans/the art museum is?*)

Note: Notice the comma after the first clause. In German, you need this comma to separate the subordinate clause (. . . **wo der Bahnhof ist?**) from the main clause (**Können Sie mir sagen, . . .**). Subordinate clauses often begin with words like **wo** (*where*), **was** (*what*), **wie viel** (*how much*), **wer** (*who*), and **warum** (*why*). The conjugated verb in the subordinate clause, **ist** (*is*), gets the boot and lands at the end of the sentence. (For more on subordinate clauses, see Chapter 12.)

Look at the conjugation of **können**. It's irregular in the singular forms: **ich, du, and er/sie/es.** The irregular forms are bold, and the regular forms show the endings in bold.

könn-en (can, to be able to, to know how to)

ich **kann**	wir könn**en**
du **kannst**	ihr könn**t**
er/sie/es kann	sie könn**en**

Sie könn**en**

Here is **können** in action:

> **» Ich kann Ihnen mit ihrem Gepäck helfen.** (*I can help you with your luggage.*)

DIFFERENCES

One striking difference between English and German is that German sometimes describes what can or can't be done using **können** but no main verb. Typically, you hear the following expressions in spoken, casual conversation. Table 7-3 lists the situation, an example sentence in German, and its equivalent in English.

REMEMBER

Several common **können** expressions are reflexive (they use a reflexive pronoun [*me, you, us,* and so on] with the verb) in German but not in English. German uses the reflexive much more frequently than English. (For more information on reflexive verbs, check out Chapter 9.) Table 7-4 lists these common expressions, an example sentence in German, and the English translation.

Table 7-3   Uses of Können without a Main Verb

Situation	Example	English Equivalent
To say that someone can speak a language	Meine Frau **kann** sehr gut Französisch.	*My wife can speak French very well.*
To say that you give up trying	Ich **kann nicht** weiter. Es ist zu schwer.	*I can't go on. It's too difficult.*
To explain what you can't help doing (excusing yourself for taking a third piece of chocolate cake)	Ich **kann nichts** dafür. Es schmeckt so gut!	*I can't help it. It tastes so good!*
To interject that you can do something	Das **kann** ich wohl!	*Of course I can do that!*

Table 7-4   Uses of Können with a Reflexive Verb

Situation	Example	English Equivalent
To say you can('t) decide	Ich **kann mich** nicht entscheiden.	*I can't decide.*
To express that you can get away with something	Wie **kannst** du **dir** so etwas erlauben?	*How can you get away with something like that?*
To be able (or unable) to afford something	Wir **können uns** kein teueres Auto leisten.	*We can't afford an expensive car.*
To give assurance that someone/ something can be trusted	Sie **können sich** auf mich verlassen.	*You can depend on me.*

PRACTICE

Decide whether the word order for the following expressions is correct. If not, make the necessary correction in word order. Remember that when there are two verbs, the main verb (the one that's in infinitive form) gets kicked to the end of the sentence. (Harsh treatment for some decent, upstanding verbs, but it's true!)

Q. Sie kann spielen Klarinette.

A. Sie kann Klarinette spielen. *(She can play the clarinet.)* The word order needs to have the conjugated verb **kann** in second position and the main verb **spielen** (in the infinitive form) at the end of the sentence.

6   Können Sie helfen mir?

_____

7   Sara kann sich kein neues Auto leisten.

_____

8   Könnt ihr gut Tennis spielen?

_____

9   Ich kann Englisch, Deutsch, und Spanisch.

_____

10   Ich kann spielen Fußball.

_____

I Like That: Mögen, the Likeable Verb

Want to talk about likes and dislikes? **Mögen** is the verb for you. Consider these sentences: **Magst du kaltes Wetter?** *(Do you like cold weather?)* **Nein, ich mag den Winter überhaupt nicht.** *(No, I don't like the winter at all.)* Want to express your feelings toward someone? Try **ich mag dich** *(I like you).*

The main definition of **mögen** is that of liking or disliking someone or something. When talking about such preferences, you usually don't need an additional verb:

>> **Magst du diese Sängerin?** *(Do you like this female singer?)*

>> **Er mag kein Starkbier.** *(He doesn't like strong beer.)*

The modal verb **mögen** comes as a double dipper. Why? Because **mögen** *(to like, to care for)* is so likeable that it has a sidekick, **möchten** *(would like, would like to do),* which is similar in meaning to **mögen**. (Check out the next section for more on **möchten**.)

This verb minitable shows you the conjugation of **mögen**. It follows the typical pattern of modal verbs: the singular verb forms are the irregular ones — **ich mag, du magst, er/sie/es mag**. The irregular forms are shown in bold, and the regular forms show the endings in bold.

mögen (to like, to care for)

ich **mag**	wir mög**en**
du **magst**	ihr mögt
er/sie/es mag	sie mög**en**
Sie mög**en**	

Here is **mögen** in action:

>> **Ich mag klassische Musik.** (*I like classical music.*)

When you want to express dislike for someone or something, you put **nicht** at the end of the sentence when no other verb is along for the ride:

>> **Lotte mag diese Musik nicht.** (*Lotte doesn't like this music.*)

>> **Mögen sie Schokoladeneis nicht?** (*Don't they like chocolate ice cream?*)

REMEMBER

To add some oomph to **mögen**, you can tack on some modifiers. The first two in the following list are with **gern** (**gern** is similar to *a lot* when you add it to other words). I arranged the list in order of most positive to most negative:

>> **mögen . . . besonders gern** (*to especially like*): **Ich mag Bratkartoffeln besonders gern.** (*I especially like roast potatoes.*) They're similar to home fries.

>> **mögen . . . (sehr) gern** (*to like [very much]*): **Ich mag Kartoffelklöße (sehr) gern.** (*I like potato dumplings very much.*) In southern Germany and Austria, **Klöße** are referred to as **Knödel**, both of which are *dumplings*.

>> **mögen . . . gar nicht** (*not to like very much*): **Ich mag Pommes frites gar nicht.** (*I don't like French fries very much.*)

>> **mögen . . . überhaupt nicht.** (*not to like at all*): **Ich mag Salzkartoffeln überhaupt nicht.** (*I don't like boiled potatoes at all.*)

A few idiomatic expressions use **mögen**:

>> **Das mag sein.** (*That could be true.*)

>> **Ich mag ihn leiden.** (*I'm fond of him.*) You can also leave off **leiden** without changing the meaning much, but **leiden** stresses the emotion of caring for someone.

>> **Darin mögen Sie Recht haben.** (*You have a point there.*)

Take a crack at these exercises. Put the correct form of **mögen** into the sentence. The example gets you started.

Q. Meine Eltern _____ die Oper sehr gern.

A. Meine Eltern **mögen** die Oper sehr gern. (*My parents like the opera very much.*)

11 _____ du die Suppe?

12 Nein, ich _____ Suppen überhaupt nicht.

13 Er _____ Horrorfilme.

14 _____ ihr Klaviermusik nicht?

15 Doch, aber wir _____ alle Musikarten.

What Would You Like?: Möchten, the Preference Verb

Life is full of choices, and you're likely to have some opinions on what you like best. When the **Kellner/Kellnerin** (*waiter/waitress*) in a German restaurant asks me **"Was möchten Sie?"** (*What would you like?*), I make sure that I order something to drink first — **"Ich möchte eine Apfelsaftschorle"** (*I'd like an apple juice/mineral water drink*). That way, I have time to peruse the eight-page menu and order the meal later.

To say you'd like to do something in German, you use the modal verb **möchten**. Although **möchten** (*would like [to do]*) is often lumped together with **mögen** (*to like, care for*) (see the preceding section for more info), it's definitely important enough to get top billing in the modal-verb lineup. Look at the conjugation of **möchten**. The verb endings are in bold.

möchten (would like [to])	
ich möcht**e**	wir möcht**en**
du möcht**est**	ihr möcht**et**
er/sie/es möcht**e**	sie möcht**en**
Sie möcht**en**	

Here's **möchten** in action:

>> **Ich möchte am Wochenende Fahrrad fahren.** (*I'd like to go bicycling on the weekend.*)

REMEMBER

The important similarity between **möchten** and **mögen**, aside from their meanings, is that neither modal verb needs a main verb to express something clearly when the context makes the meaning understandable. When you're ordering in a restaurant, for example, the context typically indicates what you'd like to have. Using **möchten** as the modal verb, you can omit the following main verbs:

>> **essen** *(to eat)*

>> **trinken** *(to drink)*

>> **haben** *(to have)*

>> **fahren** *(to drive)*

>> **gehen** *(to go, walk)*

Look at the two example sentences, one with and one without the main verb. Assuming you know they're spoken in a restaurant, the meaning of the first sentence, which has no main verb, is clear:

>> **Ich möchte ein Glas Rotwein, bitte.** *(I'd like a glass of red wine, please.)*

>> **Ich möchte ein Glas Rotwein trinken, bitte.** *(I'd like to drink a glass of red wine, please.)* Or you can use **haben** *(to have)* instead of **trinken**, and you'd still get a glass of red wine.

PRACTICE

It's your turn to see how polite you sound in German and how good you are at expressing things people would like to do. Write the sentences or questions in German, using the English cues. To help you, I've indicated some difficult elements in bold.

Q. I'd like a cup of coffee.

A. Ich möchte eine Tasse Kaffee.

16 I'd like a pizza, please.

_____

17 We'd like to learn German.

_____

18 I'd like to stay here. (**hierbleiben** means *to stay here*.)

_____

19 She'd like to dance with Andreas.

_____

20 Would you like a glass of water? (s., fam.)

_____

Do I Have To?: Müssen, the Verb of Necessity

As a child, you may have heard something along the lines of "No, you don't have to finish your broccoli au gratin, but you have to try at least three bites." So now that you've grown up — or at least other people think you have — far more serious obligations haunt you, such as paying taxes, mowing the lawn, and having the first local strawberries of the season before anyone else.

Müssen bears a vague resemblance to *must*, making it easier to get down to the nitty-gritty of how this modal works, when you *need* it, when you *have to* use it, when it's a *must*, and when you *don't have to* deal with it. What about *must not*? Oddly enough, *must not* is **darf nicht** in German, with the modal verb **dürfen** *(to be allowed to)*. (Check out the earlier section on **dürfen** if you're a bit foggy on the difference between the two verbs.)

REMEMBER

Necessity and obligation are the core meanings of **müssen** in both English and German, although in the English-speaking world and among North Americans in particular, there's a tendency to downplay the use of *must* because it sounds so strong to the ear. *Do I have to?* works just fine at getting the obligation message across (especially when uttered by whining 12-year-olds after you've told them to stop texting and go to bed).

Take a look at the conjugation of **müssen**. Like most of its fellow modal verbs, it's irregular in the singular forms: **ich, du, and er/sie/es**. The irregular forms are in bold, and the regular forms show the endings in bold.

müssen (must, to have to, need to)

ich **muss**	wir müss**en**
du **musst**	ihr müss**t**
er/sie/es **muss**	sie müss**en**
Sie müss**en**	

Here is **müssen** in action:

>> **Er muss morgen früh aufstehen.** *(He has to get up early tomorrow.)*

DIFFERENCES

Don't get lulled into thinking that **muss nicht** is equivalent to *must not*. When you turn **müssen** into a negative expression, the similarities between German an English go down the drain. German has two expressions for indicating whether something is forbidden or simply not necessary:

>> **nicht dürfen** *(not allowed, must not, not permitted)*: A no-no; strong prohibition, such as **Du darfst das nicht essen** *(You mustn't eat that)*.

>> **nicht müssen** *(not necessary, don't need to)*: An absence of necessity or obligation, such as **Du musst das nicht essen** *(You don't need to eat that)*.

PRACTICE

We all have things we *have to do*, and *don't need to do*, right? In the following situations, you *need to* insert the right conjugated form of **müssen** into the German sentence. The sample exercise shows you how this works.

Q. Alex's garage is a mess. **Er** _____ **die Garage aufräumen** (*straighten up*).

A. Alex's garage is a mess. **Er <u>muss</u> die Garage aufräumen.** (*Alex's garage is a mess. He has to straighten up the garage.*)

21 You caused a car accident. Someone says to you: Sie _____ die Polizei anrufen.

22 Your fridge is empty. You say: Ich_____ zum Supermarkt gehen.

23 You offer to help wash the dishes. Your friend says: Nein, danke. Die Kinder _____ abwaschen.

24 You ask your friend if he really has to buy a new laptop. You say: _____ du wirklich (*really*) einen neuen Laptop kaufen?

25 Kristof doesn't have to work tomorrow. Morgen _____ er nicht arbeiten.

Should I or Shouldn't I?: Sollen, the Duty Verb

There are things in life that you have to do and things you're supposed to do. I prefer the latter because they're easier to put off. But wasting valuable vacation time to accomplish everything on your checklist is something you really shouldn't do. So the to-do list just gets longer and longer until the day it fortuitously gets lost in the trash.

When you want to describe an action you *should* or *shouldn't do* or that you're *supposed to* or *not supposed to do*, **sollen** is the verb to use. Look at the conjugation of this modal verb in the minitable that follows. **Sollen** is irregular only in two places: the **ich and er/sie/es** forms. The irregular forms are in bold, and the regular forms show the endings in bold.

sollen (should, to be supposed to)

ich **soll**	wir soll**en**
du soll**st**	ihr soll**t**
er/sie/es **soll**	sie soll**en**
Sie soll**en**	

Here is **sollen** in action:

>> **Du sollst die Katze füttern.** (*You should feed the cat.*)

TIP

You, the non-native speaker of German, should be careful not to sound too forceful when it isn't necessary. **Sollen,** the modal duty verb, is the verb you use for giving advice or expressing a duty that's an expected, right-kind-of-thing-to-do action. The negative version, **nicht sollen,** expresses what you shouldn't do. The cousin **müssen** is the modal verb of necessity and strong directives; see the earlier section on **müssen.**

PRACTICE

How's your sense of duty in German? Finish the sentences with the right conjugated form of **sollen** or **nicht sollen.** The second sentence in each of these exercises has a clue to help you decide which one is logical. The sample exercise shows how to proceed.

Q. Ich _____ um sieben Uhr bei ihm vorbeikommen. Hartmut hat das gesagt.

A. Ich <u>soll</u> um sieben Uhr bei ihm vorbeikommen. Hartmut hat das gesagt. (*I should arrive at his place at 7am. Hartmut said so.*)

26. Wir _____ mehr Sport machen. Wir sind sehr faul (*lazy*).

27. Du _____ spät ins Bett gehen. Du siehst sehr müde (*tired*) aus.

28. Ich _____ den neuen Film sehen. Er ist super.

29. Maria _____ ein kleineres Auto kaufen. Das Benzin (*gas*) ist sehr teuer.

30. Du _____ zum Konzert gehen. Die Gruppe ist wirklich schlecht (*bad*).

I Want to Be Famous: Wollen, the Intention Verb

When you were little, did you want to travel around the world? Chances are that by now, you've scaled back such grand intentions: You just want to be able to sleep late Saturday mornings. You do intend to travel more, however — to your teenager's soccer games. No matter how grandiose or mundane your wants and desires may be, you can express them all with **wollen,** the intention verb.

Expressing your wants (as well as intentions, desires, and a secret wish or two) in German is simple when you know how to use **wollen.** Like some others in the band of modal verbs, it's irregular in the following forms: **ich, du, and er/sie/es** (the singular forms). The irregular forms are in bold, and the regular forms show the endings in bold. Look at the verb conjugation.

wollen (to want to, intend to, wish)

ich **will**	wir woll**en**
du **willst**	ihr woll**t**
er/sie/es **will**	sie woll**en**
Sie woll**en**	

Here is **wollen** in action:

>> **Ich will jetzt nach Hause fahren.** (*I want to drive home now.*)

When you're expressing something you *want to do* or *intend to do*, you can substitute **möchten** for **wollen** and come up with virtually the same results (see the earlier section "What Would You Like? Möchten, the Preference Verb"). Look at the following examples. The difference between them is minimal in both languages. The speaker could be talking to someone or doing some wishful thinking:

>> **Ich will ein neues Auto kaufen.** (*I want to buy a new car.*)

>> **Ich möchte ein neues Auto kaufen.** (*I would like to buy a new car.*)

When you want something from someone else, the two verbs aren't interchangeable. **Wollen** is direct: You *want* something. **Möchten** does express a want in the form of *would like to*, but it carries the ring of politeness. Compare the two example sentences that follow. The speaker is a dinner guest in someone's living room.

>> **Ich will Musik hören.** (*I want to listen to music.*) The guest is simply stating what they want or intend to do. There's no hint of politeness; it sounds blunt, even to the point of being rude.

>> **Ich möchte Musik hören.** (*I would like to listen to music.*) The guest sounds polite by using **möchte**. A request is likely to follow the stated intention with a question, such as **Haben Sie etwas dagegen?** (*Do you mind?*).

TIP

The expressions using **wollen** in the following sentences show how its meaning can bend slightly in conjunction with another word or words:

>> **wollen . . . unbedingt:** Underscores that you absolutely want something, without fail, such as **Ich will unbedingt nach Australien reisen** (*I'm dying to travel to Australia*).

>> **wie + subject + wollen:** Notes that a decision is up to somebody else, such as **Wie du willst** (*It's up to you*). The German title of Shakespeare's *As You Like It* is **Wie Ihr Wollt**.

>> **wollen nichts damit zu tun haben:** Notes that the subject doesn't want to be involved with something, such as **Ich will nichts damit zu tun haben** (*I want no part of that* or *I don't want anything to do with it*).

PRACTICE

Check that you know how to use the modal verb **wollen** in the following exercise. What do these people want to do? Change the German sentence by adding the correct form of the modal verb **wollen**. Word order is important here: Remember to replace the main verb with the conjugated form of **wollen**; then throw the main verb to the back (of the sentence, that is), changing it in midair into the infinitive form. Look at the example to get you going.

Q. Du machst einen Salat.

A. Du <u>willst</u> einen Salat <u>machen</u>. *(You want to make a salad.)* **Machst** changes to **machen** before it lands at the end of the sentence.

 Ich spiele morgen um 17.00 Uhr Tennis.

_____

 Wir trinken Orangensaft.

_____

 Ihr geht in die Stadt.

_____

34 Heidi und Thomas gehen heute Abend ins Restaurant.

_____

35 Sophie isst ein Stück Apfelkuchen.

_____

PRACTICE Now you can flex your modal muscles with the following question/answer pairs, in which you see all seven modal verbs in action. You have two modal verbs in the parentheses after each sentence. Choose the logical one and put it into the right conjugated form in the space provided. Look at the example to get you on track. Notice that it includes both a question and an answer.

Q. _____ du morgen früh aufstehen? (dürfen/müssen)

Nein, morgen _____ ich länger schlafen. (können/müssen)

A. <u>Musst</u> du morgen früh aufstehen? *(Do you have to get up early tomorrow morning?)*

Nein, morgen <u>kann</u> ich länger schlafen. *(No, tomorrow I can sleep later/longer.)*

36 _____ Sie mir bitte helfen? (können/sollen)

37 Ja, schon. Was _____ ich machen? (möchten/sollen)

38 Warum _____ du nicht fernsehen? (dürfen/wollen)

39 Ich bin sehr müde. Ich _____ ins Bett. (dürfen/müssen)

40 Was _____ es sein? (dürfen/wollen)

41 Ich _____ ein Bier, bitte. (möchten/dürfen)

42 _____ Sie klassische Musik? (mögen/möchten)

43 Ja, ich _____ Mozart besonders gern. (wollen/mögen)

44 Warum _____ die Kinder später ins Bett gehen? (dürfen/müssen)

45 Morgen _____ sie nicht in die Schule. (können/müssen)

46 Was _____ du am Wochenende machen? (sollen/möchten)

47 Ich _____ nach Budapest. (sollen/möchten)

48 _____ wir jetzt (now) nach Hause gehen? (dürfen/wollen)

49 Nein, noch (another) ein Glas Wein _____ wir trinken. (können/müssen)

50 Morgen _____ es regnen. (sollen/müssen)

51 Wirklich (Really)? Das _____ ich mir nicht vorstellen (imagine). (können/wollen)

52 _____ Hubert gut Italienisch? (können/möchten)

53 Ja, er _____ auch relativ gut Spanisch. (wollen/können)

54 Wir haben drei Tage frei. Wo _____ wir hinfahren? (müssen/sollen)

55 Ich _____ unbedingt nach Wien. (können/wollen)

Answers to "In the Mood: Combining Verbs with Modal Auxiliaries" Practice Questions

1. **Uwe hat eine Allergie gegen Nüsse. Er darf Erdnussbutter nicht essen.** (*Uwe has an allergy to nuts. He must not eat peanut butter.*)

2. **Gabi ist in einem Biergarten. Sie fragt: Darf ich hier sitzen?** (*Gabi is in a beer garden. She asks: May I sit here?*) **Note:** It's completely normal to sit with others at the long tables with benches in a beer garden. Just ask first.

3. **Dieser Fluß ist sehr schmutzig. Sie dürfen hier nicht schwimmen.** (*This river is very dirty. You may not swim here.*)

4. **Ich bin erst 17. Ich darf noch nicht wählen** (*I'm only 17. I'm not allowed to vote*).

5. **Die Bedienung sagt: Was darf es sein?** (*The server says: What are you having/What will it be?*)

6. **Können Sie mir helfen?** (*Can you help me?*) **Können** is the conjugated verb, and in a yes/no question, it's first; the verb **helfen** needs to be at the end.

7. **Sara kann sich kein neues Auto leisten.** (*Sara can't afford a new car.*) The word order is correct.

8. **Könnt ihr gut Tennis spielen?** (*Can you play tennis well?*) The word order is correct.

9. **Ich kann Englisch, Deutsch, und Spanisch.** (*I can speak English, German, and Spanish.*) The sentence is correct. **Können** needs no other verb here. But you can add **sprechen** (*to speak*) at the end of the sentence, especially if you want to go on and say something different about another language: **Ich kann Französisch verstehen, aber nicht sprechen.** (*I can understand French but not speak it.*)

10. **Ich kann Fußball spielen.** (*I can play soccer.*) The word order is incorrect; in the correct order, the conjugated modal verb **kann** is in second position, and the main verb **spielen** (in infinitive form) is at the end of the sentence.

11. **Magst du die Suppe?** (*Do you like the soup?*)

12. **Nein, ich mag Suppen überhaupt nicht.** (*No, I don't like soups at all.*) The strong negative is expressed with **überhaupt nicht**.

13. **Er mag Horrorfilme.** (*He likes horror movies.*)

14. **Mögt ihr Klaviermusik nicht?** (*Don't you like piano music?*) Notice that **nicht** is at the end of the sentence.

15. **Doch, aber wir mögen alle Musikarten.** (*Yes, but we like all kinds of music.*)

16. **Ich möchte eine Pizza, bitte.**

17. **Wir möchten Deutsch lernen.**

18 Ich möchte hierbleiben.

19 Sie möchte mit Andreas tanzen.

20 Möchtest du ein Glas Wasser?

21 Sie müssen die Polizei anrufen. (*You have to call the police.*)

22 Ich muss zum Supermarkt gehen. (*I have to go to the supermarket.*)

23 Nein, danke. Die Kinder müssen abwaschen. (*No, thank you. The children have to do the dishes.*)

24 Muss du wirklich einen neuen Laptop kaufen? (*Do you really have to buy a new laptop?*)

25 Morgen muss er nicht arbeiten. (*He doesn't have to work tomorrow.*)

26 Wir sollen mehr Sport machen. Wir sind sehr faul. (*We should do more sports. We're very lazy.*)

27 Du sollst nicht spät ins Bett gehen. Du siehst sehr müde aus. (*You shouldn't go to bed late. You look very tired.*)

28 Ich soll den neuen Film sehen. Er ist super. (*I should see the new movie. It's super.*)

29 Maria soll ein kleineres Auto kaufen. Das Benzin ist sehr teuer. (*Maria should buy a smaller car. Gas is very expensive.*)

30 Du sollst nicht zum Konzert gehen. Die Gruppe ist wirklich schlecht. (*You shouldn't go to the concert. The group is really bad.*)

31 Ich will morgen um 17.00 Uhr Tennis spielen. (*I want to play tennis tomorrow at 5 p.m.*)

32 Wir wollen Orangensaft (trinken). (*We want to drink [some] orange juice.*)

33 Ihr wollt in die Stadt (gehen). (*You want to go into the city.*) **In die Stadt gehen** usually means *to the city center*, which typically has a pleasant pedestrian area with stores and cafés.

34 Heidi und Thomas wollen heute Abend ins Restaurant (gehen). (*Heidi and Thomas want to go to a/the restaurant this evening.*)

35 Sophie will ein Stück Apfelkuchen (essen). (*Sophie wants to eat a piece of apple cake.*) German **Apfelkuchen** is *excellent* (**hervorragend**).

36 Können Sie mir bitte helfen? (*Can/Could you help me, please?*)

37 Ja, schon. Was soll ich machen? (*Yes, of course. What shall/should I do?*)

38 Warum willst du nicht fernsehen? (*Why don't you want to watch TV?*)

39 Ich bin sehr müde. Ich muss ins Bett. (*I'm really tired. I have to go to bed.*) You don't need the additional verb **gehen**.

40 Was darf es sein? (*What would you like?*) The server in a restaurant asks this.

41 Ich möchte ein Bier, bitte. (*I'd like/I'll have a beer, please.*) **Ich möchte . . .** is how you order.

(42) **Mögen Sie klassische Musik?** (*Do you like classical music?*) **Mögen** usually stands alone.

(43) **Ja, ich mag Mozart besonders gern.** (*Yes, I especially like Mozart.*)

(44) **Warum dürfen die Kinder später ins Bett gehen?** (*Why are the children allowed to go to bed later?*)

(45) **Morgen müssen sie nicht in die Schule.** (*Tomorrow they don't have to go to school.*) Keep in mind that **nicht müssen** means *don't have* to in English.

(46) **Was möchtest du am Wochenende machen?** (*What would you like to do on the weekend?*)

(47) **Ich möchte nach Budapest.** (*I'd like to go to Budapest.*) The second verb **fahren** is optional.

(48) **Wollen wir jetzt nach Hause gehen?** (*Shall we go home now?*)

(49) **Nein, noch ein Glas Wein können wir trinken.** (*No, we can drink another glass of wine.*)

(50) **Morgen soll es regnen.** (*It's supposed to rain tomorrow.*)

(51) **Wirklich? Das kann ich mir nicht vorstellen.** (*Really? I can't imagine that.*)

(52) **Kann Hubert gut Italienisch?** (*Can Hubert speak Italian well?*) You don't need the second verb **sprechen** (*to speak*).

(53) **Ja, er kann auch relativ gut Spanisch.** (*Yes, he can also speak Spanish relatively well.*)

(54) **Wir haben drei Tage frei. Wo sollen wir hinfahren?** (*We have three days off. Where shall/should we go?*)

(55) **Ich will unbedingt nach Wien.** (*I'm dying to go to Vienna.*)

Chapter **8**

Sorting Out Separable- and Inseparable-Prefix Verbs

A ll you couch potatoes: Use it or lose it! *Get up* off the couch, *put* your shoes *on*, *breathe* some air *in*, and get ready to *work out*! Why the exercise hype in a chapter on separable- and inseparable-prefix verbs? Wouldn't it be more appropriate as a pep talk in a health magazine? Actually, the verbs I deal with in this chapter are the types you see in italics here. In English, they're called *two-part* or *phrasal verbs*, and their German counterparts are called *separable-* or *inseparable-prefix* verbs. *Separable prefixes* can separate from the verb itself, depending on the verb tense you use, and the *inseparable prefixes* never separate from the verb. These verb types are equally common in German and English.

In addition to showing you how to use these prefix verbs when you're talking about events in the present, I include the lowdown on how to use them in the simple past and present perfect. Why? As you will see, those itty-bitty prefixes need special treatment when figuring out how and where to place them in your sentence.

Looking at the Prefix

The German *prefix* (which corresponds to the second part of a two-part verb in English) may stand for a preposition like *up* or an adverb like *away*. In both English and German, the prefix alters the meaning of the original verb, sometimes only slightly, sometimes radically.

TIP

To remember whether these verbs are separable- or inseparable-prefix verbs, practice pronouncing them aloud. The separable-prefix verbs stress the prefix in spoken German, but the inseparable-prefix verbs don't stress the prefix. For instance, **umsteigen** (*to change* [*trains, planes, and so on*]) is separable, so when you say it, stress the prefix **um-** like this: *UM-steig-en*. **Unterbrechen** (*to interrupt*) is inseparable, so you don't stress the prefix, but you do stress the first syllable of the verb **brechen** like this: *un-ter-BRECH-en*.

REMEMBER

Two-part verbs in English are generally exactly that — in two parts, as in *get + up = get up*. They're a dime a dozen: *turn away, put on, take off* — you get the picture. The German equivalent is different because it has the prefix attached directly to the infinitive (the base verb form). For example, **aufstehen** (*to get up*) has the prefix **auf-**. (Literally, **auf-** + **stehen** is up + stand.) Such German verbs are extremely common.

Simplifying Separable-Prefix Verbs

With separable-prefix verbs, the verb and the prefix can — drum roll please — split up (surprise, surprise). Of the three groups of verbs that I discuss in this chapter, this group is the largest because it has the largest number of prefixes as well as the largest number of verbs that connect with these prefixes. Knowing the meaning of the verb without the prefix can help, but make sure you know the separable-prefix verb and its English meaning. Take a look at the following example. **Aufstehen** (*to get up*) is a separable-prefix verb. Its prefix, **auf-**, means *up* in this context. The verb **stehen** means *to stand* or *stay*. Notice that the prefix **auf-**, appears at the end of the sentence: **Ich stehe meistens um sechs Uhr auf** (*I usually get up at six a.m.*).

You get your money's worth with the prefixes in this section. They're a great help when you're expanding your vocabulary. Why? Not only do they combine with verbs, but some also combine with nouns and adjectives. Most verb prefixes have more than one specific meaning, and as you become familiar with them, you start seeing a pattern in the way a prefix alters the meaning of the verbs it combines with. When you come across a new German verb with the same prefix, you can make an educated guess about its meaning. These itty bitty sound bites are very influential, so start your own collection right away.

Table 8-1 shows separable prefixes, their English meanings, and some verbs that use the prefix. Although this prefix list is fairly complete, the number of separable-prefix verbs is huge. This sample list contains high-frequency verbs.

The next sections show you how to use separable-prefix verbs in the present, the past, and the present perfect. I break it down by these three tenses; for each verb tense, you find out whether to do separation work or not, details on how to form the verb tense, and where to place the two verb parts in the sentence.

Table 8-1   Separable Prefixes and Verb Combinations

Prefix	English Definition	Example Verb	English Equivalent
ab-	*from*		
		abbrechen	*to break away, stop*
		abfahren	*to drive away*
		abfliegen	*to take off (plane)*
		abnehmen	*to pick up, reduce, take off*
		abschaffen	*to do away with*
an-	*at, to, on*		
		anfangen	*to begin, start*
		anhaben	*to have on, wear*
		ankommen	*to arrive*
		anrufen	*to phone*
auf-	*on, out, up*		
		aufbauen	*to put up, build up*
		aufgeben	*to give up, check (bags)*
		aufmachen	*to open, open up*
		aufstehen	*to get up, stand up*
aus-	*from, out*		
		ausbilden	*to train, educate*
		ausfallen	*to cancel, fall out (hair)*
		ausgehen	*to go out*
		aussehen	*to look (like), appear*
		aussteigen	*to get out, off (train, car and so on)*
bei-	*with, along*		
		beilegen	*to insert (in a document)*
		beitreten	*to join, enter into (a pact)*
da-	*there*		
		dableiben	*to stay behind*
dabei-	*there*		
		dabeibleiben	*to stay with, stick with (it)*
daran-	*on*		
		daranmachen	*to get down to (it)*
ein-	*in, into, down*		
		einkaufen	*to go shopping, to buy*
		einladen	*to invite*
		einschlafen	*to go to sleep*
		einsteigen	*to get in, on (train, car and so on)*
entgegen-	*against, toward*		
		entgegenkommen	*to approach, accommodate*
fehl-	*wrong*		
		fehlschlagen	*to go wrong*

(continued)

TABLE 8-1 *(continued)*

Prefix	English Definition	Example Verb	English Equivalent
fest-	*fixed*		
		festhalten	*to hold on, keep hold of*
fort-	*onward, away*		
		fortbilden	*to continue education*
		fortführen	*to carry on, continue*
gegenüber-	*across from*		
		gegenüberstehen	*to be opposite, face*
gleich-	*equal*		
		gleichstellen	*to treat as equal*
her-	*from, here*		
		herstellen	*to manufacture, establish*
heraus-	*from, out of*		
		herausfinden	*to find out*
		herausreden	*to talk one's way out of*
		herausfordern	*to challenge*
hin-	*to, towards, there*		
		hinfahren	*to drive there, go there*
hinzu-	*in addition*		
		hinzufügen	*to add (details), enclose*
kennen-	*know*		
		kennenlernen	*to get to know, meet*
los-	*start, away*		
		losbrechen	*to break off*
		losfahren	*to drive off*
		loslassen	*to let go of*
mit-	*along, with (similar to English prefix co-)*		
		mitarbeiten	*to collaborate*
		mitbringen	*to bring (something) with*
		mitfahren	*to travel with*
		mitkommen	*to come with*
		mitmachen	*to go along with, join in*
		mitteilen	*to inform (someone)*
nach-	*after, copy (similar to English prefix re-)*		
		nachahmen	*to imitate*
		nacharbeiten	*to revise, rework*
		nachfragen	*to ask, inquire*
		nachgeben	*to give way, give in*
statt-	*no equivalent*		
		stattfinden	*to take place (event)*

Prefix	English Definition	Example Verb	English Equivalent
vor-	*before* (similar to English prefixes *pre-* and *pro-*)		
		vorbereiten	*to prepare*
		vorführen	*to present, perform*
		vorlesen	*to read aloud*
		vormachen	*to show someone how to do something, fool someone*
		vorstellen	*to introduce, present*
weg-	*away, off*		
		wegbleiben	*to stay away*
		wegfahren	*to drive away*
zu-	*shut, to, upon*		
		zulassen	*to authorize, license*
		zunehmen	*to increase*
		zusichern	*to assure someone*
		zusteigen	*to get on, board*
zurück-	*back*		
		zurückkommen	*to return, come back*
		zurücktreten	*to step back, resign*
		zurückzahlen	*to pay back*
zusammen-	*together*		
		zusammenarbeiten	*to work together*
		zusammenfassen	*to summarize*
		zusammenwachsen	*to grow together*
zwischen-	*between*		
		zwischenlanden	*to stop over (flight)*

Using separable-prefix verbs in the present tense

When you write an e-mail to your friend in Berlin or speak to your German neighbor, you'll probably end up using separable-prefix verbs in the present tense. When doing so, word order is a really big deal. Why? If you mix up word order, the reader or listener may not get your intended message. Also, keep in mind that the prefix alters the basic verb's meaning, so if you leave it out, you're likely to cause confusion. (For more on word order in present tense, see Chapter 5.)

REMEMBER

With separable-prefix verbs in the present tense, keep the following two points in mind:

>> The prefix — such as **fest-** in **festhalten** (*to hold on*) — goes to the end of the sentence. In spoken German, you stress the prefix.

>> The verb itself, which is the part you conjugate, is generally in second position in the sentence, as in **Ich halte mich fest** (*I'm holding on tight*). **Halte**, the conjugated part of the verb, is in second position.

Here are some guidelines for word order, depending on the type of sentence:

>> **Statements, both positive and negative:** The verb is generally in second position, such as in **Wir haben viel vor** (*We're planning to do a lot [of activities]*). The verb is **vorhaben** (*to plan*). The conjugated part of the verb **haben** is in second position, and the prefix **vor-** is at the end of the sentence. The same sentence expressed negatively would look like this: **Wir haben nicht viel vor** (*We're not planning to do much*).

>> **Yes/no questions and commands:** The verb and subject are inverted, meaning that the verb is first, followed by the subject, such as with **Kommst du am Sonntag vom Urlaub zurück?** (*Are you coming back from vacation on Sunday?*). The verb is **zurückkommen** (*to come back*). **Kommst**, the conjugated part of the verb **zurückkommen**, is in first position in a yes/no question, and the prefix **zurück** is at the end of the question. (Go to Chapter 6 for more information on questions and commands.)

>> **Sentences or questions with a modal verb (such as** dürfen **or** möchten**) in addition to the separable-prefix verb:** Conjugate the modal verb, put it (usually) in second position, and place the separable-prefix verb in the infinitive form at the end of the phrase, such as with **Alle Gäste dürfen mitmachen** (*All the guests may join in*). The verb is **mitmachen** (*to join in*). The conjugated part of the modal verb **dürfen** (*may, to be allowed to*) is in second position, and **mitmachen**, the infinitive form of the separable-prefix verb, goes to the end of the sentence. (See Chapter 7 for info on modal verbs.)

For sentences that have more than one clause, the guidelines follow those for two-part sentences, see Chapter 12.

PRACTICE

Use the verb list in Table 8-1 and the preceding guidelines to rewrite the statements, questions, or commands in the present tense, making sure you use the correct word order. The separable-prefix verb is in parentheses in the infinitive form. Be careful: The verb may be in one part only.

Q. du schnell? (einschlafen)

A. **Schläfst du schnell ein?** (*Do you go to sleep quickly?*)

 wir viele Gäste zum Fest (einladen).

_____

 diese Firma viele Produkte im Ausland (herstellen).

_____

3 die besten Pläne oft (fehlschlagen).

_____

4 können Sie mir die Details? (mitteilen)

_____

5 der Garten sehr gut (aussehen)

_____

6 warum Martina heute? (einkaufen)

_____

7 ich muß mich auf das Interview (vorbereiten)

_____

8 in welchem Hotel die Konferenz? (stattfinden)

_____

9 wir sollen (zusammenarbeiten)

_____

10 wann wir mit dem Projekt? (anfangen)

_____

11 Sie Blumen! (mitbringen)

_____

12 wir Onkel Fritz? (einladen)

_____

PRACTICE In German public transportation, you see and hear information that helps you navigate safely and (hopefully) successfully. Using the word bank below, figure out which verb fits into the situations described. Don't be shocked by the exclamation marks! Remember: German uses them in writing to indicate a command or a directive, or, as in English, to express surprise.

abfahren	ankommen (2)	anrufen
einsteigen	festhalten	hinfahren

Q. You ask when you may call your German friend tomorrow. You say:

A. Wann kann ich dich anrufen?

13 Your German host offers to drive you to the airport. She says: Ich kann Sie zum Flughafen _____.

14 After 15 minutes, the tram (streetcar) you've been waiting for is approaching. Your new German friend says: Endlich (_At last_) _____ die Straßenbahn _____!

15. In the subway station you are hesitating about whether to get on the train. Someone tells you: _____ Sie schnell _____! Die Türen werden geschlossen. (*The doors are about to close.*)

16. You are at the train station. You want to know when the train arrives. You ask: Wann _____ der Zug _____?

17. You want to know what time your friend's train is leaving. You ask: Um wieviel Uhr _____ der Zug _____?

18. You are about to fall in a crowded bus and someone warns you to hold on (to something.) They say: _____!

Using separable-prefix verbs in the past tense

The simple past (also referred to as the narrative past) is used mainly by speakers in the north and east of Germany and in the written language of the media, especially for narrating a sequence of events in the past. (For information on how to form the simple past, see Chapter 15.) When you use separable-prefix verbs in the simple past, word order is just as important as with the present (and present perfect as well). The good news is that the guidelines for using the simple past are the same as those for present. Refer to the information in the preceding section, "Using separable-prefix verbs in the present tense."

The following examples are the same as those in the present tense section except they're in the simple past. Note that the command form doesn't exist in simple past.

Wir hatten viel vor. (*We were planning/planned to do a lot [of activities].*)

Kamst du am Sonntag vom Urlaub zurück? (*Did you come back from vacation on Sunday?*)

Alle Gäste durften mitmachen. (*All the guests were allowed join in.*)

PRACTICE

The verbs in this exercise are all in simple past. The infinitive verb form is shown in parentheses. Write the parts of the sentence in the correct word order. For help with word order, refer to the examples and the guidelines for present. You can find the separable-prefix verbs in Table 8-1. *Hint:* Remember to choose a capitalized (upper case) word to start the sentence.

Q. ein / Helena / schwarzes Kleid / an / hatte (anhaben)

A. Helena <u>hatte</u> ein schwarzes Kleid <u>an</u>. (*Helena was wearing/wore a black dress.*)

19. fuhr / nach einer Pause / fort / der Redner (fortfahren)

_____

20. ab / ihre Arbeit / Markus und Jonathan / brachen ? (abbrechen)

_____

21. sahen / m Herbst / aus / sehr schön / die Bäume (aussehen)

_____

22 Nach dem Krieg / bei / Polen / dem Warschauer Pakt / trat (beitreten)

_____

23 forderte / Der Boxer / heraus / seinen Gegner (herausfordern)

_____

24 vor / die Geschichte / Regina / las (vorlesen)

_____

25 der Bus / los / fuhr / Johanna / ohne ? (losfahren)

_____

Using separable-prefix verbs in present perfect tense

To make a sentence in present perfect using a separable-prefix verb, you need to know how to form this tense and where to place the two verb parts. Word order is the name of the game. (For more on how to form the present perfect tense and the past participle, go to Chapter 14.)

With separable-prefix verbs in the present perfect tense in general, keep the following points in mind:

» The past participle is at the end of the sentence. For example, the past participle of **hinfahren** _(to drive there, go there)_ is **hingefahren** _(driven there)_. Here's how you get it:

Split the prefix (**hin-**) from the main part of the verb (**fahren**).

Form the past participle with **ge-** by squeezing the **ge-** into the middle of the past participle: **hin- + ge- + fahren**.

» The auxiliary verb, either **haben** or **sein**, is conjugated in present tense, and it's generally in second position in the sentence. Exceptions are yes/no questions, which have inverted order: The auxiliary verb is placed first, and the subject is second.

» In spoken German, you stress the prefix in the verb. For example:

Meine Schwester hat mich angerufen. (pronounced **ANgerufen**) (_My sister called me._) The verb is **anrufen** _(to call, phone)_. The auxiliary verb **hat** is in second position. The past participle is formed with **an- + ge- + rufen**: **Ge-** is squeezed in the middle of **an-** and **-rufen**.

Der Präsident ist zurückgetreten (pronounced **zuRÜCKgetreten**). (_The president resigned._) The verb is **zurücktreten** _(to step down, resign)_. The auxiliary verb **ist** is in second position. The past participle is formed with **zurück- + ge- + treten**: **Ge-** is squeezed in the middle of **zurück-** and **-treten**.

Ist der Zug schon abgefahren? (pronounced **ABgefahren**) (_Has the train already left?_) The verb is **abfahren** _(to leave)_. The auxiliary verb **ist** is in first position because the sentence is a question. The past participle is formed with **ab + ge- + fahren**: **Ge-** is squeezed in the middle of **ab-** and **-fahren**.

Rewrite the sentences in the present. Then try your hand at writing the English equivalent in parentheses. *Note:* Verbs use either the auxiliary verb **haben** or **sein**. (See Chapter 14 for more on forming verbs in present perfect.)

Q. Ich <u>habe</u> an diesem Projekt <u>mitgemacht</u>. (mitmachen)

A. Ich <u>mache</u> an diesem Projekt <u>mit</u>. *(I am working on this project.)*

26 Ich habe 20 Freunde zur Party eingeladen. (einladen)

_____

(_____)

27 Die Firma hat seine neuen Mitarbeiter ausgebildet. (ausbilden)

_____

(_____)

28 Wir haben nicht viel eingekauft. (einkaufen)

_____

(_____)

29 Das Flugzeug ist in Bangkok zwischengelandet. (zwischenlanden)

_____

(_____)

30 Das Rockkonzert hat im Olympiastadion stattgefunden. (stattfinden)

_____

(_____)

31 Habt ihr das Gepäck (*luggage*) aufgegeben? (aufgeben)

_____

(_____)

32 Um wie viel Uhr hat der Film angefangen? (anfangen)

_____

(_____)

33 Wir sind schnell losgefahren. (losfahren)

_____

(_____)

34 Hast du ein Geschenk mitgebracht? (mitbringen)

_____

(_____)

35 Das Flugzeug ist um 15.40 abgeflogen. (abfliegen)

_____

(_____)

36 Ich habe das Geld zurückbezahlt. (zurückzahlen)

_____

(_____)

Investigating Inseparable-Prefix Verbs

Although the number of inseparable-prefix verbs isn't as large as that of separable-prefix verbs, you still need to be aware of these verbs so you can include them in your verb collection. The good news is that many of these inseparable-prefix verbs are common German verbs. In addition, some equivalent verbs in English have the same prefix. For these reasons, recognizing many of these inseparable-prefix verbs is fairly simple.

REMEMBER

The following points define inseparable-prefix verbs:

>> You don't stress the prefix in spoken German.

>> The prefix alters the original meaning of the verb.

>> The prefix sticks with the verb stem in all tenses. For instance, consider the verb **vollenden** (_to finish, complete_). The prefix is **voll-** (_full_), and the verb is **enden** (_to finish_). In the third-person singular, the present tense is **vollendet** (_finish_), the simple past is **vollendete** (_finished_), and the present perfect is **hat . . . vollendet** (_has finished_).

>> Word order in these tenses follow the same rules as verbs that have no prefix. (See Chapters 5, 14, and 15 for details on word order in present, present perfect, and simple past tenses.)

>> The past participle doesn't have the prefix **ge-**.

>> The ending of the past participle may be

Weak (formed with **-t**): For instance, the past participle of **entdecken** (_to discover_) is **entdeckt** (_discovered_).

> *Strong (formed with **-en**):* For instance, the past participle of **empfehlen** (*to recommend*) is **empfohlen** (*recommended*).

The following sentences show inseparable prefix verbs in action:

> **Wer entdeckte Nordamerika?** (*Who discovered North America?*) **Entdecken** (*to discover*) is an inseparable-prefix verb. Its prefix, **ent-**, means *away from*, and it corresponds to the English prefix *de-* or *dis-*. The verb **decken** means to cover.

> **Ich verspreche dir einen Rosengarten.** (*I promise you a rose garden.*) The verb is **versprechen** (*to promise*).

> **Verfahren sich viele Touristen in der Stadt?** (*Do many tourists get lost in the city?*) The verb **verfahren** means to get lost. In yes/no questions, the verb is at the beginning of the question.

Table 8-2 lists inseparable prefixes, their English meanings, and some verbs that use the prefix. A number of the prefixes have direct comparable usages in English, and many of the verbs are frequently used. **Erkennen Sie einige Verben?** (*Do you recognize some verbs?*)

Table 8-2　Inseparable Prefixes and Verb Combinations

Prefix	English Definition	Example Verb	English Equivalent
be-	similar to English prefix *be-*		
		sich befinden (reflexive)	*to be located*
		befreunden	*to befriend*
		bekommen	*to get*
		bemerken	*to notice*
		besuchen	*to visit/attend*
emp-	no equivalent		
		empfehlen	*to recommend*
		empfinden	*to feel*
ent-	similar to English prefixes *de-* and *dis-*		
		entbehren	*to do without*
		entdecken	*to discover*
		entkommen	*to escape*
		entscheiden	*to decide, determine*
		entstehen	*to originate*
er-	sometimes no equivalent, sometimes similar to the English prefix *re-* or the meaning of fatal		
		erfinden	*to invent, make up*
		erhängen	*to hang (execute)*
		erkennen	*to recognize*
		erklären	*to explain, declare*
		erschiessen	*to shoot dead*
		ertrinken	*to drown*

Prefix	English Definition	Example Verb	English Equivalent
		erwarten	to expect, anticipate
		erzählen	to tell
ge-	no equivalent		
		gebrauchen	to use, make use of
		gefallen	to like
		gehören	to belong to
		gestalten	to form, shape
miss-	Similar to English prefix *mis-*		
		missbrauchen	to misuse, abuse
		misstrauen	to mistrust
		missverstehen	to misunderstand
ver-	similar to English prefix *for*		
		verbieten	to forbid
		vergeben	to forgive
		vergessen	to forget
ver-	*(go) awry*		
		sich verfahren (reflexive)	to get lost
		verkaufen	to sell
		verkommen	to go to ruin
ver-	*away, lose*		
		verlassen	to leave, abandon
		verlieren	to lose
ver-	no equivalent		
		vergrößern	to enlarge
		verhaften	to arrest
		versprechen	to promise
		verstehen	to understand
voll-	*complete*		
		vollenden	to complete, come to an end
		vollführen	to execute, perform
zer-	*completely (ruin)*		
		zerbrechen	to shatter
		zerstören	to destroy

PRACTICE

You were about to read the synopsis of a German movie, but your puppy ripped it to shreds. Piece it back together by putting the sentences in the correct order. (Use the corresponding letters instead of rewriting the entire sentence.) After that, write a brief English summary of the story. *Hint:* It's a lowbrow love story with a tragic ending. **Viel Spaß!** (Have fun!) Look at the list of inseparable-prefix verbs in Table 8-2 to help you. *Note:* The Lüneburger Heide is a large heath near the city of Lüneburg.

A. Der Film beginnt mit Leo der Lugner (*Leo the Liar*) als er aus einem Gefängnis (*prison*) **entkommt.**

B. Nach zwei Monaten zusammen, **verkommt** das Verhältnis (*relationship*) der beiden.

C. Am Anfang (*In the beginning*) **misstraut** er dieser Frau in schwarz, . . .

D. Das Gefängnis **befindet sich** in der Nähe von der Lüneburger Heide im Norddeutschland.

E. Plötzlich (*Suddenly*) **bemerkt** er eine schöne Frau in einem schwarzen Kleid.

F. Bald kommt die Polizei und **verhaftet** Leo Lügner.

G. Eines Nachts (*One night*) **zerbricht** Leo eine Flasche (*bottle*) Bier über Silkes Kopf.

H. Dann **erschiesst** er die schöne Silke.

I. Leo Lügner **entdeckt** ein altes Fahrrad, in der Heide und **fährt** damit **los.**

J. . . . ich **werde** (*will*) dich nie (*never*) **verlassen.**

K. Die beiden (*The two of them*) sprechen über das Leben im Gefangnis, und **vergessen** ihre schreckliche Situation.

L. Schreckliche Silke sagt, "Ich **verspreche** dir. . .

M. . . . aber sie sagt, "Mein Name ist Schreckliche Silke (*Horrible Silke*), und ich bin aus dem Gefangnis **entkommen.**"

N. Bald (*Soon*) **verfährt** er sich in der Heide.

Q. **Was passiert in dem Film?** (*What happens in the movie?*)

A. **Der Film beginnt mit Leo der Lügner** (*Leo the Liar*) **als er aus einem Gefängnis** (*prison*) **entkommt.**

37._____	42._____	47._____
38._____	43._____ ***Hint:*** Die beiden . . .	48._____
39._____	44._____	49._____
40._____ ***Hint:*** Plötzlich . . .	45._____	
41._____	46._____	

Summary of the movie in English:

Answers to "Sorting Out Separable- and Inseparable-Prefix Verbs" Practice Questions

(1) **Wir laden viele Gäste zum Fest ein.** (*We're inviting many guests to the party.*)

(2) **Diese Firma stellt viele Produkte im Ausland her.** (*This company produces many products in foreign countries.*)

(3) **Die besten Pläne schlagen oft fehl.** (*The best plans often go wrong.*)

(4) **Können Sie mir die Details mitteilen?** (*Can you inform me of the details?*) This is a question, and it has a modal verb. Put the conjugated modal verb in first position and the verb in its infinitive form at the end.

(5) **Der Garten sieht sehr gut aus.** (*The garden looks really good.*)

(6) **Warum kauft Martina heute ein?** (*Why is Martina shopping today?*)

(7) **Ich muß mich auf das Interview vorbereiten.** (*I have to prepare [myself] for the interview.*) This sentence has a modal verb. Put the conjugated modal verb in the second position and the verb in its infinitive form at the end.

(8) **In welchem Hotel findet die Konferenz statt?** (*In which hotel is the conference taking place?*)

(9) **Wir sollen zusammenarbeiten.** (*We should work together.*)

(10) **Wann fangen wir mit dem Projekt an?** (*When do we start the project?*)

(11) **Bringen Sie Blumen mit!** (*Bring flowers along.*) This sentence is a command. The verb is first, followed by the subject.

(12) **Laden wir Onkel Fritz ein?** (*Are we inviting Uncle Fritz?*) This is a yes/no question, so the verb comes first, followed by the subject.

(13) **Ich kann Sie zum Flughafen hinfahren.** (*I can take [drive] you to the airport.*)

(14) **Endlich kommt die Straßenbahn an!** (*At last the tram is approaching [arriving].*)

(15) **Steigen Sie schnell ein! Die Türen werden geschlossen.** (*Get in fast! The doors are about to close.*)

(16) **Wann kommt der Zug an?** (*When does the train arrive?*)

(17) **Um wieviel Uhr fährt der Zug ab?** (*What time does the train leave?*)

(18) **Festhalten!** (*Hold on tight!*)

(19) **Nach einer Pause fuhr der Redner fort.** (*After a break, the speaker continued.*)

(20) **Brachen Markus und Jonathan ihre Arbeit ab?** (*Did Markus and Jonathan stop their work?*)

(21) **Im Herbst sahen die Bäume sehr schön aus.** (*The trees looked very pretty in the fall.*)

(22) **Nach dem Krieg trat Polen dem Warschauer Pakt bei.** (*After the war, Poland entered into the Warsaw Pact.*)

(23) Der Boxer forderte seinen Gegner heraus. (*The boxer challenged his opponent.*)

(24) Regina las die Geschichte vor. (*Regina read the story aloud.*)

(25) Fuhr der Bus ohne Johanna los? (*Did the bus leave without Johanna?*)

(26) Ich lade 20 Freunde zur Party ein. (*I'm inviting 20 friends to the party.*)

(27) Die Firma bildet seine neuen Mitarbeiter aus. (*The company trains its new staff.*)

(28) Wir kaufen nicht viel ein. (*We don't buy much.*)

(29) Das Flugzeug landet in Bangkok zwischen. (*The plane is stopping over in Bangkok.*)

(30) Das Rockkonzert findet im Olympiastadion statt. (*The rock concert takes place in the Olympic Stadium.*)

(31) Gebt ihr das Gepäck auf? (*Are you checking the bags?*)

(32) Um wie viel Uhr fängt der Film an? (*At what time does the movie start?*)

(33) Wir fahren schnell los. (*We're driving away fast.*)

(34) Bringst du ein Geschenk mit? (*Are you bringing a present [along]?*)

(35) Das Flugzeug fliegt um 15.40 ab. (*The plane is taking off at 3:40pm.*)

(36) Ich zahle das Geld zurück. (*I'm paying the money back.*)

(37) D. Das Gefängnis befindet sich in der Nähe von der Lüneburger Heide (*name of a large heath near Lüneburg*) im Norddeutschland.

(38) I. Leo Lügner entdeckt ein altes Fahrrad in der Heide und fährt damit los.

(39) N. Bald (*Soon*) verfährt er sich (*he gets lost*) in der Heide.

(40) E. Plötzlich (*Suddenly*) bemerkt er eine schöne Frau in einem schwarzen Kleid.

(41) C. Am Anfang (*In the beginning*) misstraut er dieser Frau in schwarz, . . .

(42) M. . . . aber sie sagt, "Mein Name ist Schreckliche Silke (*Horrible Silke*), und ich bin aus dem Gefängnis entkommen."

(43) K. Die beiden (*The two of them*) sprechen über das Leben im Gefängnis, und vergessen ihre schreckliche Situation.

(44) L. Schreckliche Silke sagt, "Ich verspreche dir . . .

(45) J. . . . ich werde (*will*) dich nie (*never*) verlassen."

(46) B. Nach zwei Monaten zusammen, verkommt das Verhältnis (*relationship*) der beiden.

(47) G. Eines Nachts (*One night*) zerbricht Leo eine Flasche (*bottle*) Bier über Silkes Kopf.

(48) H. Dann erschiesst er die schöne Silke.

F. Bald kommt die Polizei und verhaftet Leo Lügner.

Leo Lügner escapes from a prison near the Lüneburger Heide, where he discovers a bicycle that he uses to escape. He soon gets lost in the heath but all of a sudden, he notices a beautiful woman in a black dress; he's suspicious of her at first. However, when Leo discovers that this woman named Schreckliche Silke is also an escaped convict, they begin talking about life in prison and forget the terrible situation they're in. Schreckliche Silke promises Leo Lügner that she'll never leave him, but after two months together, their relationship falls apart. One night, Leo breaks a beer bottle over Silke's head and shoots her dead; soon, the police come and arrest Leo Lügner.

3

Adding Flair to Your Conversations

Chapter **9**

Sounding More Like a Native with Verb Combinations

What, exactly, marks the difference between the dabbler in German who is struggling to order a cup of coffee and the customer in a top-notch restaurant who has the wait staff surrounding the table, offering yet another sample from the chef's newest concoction? The customer's sway over the servers may have to do with their command of native German expressions. You can notice how well a person has mastered German — or any language — by observing their timely use of idiomatic language, which is the ability to insert fixed expressions into spoken and written language with ease. This chapter takes a closer look at idiomatic expressions that involve verbs. By using these expressions, you can take your German to the next level and come across like a native speaker.

Set in Their Ways: Grasping Idiomatic Verb Expressions

Idiomatic language involves stringing words together into a fixed expression that's more than the sum of its parts. One group of fixed expressions is the vast family of *idiomatic verb expressions*: combinations of verbs and other words to form a slightly different meaning. Left to its own devices, the preposition **um**, for example, generally means *around*: **Wir haben einen Zaun um das ganze Haus** *(We have a fence around the whole house)*. But in the expression **Er bittet um Hilfe** *(He's asking for help)*, the preposition **um** takes on a special meaning in combination with **bitten**.

Idiomatic German flows easily from the mouths of native speakers, who know when and how much to season their language with verb expressions. You can add some flair to your German by using the following major types of idiomatic verb expressions:

>> **Reflexive verbs**: Verbs are reflexive when you use them with reflexive pronouns, which include words such as *myself, themselves,* and *himself* in English. Look at the following example: **Ich erinnere mich an unserem ersten Tanz** *(I remember our first dance;* literally: *I recall to myself at our first dance)*. German expresses a great deal of actions using reflexive pronouns linked to the verb, an area in which English makes minimal use.

>> **Verbs associated with certain prepositions**: In this chapter, you find out about idiomatic expressions that pair the verb with a particular preposition in either the dative or accusative case. The preposition **vor**, for example, usually means *in front of*, but in the example **Ich habe Angst vor Schlangen** *(I'm afraid of snakes)*, the fixed expression combines the verb **haben** *(to have)* with **Angst** *(fear)* and the dative preposition **vor**.

>> **Verbs with separable or inseparable prefixes**: A *separable verb* is a verb with a prefix that detaches from the verb when it's conjugated. The confusion comes about because more often than not, these prefixes are nothing more than prepositions in disguise. (For more on verbs with separable and inseparable prefixes, see Chapter 8.)

To add more factors to this equation, you find combos of combos; some verb/preposition combos are actually separable or inseparable verb combos at the same time. In the following verb/preposition expression, the verb **ankommen** *(to arrive)* is a case in point because it has a separable verb prefix **an-**. When you add the preposition **auf** *(on)* to the expression, the meaning changes. Look at this example: **Es kommt darauf an** *(It depends)*. The prefix **an-** is separated from **-kommen,** the word **darauf** (literally: *on it*) accompanies the verb, and the sum of its parts is no longer *to arrive* but *to depend on*. The preposition **auf** *(on)* in the word **darauf** is a combination of **da- + (r) + auf.**

In the following sections, I show you various ways of using verb combinations to talk about yourself, others, and things. These idiomatic expressions combine a verb with another word (or words), such as a reflexive pronoun or a preposition, to form expressions.

In the Looking Glass: Reflecting on Reflexive Verbs

Look at yourself in the mirror and smile. What do you see (besides a stunningly beautiful or handsome person)? You are, grammatically speaking, *reflecting on yourself*. *Reflexive verbs* have a subject that carries out an action directed at itself. Typically, the verb combines with a reflexive pronoun to describe an action. The reflexive pronoun refers to the subject of the sentence, which is carrying out the action indicated by the verb.

German and English both have reflexive verbs, but German uses them much more liberally. To make a long story short, your German can benefit from flexing (yourself) at the reflexive-verb gym. This section helps you understand reflexive verbs and how you can use them correctly.

Self-ish concerns: Meeting the reflexive pronouns

A reflexive verb has two elements: the verb and the reflexive pronoun. In English, a reflexive pronoun has the ending *-self* (*myself, yourself*) for singular forms and *-selves* for plural forms (*ourselves, yourselves*). Both English and German have two cases of reflexive pronouns: the accusative and the dative case. The two cases are identical in English; in German, there are only two variations between the two cases, namely in the first- and second-person singular forms. (To find out more about cases, go to Chapter 3.)

Table 9-1 shows the reflexive pronouns together with their translations. As a guide, I list the corresponding nominative pronouns in the left column. Notice how frequently **sich** steps up to bat. Here's the key to the abbreviations: s. = singular, pl. = plural, inf. = informal, and form. = formal.

Table 9-1   Reflexive Pronouns: Accusative and Dative Case

Nominative (nom.) Pronouns for Reference	Accusative (acc.)	Dative (dat.)
ich *(I)*	**mich** *(myself)*	**mir** *(myself)*
du *(you)* (s., inf.)	**dich** *(yourself)*	**dir** *(yourself)*
er/sie/es *(he/she/it)*	**sich** *(himself/herself/itself)*	**sich** *(himself/herself/itself)*
wir *(we)*	**uns** *(ourselves)*	**uns** *(ourselves)*
ihr *(you)* (pl., inf.)	**euch** *(yourselves)*	**euch** *(yourselves)*
sie *(they)*	**sich** *(themselves)*	**sich** *(themselves)*
Sie *(you)* (s. or pl., form.)	**sich** *(yourself or yourselves)*	**sich** *(yourself or yourselves)*

On the case! Choosing the right form of reflexive pronoun

Reflexive pronouns are either in the accusative case or the dative case. The case you use depends on how the pronoun functions in the sentence. It may be the direct object (accusative case) or the indirect object (dative case) of the verb. Case shows the relationship of words to one another in a sentence, such as who's doing what (where the reflexive pronoun is in the accusative case) or who's doing what to what/whom (where the reflexive pronoun is in the dative case). Look at this example: **Ich putze mir die Zähne** (*I brush my teeth* [Literally: *I brush myself the teeth*]). It explains who's doing what to what, so German expresses this activity with a reflexive pronoun in dative case, **mir. Die Zähne** is the direct object, the receiver of the action, and it's in the accusative case. (See Chapter 3 for more on cases.)

REMEMBER

You may find the literal translation *I brush myself the teeth* a bit odd. Well, it's just one of the quirks of German grammar. Another thing: It shows you how word-for-word translations are often inaccurate in providing the real meaning of an expression.

Check out these examples of reflexive pronouns in action:

>> **Ich fühle mich viel besser.** *(I feel/I'm feeling much better.)* **Mich** *(myself)* is the accusative form of the reflexive pronoun; it's the direct object that refers to the subject performing the action of the verb **fühlen**. (The information answers the question *who's doing what?* Therefore, the reflexive pronoun is in the accusative case.)

>> **Ich ziehe mir eine Jeans an.** *(I put on/I'm putting on a pair of jeans.)* **Mir** is the dative form of the reflexive pronoun; **eine Jeans** is the direct object (accusative case) in the sentence. (The information answers the question "Who's doing what to what/whom?" Therefore, the reflexive pronoun is in the dative case.)

REMEMBER

The verbs using the dative reflexive pronoun are those in sentences that have a separate direct object; the verbs using an accusative reflexive pronoun have no separate direct object in the sentence.

The reflexive pronoun can also be a part of a *verb + preposition* expression, and certain prepositions can require either the accusative or the dative case, as with **Wir freuen uns auf den Feiertag nächste Woche** *(We're happy about the holiday next week)*. The preposition **auf** *(about)* requires the accusative case, as do time expressions. (I talk more about verb/preposition idioms in the upcoming section "Combining Verbs with Prepositions.")

Placing your pronoun

REMEMBER

Word order plays an important role in sentence construction with reflexive pronouns. Check out the following important points to remember with word order and reflexive pronouns:

>> In a statement, the reflexive pronoun immediately follows the conjugated verb; **sich** comes right after **haben** in this example: **Die Touristen haben sich die schöne Umgebung angesehen** *(The tourists looked at the beautiful surroundings)*.

>> In a question, if the subject is a pronoun (**du** *[you]*, for example), you place the reflexive pronoun (**dich** *[you]*) directly after it, as in this example: **Erkältest du dich schon wieder?** *(Are you catching a cold again?)*.

>> In the present tense, you push the prefix of a separable-prefix verb to the end of the sentence. In the following example, the verb **anziehen** *(to get dressed)* is a separable-prefix verb; the reflexive pronoun **mich** comes after the conjugated verb **ziehe,** and the prefix **an-** goes to the end of the sentence (refer to Chapter 8): **Ich ziehe mich an** *(I get/I'm getting dressed)*.

Identifying which verbs need to be reflexive

Many German verbs require a reflexive pronoun such as **mich** *(myself)*, **dich** *(yourself)*, or **uns** *(ourselves)* in situations when you don't use a reflexive pronoun in English, such as with **Beeilen Sie sich!** *(Hurry up!)*.

DIFFERENCES

In German, you frequently find the reflexive in references to parts of the body. These verbs often describe what you do to yourself when you're in the bathroom. Shaving (**sich rasieren** *[to shave oneself]*), for example, uses a reflexive verb. In English, you can say *The man shaved himself*, although it's more common to say *He shaved*, period. The first version is expressed reflexively, using *himself*. The second statement, *he shaved*, is just as understandable, and it isn't reflexive in structure. But German has only one, reflexive way of expressing this action: **Er rasiert sich** *(He shaves himself)*.

To add further to the mix, some German verbs can go either way: with or without the reflexive pronoun. With such verbs, the reflexive format is different from the verb without the reflexive pronoun. The next three examples show you **waschen** *(to wash)* expressed with a reflexive pronoun in the accusative case, then in the dative case, and finally without a reflexive pronoun:

>> **Ich wasche mich am Abend.** *(I wash myself in the evening.)* **Mich**, the reflexive pronoun in accusative case, refers to the subject of the sentence, **ich**. And **ich** *(I)* is carrying out the action on **mich** *(myself)*.

>> **Waschbären waschen sich oft die Hände.** *(Raccoons often wash their hands.)* Notice that German speakers express their hands with **die Hände** *(the hands)*, so if you want to say *I wash my hands* in German, it looks like this: **Ich wasche mir die Hände. Mir** is the dative case reflexive pronoun *myself*, and **die Hände** is the accusative case (direct object) *the hands*.

>> **Christian wäscht sein Auto jeden Samstag.** *(Christian washes his car every Saturday.)* In both the English and the German sentences, the verb **wäscht** *(washes)* is followed by a direct object that refers to another living being or thing.

Table 9-2 lists some of the most common reflexive verbs, many of which have to do with daily routine, especially personal hygiene. In German, you express the verbs in this list with a reflexive pronoun. The helpful grammar details give you clues about case and whether you have a separable-prefix verb.

Table 9-2   Reflexive Verbs: The Daily Routine

German Expression	English Equivalent	Helpful Grammar Details
sich abschminken (acc.)	*to take off one's makeup*	Separable-prefix verb; accusative reflexive pronoun
sich abtrocknen (acc.) **sich (die Hände) abtrocknen** (dat.)	*to dry oneself off* *to dry (one's hands)*	Separable-prefix verb; accusative or dative reflexive pronoun
sich anziehen (acc.) **sich (das Hemd) anziehen** (dat.)	*to get dressed* *to put on (one's shirt)*	Separable-prefix verb; accusative or dative reflexive pronoun
sich ausziehen (acc.) **sich (die Stiefel) ausziehen** (dat.)	*to get undressed* *to take off (one's boots)*	Separable-prefix verb; accusative or dative reflexive pronoun
sich beeilen (acc.)	*to hurry (up)*	Accusative reflexive pronoun
sich duschen (acc.)	*to take a shower*	Accusative reflexive pronoun
sich freuen auf den Tag (acc.)	*to look forward to the day*	Accusative reflexive pronoun
sich freuen auf das Frühstück (acc.)	*to look forward to (having) breakfast*	Accusative reflexive pronoun

(continued)

TABLE 9-2 *(continued)*

German Expression	English Equivalent	Helpful Grammar Details
sich kämmen (acc.) **sich (die Haare) kämmen** (dat.)	*to comb oneself* *to comb (one's hair)*	Accusative or dative reflexive pronoun
sich die Zähne putzen (dat.)	*to brush/clean one's teeth*	Dative reflexive pronoun
sich rasieren (acc.) **sich (das Gesicht) rasieren** (dat.)	*to shave oneself* *to shave (one's face)*	Accusative or dative reflexive pronoun
sich schminken (acc.)	*to put on one's makeup*	Accusative reflexive pronoun
sich waschen (acc.) **sich das Gesicht waschen** (dat.) **sich die Haare waschen** (dat.) **sich die Hände waschen** (dat.)	*to wash oneself* *to wash (one's face)* *to wash (one's hair)* *to wash (one's hands)*	Accusative or dative reflexive pronoun

PRACTICE

Write about your daily routine, using the German expressions provided in Table 9-2. Remember that with separable-prefix verbs, you place the prefix at the end of the sentence. Make sure to pay attention to whether the reflexive pronoun is expressed in the accusative case (**mich** [*myself*]) or dative case (**mir** [*myself*]).

Q. sich das Gesicht rasieren

_____

A. **Ich rasiere mir das Gesicht.** (*I shave my face.*)

① sich das Gesicht waschen

_____

② sich die Zähne putzen

_____

③ sich duschen

_____

④ sich die Haare waschen

_____

⑤ sich abtrocknen

_____

TIP

To become familiar with this group of reflexive-verb expressions, talk to yourself in the bathroom as you're getting ready in the morning: **Ich kämme mir die Haare** (*I'm combing my hair*). Remember to take one last look in the mirror, smile, and say **Ich freue mich auf den Tag** (*I'm looking forward to the day*).

PRACTICE

Markus (M) and Julia (J) are getting ready to go out to a new restaurant. Read the following passage, and choose the correct reflexive pronoun for each blank space. Look at the section on reflexive verbs, including tables 9-1 and 9-2, to decide which reflexive pronoun to use.

Q. **Markus und Julia freuen** _____ **das neue Restaurant.**

A. **Markus und Julia** <u>freuen sich</u> **auf das neue Restaurant.** (Markus und Julia are looking forward to the new restaurant.)

6 J: Markus, **freust** du _____ auf heute Abend?

7 M: Ja sicher, Julia. Ich **freue** _____ schon darauf (*to it*).

8 Markus **duscht** _____ . . .

9 . . . und **trocknet** _____ **ab.**

10 Dann **rasiert** er _____ . . .

11 . . .und **zieht** _____ ein neues Hemd **an.**

M: Julia, bist du schon fertig? (*Julia, are you ready yet?*)

12 J: Nein, ich **schminke** _____ . . .

13 . . . und dann **ziehe** ich _____ das schwarze Kleid **an.**

14 M: Dann **beeile** _____ !

Endlich sind sie fertig. (*At last they're ready.*)

15 Markus und Julia **ziehen** _____ die Schuhe **an** und gehen ins Restaurant.

Combining Verbs with Prepositions

Prepositions are short, cute words that can have a great influence on other parts of a sentence. Some German cuties and their English counterparts look similar at times, such as **in** (*in*), **an** (*on*), or **für** (*for*).

Having said that, however, I need to add that they can be sly little creatures that change their tune when they hook up with different verbs, changing the verb's meaning. One other thing you need to keep in mind is that all German prepositions use case to indicate the relationship they have with other parts of the sentence — namely, the object of the preposition. Some prepositions use the accusative case; others use the dative case. No matter how you cut the cake, certain prepositions that work together with certain verbs make for powerful, effective means of expression in German and English. You may refer to them as *idioms, idiomatic expressions,* or the bare-bones term *verb/preposition combos*. I prefer the latter. When you want to sound like German is your mother tongue, you need to acquire as many of these combos as you can fit into your repertoire. (To find out about dative and accusative terminology, go to Chapter 3.)

REMEMBER

Verb/preposition combinations are more than the sum of their parts. Why? These prepositions are slick: When combined with a verb to form a fixed expression, they can alter the meaning of the verb they appear with. That's why mastering the verb/preposition combos as a unit is important. You can't predict which preposition partners with which verb, and you can't know ahead what the whole shebang means, even if you know the meaning of the verb alone, without a preposition.

Identifying common combos in the accusative case

In this section, I show you an important group of verb/preposition combos you can use to add real German sparkle to your written and spoken language. Verbs that combine with prepositions using the accusative case make up this useful group. These common verb/preposition combos are fixed expressions for which you need to remember which preposition partners with which verb, which case the preposition takes (accusative for this list), and what the expression means. (Check out Chapter 13 for more info on prepositions.)

Table 9-3 lists some commonly used verb/preposition combos with prepositions in the accusative case. Used alone, these prepositions may be switch hitters, the kind that can work in both the accusative and dative case, but in combination with these verbs, they go to up to bat as accusatives. The expressions are listed alphabetically by verb.

Table 9-3   Idiomatic Verb Expressions with Accusative Prepositions

Verbal Expression	Example Sentence	English Equivalent
ankommen auf *(to depend on)* *Note:* **Ankommen** has a separable prefix **an-**.	**Es kommt auf das Wetter an.**	*It depends on the weather.*
bitten um *(to ask for)*	**Wir bitten um Ihre Unterstützung.**	*We're asking for your support.*
denken an *(to think of/about)*	**Denkst du oft an deine Kindheit?**	*Do you often think about your childhood?*
glauben an *(to believe in)*	**Sie glauben nicht an Gott.**	*They don't believe in God.*
halten für *(to take someone for/consider)*	**Hältst du ihn für einen Dieb?**	*Do you take him for a thief?*
reden über *(to talk about)*	**Sie redet über diverse Themen.**	*She talks about different topics.*
schreiben an *(to write to)*	**Ich schreibe an die Zeitung.**	*I'm writing to the newspaper.*
schreiben über *(to write about)*	**Schreibst du über mich?**	*Are you writing about me?*
sorgen für *(to take care of)*	**Wir sorgen für unsere Oma.**	*We're taking care of our grandma.*
sich verlieben in *(to fall in love with)*	**Ich habe mich in ihn verliebt.**	*I fell in love with him.*
verzichten auf *(to do without)*	**Ich kann auf meinen Urlaub verzichten.**	*I can do without my vacation.*
warten auf *(to wait for)*	**Wartest du auf uns?**	*Are you waiting for us?*

Read the following text, and fill in the two spaces (one for the verb, one for the preposition) with the missing parts of the verb/preposition combos you find in Table 9-3. The missing expression is written in parentheses in English. To make your task easier, read through the text first, checking out the context of each blank space. The paragraph is a love letter written by a completely unknown writer of romantic fiction. **Viel Vergnügung!** *(Have a good time!)*

Mein Liebling,

Q. Ich _____ diesen Brief _____ (to write to) dich, weil ich dich liebe.

A. Ich schreibe diesen Brief an dich, weil ich dich liebe. *(I'm writing you this letter because I love you.)*

Ich weiß, du (16) _____ oft _____ (to think about) mich, und ich

(17) _____ oft _____ (to think about) dich. Jeden Tag

(18) _____ ich _____ (to wait for) deinen Telefonanruf. Ich kann nicht

(19) _____ deine täglichen Anrufe _____ (to do without). In der Arbeit

(20) _____ ich immer _____ (to talk about) dich. Meine Kollegen

(21) _____ mich _____ (to take me for/consider) eine Idiotin, aber

das ist nicht wichtig. Wichtig ist nur eins: ich (22) _____ mich _____

dich verliebt *(to fall in love with)*. Ich (23) _____ _____ (to ask for)

einen Anruf von dir heute Abend.

Deine Sarah

Eyeing common combos in the dative case

Verbs that combine with prepositions using the dative case are another commonly used group of verb/preposition combos. When you're able to plunk these expressions into your German, you're well on the way to sounding like you're originally from a German-speaking country. These frequently used combos are fixed expressions for which you need to remember which preposition combines with which verb, which case the preposition takes (dative for this list), and what the expression means.

Table 9-4 lists some commonly used expressions with prepositions in the dative case. Used alone, these prepositions may be accusative or dative, but in these expressions, they require the dative. I list the expressions alphabetically by verb.

Look at Adventure Tours Unlimited's description of its most exciting trip on offer. Fill in the two spaces with verb expressions you find in Table 9-4. The missing expression is written in parentheses in English. First, read through the exercise to grasp the gist of the description. **Viel Spaß!** *(Have fun!)*

Table 9-4 Idiomatic Verb Expressions with Dative Prepositions

Verbal Expression	Example Sentence	English Equivalent
abhängen von (to depend on) *Note:* Abhängen has a separable prefix **ab-**.	**Es hängt von dem Wetter ab.**	*It depends on the weather.*
Angst haben vor (to be afraid of)	**Hast du Angst vor Grizzlybären?**	*Are you afraid of grizzly bears?*
arbeiten an (to work on)	**Ich arbeite sehr fleißig an dem Projekt.**	*I'm working very diligently on the project.*
bestehen aus (to consist of)	**Die Schweiz besteht aus vier Sprachregionen.**	*Switzerland consists of four language regions.*
erzählen von (to talk about)	**Er erzählt oft von seinen Reisen.**	*He often talks about his trips.*
fahren mit (to go/ride with)	**Ich fahre mit der U-Bahn.**	*I'll go (or ride) with the subway.*
gehören zu (to belong to)	**Sie gehören zu unserer Mannschaft.**	*They belong to our team.*
halten von (to think of, have an opinion about)	**Sie hält nicht viel von der neuen Regierung.**	*She doesn't think much of the new government.*
rechnen mit (to count on)	**Sie rechnen mit einer langen Nacht.**	*They're counting on a long night.*
sprechen von (to talk about)	**Ich spreche nicht von dir.**	*I'm not talking about you.*
studieren an (to study at)	**Viele Studenten studieren an technischen Universitäten.**	*Many students study at technical universities [usually engineering schools].*
verstehen von (to understand about)	**Verstehst du etwas von Motorrädern?**	*Do you know something about motorcycles?*

Q. _____ Sie etwas _____ (to know something about) Reisen?

A. **Verstehen** Sie etwas **von** Reisen? (*Do you know something about traveling?*)

Was (24) _____ Sie _____ (*to think of*) einer Traumreise? Na, ja. Ich (25) _____ jetzt _____ (*to talk about*) meiner speziellen Reise. Sie (26) _____ _____ (*to consist of*) einem Besuch auf drei Inseln: Banga, Tanga, und Zanga. Zuerst (27) _____ wir _____ (*to go by* [*means of*]) einem Ruderboot (*rowboat*) von Banga nach Tanga. Dort (28) _____ Sie Haifische (*sharks*) _____ (*to study at*) der Tanga Universität. Dann (29) _____ ich zusammen mit Ihnen _____ (*to work on*) einem Segelboot (*sailboat*) – wir bauen das Boot! (30) _____ Sie Angst _____ (*to be afraid of*) dem Segeln? Dann (31) _____ Sie _____ (*to belong to*) der Gruppe, die ein Haus auf Zanga baut. . . .

PRACTICE

Fill in the spaces with the missing prepositions you find in the following word bank. Refer to the idiomatic verb expressions in tables 9-3 and 9-4 for help. Then try your hand at writing the equivalent sentences in English.

an	auf(2)	für	mit(2)	über	um	von(3)	vor

Q. Es **hängt** _____ der Jahreszeit **ab**.

A. Es **hängt von** der Jahreszeit **ab**. *(It depends on the season.)*

32 Wir **rechnen** _____ jedem *(every)* Cent.

_____

33 Josef kann nicht _____ Kaffee **verzichten**.

_____

34 Ich **verstehe** nicht viel _____ der Philosophie.

_____

35 Sie **denken** oft _____ die Arbeit.

_____

36 **Sorgt** ihr _____ das Essen heute Abend?

_____

37 Es **kommt** _____ jede *(every)* Minute **an**.

_____

38 **Fährt** Bettina _____ dem Zug?

_____

39 Sie **haben** Angst _____ dem Krieg *(war)*.

_____

40 Wir **bitten** _____ ihre Hilfe.

_____

41 Der alte Mann **erzählt** viel _____ seiner Jugend *(youth)*.

_____

Answers to "Sounding More Like a Native with Verb Combinations" Practice Questions

(1) **Ich wasche mir das Gesicht.** *(I wash my face.)* The reflexive pronoun **mir** is in the dative case, and the direct object **das Gesicht** is in accusative case.

(2) **Ich putze mir die Zähne.** *(I brush my teeth.)* The reflexive pronoun **mir** is in the dative case, and the direct object **die Zähne** is in accusative case.

(3) **Ich dusche mich.** *(I take a shower.)* The reflexive pronoun **mich** is in the accusative case. It refers to the action of the subject, **ich**.

(4) **Ich wasche mir die Haare.** (I wash my hair.) The reflexive pronoun **mir** is in the dative case, and the direct object **die Haare** is in accusative case.

(5) **Ich trockne mich ab.** *(I dry myself.)* The reflexive pronoun **mich** is in the accusative case. It refers to the action of the subject, **ich**. The separable-prefix verb requires the prefix **ab** at the end of the sentence.

(6) J: **Markus, freust du dich auf heute Abend?** *(J: Markus, are you looking forward to this evening?)*

(7) M: **Ja sicher, Julia. Ich freue mich schon darauf.** *(M: Yes, of course, Julia. I'm really looking forward to it.)*

(8) **Markus duscht sich . . .** *(Markus takes a shower . . .)*

(9) **. . . und trocknet sich ab.** *(. . . and dries himself off.)* The separable-prefix verb requires the prefix **ab** at the end of the sentence.

(10) **Dann rasiert er sich . . .** *(Then he shaves . . .)*

(11) **. . . und zieht sich ein neues Hemd an.** *(. . . and puts on a new shirt.)* The separable-prefix verb requires the prefix **an** at the end of the sentence.

M: **Julia, bist du schon fertig?** *(Julia, are you ready yet?)*

(12) J: **Nein, ich schminke mich . . .** *(No, I'm putting on makeup . . .)*

(13) **. . . und dann ziehe ich mir das schwarze Kleid an.** *(. . . and then I'll put on the black dress.)* The separable-prefix verb requires the prefix **an** at the end of the sentence.

(14) M: **Dann beeile dich!** *(Then hurry up!)*

Endlich sind sie fertig. *(At last they're ready.)*

(15) **Markus und Julia ziehen sich die Schuhe an und gehen zur Restaurant.** *(Markus and Julia put on their shoes and go to the restaurant.)* The separable-prefix verb requires the prefix **an** at the end of the sentence.

Mein Liebling,

Ich weiß, du (16) **denkst oft an** mich, und ich (17) **denke oft an** dich. Jeden Tag (18) **warte** ich **auf** deinen Telefonanruf. Ich kann nicht (19) **auf** deine täglichen Anrufe **verzichten.** In der Arbeit (20) **rede** ich immer **über** dich. Meine Kollegen (21) **halten** mich **für** eine Idiotin, aber das ist nicht wichtig. Wichtig ist nur eins: ich (22) **habe** mich **in** dich **verliebt.** Ich (23) **bitte um** einen Anruf von dir heute Abend.

Deine Sarah

My darling,

I know you often think about me, and I often think about you. Every day I wait for your telephone call. I can't do without your daily calls. At work I always talk about you. My colleagues take me for an idiot, but that's not important. Only one thing is important: I've fallen in love with you. I'm asking for a call from you this evening.

Your Sarah

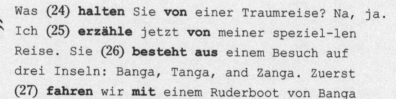 Was (24) **halten** Sie **von** einer Traumreise? Na, ja. Ich (25) **erzähle** jetzt **von** meiner speziel-len Reise. Sie (26) **besteht aus** einem Besuch auf drei Inseln: Banga, Tanga, and Zanga. Zuerst (27) **fahren** wir **mit** einem Ruderboot von Banga nach Tanga. Dort (28) **studieren** Sie Haifische **an** der Tanga Universität. Dann (29) **arbeite** ich zusammen mit Ihnen **an** einem Segelboot — wir bauen das Boot! (30) **Haben** Sie Angst **vor** dem Segeln? Dann (31) **gehören** Sie **zu** der (or **zur**: **zu** + **der** = **zur**) Gruppe, die ein Haus auf Zanga baut. . . .

What do you think of a dream trip? Good. I'll talk about my special trip. It consists of a visit to three islands: Banga, Tanga, and Zanga. First we travel by rowboat from Banga to Tanga. There we study sharks at Tanga University. Then I'll work together with you on a sailboat — we'll build the boat! Are you afraid of sailing? Then you'll be a part of the group that builds a house on Zanga. . . .

(32) **Wir rechnen mit jedem Cent.** *(We count on/are counting on every penny.)*

(33) **Josef kann nicht auf Kaffee verzichten.** *(Josef can't do without coffee.)*

(34) **Ich verstehe nicht viel von der Philosophie.** *(I don't understand much about philosophy.)*

(35) **Sie denken oft an die Arbeit.** *(They often think about work.)*

(36) **Sorgt ihr für das Essen heute Abend?** *(Are you taking care of dinner this evening?)*

(37) **Es kommt auf jede Minute an.** *(Every minute counts; literally: It depends on every minute.)*

(38) **Fährt Bettina mit dem Zug?** *(Is Bettina taking the train?)*

(39) **Sie haben Angst vor dem Krieg.** *(They're afraid of war.)*

(40) **Wir bitten um ihre Hilfe.** *(We ask/are asking for your help.)*

(41) **Der alte Mann erzählt viel von seiner Jugend.** *(The old man talks a lot about his youth.)*

Chapter **10**

Adding Adjectives for Description

A djectives add spice, distinctive flavor, and creativity to a sentence. They dress up nouns for a vigorous winter workout in Arlberg. What's in it for you? Why not be content with the basics? Cross out *vigorous* from *vigorous winter workout*, and you still get the picture. But the listener doesn't perk up and become involved. Adjectives add depth and character to the power of a noun. Besides, they're **interessant** *(interesting)*, **lustig** *(funny)*, **unglaublich** *(incredible)*, **ruhig** *(quiet)*, and **praktisch** *(practical)*.

I have good news and not-so-good news. First, the good news: There are a large number of cognates among German adjectives. In the first paragraph, you probably recognize **interessant**, and you may get the meaning of **praktisch** if you know that the ending **-isch** often stands in for English adjective endings like *-ic* and *-ical*. The not-so-good news is that you have to address grammar — gender, number, and case — when handling adjectives. Depending on where you place the adjective in the sentence, you may or may not need to put the adjective in synch with the noun it modifies. How? By adding the appropriate endings to indicate agreement with the noun.

Keine Sorge. *(Not to worry.)* This chapter explains how to categorize types of adjectives in German for easy reference, form case endings of adjectives, and use possessive adjectives. You discover how to wade through these adjective pitfalls so you can use them comfortably and safely in your speech and writing.

Organizing Adjectives: Opposites, Cognates, and Collocations

Adjectives are so numerous that it's essential to find a system for categorizing them as a means of easy reference. When you encounter a new adjective, try to find a hook to hang it on. You may be able to group them in three ways:

>> **Opposites:** Some adjective types lend themselves to pairing with an adjective of the opposite meaning.

>> **Cognates:** Cognates, which are similar words in English and German, are instantly recognizable; after you check that the meaning is the same in both languages, you need to know only how to form their endings in sentences.

>> **Collocations:** *Collocations* are semi-fixed, frequently used word combinations, so look for adjective + noun phrases.

Get into the habit of recognizing collocations that adjectives occur in. It takes a bit more work than figuring out what an adjective alone means, but in the end, it saves time. Add collocations to your range of expression, and you're on the path to successful, idiomatic German.

This section helps you place adjectives in these three groupings. By doing so, you can more easily remember these descriptors; then you can use them when you want to discuss appearance, personal traits, weather, and more.

Letting opposites attract

You can master many groups of descriptive adjectives as opposite pairs. Two common groups I deal with in this section are adjectives that describe people's appearance and personal traits, and adjectives that describe the weather.

Describing appearance and personal traits

When you want to say what people are like, you use descriptive adjectives to describe them, such as **sie ist groß** (*she's tall*) or **er ist freundlich** (*he's friendly*). In Table 10-1, you see such adjectives grouped as opposites; looking at them this way saves you time when you're remembering them.

Refer to Table 10-1 and match the adjective with its opposite. The adjectives describe appearance and personal traits of Max and Moritz, twins who couldn't be more opposite.

PRACTICE

Table 10-1   Adjectives of Personal Appearance and Traits

German	English	German Opposite	English Opposite
attraktiv	*attractive*	unattraktiv	*unattractive*
freundlich	*friendly*	unfreundlich	*unfriendly*
glücklich	*happy*	traurig/unglücklich	*sad, unhappy*
heiter, lustig	*cheerful, funny*	ernst	*serious*
interessant	*interesting*	uninteressant/langweilig	*uninteresting/boring*
jung	*young*	alt	*old*
klein	*short*	groß	*tall*
neu	*new*	alt	*old*
ruhig	*quiet*	laut	*loud*
schlank	*thin/slim*	mollig	*plump/chubby*
stark	*strong*	schwach	*weak*
sportlich	*athletic*	unsportlich	*unathletic*
sympathisch	*likable, friendly*	unsympathisch	*unpleasant, disagreeable*
tolerant	*tolerant*	intolerant	*intolerant*
zuverlässig	*reliable*	unzuverlässig	*unreliable*

Q. Max ist zuverlässig, aber Moritz ist _____.

A. Max ist zuverlässig, aber Moritz ist **unzuverlässig.** *(Max is reliable, but Moritz is unreliable.)* Notice that German also uses the prefix **un-** to mean *not.*

1. Moritz ist klein, aber Max ist _____.

2. Moritz ist attraktiv, aber Max ist _____.

3. Max ist sympathisch, aber Moritz ist _____.

4. Max ist stark, aber Moritz ist _____.

5. Moritz ist sportlich, aber Max ist _____.

6. Max ist laut, aber Moritz ist _____.

PRACTICE

Now that you're becoming familiar with some adjectives as shown in Table 10-1, you see them in a different context in the following exercise. Some look different; word endings appear, or the adjective has changed into a noun. Try figuring out what these sentences might mean in English and write your educated guess in the space provided. I give you some hints along the way.

Q. Das ist mein Ernst. _____.

A. Das ist mein Ernst. *(I mean that seriously/in all seriousness.)*

7 Die Züge (*the trains*) in der Schweiz sind sehr zuverlässig.

_____.

 8 Wir haben eine sehr glückliche Kindheit (*childhood*) gehabt.

_____.

 9 Das Haus ist klein aber fein.

_____.

10 Es war ein attraktives Angebot (*offer*).

_____.

11 Dann beginnt der Ernst des Lebens.

_____.

12 Das ist aber eine schwache Ausrede (*excuse*).

_____.

13 In Düsseldorf, bestellt man ein Düsseldorfer Alt zu trinken.

_____.

 14 Ich hatte einen ruhigen Schlaf.

_____.

15 Geld allein macht nicht glücklich.

_____.

16 Heute ist es heiter bis wolkig. (Look at the next section for adjectives of weather.)

_____.

Describing the weather

No matter where you are, talking about das **Wetter** (*the weather*) is the perfect icebreaker. It also provides you ammunition to make your friends jealous when you're writing them **Ansichtskarten** (*postcards*) while you're **im Urlaub** (*on vacation*). Look at the weather vocabulary in Table 10-2. Great news: Most of the adjectives have near opposites, so it's economical to remember them in pairs.

More weather-related adjectives include **frostig** (*chilly*), **heiter** (*fine*), **schön warm** (*nice and warm*), **neb(e)lig** (*foggy*), **regnerisch** (*rainy*), **schwül** (*humid*), and **stürmisch** (*gusty, blustery*).

Table 10-2   Adjectives of Weather

German	English	German Opposite	English Opposite
gut, schön	good, nice	schlecht	bad
sonnig	sunny	wolkig, bewölkt	cloudy
wunderschön	delightful, lovely	furchtbar	awful
warm	warm	kühl	cool
heiß	hot	kalt	cold
trocken	dry	nass	wet

PRACTICE

You're on vacation. Finish the postcard, describing the weather and someone you met there. Fill in the blanks, using some adjectives describing weather and people. *Note:* The first word in a letter isn't capitalized unless it's a noun.

Q. Hier ist es sehr _____.

A. Hier ist es sehr <u>heiß</u>. *(It's very hot here.)*

Postcard
18/2/08

DEUTSCHE POST WORLD NET
50

Liebe Christine,

wie geht es dir? Ist das Wetter zu Hause
(17)_____? Heute ist es
(18)_____, aber gestern war es
(19)_____ und (20)_____.
Ich bin sehr (21)_____!
Im Hotel gibt es einen Mann, der sehr
(22)_____ ist. Er ist auch
(23)_____. Wenn das Wetter
morgen (24)_____ ist, machen wir
eine Bergtour.

Alles Gute, Siggi

Christine Schroeder

Holtstr. 95

10472 Berlin Deutschland

A family resemblance: Describing with cognates

Although German does have some incredibly foreign-sounding words, the number of cognates is surprisingly large. You can put them in several categories for easy access. Some example categories are based on the adjective's ending. See Table 10-3.

Table 10-3   Common Endings of German Adjectives

German Ending	Usual English Ending	Examples
-al	same	**diagonal, digital, emotional, formal, ideal, integral, interkontinental, international, irrational, kollegial, liberal, national, normal, optimal, original, sentimental, sozial, total, universal**
-ant or **-ent**	same	**elegant, exzellent, intelligent, interessant, intolerant, kompetent, tolerant, uninteressant**
-ell	-al	**generell, individuell, informell, konventionell, kriminell, offiziell, partiell, rationell, sensationell, visuell**
-isch	-ic or -ical	**allergisch, alphabetisch, analytisch, charakteristisch, chemisch, dynamisch, egoistisch, elastisch, elektrisch, elektronisch, ethisch, exotisch, exzentrisch, fanatisch, fantastisch, klassisch, harmonisch, hygienisch, identisch, idiomatisch, idyllisch, ironisch, logisch, lyrisch, melodisch, militärisch, musikalisch, mythisch, patriotisch, philosophisch, politisch, praktisch, romantisch, sarkastisch, sporadisch, symmetrisch, systematisch, tropisch**
-iv	-ive	**aktiv, alternativ, exklusiv, explosiv, intensiv, interaktiv, kreativ, massiv, passiv**
-lich or **-ig**	-y, -ly, or -ally	**freundlich, frostig, hungrig, persönlich, sportlich, sonnig, unfreundlich, unpersönlich, unsportlich, windig**

REMEMBER

Some cognates — such as **bitter, blind, blond, fair, golden, human, illegal, legal, liberal, mild, modern, neutral, parallel, solid, uniform, warm,** and **wild** — have the same meaning and the same spelling. Others have a few spelling changes from English to German, such as

>> *c* → k: **direct, exakt, intakt, komplex, konstant, korrekt, nuklear**

>> *c* → k; *ve* → v: **aktiv, effektiv, exklusiv, kreativ**

>> *le* → el: **flexibel, kompatibel, miserabel, variabel**

>> *d* → t: **hart, laut** *(loud)*

>> *y* → ig: **frostig, hungrig, sonnig, windig**

TIP

Get in the habit of remembering cognates in groups such as those in Table 10-3. Repeat them out loud, alphabetically and rhythmically. They'll stick with you and serve you well when you need them.

PRACTICE

The exercise shows possible adjective/noun combinations. The adjectives are cognates from Table 10-3. Choose one or more adjectives in parentheses that fit best with the corresponding noun and then write your choice(s) in the space provided. (You see endings on the adjectives. The section "Helping Adjectives Meet a Satisfying End" later in this chapter explains how these endings work.)

Q. eine _____ Rakete (**interkontinentale/dynamische/sportliche**)

A. eine <u>interkontinentale</u> **Rakete** (*an intercontinental missile/rocket*)

25 eine _____ Krankheit (systematische/chronische/universale/tropische)

26 _____ Musik (klassische/tolerante/romantische)

27 der _____ Vulkan (aktive/interaktive/explosive)

28 ein _____ Restaurant (hungriges/exklusives/exzellentes)

29 _____ Wetter (wildes/ideales/direktes/sonniges)

30 die _____ Partei (generelle/liberale/alternative)

31 die _____ Kleidung (normale/sportliche/elegante)

32 eine _____ Insel in dem Pazifik (idyllische/aktive/romantische)

33 die _____ Atmosphäre (offizielle/passive/kollegiale/digitale)

34 ein _____ Mädchen (identisches/emotionales/freundliches)

Traveling companions: Describing with collocations

Acquiring word chunks is far more economical than studying isolated words. *Collocations* are chunks of words that are very predictable, some so predictable that they nearly always stick together. By some definitions, collocations include idioms and other fixed expressions. Collocations are made up of all kinds of word combinations: adjective + noun, noun + noun, adverb + adjective, and so on. In this section, I deal with adjective combos.

Some collocations translate well: **Starke Nerven** is the same as *strong nerves*. Other expressions aren't as close: **Das ist ein starkes Stück** in literal English means *that's a strong piece*. Yet in German, it's like saying *that's a bit too much*, as in *that's over the top*. Take a look at some example collocations:

>> **Unsere Produkte werden nur in umweltfreundlichen Verpackungen verkauft.** *(Our products are sold only in environmentally friendly packaging.)* The collocation is the combination of **umweltfreundlich(en) + Verpackung(en)** *(environmentally friendly + packaging).* Notice that the fixed combination *environmentally friendly* is an adverb + adjective in English; in German, it's a noun + adjective: **die Umwelt** *(the environment)* + **freundlich** *(friendly).*

>> **Ich ärgere mich grün und blau.** *(I'm hopping mad.* Literally, it's something like *I'm annoyed green and blue.)* You can also describe this expression as an idiom. Whatever the terminology, if you were to ask a German speaker to finish the sentence ich **ärgere mich . . . und . . .**, they wouldn't hesitate to add the right colors.

TIP

Read and listen actively to German. Make it your goal to recognize chunks of language, not only single words. Knowing a stack of collocations with adjectives offers you great opportunities for expressing yourself clearly and succinctly.

Brighten your language with colorful collocations/expressions. In the following mini-table, look at the expressions that use colors. Match the English equivalents and write them next to the German expression. Try matching the ones that seem logical first. When you finish, look at the answer key to see whether your educated guesses were right.

PRACTICE

Q. Sie treffen ins Schwarze.

A. *They hit the bull's eye.*

They hit the bull's eye.	They're drunk.	They're working illegally, not paying taxes.
They get off lightly, with a slap on the wrist.	They're blushing.	They're riding (the train) without a ticket.
They're hopping mad.	They're outdoors.	They're getting tan.

35 Sie sind blau. _____

36 Sie fahren schwarz. _____

37 Sie sind im Grünen (**Im Grünen** shows the noun form of the adjective **grün.**)

_____

38 Sie werden rot. _____

39 Sie arbeiten schwarz. _____

40 Sie werden braun. _____

41 Sie ärgern sich grün und blau. _____

42 Sie kommen mit einem blauen Auge davon. _____

For the majority of the adjective/noun combos in this exercise, the adjective, the noun, for both are cognates with English. That fact will help you figure out the English equivalents. Write your educated guess next to the German expressions.

PRACTICE

Q. ein gemütlicher Biergarten

A. ein gemütlicher Biergarten *(a congenial/cozy/comfy beer garden).* **Gemütlich** is similar in meaning to *hygge,* a noun borrowed from Danish. A living room, balcony, restaurant, ski lodge, and so on, and even a person, can be described as **gemütlich.** (The noun form is **die Gemütlichkeit.**) It's one of those words that has no real equivalent in English.

43 eine tiefe Krise _____

44 der politische Gegner _____

45 die wahre Liebe _____

46   die internationale Zusammenarbeit _____

47   die kostenlose Software _____

48   ein fester Job _____

49   in den guten alten Zeiten _____

50   eine effektive Methode _____

51   ein normales Leben _____

52   die flexiblen Arbeitszeiten _____

53   eine bittere Pille _____

54   mit freundlichen Grüßen (a relatively formal email/letter closing) _____
_____

Helping Adjectives Meet a Satisfying End

Expanding your adjective arsenal is the first step; knowing how to form and use adjectives correctly in a sentence is your next goal. This section entails deciding whether the adjectives need endings and, if so, how to form these endings.

DIFFERENCES

English uses adjectives as is, straight up, with no changes needed to plunk them into a combination with a noun. German is quite different. Before a German adjective can sidle up to a noun, it quite often needs an ending that reflects the gender and case of the noun it modifies. As in English, a German adjective usually comes right before the noun it describes: **eine wunderbare Gegend** (a wonderful area/region).

Not all adjectives in all sentences need special attention as far as necessary ending changes are concerned. An adjective has no ending when it follows the verbs **sein** (to be), **werden** (to become), or *bleiben* (to remain) and modifies the subject. See these two examples:

Das Wetter bleibt warm. (The weather remains warm.)

Die Berge in Bayern sind wunderschön. (The mountains in Bavaria are gorgeous.)

Work at recognizing the case and gender of nouns in the sentence and knowing how to add the correct endings. In this section, you need to know the difference between endings when an adjective stands alone in front of the noun — such as **frisches Obst** (fresh fruit) — and when an adjective has a word such as **der, ein,** or **dieser** at the beginning of the phrase — as in **das frische Obst** (the fresh fruit).

Forming endings on adjectives not preceded by der- or ein- words

When you describe something in general, such as food prices, you simply say something like *fresh pineapples are expensive*. You don't need to add *the, those,* or *our.* It's the same in German, except you have the added factor of case endings for adjectives. In other words, when you say **frische Ananas sind teuer** (*fresh pineapples are expensive*), you need to know that the ending for **frisch** is **-e**. *Note:* In phrases that do have an article or modifier such as *the, those,* or *our* (as in *those fresh pineapples*), the adjective endings are different. Check out the following section, "Preceded adjectives: Forming the endings," for details.

This section deals with endings for an adjective that modifies and precedes a noun, but the adjective isn't preceded by an article (such as **der/die/das** or **ein/eine**) or other modifiers (**der-** words, such as **dieser** and **solcher**, and **ein-** words, such as **mein** and **kein**).

REMEMBER

Here are the characteristics that define adjectives without **der-** or **ein-** words preceding them:

>> Because no article or other modifier precedes the noun, the adjective must indicate gender and case of the noun; it has a double duty of adjective and article.

>> These adjectives have mostly the same endings as **der-** words, with the exception of the masculine and neuter genitive, where the ending is **-en**.

TIP

To form these adjective endings, you need to know the gender, case, and number of the noun that the adjective modifies. Take the adjective **gut** (*good*). To say **guter Käse ist teuer** (*good cheese is expensive*), you need to know that **Käse** is masculine singular (**der Käse**) and that in this sentence, it's in the nominative case (subject). You add that nominative masculine ending **-er** to **gut,** so you have **gut + -er = guter Käse.**

The four adjectives in Table 10-4 deal with food: **gut** (*good*), **schmackhaft** (*tasty*), **lecker** (*delicious, mouth-watering, scrumptious*), and **köstlich** (*delicious, luscious, exquisite*). The endings that agree in case, number, and gender with the noun they modify are in bold. For easy reference, I also list the adjective ending separately in bold with each example. Add these endings to adjectives that aren't preceded by **der-** or **ein-** words.

Table 10-4   Adjective Endings Not Preceded by Der- or Ein- Words

Case	Masculine	Feminine	Neuter	Plural
Nominative (subject)	gut**er** Käse (*good cheese*) **-er**	schmackhaft**e** Wurst (*tasty sausage*) **-e**	lecker**es** Brot (*delicious bread*) **es**	köstlich**e** Kuchen (*delicious cakes*) **-e**
Accusative (direct object)	gut**en** Käse **-en**	schmackhaft**e** Wurst **-e**	lecker**es** Brot **-es**	köstlich**e** Kuchen **-e**
Dative (indirect object)	gut**em** Käse **-em** schmackhaft**er** Wurst **-er**	lecker**em** Brot **-em**	köstlich**en** Kuchen **-en**	
Genitive (possessive)	gut**en** Käse**s** **-en**	schmackhaft**er** Wurst **-er**	lecker**en** Brot**es** **-en**	köstlich**er** Kuchen **-er**

Check out some examples:

>> **Leckeres Brot findet man überall in deutschen Bäckereien.** *(You can find delicious bread everywhere in German bakeries.)* The adjective **lecker + -es** *(delicious)* describes the noun **(das) Brot** *(bread)*; **leckeres Brot** is in the accusative case because it's the direct object. The neuter singular accusative ending for unpreceded adjectives is **-es**.

>> **Es gibt köstliche Kuchen in österreichischen Cafés.** (There are luscious cakes in Austrian cafés.) The adjective **köstlich + -e** describes the noun **(der) Kuchen,** in plural form. **Köstliche Kuchen** is in the accusative case because it's the direct object. The plural accusative ending for unpreceded adjectives is **-e**.

PRACTICE

Add the correct ending to the adjectives in parentheses. Write the adjective in the space provided. Use Table 10-4 for reference. The abbreviations in italics in parentheses following the noun guide you to choose the correct ending. Here is the key to the abbreviations: *m. = masculine, f. = feminine, n. = neuter, pl. = plural, nom. = nominative, acc. = accusative, dat. = dative, gen. = genitive*

Q. Im Winter trinken wir gern _____ **Tee.** (*m., acc.*) (**heiß**)

A. Im Winter trinken wir gern <u>heißen</u> **Tee.** *(We like to drink hot tea in the winter.)* **Tee** is masculine. **Heißen Tee** is in accusative case; it's the direct object of the sentence.

55 Im Sommer schmeckt mir _____ Bier *(n., nom.)* vom Faß. (erfrischend)

56 Ich trinke auch gern _____ Getränke. *(pl., acc.)* (alkoholfrei)

57 Mögen Sie _____ Wein? *(m., acc.)* (deutsch)

58 Ja, _____ Weißweine *(pl., nom.)* gefallen mir. (trocken)

59 Essen Sie _____ Obst *(n., acc.)* zum Nachtisch? (frisch)

60 Aber nein! _____ Schokoladeneis *(n., nom.)* ist meine Lieblingsnachspeise. (lecker)

61 Bestellen Sie _____ Kaffee *(m., acc.)* am Abend? (koffeinfrei)

62 Nein, ich trinke gern _____ Espresso *(m., acc.)* mit etwas Zucker. (italienisch)

63 Welches Restaurant serviert _____ Käsespätzle? *(pl., acc.)* (schwäbisch)

64 _____ Wurst *(f., nom.)* ist sehr schmackhaft. (deutsch)

65 Wir bekommen _____ Eier *(pl., acc.)* vom Bauernhof. (frisch)

66 _____ Spargel *(m., nom.)* schmeckt sehr gut (weiß) . . .

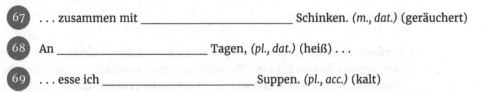

67 . . . zusammen mit _____ Schinken. *(m., dat.)* (geräuchert)

68 An _____ Tagen, *(pl., dat.)* (heiß) . . .

69 . . . esse ich _____ Suppen. *(pl., acc.)* (kalt)

Preceded adjectives: Forming the endings

When you want to be specific about something, you use articles and modifiers like *the, those,* or *a* to say something like *the modern painting, those violent movies,* or *a fantastic restaurant*. In English, you simply add the adjective of your choice, and you're all set. Not so in German. Both the article/modifier and the adjective need to reflect the gender, number, and case of the noun they modify.

This section deals with endings for an adjective that modifies and precedes a noun that's preceded by an article (such as **der/die/das** or **ein/eine**) or other modifiers (**der-** words such as **dieser** and **solcher**, and **ein-** words such as **mein** and **kein**). (See Chapter 3 for information on articles and **der-** and **ein-** words.) Preceded adjectives appear in phrases with an article or other modifier, an adjective, and a noun.

Take the example **das brave Kind hilft seiner Mutter** *(the good [well-behaved] child helps its mother)*. **Kind** is singular, neuter, and in the nominative case because it's the subject of the sentence, so the article **das** and the adjective **brave** reflect the neuter gender, number, and case of **Kind**. Check out Table 10-5.

Table 10-5 Preceded Adjective Endings

Case	Masculine	Feminine	Neuter	Plural
Nominative (subject)	**der** lustige Mann ein lustiger Mann	**die** glückliche Frau eine glückliche Frau	**das** brave Kind ein braves Kind	**die** braven Kinder keine braven Kinder
Accusative (direct object)	**den** lustigen Mann einen lustigen Mann	**die** glückliche Frau eine glückliche **Frau**	**das** brave Kind ein braves Kind	**die** braven Kinder keine braven Kinder
Dative (indirect object)	**dem** lustigen Mann einem lustigen Mann	**der** glücklichen Frau **einer** glücklichen **Frau**	**dem** braven Kind einem braven Kind	**den** braven Kindern keinen braven Kindern
Genitive (possessive)	**des** lustigen Mannes eines lustigen Mannes	**der** glücklichen Frau einer glücklichen Frau	**des** braven Kindes eines braven Kindes	**der** braven Kinder keiner braven Kinder

PRACTICE

Choose the correct form of the definite article (**der/die/das**) and the correct ending to the adjective in parentheses. Write the article and adjective in the space provided. Use Table 10-5 for reference. The abbreviations in italics in parentheses following the noun guide you to choose the correct ending. Here is the key to the abbreviations: *m.* = *masculine, f.* = *feminine, n.* = *neuter, sing.* = *singular, pl.* = *plural, nom.* = *nominative, acc.* = *accusative, dat.* = *dative, gen.* = *genitive*

Q. Oje! _____ Hemd (n., sing., nom.) ist schmutzig. (weiß)

A. Oje! <u>Das weiße Hemd</u> **ist schmutzig.** *(Oh dear! The white shirt is dirty.)*

70. Ich mag _____ Musik *(f., sing., acc.)* überhaupt nicht. (laut)

71. Warum hat er _____ Auto *(n., sing., acc.)* verkauft? (alt)

72. Er will _____ BMW540i *(m., sing., acc.)* kaufen. (neu)

73. Das ist das Fahrrad _____ Kindes. *(n., sing., gen.)* (klein)

74. Achtung! Ich sehe _____ Bären *(pl., acc.)* schon wieder! (hungrig)

In the following five exercises, you follow the same instructions as in the previous five sentences, except that you need to choose the correct form of the indefinite article (**ein**).

75. Die Familie Sandner verbringt den Urlaub in _____ Dorf. *(n., dat.)* (gemütlich)

76. Guck mal! Ist das _____ Katze da drüben? *(f., nom.)* (klein)

77. Er trägt _____ Hut. *(m., acc.)* (australisch)

78. Sie hat _____ Onkel, *(m., acc.)* der in Österreich lebt. (alt)

79. Endlich haben wir _____ Wochenende *(n., acc.)* ohne Regen. (schön)

PRACTICE

You're on vacation on the island of **Rügen, in der Ostsee** *(Rügen, in the Baltic Sea)*. Write a letter describing some activities you're doing there. Fill in the blanks using the adjectives in parentheses. Look at Table 10-5 for the adjective endings needed. *Note:* The first word in a letter after the salutation isn't capitalized unless it's a noun.

Q. Die Insel Rügen hat eine _____ (herrlich) Küste.

A. Die Insel Rügen hat eine <u>herrliche</u> **Küste.** *(The island of Rügen has a wonderful coastline.)* **Eine herrliche Küste** is singular accusative; it's the object of the sentence. **Eine** is the hint that **Küste** is feminine; you indicate the agreement with **-e** tacked onto **herrlich.**

Hallo Margit und Thomas,

was macht ihr mit den (80) _____ (klein) Kindern zu Hause? Hier auf
der Insel Rugen gibt es leider keine (81) _____ (exotisch) Blumen,
aber gestern haben wir die (82) _____ (spektakular) (83) _____
(weiß) Felsen gesehen. Kennst du die Bilder von dem (84) _____
(bekannt) Maler Caspar David Friedrich? Diese (85) _____ (herrlich)
Landschaft hat er oft gemalt. Wir geniessen die (86) _____ (gesund)
Luft, und morgen machen wir einem (87) _____ (lang) Spaziergang
bei Binz. Heute Abend essen wir mit einem (88) _____ (interessant)
Ehepaar aus Ostdeutchland. Sie sagen, diese (89) _____
(wunderschön) Insel ist ihr Urlaubziel seit vielen Jahren. Am Donnerstag
fahren wir zu einer (90) _____ (klein) Insel mit einem (91) _____
(komisch) Namen - Hiddensee. Dort gibt es einen (92) _____ (lang)
Strand und einen (93) _____ (schön) Leuchturm.

Machts gut, Liesl und Hansi

Using Possessive Adjectives: My Place or Your Place?

Possessive adjectives are the words describing ownership, possession, or relationship, such as *my*, *your*, *his*, *her*, and so on. They're also referred to as *possessive pronouns*. (That's because, technically speaking, a possessive adjective is a pronoun that's used as an adjective to show who "owns" the noun following it.) Identifying possessive adjectives is easy because they're grouped together with the **ein-** words (they have the same endings, even if they don't rhyme with **ein**). The **ein-** words include **ein**, **kein**, and all the possessive adjectives.

The singular possessive adjectives are **mein** (*my*), **dein** (*your*), **sein** (*his*), **ihr** (*her*), and **sein** (*its*). The plural possessive adjectives are **unser** (*our*), **euer** (*your*), **ihr** (*their*), and **Ihr** (*your* — formal, singular and plural).

Table 10-6 shows possessive adjective endings in all cases and genders. This is the same pattern for **ein-** and **kein-** in Table 10-5. The following table shows **mein** and **unser** together. All other possessive adjectives use these same endings. The endings are shown separately in bold.

Table 10-6 Possessive Adjective Endings and First-Person Examples

Case	Masculine	Feminine	Neuter	Plural
Nominative (subject)	mein, unser -	meine, unsere -e	mein, unser -	meine, unsere -e
Accusative (direct object)	meinen, unseren -en	meine, unsere -e	mein, unser -	meine, unsere -e
Dative (indirect object)	meinem, unserem -em	meiner, unserer -er	meinem, unserem -em	meinen, unseren -en
Genitive (possessive)	meines, unseres -es	meiner, unserer -er	meines, unseres-es	meiner, unserer -er

PRACTICE

Using Table 10-6, complete the sentences in the exercise. Put the adjectives in parentheses in the sentences, being mindful of the endings. The abbreviations in italics in parentheses following the noun guide you to choose the correct ending for the adjective. Here is the key to the abbreviations: *m. = masculine, f. = feminine, n. = neuter, sing. = singular, pl. = plural, nom. = nominative, acc. = accusative, dat. = dative*

Q. Ich kann _____ Schlüssel *(pl., acc.)* **nicht finden. (mein)**

A. Ich kann <u>meine</u> Schlüssel nicht finden. *(I can't find my keys.)* **Meine** is plural accusative.

94 _____ Schlüssel (pl., nom.) liegen auf dem Tisch. (dein)

95 Und ist _____ Gepäck (n., sing., nom.) schon fertig? (unser)

96 Nein. Uli hat _____ Koffer (m., sing., acc.) noch nicht gepackt. (sein)

97 Na ja, _____ Urlaub (m., sing., nom.) fängt schon mit vielen Problemen an. (unser)

98 In einem Monat wird _____ Großmutter (f., sing., nom.) 90 Jahre alt. (mein)

99 Zu _____ Geburtstag (m., sing., dat.) organisieren die Enkelkinder eine grosse Überraschung. (ihr)

100 Wir laden viele _____ Verwandten (pl, acc.) in ein Restaurant ein. (unser)

101 _____ Cousin (m., sing., nom.) Jonathan ist Mitglied einer Musikgruppe. (mein)

102 Er wird die ganze Nacht im Restaurant mit _____ Gruppe *(f., sing., dat.)* Musik machen. (sein)

Answers to "Adding Adjectives for Description" Practice Questions

(1) **Moritz ist klein, aber Max ist groß.** (*Moritz is short, but Max is tall.*)

(2) **Moritz ist attraktiv, aber Max ist unattraktiv.** (*Moritz is attractive, but Max is unattractive.*)

(3) **Max ist sympathisch, aber Moritz ist unsympathisch.** (*Max is likable, but Moritz is disagreeable.*)

(4) **Max ist stark, aber Moritz ist schwach.** (*Max is strong, but Moritz is weak.*)

(5) **Moritz ist unsportlich, aber Max ist sportlich.** (*Moritz is unathletic, but Max is athletic.*)

(6) **Max ist laut, aber Moritz ist ruhig.** (*Max is loud, but Moritz is quiet.*)

(7) **Die Züge in der Schweiz sind sehr zuverlässig.** (*The trains in Switzerland are very reliable.*) They're definitely punctual. Oh, and the scenery in Switzerland!

(8) **Wir haben eine sehr glückliche Kindheit gehabt.** (*We had a very happy childhood.*)

(9) **Das Haus ist klein aber fein.** (*The house is small, but fine.*) In other words, it's just right.

(10) **Es war ein attraktives Angebot.** (*It was an attractive offer.*)

(11) **Dann beginnt der Ernst des Lebens.** (*Then life begins in earnest.*)

(12) **Das ist aber eine schwache Ausrede.** (*That is a really poor excuse.*)

(13) **In Düsseldorf, bestellt man ein Düsseldorfer Alt zu trinken.** (*In Düsseldorf, people order a Düsseldorfer Alt to drink.*) It's a kind of beer, **Altbier**, special to the region.

(14) **Ich hatte einen ruhigen Schlaf.** (*I had a quiet/restful sleep.*)

(15) **Geld allein macht nicht glücklich.** (*Money alone won't buy happiness.*)

(16) **Heute ist es heiter bis wolkig.** (*Today it's [generally] fine but cloudy [in places.]*)

Postcard

18/2/08

Liebe Christine,

wie geht es dir? Ist das Wetter zu Hause
(17) kalt? Heute ist es (18) wunderschön, aber
gestern war es (19) kühl und (20) windig. Ich bin
sehr (21) glücklich! Im Hotel gibt es einen
Mann, der sehr (22) sympathisch ist. Er ist
auch (23) sportlich. Wenn das Wetter morgen
(24) schön warm ist, machen wir eine
Bergtour.

Alles Gute, Siggi

Christine Schroeder

Holtstr. 95

10472 Berlin Deutschland

DEUTSCHE POST WORLD NET 50

Dear Christine,

How are you? Is the weather cold at home? Today it's lovely, but yesterday it was cool and windy. I'm really happy! There's a man in the hotel who is very friendly. He's also athletic. If the weather's nice and warm tomorrow, we're going climbing.

All the best, Siggi

25. eine **chronische/tropische** Krankheit (*a chronic/tropical disease*),

26. **klassische/romantische** Musik (*classical/romantic music*),

27. der **aktive** Vulkan (*the active volcano*). You could, however, say **der Vulkan explodiert.** (*explodes*).

28. ein **exklusives/exzellentes** Restaurant (*an exclusive/excellent restaurant*).

29. **wildes/ideales/sonniges** Wetter (*wild/ideal/sunny weather*).

30. die **liberale** Partei (*the liberal party*). You can consider **die Grünen** (*the Greens*) to be an alternative party.

31. die **sportliche/elegante** Kleidung (*the sporty/elegant clothes*).

32. eine **idyllische/romantische** Insel in dem Pazifik (*an idyllic/romantic island in the Pacific*).

33. die **kollegiale** Atmosphäre (*a helpful, congenial atmosphere*), such as at the workplace, when **die Kollegen** (*the colleagues*) are helpful and considerate.

34. ein **emotionales/freundliches** Mädchen (*an emotional/friendly girl*).

35. **Sie sind blau.** (*They're drunk.*) Literally: *They're blue.*

36. **Sie fahren schwarz.** (*They're riding [the train] without a ticket.*) Literally: *They're riding black.*

37. **Sie sind im Grünen.** (They're outdoors.)

38. **Sie werden rot.** (They're blushing.)

39. **Sie arbeiten schwarz.** (*They're working illegally, not paying taxes.*) Literally: *They're working black.*

40. **Sie werden braun.** (*They're getting [a] tan.*)

41. **Sie ärgern sich grün und blau.** (*They're hopping mad.*) Literally: *They're green and blue mad.*

42. **Sie kommen mit einem blauen Auge davon.** (*They're getting off with a slap on the wrist.*) Literally: *They come away with a blue eye.*

43. **eine tiefe Krise** (*a deep, serious crisis*).

44. **der politische Gegner** (*the political opponent*).

45. **die wahre Liebe** (*true love*).

46. **die internationale Zusammenarbeit** (*the international cooperation*).

47. **die kostenlose Software** (*free software*).

48. **ein fester Job** (*a steady job*).

49. **in den guten alten Zeiten** (*in the good old days*).

50. **eine effektive Methode** (*an effective method*).

51. **ein normales Leben** (*a normal life*).

52. **die flexiblen Arbeitszeiten** (*flexible working hours*).

53. **eine bittere Pille** (*a bitter pill [to swallow]*).

54. **mit freundlichen Grüßen** (*Sincerely*). Literally: *with friendly greetings.* This is a relatively formal email/letter closing.

55. Im Sommer schmeckt mir **erfrischendes** Bier vom Faß. (*In the summer, I enjoy refreshing beer on tap/from the barrel.*)

56. Ich trinke auch gern **alkoholfreie** Getränke. (*I also enjoy drinking alcohol-free beverages.*)

57. Mögen Sie **deutschen** Wein? (*Do you like German wine?*)

58. Ja, **trockene** Weißweine gefallen mir. (*Yes, I like dry white wine[s].*)

59. Essen Sie **frisches** Obst zum Nachtisch? (*Do you eat fresh fruit for dessert?*)

60 Aber nein! **leckeres** Schokoladeneis ist meine Lieblingsnachspeise. *(No way! Delicious chocolate ice cream is my favorite dessert.)*

61 Bestellen Sie **koffeinfreien** Kaffee am Abend? *(Do you order decaffeinated coffee in the evening?)*

62 Nein, ich trinke gern **italienischen** Espresso mit etwas Zucker. *(No, I like to drink Italian expresso with a little sugar.)*

63 Welches Restaurant serviert **schwäbische** Käsespätzle? *(Which restaurant serves Swabian cheese noodles?)* **Spätzle** are a cross between noodles and gnocchi. **Schwaben** *(Swabia)* is a region in the southwest of Germany.

64 **Deutsche** Wurst ist sehr schmackhaft. *(German sausages are very tasty.)*

65 Wir bekommen **frische** Eier vom Bauernhof. *(We get fresh eggs from the farm.)*

66 **Weißer** Spargel schmeckt sehr gut *(White asparagus tastes very good)* . . .

67 . . . zusammen mit **geräuchertem** Schinken *(together with smoked ham)*.

68 An **heißen** Tagen, *(pl., dat.)* *(On hot days,)* . . .

69 . . . esse ich **kalte** Suppen. *(. . . I eat cold soups.)*

70 Ich mag **die laute** Musik überhaupt nicht. *(I don't like the loud music at all.)*

71 Warum hat er **das alte** Auto verkauft? *(Why did he sell the old car?)*

72 Er will **den neuen** BMW540i kaufen. *(He wants to buy the new BMW540i.)*

73 Das ist das Fahrrad **des kleinen** Kindes. *(That's the small child's bicycle.)*

74 Achtung! Ich sehe **die hungrigen** Bären schon wieder! *(Look out! I see the hungry bears again!)*

75 Die Familie Sandner verbringt den Urlaub in **einem gemütlichen** Dorf. *(The Sandner family is spending the vacation in a cozy village.)*

76 Guck mal! Ist das **eine kleine** Katze da drüben? *(Hey, look! Is that a little cat over there?)* **Gucken** *(to look)* is a colloquial expression.

77 Er trägt **einen australischen** Hut. *(He's wearing an Australian hat.)*

78 Sie hat **einen alten** Onkel, der in Österreich lebt. *(She has an old uncle who lives in Austria.)*

79 Endlich haben wir **ein schönes** Wochenende ohne Regen. *(At last we're having a nice weekend without rain.)*

Hallo Margit und Thomas,

was macht ihr mit den (80) kleinen Kindern zu Hause? Hier auf der Insel
Rügen gibt es leider keine (81) exotischen Blumen, aber gestern haben
wir die (82) spektakulären (83) weißen Felsen gesehen. Kennst du die Bilder
von dem (84) bekannten Maler Caspar David Friedrich? Diese (85) herrliche
Landschaft hat er oft gemalt. Wir geniessen die (86) gesunde Luft, und
morgen machen wir einem (87) langen Spaziergang bei Binz. Heute Abend
essen wir mit einem (88) interessanten Ehepaar aus Ostdeutchland. Sie
sagen, diese (89) wunderschöne Insel ist ihr Urlaubziel seit vielen Jahren.
Am Donnerstag fahren wir zu einer (90) kleinen Insel mit einem (91) komischen
Namen - Hiddensee. Dort gibt es einen (92) langen Strand und einen
(93) schönen Leuchturm.

Machts gut, Liesl und Hansi

Hi Margit and Thomas,

What are you doing with the little children at home? Here on the island of
Rügen, there aren't any exotic flowers, but yesterday we saw the spectacular
white cliffs. Do you know the paintings by the famous painter Caspar David
Friedrich? He often painted this wonderful landscape. We're enjoying the
healthy air, and tomorrow we're going on a long walk near Binz. This evening
we're having dinner with an interesting couple from eastern Germany. They
say this beautiful island is where they've been spending their vacations for
many years. On Thursday we're going to a small island with a funny name —
Hiddensee. There's a long beach there and a nice lighthouse.

See you soon, Liesl and Hansi

94 **Deine** Schlüssel liegen auf dem Tisch. *(Your keys are lying in the table.)*

95 Und ist **unser** Gepäck schon fertig? *(And is our luggage ready yet?)*

96 Nein. Uli hat **seinen** Koffer noch nicht gepackt. *(No. Uli hasn't packed his suitcase yet.)*

97 Na ja, **unser** Urlaub fängt schon mit vielen Problemen an. *(Oh, well. Our vacation is already starting with a lot of problems.)*

98 In einem Monat wird **meine** Großmutter 90 Jahre alt. *(My grandmother will be 90 in one month.)*

99 Zu **ihrem** Geburtstag organisieren die Enkelkinder eine grosse Überraschung. *(For her birthday, the grandchildren are organizing a big surprise.)*

100 Wir laden viele **unserer** Verwandten in ein Restaurant ein. *(We're inviting a lot of our relatives to a restaurant.)*

101 **Mein** Cousin Jonathan ist Mitglied einer Musikgruppe. *(My cousin Jonathan is a member of a band [music group].)*

102 Er wird die ganze Nacht im Restaurant mit **seiner** Gruppe Musik machen. *(He's going to play music with his group the whole night in the restaurant.)*

Chapter **11**

Comparing with Adjectives and Adverbs

You may be wondering why I mix adjectives and adverbs in the same chapter, especially after Chapter 10 deals with adjectives. I have some very good reasons. Both have the power to make comparisons. What's even better is that German adjectives and adverbs are one and the same word in most cases. Take the adjective *good* and its adverbial counterpart *well*. The German equivalents are exactly the same for both adjective and adverb: **gut**. Best of all, using comparative and superlative forms of adjectives and adverbs offers great opportunities for making your language more precise, useful, and interesting.

In this chapter, you make comparisons by using adjectives and adverbs, such as **freundlich, freundlicher,** and **am freundlichsten** (*friendly, friendlier, friendliest*). Many adjectives and adverbs follow a regular pattern for making words of comparison. Some forms are irregular; they need more attention to master. Grammar comes into play with comparative adjectives that precede a noun. (See Chapter 10 for preceded adjectives.) Some types of adjectives and adverbs have a unique grammatical structure; I explain these word groups in this chapter. These groups include adjectives that omit the noun, participles (verb forms like *loving* or *loved*) that function as adjectives or adverbs, and adverbs that modify adjectives. The last section in this chapter deals with comparing equals/unequals, such as **(nicht) so teuer wie** (*[not] as expensive as*).

Comparing Regular Adjectives and Adverbs: Fast, Faster, Fastest

Adjectives modify or describe nouns; *adverbs* modify or describe verbs, other adverbs, or adjectives. (The verb **sein** *[to be]* is an exception: Adverbs can't modify the verb **sein**.) When you're using comparative and superlative forms, German makes adjectives and adverbs in similar ways. *Comparative* means that you compare two objects, people, activities, ideas, and so on (*longer* is the comparative form of *long*, for example); *superlative* means that you compare three or more objects, people, activities, ideas, and so on (*longest* is the superlative form).

Forming the comparative and superlative forms of adjectives and adverbs from the basic form isn't difficult when you see the similarities to English. The endings that vary from the most-frequent pattern mostly have to do with facilitating pronunciation. The following guidelines show how to add **-er** and **-(e)st** endings as well as the endings for adjectives that come before nouns. (See Chapter 10 for details on adjective agreement.)

Comparing two things

For both adjectives and adverbs, when you want to compare two things, people, and so on, take the base form (the adjective or adverb as you see it in the dictionary) and form the comparative by adding **-er** to the base form, as in **witzig ⇨ witziger** (*witty ⇨ wittier*). To express *than* in a comparison, the German equivalent is **als**.

>> **Mein Onkel Richard ist nett, aber meine Tante Christel ist netter als Onkel Richard.**
(My Uncle Richard is nice, but my Aunt Christel is nicer than Uncle Richard.) The adjective **nett** is the base form; **netter als** *(nicer than)* is the comparative form.

>> **Onkel Richard fährt schnell, aber Tante Christel fährt schneller als Onkel Richard.**
(Uncle Richard drives fast, but Aunt Christel drives faster than Uncle Richard.) The adverb **schnell** is the base form; **schneller als** *(faster than)* is the comparative form. ***Note:*** **Schnell** is both an adjective and an adverb, just as *fast* is in English.

Adjectives ending in **-el** and **-er** leave the last **-e** off the base form and then add **-er** to make the comparative: **dunkel ⇨ dunkler** *(dark ⇨ darker)*, **teuer ⇨ teurer** *(expensive ⇨ more expensive)*.

REMEMBER When you want to use a comparative adjective that precedes the noun, you follow the same guidelines as with other adjectives that precede the noun. (See Chapter 10 for more on preceded adjectives.) Look at the following examples, which show three scenarios for preceded adjective endings:

>> **Du hast ein neueres Auto als ich.** *(You have a newer car than I do.)* The direct object, **ein neueres Auto**, is in accusative case, and it's singular. The indefinite article **ein** *(a)* has no ending in accusative singular case: It's neuter to reflect the neuter noun **(das) Auto**. The base form of the adjective **neu** *(new)* has the comparative ending **-er** + the neuter, singular ending **-es** to form **neueres** (**neu** + **-er** + **-es**). In the example sentence, the indefinite article **ein** "falls down on the job" of marking the gender/case of **Auto**, so the adjective **neueres** has to pick up the slack.

» **Ich habe den kleineren Wagen.** *(I have the smaller car.)* The direct object, **den kleineren Wagen,** is in accusative case, and it's singular. The definite article **den** *(the)* has the accusative masculine ending: It's masculine to reflect the masculine noun **(der) Wagen.** The base form of the adjective **klein** *(small)* has the comparative ending **-er** + the masculine, singular, accusative ending **-en** to form **kleineren (klein** + **-er** + **-en).** Notice that in the example sentence, **kleineren** mirrors the **-en** ending of **den.** If you see **den,** you'll need that **-en** ending on the adjective, so the result is **kleineren.**

» **Köstlicheres Brot ist kaum zu finden.** *(It's hard to find more delicious bread.)* The subject of the sentence, **köstlicheres Brot,** is in nominative case, and it's singular. The base form of the adjective **köstlich** *(delicious)* has the comparative ending **-er** + the neuter, singular ending **-es** to reflect the neuter noun **(das) Brot.** The comparative **köstlicheres** is formed like this: **köstlich** + **-er** + **-es** = **köstlicheres.** In the phrase **köstlicheres Brot,** there is no article to help you determine case/gender, so the adjective **köstlicheres** has to step up to the plate.

DIFFERENCES

German doesn't use **mehr** *(more)* together with the **-er** ending. In English, the comparative adjective form can look like this: *more intelligent* or *more interesting.* German uses only the **-er** ending: **intelligenter** or **interessanter.**

Absolutely the most!: Discussing superlatives

The superlative form for adverbs as well as for adjectives that follow a noun in a sentence is the following: **am** + adjective/adverb + **-sten:**

> **Dieser Supermarkt ist am billigsten.** (This supermarket is the cheapest/most inexpensive.) **Billig** is the base form of the adjective and **am billigsten** is the superlative.

> **Tante Gisela kocht am besten.** *(Aunt Gisela cooks the best.)* **Gut** is the base form of the adverb; **am besten** is the superlative form.

A superlative adjective often precedes the noun it modifies, which means it needs to reflect the noun's gender, number, and case. You get the superlative form of such adjectives by adding **-st** to the base form and then adding the adjective ending (see Chapter 10): **höflich ⇨ höflichst-** + adjective ending *(polite ⇨ most polite).*

> **Manuela ist die höflichste Kollegin im Büro.** (Manuela is the most polite colleague in the office.) **Höflich** is the base form of the adjective; **die höflichst-** + **-e (Kollegin)** is feminine, singular, nominative case.

> **Onkel Kalle hat das schönste Haus.** (Uncle Kalle has the nicest house.) **Schön** is the base form of the adjective; **das schönst-** + **-e (Haus)** is the superlative form that reflects the neuter, singular accusative noun **das Haus.** *Note:* Here's the alternative form, which uses an adjective that follows the noun: **Sein Haus ist am schönsten** *(His house is the nicest).*

TIP

You make the superlative form for adjectives ending in **-t** or **-z** (and a few others) by adding **-e** + **-st** = **-est** for ease of pronunciation: **elegantest-** *(most elegant).* An example is **Du findest die elegantesten Schuhe bei Salamander** *(You find the most elegant shoes at Salamander* [a well-known shoe store]). **Elegant** is the base form of the adjective; **die elegant-** + **est-** + **-en** is the superlative form that reflects the accusative plural noun **Schuhe.**

Considering common comparisons

Table 11-1 contains a list of some adjectives and adverbs that are frequently used for making comparisons of people and things. The fourth column shows any differences in spelling, as in **nett ⇨ netter ⇨ am nettesten**, where you add the **-e** in front of **-st**. The superlative form for all words is shown at first as **am + (e)sten**. You use this form when the adjective follows the noun and for adverbs. The form shown in parentheses is the form that you use when a superlative adjective precedes the noun. You add the adjective endings to this form.

Table 11-1   Regular Comparison Forms

English	Base	Comparative	Superlative	Spelling Changes
modest	bescheiden	bescheidener	am bescheidensten (bescheidenst-)	
cheap, inexpensive	billig	billiger	am billigsten (billigst-)	
dark	dunkel	dunkler	am dunkelsten (dunkelst-)	Drop the last -e in the comparative.
elegant	elegant	eleganter	am elegantesten (elegantest-)	Add -e + st in the superlative.
fit, in shape	fit	fitter	am fittesten (fittest-)	Double the t; add -e + st in the superlative.
hard-working, industrious	fleißig	fleißiger	am fleißigsten (fleißigst-)	
flexible	flexibel	flexibler	am flexibelsten (flexibelst-)	Drop the last -e in the comparative.
friendly	freundlich	freundlicher	am freundlichsten (freundlichst-)	
happy	glücklich	glücklicher	am glücklichsten (glücklichst-)	
generous	großzügig	großzügiger	am großzügigsten (großzügigst-)	
ugly	hässlich	hässlicher	am hässlichsten (hässlichst-)	
polite	höflich	höflicher	am höflichsten(höflichst-)	
pretty	hübsch	hübscher	am hübschesten (hübschest-)	Add -e + st in the superlative.
intelligent	intelligent	intelligenter	am intelligentesten (intellegentest-)	Add -e + st in the superlative.
musical	musikalisch	musikalischer	am musikalischsten (musikalischst-)	
brave	mutig	mutiger	am mutigsten (mutigst-)	
nice	nett	netter	am nettesten (nettest-)	Add -e + st in the superlative.
neat	ordentlich	ordentlicher	am ordentlichsten (ordentlichst-)	
chic, stylish	schick	schicker	am schicksten (schickst-)	
pretty, beautiful	schön	schöner	am schönsten (schönst-)	
athletic	sportlich	sportlicher	am sportlichsten (sportlichst-)	
expensive	teuer	teurer	am teuersten (teuerst-)	Drop the last -e in the comparative.
sensible	vernünftig	vernünftiger	am vernünftigsten (vernünftigst-)	
witty	witzig	witziger	am witzigsten (witzigst-)	

REMEMBER

All adjectives that precede the noun take adjective endings that reflect the noun's gender, number, and case.

When making a sentence, remember to add the appropriate endings to adjectives of comparison when needed. Adjectives following a noun don't need to reflect the gender, number, and case of the noun, but adjectives that precede the noun do need agreement. (See Chapter 10 for more on adjectives.)

PRACTICE

Complete the sentences, using the comparative or superlative form of the word in parentheses. The context of the sentence gives clues as to whether you need the comparative or superlative form. Then try your hand at translating the sentences into English.

Q. Im Frühling gibt es die _____ Blumen. *(pretty)*

_____

A. Im Frühling gibt es die <u>schönsten/hübschesten</u> **Blumen.** *(The prettiest flowers are in spring.)* The adjective **(die) schönsten/hübschesten** is in the accusative plural form to reflect number and case of **(die) Blumen.**

 1 Claudia fährt am _____. *(sensible)*

_____

2 Mein Bruder ist _____ als ich. *(witty)*

_____

3 Wir waren vorher _____ als jetzt. *(brave)*

_____

4 Siegbert machte den _____ Eindruck *(impression)*. *(nice)*

_____

5 Ich bin _____ als du. *(fit)*

_____

6 Am _____ bin ich mit meiner Familie. *(happy)*

_____

7 Wiebke hat jetzt _____ Haar als früher. *(dark)*

_____

8 Du hast _____ Antworten als Hermann. *(intelligent)*

_____

9 Welche Insekten sind _____, Bienen *(bees)* oder Ameisen *(ants)*? *(fleißig)*

_____

10 Ich denke, Bienen sind die _____ Insekten. *(intelligent)*

_____

11 Ich habe einen _____ Arbeitsplatz *(workplace/station)* als mein Chef. *(neat)*

_____

12 Am _____ ist die Knastlinger Familie. *(generous)*

_____

13 Karl-Heinz arbeitet _____ als seine Kollegen. *(hard-working)*

_____

14 Schuh Weber hat _____ Schuhen als Schuh Knecht. *(stylish)*

_____

15 Die _____ Person im Büro ist Frau Hufnagel. *(modest)*

_____

16 Sport Scheck hat die _____ Sportartikel. *(expensive)*

_____

Adding the umlaut in regular comparisons

German wouldn't be the same without its three interesting-looking letters that have umlauts (not to mention that cool **ess-tset**, the letter ß). When forming the comparative and superlative forms of some adjectives and adverbs, be careful to add the umlaut when you need it.

REMEMBER

The general guideline for adding umlauts in comparisons is simple:

» Many adjectives and adverbs with one syllable and with an **-a, -o,** or **-u** in the base form add an umlaut in the comparative and superlative forms: **alt** ⇨ **älter** ⇨ **ältest-** *(old* ⇨ *older* ⇨ *oldest).*

» Some common one-syllable words with an **-a, -o** or **-u** in the base form don't have an umlaut: **blond** *(blond[e])*, **bunt** *(colorful)*, **falsch** *(wrong)*, **froh** *(glad)*, **klar** *(clear)*, **toll** *(amazing, great)* **wahr** *(true)*, and **laut** *(loud, noisy)*. **Note**: **Laut** has **-au** in the base form, unlike the others in this list. I include it here because it doesn't add an umlaut in the comparative and superlative forms.

Herr Diefenbacher ist alt, aber Frau Kolbe ist noch älter. *(Herr Diefenbacher is old, but Frau Kolbe is even older.)* The adjective **alt** (base form) changes to **älter**, with an umlaut in the comparative form.

Die ärmsten Länder brauchen sehr viel Unterstützung. *(The poorest countries need a lot of aid.)* The adjective **ärmsten** is the superlative form; **die ärmsten Länder** is the subject (nominative case), and it's plural. **Ärmsten** precedes the noun, so it needs the adjective ending to reflect **Länder**. You form it like this: **arm-** (base form) changes to **ärm-** (add the umlaut) + **-est** (superlative ending) + **en** (nominative plural ending).

PRACTICE

Complete the following with the forms of the adjectives and adverbs that are missing. Remember to include the umlaut and –**e** with –**st** if needed. Some exercises have all three words missing; these are cognates.

English	Base	Comparative	Superlative

Q. *old*   alt   _____   _____

A. *old*   alt   älter   am ältesten

17. *poor* _____ _____ am ärmsten

18. *stupid* _____ dümmer _____

19. *crude, coarse* _____ gröber _____

20. *large, big, tall* groß _____ _____

21. *hard, tough* hart _____ _____

22. *young* _____ jünger _____

23. *cold* _____ _____ am kältesten

24. *warm* warm _____ _____

25. *strong* _____ stärker _____

26. *smart* _____ klüger _____

27. *short* kurz _____ _____

28. *long* _____ _____ am längsten

29. *often* oft _____ _____

30. *red* _____ röter _____

Using Irregular Comparison Forms

German has some wayward characters among adjectives and adverbs, but luckily, a few of these irregular types have parallels to English odd ducks. The classic example is **gut ⇨ besser ⇨ am besten**, which is easily recognizable in English as *good ⇨ better ⇨ best*. These words are high-frequency, and there is only a small number of them, so getting them into your active vocabulary should be a snap. All you need to do is memorize this list of commonly used irregular comparison forms. Look at Table 11-2 for the list of irregular adjectives and adverbs.

Table 11-2   Irregular Comparison Forms

English Equivalent	Base	Comparative	Superlative
soon, sooner, soonest	bald	eher	am ehesten
like/enjoy (doing something), prefer, like most of all	gern	lieber	am liebsten
good, better, best	gut	besser	am besten
high, higher, highest	hoch	höher	am höchsten
near, nearer, nearest	nah	näher	am nächsten
much, more, most	viel	mehr	am meisten

TIP

The use of **gern** (the base form of the word meaning *to like, enjoy [doing something]*) is easiest to remember in the context of some common expressions:

> » **Ich spiele gern Klavier/Ich tanze gern/Ich esse gern Fisch.** *(I like to play the piano/I like to dance/I like to eat fish.)* You use this construction to express that you like an activity, sport, game, food, and so on. Also: **Ich spiele lieber Tennis/ich trinke am liebsten Wasser.** *(I prefer playing tennis/I like drinking water most of all.)* The base form of these sentences are **Ich spiele gern Tennis and Ich trinke gern Wasser** *(I like to play tennis and I like to drink water).*

> » **Ich möchte gern wissen, ob** . . . *(I wonder if . . .)*

> » **Was möchtest du lieber . . .?** *(Which would you rather . . .?)*

> » **Am liebsten möchte ich** . . . *(Most of all, I'd like to . . .)* Use this expression to talk about an activity/food/place that you like or would like to do/eat/go to/and so on.

PRACTICE

These exercises are grouped in three sentences with the base form, comparative form, and the superlative form. Complete the three unfinished sentences in each exercise, using the irregular comparison forms in Table 11-2. The question heading each group of three questions indicates the English equivalent of the German word to use.

Which mountain is higher?

Q. Die Zugspitze ist _____.

Der Großglockner ist _____.

Der Mont Blanc ist _____.

A. **Die Zugspitze ist** <u>hoch</u>. *(The Zugspitze is high.)* Zugspitze is Germany's highest mountain.

Der Großglockner ist <u>höher</u>. *(Großglockner is higher.)* Großglockner is Austria's highest mountain.

Der Mont Blanc ist <u>am höchsten</u>. *(Mont Blanc is the highest.)* Mont Blanc, located at the border between France and Italy, is the highest mountain in the Alps.

Which dinner is more expensive?

31 Ein Abendessen im Restaurant Bei Mario kostet _____.

32 Ein Abendessen im Restaurant Chez Philippe kostet _____.

33 Ein Abendessen im Restaurant Zur Goldenen Gans kostet _____.

Who's coming home sooner?

34 Monika kommt _____ nach Hause.

35 Jennifer kommt _____ nach Hause.

36 Sarah kommt _____ nach Hause.

Which sport do you like better?

37 Ich fahre _____ Fahrrad.

38 Ich fahre _____ Wasserski.

39 Ich fahre _____ Ski.

Which supermarket is closer?

40 Der Edeka ist _____.

41 Der Rewe ist _____.

42 Der Aldi ist _____.

Who is the better friend?

43 Eric ist ein _____ Freund von mir.

44 Michael ist ein _____ Freund von mir.

45 Helmut ist der _____ Freund von mir.

What kind of potatoes do they like?

46 Babys essen _____ Kartoffelpüree.

47 Kinder essen _____ Pommes frites.

48 Erwachsene essen _____ Kartoffelgratin.

Identifying Unique Adjective and Adverb Groups

The structure and usage of some adjectives and adverbs is unique. These types include adjectives that are used as nouns, participles used as adjectives or adverbs, and adverbs that modify adjectives. Most are fairly easy to remember because they have parallel meanings and structures in English.

You need to know these groups because they're high-frequency words and expressions that you come across in everyday language, and they help you express yourself more clearly. They're easy to remember if you understand how to use these structures in sentences. This section includes the following three unique groups:

>> Naturally, adjectives used as nouns are the type that stand in for the noun; they omit the noun, as in **das Richtige** *(the right thing/decision/choice)*.

>> The second group includes participles that function as adjectives or adverbs, such as **am motiviertesten** *(the most motivated)*. The present participle of **motivieren** *(to motivate)* is **motivierend** *(motivating)*, and the past participle of is **motiviert** *(motivated)*.

>> The third group I deal with in this section is made up of adverbs that modify adjectives. The combination serves to make the adjective more descriptive. In the expression **wirklich interessant**, you use the word **wirklich** *(really, absolutely)* to modify **interessant** *(interesting)*.

Adjectives that act as nouns

Sometimes, adjectives replace a noun to represent an abstract idea, a person, an object, and so on. The noun that the adjective replaces may be singular or plural, and it may be the subject or the object of a sentence; in short, it functions the same as a noun. The same structure exists in English and German for adjectives that take over as nouns: *the poor, the brave, the lonely one, the new ones*. The only difference is that in German, nouns are capitalized; the spelling reflects gender, number, and case. In addition, there's no equivalent for *one/ones* in English; the German adjective stands alone to represent the noun.

To understand how such adjectives work, imagine that you're discussing with your friend which cat you want to take home from the animal shelter. You talk about **die Große, die Schwarze,** and **die Ruhige** *(the big one, the black one, the quiet one)*. You're replacing the word **Katze** *(cat)* by describing a characteristic of each cat and using that adjective to represent that cat. You use the feminine article **die** because **Katze** is a feminine noun. If you're talking about taking home a dog, **der Hund**, you refer to each one as **der Große, der Schwarze,** and **der Ruhige**. When you make your decision, you may say something like **Ich nehme den Schwarzen** (*I'll take the black one [dog]*). The adjective has the accusative masculine singular case ending **-en** to reflect the noun it's replacing.

WARNING

Don't make the mistake of thinking that adjectives like **das Gute** (*the good thing*) are in the superlative. Adjectives that describe something abstract are neuter nouns; das signifies the neuter noun in this case, not the superlative form. (See the earlier section "Comparing Regular Adjectives and Adverbs: Fast, Faster, Fastest" for more on superlatives.) Compare the following sentences:

Ich wünsche euch das Beste. (*I wish you the best.*) This has a superlative meaning, but **das Beste** is a noun. By contrast, **die beste Idee** (*the best idea*) is a combination of the superlative adjective **die beste** and the noun **Idee**.

Ich möchte ein Dunkles. (*I'd like a dark [beer].*) The indefinite article ein combines with **Dunkles** to stand in for **dunkles Bier** (*dark beer*). When ordering a lager beer in a restaurant, you say: *Ich möchte ein Helles.*

PRACTICE

The word bank has adjectives that act as nouns. Decide which noun fits logically into the sentence and write it in the space provided. Read the exercises before you start.

Q. **Ist das die Frau von Herrn Fischer?**

Ich bin mir nicht sicher, aber ich glaube, das ist seine _____.

A. **Ist das die Frau von Herrn Fischer?** (*Is that Herr Fischer's wife?*)

Ich bin mir nicht sicher, aber ich glaube, das ist seine <u>Geliebte</u>. (*I'm not sure, but I think that's his mistress.*)

Geliebte	Bekannte (*acquaintance*)	Blaues
Gebrauchten (*used*)	Kalte	Kleinen
Kranken	Neue	Kriminelle
Neues	Teueren	

 49 Haben wir eine neue Kollegin?

Ja, die _____ ist sehr nett.

 50 Im Selbstbedienungsrestaurant gibt es Gerichte in großen und kleinen Portionen.

Ich nehme immer die _____.

51 Ist Helena deine neue Freundin?

Nein, Sie ist eine _____ von mir.

52 Möchten Sie eine kalte Limonade?

Ja, ich nehme die _____.

53 Maria, hast du ein Handtuch für mich?

Ja, möchtest du ein Rotes oder ein _____?

54 Die Verkäuferin im Schuhgeschäft zeigt (*is showing*) Jonas ein teueres und ein billiges Paar Schuhe.

Jonas kauft die _____.

55 Ist das die neue Klinik?

Ja, in dieser kann man sehr viele _____ helfen.

56 Gibt es viel Kriminalität in der Stadt?

Nein, es gibt nur wenige _____.

57 Dieser BMW ist ein Gebrauchtwagen, oder bevorzugen (*prefer*) Sie einen Neuwagen?

Ich kaufe den _____.

58 Was gibt es in den Nachrichten (*news*)?

Ach, nichts _____.

Participles that function as adjectives or adverbs

In German, as in English, present and past participles can function as adjectives or adverbs. If the adjectives precede a noun, they agree in gender, number, and case with the noun they modify. A *present participle* is the infinitive (such as *fly, tumble,* or *seethe*) with the ending *-ing*. When you use it in English as an adjective, you combine it with the noun you want to modify, such as *the flying squirrels, the tumbling acrobats,* or *the seething volcano*.

TIP

To create the present participle in German, start with a verb, such as **laufen** (*to run*). Verbs form the present participle by dropping the infinitive ending **-en** and adding **-end** to the infinitive form (**lauf-** + **-end** = **laufend**). So the present participle of **laufen** is **laufend** (the closest thing to the English word *running*). Look at an example:

> **Er erzählte Witze am laufenden Band**. (*He told an endless stream of jokes.* Literally: He told jokes on a running band/belt.)

TIP

A past participle of a regular verb is the infinitive of a verb with *-ed* or *-d* added. For an irregular verb, it's the form such as *eaten, hidden,* or *seen* that you use to form the present perfect tense and other compound verb tenses. (An example of the present perfect tense is *Scruffy has already eaten,* in which you combine the past participle *eaten* with the auxiliary verb *have.*) You can use the past participle as a descriptive word: *the drenched cat, sunken treasure,* or *forbidden fruit.*

Verbs form past participles differently, depending on the verb type (see Chapter 14). The past participle of **pflegen**, for example, is **gepflegt** (*groomed, taken care of*). The phrases **gepflegtes**

Essen (*first-rate food*) and **gepflegte Weine** (*quality wines*) are typical descriptions that restaurants use to impress their clientele. Literally speaking, these expressions mean *groomed food/wines* in the sense that the restaurant has a carefully selected menu or wine list.

Some German verbs, namely the verbs ending in **-ieren**, have the same meanings in English, making them easily recognizable. The past-participle form of these verbs is formed with **-iert** at the end; the ending is the same, whether you're using the past participle as an adjective or adverb.

Many of these common adjectives have comparative and superlative forms: Some common adjectives with this structure are **dekoriert** (*decorated*), **diszipliniert** (*disciplined*), **fasziniert** (*fascinated*), **frustriert** (*dissatisfied, frustrated*), **interessiert** (*interested*), **motiviert** (*motivated*), **organisiert** (*organized*), and **talentiert** (*talented*). They can all form comparative and superlative adjectives (and possibly adverbs):

> **In der Schule war ich motivierter als meine Schwester.** *(I was more motivated than my sister when I was in school.)* **Motivierter** is a comparative adjective.

> **Wir schauten die Olympische Spiele fasziniert zu.** *(We watched the Olympic Games with fascination.)* **Fasziniert** is an adverb describing how (we) watched.

PRACTICE

The words in bold are participles functioning as adjectives or adverbs. In the spaces provided, write the infinitive form of the verb; then try your hand at writing the equivalent sentence in English.

Q. Die Polizei stoppte den fliehenden Mann. _____

_____

A. Die Polizei stoppte den fliehenden Mann. <u>fliehen</u>

The police stopped the fleeing man/the man who was fleeing.

 59 In der Staubinger Familie war die Politik ein viel **diskutiertes** Thema. _____

_____

60 Nächste Woche fährt unsere Familie mit dem neu **gekauften** Wohnwagen in Urlaub. _____

_____

61 Es macht Spaß, auf einem gut **trainierten** Pferd zu reiten. _____

_____

62 Meine Chefin ist eine **gestresste** Frau. _____

_____

63 In Krisenzeiten setzen die Öl **exportierenden** Länder die Preise hoch.

_____

 64 Sehen Sie das **lachende** Baby? Es ist süß. _____

_____

65 Der Bäcker holt (*takes [out]*) das frisch **gebackene** Brot aus dem Ofen.

_____

66 Der Spion hatte einen **gefälschten** Reisepass (*passport*). _____

_____

67 Bitte, wecken Sie (*wake [up]*) die **schlafenden** Kinder nicht auf. _____

_____

68 Ich besuche meine Eltern am **kommenden** Wochenende. _____

_____

Adverbs that modify adjectives

Adverbs modify verbs, but they can also modify adjectives. In order to express that something or someone is quite good, especially interesting, or *really motivated,* you use adverbs to modify the adjective. Those adverbs frequently used in German are **besonders** (*especially*), **echt** (*really*), **etwas** (*somewhat*), **relativ** (*relatively*), **sehr** (*very*), **total** (*totally, absolutely*), **ungewöhnlich** (*unusually*), **viel** (*much, a lot*), **wirklich** (*absolutely, really*, and **ziemlich** (*quite*). Good news here is that they don't have any changes in the endings.

TIP

To use an adverb to modify an adjective, just place the adverb in front of the adjective it's modifying, and voilà! To see how this works, imagine you're talking about the hotels you stayed at on your last trip to Europe. One hotel was especially luxurious. To express this in German, you place the adverb **wirklich** (*really*) in front of **luxuriös** (*luxurious*), and if the adjective precedes the noun that it modifies, add the appropriate adjective ending, such as **Wir haben zwei Nächte in einem wirklich luxuriösen Hotel übernachtet** (*We spent two nights in a really luxurious hotel*). Check out these examples:

>> **Der Sommer war etwas wärmer als in vergangenen Jahren.** (The summer was somewhat warmer than in previous years.) The adverb **etwas** modifies the adjective **wärmer**, which is in the comparative form. The adjective **wärmer** needs no ending because it doesn't precede the noun that it modifies, **der Sommer**.

>> **Letztes Jahr hatten wir einen ziemlich langen Winter.** *(Last year we had quite a long winter.)* The adverb **ziemlich** modifies the adjective **lang: einen ziemlich langen. Winter** is the direct object of the sentence, so the other modifiers — **einen** and **langen** — have masculine, singular, accusative endings to reflect **(der) Winter**.

PRACTICE

The word bank has adverb + adjective pairs to fit into the sentences in the exercise. The context of the sentence will help you decide which pair to put in the space provided.

Q. Wir haben _____ Nachbarn.

A. Wir haben <u>total nette</u> **Nachbarn.** *(We have totally kind/nice neighbors.)* **Total** is colloquial; it adds color to the bland adjective **nett.**

total nette	sehr schöne	viel teuerer	echt cool
besonders früh	relativ gute	wirklich heißen	wirklich lustiger
ziemlich schnell	etwas besser	ungewöhnlich hässliches *(ugly)*	

69 Im Dezember wird es _____ dunkel.

70 Ich schwimme gern an _____ Tagen.

71 Die Deutschen fahren _____ auf der Autobahn.

72 Van Gogh hat _____ Bilder gemalt.

73 Die neue Kneipe *(bar/pub,* colloquial) ist _____.

74 In Europa ist das Benzin *(gasoline)* _____ als in den USA.

75 Nach der Operation geht es dem Patienten _____.

76 in diesem Semester habe ich _____ Noten *(grades)* bekommen.

77 Dieser Hund hat ein _____ Gesicht *(face).*

78 Charlie Chaplin war ein _____ Komiker.

Answers to "Comparing with Adjectives and Adverbs" Practice Questions

1. Claudia fährt **am vernünftigsten**. (*Claudia drives the most sensibly.*)

2. Mein Bruder ist **witziger** als ich. (*My brother is wittier than I.*)

3. Wir waren vorher **mutiger** als jetzt. (*We were braver then than now.*)

4. Siegbert machte den **nettesten** Eindruck. (*Siegbert made the nicest impression.*)

5. Ich bin **fitter** als du. (*I'm in better shape than you.*)

6. Am **glücklichsten** bin ich mit meiner Familie. (*I'm happiest [when I'm] with my family.*)

7. Wiebke hat jetzt **dunkleres** Haar als früher. (*Wiebke now has darker hair than before.*)

8. Du hast **intelligentere** Antworten als Hermann. (*You have more intelligent answers than Hermann.*)

9. Welche Insekten sind **fleißiger**, Bienen oder Ameisen? (*Which insects are more hard-working, bees or ants?*)

10. Ich denke, Bienen sind die **intelligentesten** Insekten. (*I think bees are the most intelligent insects.*)

11. Ich habe einen **ordentlicheren** Arbeitsplatz als mein Chef. (*I have a neater workstation than my boss.*)

12. Am **großzügigsten** ist die Knastlinger Familie. (*The Knastlinger family is the most generous.*)

13. Karl-Heinz arbeitet **fleißiger** als seine Kollegen. (*Karl-Heinz works harder than his colleagues.*)

14. Schuh Weber hat **schickere** Schuhen als Schuh Knecht. (*Schuh Weber has more stylish shoes than Schuh Knecht.*)

15. Die **bescheidenste** Person im Büro ist Frau Hufnagel. (*The most modest person in the office is Frau Hufnagel.*)

16. Sport Scheck hat die **teuersten** Sportartikel. (*Sport Scheck [a sports store] has the most expensive sporting goods.*)

17. *poor* **arm** **ärmer** am ärmsten

18. *stupid* **dumm** dümmer **am dümmsten**

19. *crude, coarse* **grob** gröber **am gröbsten**

20. *large, big, tall* **groß** **größer** **am größten**

21. *hard, tough* **hart** **härter** **am härtesten**

22. *young* **jung** **jünger** **am jüngsten**

23. *cold* **kalt** **kälter** **am kältesten**

24. *warm* **warm** **wärmer** **am wärmsten**

(25) *strong* **stark stärker am stärksten**

(26) *smart* **klug klüger am klügsten**

(27) *short* **kurz kürzer am kürzesten**

(28) *long* **lang länger am längsten**

(29) *often* **oft öfter am öftesten**

(30) *red* **rot röter am rötesten**

(31) Ein Abendessen im Restaurant Bei Mario kostet **viel**. (*A dinner in Mario's restaurant is expensive.*)

(32) Ein Abendessen im Restaurant Chez Philippe kostet **mehr**. (*A dinner in Philippe's restaurant is more expensive.*)

(33) Ein Abendessen im Restaurant Zur Goldenen Gans kostet **am meisten**. (*A dinner in the Goldenen Gans restaurant is the most expensive.*)

(34) Monika kommt **bald** nach Hause. (*Monika is coming home soon.*)

(35) Jennifer kommt **eher** nach Hause. (*Jennifer is coming home sooner.*)

(36) Sarah kommt **am ehesten** nach Hause. (*Sarah is coming home the soonest.*)

(37) Ich fahre **gern** Fahrrad. (*I like bicycling.*)

(38) Ich fahre **lieber** Wasserski. (*I like waterskiing better.*)

(39) Ich fahre **am liebsten** Ski. (*I like skiing the most.*)

(40) Der Edeka ist **nah**. (*Edeka is close.*) Another way to describe that something is *near* is **in der Nähe von** + a place, as in **unserem Haus**. **Von** is a preposition that uses the dative case, so the ending of **unser** is **-em** to reflect the neuter noun **(das) Haus.**

(41) Der Rewe ist **näher**. (*Rewe is closer.*)

(42) Der Aldi ist **am nächsten**. (Aldi is the closest.)

(43) Eric ist ein **guter** Freund von mir. (*Eric is a good friend of mine.*) The adjective expression includes **ein + gut** + ending **-er**, which reflects the masculine singular noun **Freund** in nominative case.

(44) Michael ist ein **besserer** Freund von mir. (*Michael is a better friend of mine.*) The adjective expression includes **ein + besser** + ending **-er,** which reflects the masculine singular noun **Freund** in nominative case.

(45) Helmut ist der **beste** Freund von mir. (*Helmut is my best friend.*) The adjective expression includes **der + best + -e**, which reflects the masculine singular noun **Freund** in nominative case. The adjective ending for **best–** is different because of the switch from the indefinite article ein to the definite article **der.**

(46) Babys essen **gern** Kartoffelpüree. (*Babies like mashed potatoes.*)

(47) Kinder essen **lieber** Pommes frites. (*Children prefer French fries.*)

(48) Erwachsene essen **am liebsten** Kartoffelgratin. (*Adults like potatoes au gratin most of all.*) Well, at least some do . . .

(49) **Haben wir eine neue Kollegin?** (*Do we have a new colleague?*)

Ja, die **Neue** ist sehr nett. (*Yes, the new one is really nice.*)

(50) **Im Selbstbedienungsrestaurant gibt es Gerichte in großen und kleinen Portionen.** (*In the self-service restaurant there are meals in large and small servings/portions.*)

Ich nehme immer die **Kleinen**. (*I always take the small servings.*)

(51) **Ist Helena deine neue Freundin?** (*Is Helena your new girlfriend?*)

Nein, Sie ist eine **Bekannte** von mir. (*No, she's an acquaintance of mine.*)

(52) **Möchten Sie eine kalte Limonade?** (*Would you like a cold lemonade?*)

Ja, ich nehme die **Kalte**. (*Yes, I'll take the cold one.*)

(53) **Maria, hast du ein Handtuch für mich?** (*Maria, do you have a towel for me?*)

Ja sicher. Möchtest du ein Rotes oder ein **Blaues**? (*Yes, of course. Would you like a red one or a blue one?*)

(54) **Die Verkäuferin im Schuhgeschäft zeigt Jonas ein teueres und ein billiges Paar Schuhe.** (*The saleswoman in the shoe store is showing Jonas an expensive and an inexpensive pair of shoes.*)

Jonas kauft die **Teueren**. (*Jonas buys the expensive ones.*)

(55) Ist das die neue Klinik? (*Is that the new clinic?*)

Ja, in dieser kann man sehr vielen **Kranken** helfen. (*Yes, this clinic can help a lot of sick people.*)

(56) **Gibt es viel Kriminalität in der Stadt?** (*Is there much crime in the city?*)

Nein, es gibt nur wenige **Kriminelle**. (*No, there are only a few criminals.*)

(57) **Dieser BMW ist ein Gebrauchtwagen, oder bevorzugen Sie einen Neuwagen?** (*This BMW is a used car, or do you prefer a new car?*)

Ich kaufe den **Gebrauchten**. (*I'll buy the used car.*)

(58) **Was gibt es in den Nachrichten?** (*What's in the news?*)

Ach, nichts **Neues**. (*Oh, nothing new.*)

(59) In der Staubinger Familie war die Politik ein viel **diskutiertes** Thema. **diskutieren**

(*In the Staubinger family, politics was a frequently discussed topic/topic that was often discussed.*)

(60) Nächste Woche fährt unsere Familie mit dem neu **gekauften** Wohnwagen in Urlaub. **kaufen**

(*Next week our family is going on vacation in our newly purchased trailer/RV.*)

(61) Es macht Spaß, auf einem gut **trainierten** Pferd zu reiten. **trainieren**

(*It's a lot of fun to ride on a well-trained horse.*)

(62) Meine Chefin ist eine **gestresste** Frau. **stressen**

(*My boss is a stressed woman.*)

(63) In Krisenzeiten setzen die Öl **exportierenden** Länder die Preise hoch. **Exportieren**

(*In times of crisis, the oil exporting countries fix/set the prices high.*)

64. Sehen Sie das **lachende** Baby? Es ist süß. **lachen**

(*Do you see the baby laughing/laughing baby? It's so sweet.*)

65. Der Bäcker holt das frisch **gebackene** Brot aus dem Ofen. **backen**

(*The baker is taking the freshly baked bread out of the oven.*)

66. Der Spion hatte einen **gefälschten** Reisepass. **fälschen** The adjective is **falsch.**

(*The spy had a forged/fake passport.*)

67. Bitte, wecken Sie die **schlafenden** Kinder nicht auf. **schlafen.**

(*Please don't wake up the sleeping children.*)

68. Ich besuche meine Eltern am **kommenden** Wochenende. **kommen**

(*I'm visiting my parents this coming weekend.*)

69. Im Dezember wird es **besonders früh** dunkel. (*It gets dark especially early in December.*)

70. Ich schwimme gern an **wirklich heißen** Tagen. (*I like to go swimming on really hot days.*)

71. Die Deutschen fahren **ziemlich schnell** auf der Autobahn. (*Germans drive quite fast on the highway.*)

72. Van Gogh hat **sehr schöne** Bilder gemalt. (*Van Gogh painted very beautiful paintings.*)

73. Die neue Kneipe ist **echt cool**. (*The new bar is really cool.*) German has adopted many colloquial terms from English, including *cool, super,* and *wow!*

74. In Europa ist das Benzin **viel teurer** als in den USA. (*Gasoline is a lot more expensive in Europe than in the USA.*)

75. Nach der Operation geht es dem Patienten **etwas besser**. (*The patient is feeling somewhat better after the operation.*)

76. In diesem Semester habe ich **relativ gute** Noten bekommen. (*In this semester, I got relatively good grades.*)

77. Dieser Hund hat ein **ungewöhnlich hässliches** Gesicht. (*This dog has a really ugly face.*)

78. Charlie Chaplin war ein **wirklich lustiger** Komiker. (*Charlie Chaplin was a really funny comedian.*)

Chapter **12**

Connecting with Conjunctions

onjunctions are the glue that connects parts of a sentence, such as clauses, phrases, or words. To reach beyond basic sentence structure in German, you need these small yet important words to form more-sophisticated sentences. German uses two types of conjunctions: *coordinating conjunctions,* such as **oder** *(or),* and *subordinating conjunctions,* such as **weil** *(because.* Your choice is based on the structure of the clauses, phrases, or words that you're joining. In the first section of this chapter, I clarify the difference between these two types of conjunctions, and in the rest of this chapter, I explain how to use the most common German conjunctions to express your ideas clearly and intelligently.

Conjunctions and Clauses: Terminating Terminology Tangles

To get a good grasp on conjunctions and how to use them, first you need to understand and keep track of the basic grammatical vocab. You're probably familiar with many of the following terms, but here's a quick recap of the differences among phrases, clauses, and sentences:

» **Phrase:** A group of connected words that have neither subject nor verb, often a preposition + noun combination, such as **nach Zürich** *(to Zürich)*

>> **Clause:** A group of related words that have a subject and a verb, such as **Ich fliege** (*I'm flying*)

Main clause (independent clause): A clause that can stand on its own; it has a sentence structure, as in **der Nachrichtensprecher war enttäuscht** (*the newscaster was disappointed*). This is just about the same as a sentence except that it doesn't have a proper beginning (capitalized **D** in **der**) or a punctuation mark at the end (a period in this example).

Subordinate clause (dependent clause): This clause has a sentence structure with a subject and a verb, but it can't stand on its own; it needs some help from its friends, the independent clause and the conjunction. If you see such a clause alone without a main clause, such as **weil er seine Stimme verloren hat** (*because he lost his voice*) — you're left waiting to find out more information.

>> **Sentence:** A group of words that has it all, with a subject, a verb, and an ending such as a period, exclamation point, or question mark — the whole shebang, as in **Ich fliege nächste Woche nach Zürich** (*I'm flying to Zürich next week*).

Conjunctions are the connectors, the cement, the orangutan glue that you use to combine sentence parts. Here are the two types of conjunctions:

>> **Coordinating:** A coordinating conjunction joins main clauses, phrases, or words.

Der Nachrichtensprecher hat seine Stimme verloren, und er musste zu Hause bleiben. (*The newscaster lost his voice, and he had to stay home.*) The coordinating conjunction **und** (*and*) combines the two main clauses; a comma placed before **und** separates the two clauses.

Martin ging nach Hause und machte sich ein Käsebrot zum Abendessen. (*Martin went home and made [himself] a cheese sandwich for supper.*) **Und** (*and*) is a coordinating conjunction; it combines two actions (verbs) that Martin did without repeating the subject.

>> **Subordinating:** This conjunction introduces a subordinate clause and relates it to another clause in the sentence.

Der Nachrichtensprecher war enttäuscht, weil er seine Stimme verloren hat. (*The newscaster was disappointed because he lost his voice.*) **Weil** (*because*) is the subordinating conjunction. The subordinate clause **weil er seine Stimme verloren hat** (*because he lost his voice*) has complete meaning when it's connected to **der Nachrichtensprecher war enttäuscht** (*the newscaster was disappointed*).

Martin ging nach Hause, obwohl er sehr einsam war. (*Martin went home, although he was very lonely.*) The subordinating conjunction **obwohl** (*although*) introduces the subordinate clause that follows it and connects the two parts of the sentence: **Martin ging nach Hause** and **er sehr einsam war.**

In English, conjunctions such as *and, because, but, or,* and *when* are simple to use in a sentence; the word order comes naturally for fluent speakers. German conjunctions, however, require a conscious effort to keep in mind which type of conjunction you're dealing with and how to get the word order straight. You need to know that, with subordinating conjunctions, you kick the verb to the end of the subordinate clause. You also need to remember when and where to place the comma. Keep reading for details on using these two types of conjunctions correctly.

Connecting with Coordinating Conjunctions

Coordinating conjunctions — the ones that join main clauses, phrases, or words — are the easier of the two types to master. The number of German coordinating conjunctions is small. The conjunctions correspond well to their English counterparts in meaning and usage except for a few easy-to-understand differences.

Table 12-1 shows the common coordinating conjunctions with their English equivalents and comments relating to the conjunction in a clause.

Table 12-1   Common Coordinating Conjunctions

German	English Equivalent	Comma Separates Joined Sentence Parts?	Comment
aber	*but*	yes	Used the same way in English.
denn	*for, because*	yes	**Denn** is also used as a flavoring particle, often to interest the listener; **weil**, a subordinating conjunction, also means *because,* but it has a different word order.
oder	*or*	no (unless the writer chooses a comma for clarity)	Used the same way in English.
sondern	*but*	yes	Used to express *on the contrary, rather,* or *instead;* it's preceded by a clause that makes a negative statement.
und	*and*	no (unless the writer chooses a comma for clarity)	Used the same way in English.

Note: In German, you don't use a comma before **und** in a series (or list of words), although this practice is common in English. Example: **Wir haben Kartoffelbrei, Spinat und Kabeljau gegessen.** (*We ate mashed potatoes, spinach, and cod.*)

Working on word order: Coordinating conjunctions

When you form German sentences with coordinating conjunctions, the separate sentence parts maintain their word order. Keep in mind that in standard German word order, the active, conjugated verb is placed in second position. The standard word order is the same for English and German: Take the subject + the verb + the other information, such as an object or a prepositional phrase, and add the conjunction to combine the other sentence part. Now you have two parts combined into one sentence:

> **Luca geht ins Kaufhaus, aber sein Hund bleibt zu Hause.** (*Luca goes to the department store, but his dog stays home.*) **Aber** (*but*) is the coordinating conjunction.

Although the preceding word order is exactly the same in English and German, I can't let you go away without pointing out other German sentences using a coordinating conjunction that have a different word order from the standard subject + verb + other information structure. (Go to Chapter 2 for more on word order.)

Time expressions (descriptions of time such as *this morning, in the eighteenth century, at five o'clock,* and so on) can take the place of the subject. The verb is still in second position, but the subject goes behind the verb. This point is important because it distinguishes coordinating conjunctions from their cousins, the subordinating conjunctions. I explain the differences between these two conjunction types in the "Using subordinating conjunctions" section of this chapter. The example shows you how this word order change looks:

Wir fahren heute mit dem Zug nach Hamburg, denn morgen in der Früh möchten wir zum Fischmarkt gehen. *(We're taking the train to Hamburg today because tomorrow morning we'd like to go to the fish market.)* The time expression **morgen in der Früh** immediately follows the coordinating conjunction **denn**.

When forming a German sentence, remember *time, manner, place* — the mantra for positioning information describing when, how, and where. The standard word order is

1. Time (tells when)

2. Manner (tells how)

3. Place (tells where)

In the sentence wir fahren heute mit dem Zug nach Hamburg, heute = *time,* mit dem Zug = *manner,* and nach Hamburg = *place.* In the second clause, denn morgen in der Früh möchten wir zum Fischmarkt gehen, morgen in der Früh = *time* and zum Fischmarkt = *place.*

Some of the following sentences have the wrong word order. When that is the case, rewrite the sentence in the correct word order. Remember to use the comma if appropriate.

Q. Morgen ich möchte schwimmen, aber ich muss arbeiten.

A. **Morgen möchte ich schwimmen, aber ich muss arbeiten.** *(I'd like to go swimming tomorrow, but I have to work.)* Alternative word order: **Ich möchte morgen schwimmen, aber . . .**

 Am Freitag fahren wir nach Wien mit dem Zug und bleiben dort eine Woche.

_____

 Was für ein Auto fährt Timo? Einen Ford oder einen VW?

_____

 Timo hat kein Auto sondern ein Motorrad.

_____

 Im Sommer fährt Gretel nach Italien und Griechenland.

_____

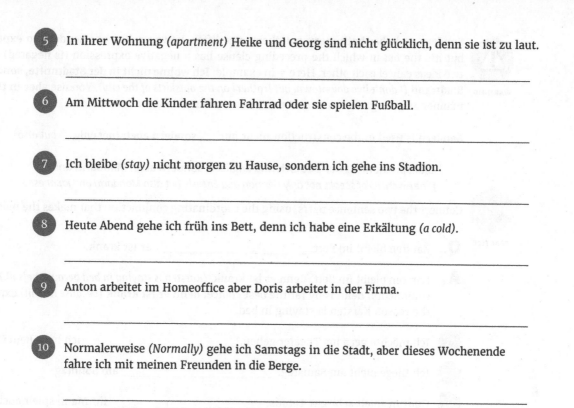

5 In ihrer Wohnung (*apartment*) Heike und Georg sind nicht glücklich, denn sie ist zu laut.

_____

6 Am Mittwoch die Kinder fahren Fahrrad oder sie spielen Fußball.

_____

7 Ich bleibe (*stay*) nicht morgen zu Hause, sondern ich gehe ins Stadion.

_____

8 Heute Abend gehe ich früh ins Bett, denn ich habe eine Erkältung (*a cold*).

_____

9 Anton arbeitet im Homeoffice aber Doris arbeitet in der Firma.

_____

10 Normalerweise (*Normally*) gehe ich Samstags in die Stadt, aber dieses Wochenende fahre ich mit meinen Freunden in die Berge.

_____

Using coordinating conjunctions

Incorporating coordinating conjunctions into your writing and speech shouldn't be too difficult. The coordinating conjunctions are straightforward in usage and meaning. You just combine two sentence parts by using the coordinating conjunction that fits what you intend to say about the relationship between them.

The common coordinating conjunctions are as follows:

aber (*but*)	**sondern** (*but*)
denn (*for, because*)	**und** (*and*)
oder (*or*)	

When you're writing in German, **oder** and **und** don't need a comma preceding them, although using a comma sometimes improves clarity. **Aber, sondern,** and **denn** do need a preceding comma to connect clauses, phrases, and words. **Denn**, however, connects clauses only; it has the same function as *because* in English. Otherwise, word order follows the guidelines as described in the preceding section for coordinating conjunctions.

> **Ich gehe zum Geldautomat, denn ich brauche Bargeld.** (*I'm going to the ATM because I need some cash.*)

> **Heute esse ich ein saftiges Steak im Restaurant, oder ich mache Pasta zu Hause.**
> (*Today I'll have a juicy steak in a restaurant, or I'll make pasta at home.*)

WARNING

Sondern and **aber** both mean *but*; their uses differ, however. You use **sondern** to express *but*, but it's the *but* in which the preceding clause has a negative expression (is negated) and the two ideas cancel each other. Here's an example: **Ich wohne nicht in der Stadtmitte, sondern am Stadtrand** (*I don't live downtown, but [rather] on the outskirts of the city*). You use **aber** in the same manner as in English: to connect two ideas that aren't mutually exclusive.

Sondern is used in the construction **nicht nur . . . sondern auch** (*not only . . . but also*).

> **Olaf spricht nicht nur Deutsch und Englisch, sondern auch Mandarin und Japanisch.** (*Olaf speaks not only German and English, but also Mandarin and Japanese.*)

Connect the two sentence parts, using the coordinating conjunction that makes the most sense.

PRACTICE

Q. Karsten bleibt im Bett, _____ er ist krank.

A. Karsten bleibt im Bett, **denn** er ist krank. (*Karsten is staying in bed because he's ill.*) The conjunction **denn** is by far the best choice; **denn er ist krank** (*because he's ill*) explains the reason Karsten is staying in bed.

 11 Ich möchte gern ins Theater gehen, _____ ich habe kein Geld.

12 Ich fliege nicht am Samstag, _____ am Sonntag.

13 Gudrun spielt sehr gut Tennis, _____ ihr Mann spielt auch sehr gut.

14 Essen wir heute Abend bei dir _____ bei mir?

15 Der Film hatte _____ gute Schauspieler (*actors*), _____ hervorragende (*excellent*) Musik.

16 Ich gehe sehr gern tanzen, _____ heute Abend muss ich babysitten.

17 Wird es am Wochenende sonnig _____ regnerisch sein?

18 Claudia hat _____ zwei Kajaks, _____ ein Segelboot.

19 Moritz ist ein fleißiger (*hard-working*) Student, _____ er möchte Ingenieur werden.

20 Wir fahren nicht mit der U-Bahn nach Hause, _____ gehen zu Fuß.

Connecting with Subordinating Conjunctions

The trick with subordinating conjunctions is remembering three things: the correct word order, where to put the comma, and (of course) the meaning of the subordinating conjunction. A *subordinate clause* (dependent clause) has a simple structure with a subject and a verb, but it can't stand on its own without help from a main clause and a subordinating conjunction. A *subordinating conjunction* introduces a subordinate clause and relates that clause to the main clause in the sentence.

Table 12-2 presents a list of commonly used German subordinating conjunctions with their English equivalents and comments on their usage.

Table 12-2 Common Subordinating Conjunctions

German	English Equivalent	Comment
als	*as, when*	Describes an event in the past. Example: **Als ich elf Jahre alt war** . . . *(When I was eleven . . .).*
bevor	*before*	Used the same way in English.
da	*since (inasmuch as)*	Not to be confused with the preposition **seit** (*since* + a point in time) or **da** *(there).*
damit	*so that*	Used to express *in order that* . . .; not to be confused with **damit**, a compound of **da + mit** to express *with that/it/them*.
dass	*that*	Rarely begins a sentence; in English, you can leave out the conjunction *that,* but you can't in German. Example: **Ich wusste, dass er** . . . *(I knew [that] he . . .).*
falls	*in case*	Used to describe *in the situation/event that* . . .
ob	*if, whether*	Not interchangeable with **wenn**; **ob** can be used to begin an indirect yes/no question.
obwohl	*although*	Used the same way in English.
weil	*because*	Same meaning as **denn** (coordinating conjunction) but with a different word order in the subordinate clause.
wenn	*if, when, whenever*	Not interchangeable with **ob**; **wenn** starts a clause that stipulates the condition of something possibly happening or not, such as *if A, then B*.

Join the two clauses in the following exercise. Choose the most logical conjunction in parentheses. Remember to include the comma in the sentence.

Q. **Wir bleiben zu Hause _____ es heute Nachmittag regnet. (bevor/falls)**

A. **Wir bleiben zu Hause, <u>falls</u> es heute Nachmittag regnet.** *(We'll stay home in case it rains this afternoon.)*

21 Ich komme nach Hause _____ es dunkel wird (bevor/obwohl)

22 Es begann zu schneien *(to snow)* _____ ich heute nach Innsbruck fuhr. (falls/als)

23 Am Abend trinke ich nur *(only)* ein einziges Glas Rotwein _____ ich Rotwein sehr mag. (obwohl/weil)

24 Wir trinken einen Kaffee _____ Peter kommt. (damit/wenn)

25 Ich fahre morgen früh nach Bremen _____ ich alles erledigen *(get [something] done)* kann. (damit/dass)

26 Ich arbeite gern _____ mir meine Arbeit Spaß *(fun)* macht. (obwohl/weil)

27 Niemand *(No one)* weiss _____ Marcel am Donnerstag kommt. (ob/falls)

28 Ich möchte wissen _____ du mich liebst. (wenn/ob)

Using subordinating conjunctions

Subordinating conjunctions have some similarities to their cousins, the coordinating conjunctions: Both types of conjunctions link ideas, both introduce one of the ideas, and both generally use commas to separate the ideas. The distinguishing characteristics of subordinating conjunctions are as follows:

>> A subordinating conjunction begins a subordinate clause: **Ich hoffe, dass du kommst** *(I hope that you come)*. **Dass** is the subordinating conjunction, and the subordinate clause is **dass du kommst.**

>> A comma always separates the main clause from the subordinate clause: **Ich hoffe** (main clause) + , (comma) + **dass** . . . (subordinate clause).

>> Subordinating conjunctions affect word order of verbs: They push the conjugated (main) verb to the end of the subordinate clause.

REMEMBER

Two subordinating conjunctions, **als** and **wenn,** have similar meanings; both can mean *when.* But **als** describes an event (a single event) in the past, and **wenn** functions the way it does in English; you can use it for an action that's repeated in any verb tense.

> **Als ich in der Stadt lebte, hatte ich kein Auto.** *(When I lived in the city, I didn't have a car.)* You don't live in the city anymore; that event is over.

> **Wenn ich nicht mehr arbeite, möchte ich noch fit bleiben.** *(When I'm no longer working, I'd like to stay in shape.)* This sentence is in present tense; it describes an imagined scenario in the future.

REMEMBER

Ob and **wenn** are similar because they can both mean *if.* But **ob** can begin an indirect yes/no question, and **wenn** starts a clause that stipulates the condition of something possibly happening or not. You use **ob** to express *whether [or not].* **Falls** and **wenn** are also similar. **Falls** can be used in such situations when you want to express *in case* or *in the case that.*

> **Ich weiß nicht, ob das richtig ist.** *(I don't know if that's right.)* You're posing a question to yourself that would have a yes/no answer.

> **Wenn/Falls es morgen regnet, bleiben wir zu Hause.** *(If/In case it rains tomorrow, we'll stay home.)*

Look at the following examples of how you use **da, bevor,** and **damit** in German sentences. In the next section, you find example sentences with **dass, obwohl,** and **weil.**

> **Da ich wenig Geld habe, hoffe ich einen reichen Partner zu finden.** (*Since I have little money, I hope to find a rich partner.*) You can also use **weil** in place of **da** in this sentence when you want to express *because.*

> **Bevor ich den richtigen Mann finde, werde ich meine Freiheit genießen.** (*Before I find the right man, I'll enjoy my freedom.*)

> **Ich brauche viel Geld, damit ich Luxusartikel kaufen kann.** (*I need a lot of money so I can buy luxury goods.*)

Using the correct word order

REMEMBER

Clarity is the name of the game, and to use subordinating conjunctions properly, you need to make sure you put everything in its proper order:

>> The conjugated verb is thrown (ruthlessly!) to the end of the end of the subordinate clause: **Ich hoffe, dass sie das Basketballspiel gewinnen** (*I hope [that] they win the basketball game*). The verb **gewinnen** (*win*) is at the end of the subordinate clause, which begins with the word **dass,** and **dass** very rarely begins a sentence.

>> When a subordinate clause begins a sentence, the word directly following the clause is the conjugated verb of the main clause. Why? The whole subordinate clause counts as one sentence element (one unit), so the verb in the main clause is in its usual second position: **Wenn ich zu spät aufstehe, verpasse ich den Zug** (*When I get up too late, I miss the train*). The verb **verpasse** (*miss,* as in *to miss an opportunity*) directly follows the subordinate clause.

Look at the annotated examples of three sentences that use subordinating conjunctions:

> **Ich hoffe, dass sie das Basketballspiel gewinnen.** (*I hope [that] they win the basketball game.*) The main clause comes first, followed by the subordinate clause.

1. **Ich hoffe** (*I hope*) = main clause

2. **dass** (*that*) = subordinating conjunction introducing the subordinate clause

3. **sie** (*they*) = subject

4. **das Basketballspiel** (*the basketball game*) = direct object, in accusative case

5. **gewinnen** (*win*) = verb at the end of the subordinate clause

> **Obwohl ich oft zu spät aufstehe, erreiche ich den Zug.** (*Although I often get up too late, I catch the train.*) The subordinate clause comes first, followed by the main clause.

1. **Obwohl** (*although*) = subordinating conjunction introducing the sentence

2. **ich oft zu spät** (*I often too late*) = subject and other information

3. **aufstehe** (*get up*) = verb at the end of the subordinate clause

4. **erreiche** *(catch)* = verb at the beginning of the independent clause (counts as second position in the sentence)

5. **ich den** Zug *(I the train)* = subject and direct object in accusative case

Weil ich viel zu spät aufgestanden bin, habe ich den Zug verpasst. *(Because I [have gotten] got up much too late, I [have] missed the train.)* The subordinate clause comes first, with the main clause in second position; both clauses use the present-perfect verb tense. (See Chapter 14 for more on present perfect.)

In the subordinate clause, the two verb parts are at the end of the clause, with the past participle (**aufgestanden**) preceding the conjugated verb (**bin**). In the main clause (**habe ich den Zug verpasst**), the word order of the verbs follows that of present perfect in a sentence with only one clause: The conjugated verb is in second position (**habe**), and the past participle is at the end of the clause/sentence. Remember that the whole subordinate clause functions as a subject, or as one unit of information, with a comma separating the two clauses. The conjugated verb is, grammatically speaking, in second position.

1. **Weil** *(because)* = subordinating conjunction introducing the sentence

2. **ich viel zu spät** *(I much too late)* = subject and other information

3. **aufgestanden** *(got up)* = past participle of aufstehen *(to get up)*

4. **bin** *(have; literally: am)* = conjugated verb thrown to the end of the subordinate clause so that it follows the past participle **aufgestanden** *(got up)*

5. **habe** *(have)* = conjugated verb at the beginning of the main clause

6. **ich den Zug** *(I the train)* = subject and direct object, accusative case

7. **verpasst** *(missed)* = past participle of verpassen *(to miss)*

In the following exercises, the first clause has the correct word order. Decide whether the word order of the following clause is correct. If not, rewrite the sentence in the correct word order.

Q. Ich weiss, dass Sie sprechen gut Deutsch.

A. Ich weiss, **dass Sie gut Deutsch sprechen**. *(I know that you speak good German.)* The word order is incorrect; the verb must go to the end of the subordinate clause.

 29   Ich möchte, dass du morgen mit mir kommst.

_____

 30   Obwohl die Fahrpreise sehr hoch sind, ich möchte mit dem Zug durch die Schweiz reisen.

_____

 31   Die Fähre *(ferry)* konnte am Vormittag nicht zur Insel fahren, weil das Wetter zu stürmisch war.

_____

32 Wenn das schlechte Wetter anhält *(continues)*, wir müssen den Urlaub abbrechen.

_____

 33 Johanna und Anja sind gestern zu Fuß in den Biergarten gegangen, da sie ihre Freunde dort treffen *(meet)* wollten.

_____

34 Erst als sie dort waren, es hat angefangen *(started)* zu regnen.

_____

35 Es ist nicht gut, dass du bist allein.

_____

Answers to "Connecting with Conjunctions" Practice Questions

1. **Am Freitag fahren wir mit dem Zug nach Wien und bleiben dort eine Woche.** *(On Friday we're taking the train to Vienna, and we're staying there for a week.)* Word order is time (**Am Freitag**), manner (**mit dem Zug**), and place (**nach Wien**).

2. **Was für ein Auto fährt Timo? Einen Ford oder einen VW?** *(What kind of car does Timo drive? A Ford or VW?)* The word order is correct.

3. **Timo hat kein Auto, sondern ein Motorrad.** *(Timo doesn't have a car, rather [he has] a motorcycle.)* You need a comma before **sondern.**

4. **Im Sommer fährt Gretel nach Italien und Griechenland.** *(Gretel is going to Italy and Greece in the summer.)* Word order is correct. **Im Sommer** is the first placeholder, so the verb **fährt** follows in second position.

5. **Heike und Georg sind nicht glücklich in ihrer Wohnung, denn sie ist zu laut.** *(Heike and Georg aren't happy in their apartment because it's too loud.)*

6. **Am Mittwoch fahren die Kinder Fahrrad oder sie spielen Fußball.** *(On Wednesday, the children ride bicycles or they play soccer.)* The verb needs to be in the second position.

7. **Ich bleibe morgen nicht zu Hause, sondern ich gehe ins Stadion.** *(I'm not staying home tomorrow; instead I'm going to the stadium.)* Time (**morgen**) precedes place (**zu Hause**).

8. **Heute Abend gehe ich früh ins Bett, denn ich habe eine Erkältung.** *(I'm going to bed early this evening because I have a cold.)* The word order is correct.

9. **Anton arbeitet im Homeoffice, aber Doris arbeitet in der Firma.** *(Anton works in his home office/at home and Doris works in the company.)* A comma precedes **aber.**

10. **Normalerweise gehe ich samstags in die Stadt, aber dieses Wochenende fahre ich mit meinen Freunden in die Berge.** (I usually go into the city on Saturdays, but this weekend I'm going to the mountains with my friends.) The word order is correct.

11. Ich möchte gern ins Theater gehen, **aber** ich habe kein Geld. *(I'd really like to go to the theater, but I don't have any money.)*

12. Ich fliege nicht am Samstag, **sondern** am Sonntag. *(I'm not flying on Saturday, but rather on Sunday.)*

13. Gudrun spielt sehr gut Tennis, **und** ihr Mann spielt auch sehr gut. *(Gudrun plays tennis very well, and her husband also plays very well.)* The hint is in the second phrase, **auch sehr gut;** the information in the two sentence parts is equal.

14. Essen wir heute Abend bei dir **oder** bei mir? *(Are we having dinner at your place or my place tonight?)*

15. Der Film hatte **nicht nur** gute Schauspieler, **sondern auch** hervorragende Musik. *(The movie had not only good actors, but also excellent music.)*

16. Ich gehe sehr gern tanzen, **aber** heute Abend muss ich babysitten. *(I really like to go dancing, but this evening I have to babysit.)*

(17) Wird es am Wochenende sonnig **oder** regnerisch sein? (*Is it going to be sunny or rainy this weekend?*)

(18) Claudia hat **nicht nur** zwei Kajaks, **sondern auch** ein Segelboot. (*Claudia has not only two kayaks, but also a sailboat.*)

(19) Moritz ist ein fleißiger Student, **denn** er möchte Ingenieur werden. (*Moritz is a hard-working student because he wants to become an engineer.*) **Und** is possible here, too.

(20) Wir fahren nicht mit der U-Bahn nach Hause, **sondern** gehen zu Fuß. (*We're not taking the subway home, but rather [we're] walking.*)

(21) Ich komme nach Hause, **bevor** es dunkel wird. (*I'll come home before it gets dark.*)

(22) Es begann zu schneien, **als** ich heute nach Innsbruck fuhr. (*It began to snow as I was driving to Innsbruck today.*)

(23) Am Abend trinke ich nur ein einziges Glas Rotwein, **obwohl** ich Rotwein sehr mag. (*I drink only one glass of red wine in the evening although I really like red wine.*)

(24) Wir trinken einen Kaffee, **wenn** Peter kommt. (*We'll drink coffee when Peter comes.*)

(25) Ich fahre morgen früh nach Bremen, **damit** ich alles erledigen kann. (*I'm driving to Bremen early tomorrow morning so that I can get everything done.*)

(26) Ich arbeite gern, **weil** mir meine Arbeit Spaß macht. (*I like to work because I enjoy my job/my job is fun.*)

(27) Niemand weiss, **ob** Marcel am Donnerstag kommt. (*No one knows whether Marcel is coming on Thursday.*)

(28) Ich möchte wissen, **ob** du mich liebst. (*I would like to know if you love me.*)

(29) Ich möchte, **dass** du morgen mit mir kommst. (*I'd like you to come with me tomorrow.*) The word order is correct.

(30) **Obwohl** die Fahrpreise sehr hoch sind, **möchte ich mit dem Zug durch die Schweiz reisen.** (*Although the ticket prices are high, I'd like to travel through Switzerland.*) **Möchte** is in the second position after the subordinate clause, all of which is one unit of information.

(31) Die Fähre konnte am Vormittag nicht zur Insel fahren, **weil** das Wetter zu stürmisch war. (*The ferry couldn't go to the island in the morning because the weather was too stormy.*) The word order is correct.

(32) **Wenn** das schlechte Wetter anhält, **müssen wir den Urlaub abbrechen.** (*If the bad weather persists, we'll have to cut our vacation short.*) The subordinate clause **Wenn das schlechte Wetter anhält** is in first position, followed by the conjugated verb **müssen** in second position.

(33) Johanna und Anja sind gestern zu Fuß in den Biergarten gegangen, **da** sie ihre Freunde dort treffen wollten. (*Johanna and Anja walked to the beer garden yesterday, since [because] they wanted to meet their friends there.*) The word order is correct. The conjugated verb **wollten** follows the infinitive verb **treffen.**

(34) Erst **als** sie dort waren, **hat es angefangen zu regnen.** (*Just as they got there, it started to rain.*) In the main clause, the conjugated verb **hat** is the second position placeholder following the subordinate clause **Erst als sie dort waren.**

(35) Es ist nicht gut, **dass du allein bist.** (*It's not good that you're alone.*) Put the verb at the end of the subordinate clause.

Chapter **13**

Your Preposition Primer

What's in a preposition? **Zwischen** *(between)* by any other name would sound as strange. A preposition is a small word that shows the relationship between its object (a noun) and another word or words in the sentence. It's part of a *prepositional phrase*, which starts with a preposition and has an article, a noun, and (sometimes) other words as well.

You find out how crucially important these little guys are in expressing such things as

>> Place/where something is located, as with **in** *(in)*: **es gibt eine Fliege in meiner Suppe** *(there's a fly in my soup)*.

>> Movement/the direction where something is going, as with **unter** *(under)*: **eine Maus läuft unter meinen Stuhl** *(a mouse is running under my chair)*.

>> Information showing relationships, as with **trotz** *(in spite of)*: **trotz dieser Überraschungen, schmeckt mir das Essen** *(in spite of these surprises, the food tastes good)*.

In this chapter, I break down German prepositions into four groups: accusative, dative, genitive, and accusative/dative prepositions. The latter group are what I call the *two-timers* because they can be either accusative or dative. I give an easy and logical explanation for these wise guys in the section pertaining to them. One more section of this chapter deals with preposition combinations, the fixed expressions such as **zu Hause** *(at home)* and **nach Hause** *(to home [going home])*.

Prepping for Prepositions: Basic Guidelines

Prepositions, such as around, before, and *with*, combine with other words to form prepositional phrases that provide information on where *(around the corner)*, when *(before noon)*, who *(with you)* and much more. Prepositions perform incredible tasks when they combine with other words to create a diverse range of expressions. But all those possibilities come at a price. Prepositions are finicky little critters, much more so in German than in English. They abide by grammar rules which — for German, at least — means they force you as the speaker/writer to pay attention to case. So how in the world do you get to feel even remotely comfortable with understanding, let alone using, German prepositions with the right case? For a start, take a look at these guidelines.

Getting the importance of case

DIFFERENCES

In German, case is one key to perfecting the fine art of prepositioning. Both English and German have many prepositions, and both languages use prepositions in similar ways. But English doesn't have much truck with cases and case endings. In fact, if you bring up the subject of case in English grammar, some people may tell you to go home, lie down for a while, and forget all about it. But case is hugely important to getting a grip on using German prepositions correctly in a prepositional phrase.

REMEMBER

As with other German words — nouns, adjectives, and verbs, for example — prepositions need to be understood together with the other trappings of language. A lowly two-letter preposition like **in** *(in, into, to)* has so much power that it forces the rest of the prepositional phrase — the noun and other words following the preposition — to take the same case endings. The preposition doesn't change; it "tells" the others to conform; in other words, it forces the prepositional phrase as a whole to follow the case of that preposition. The result is that the case endings in the prepositional phrase help you (a) recognize the links between the preposition and the words in the phrase and (b) understand the prepositional phrase in context of the whole sentence.

The three cases that prepositions identify with are accusative, dative, and genitive. Some prepositions are two-timers: They may use accusative or dative case, depending on meaning. The following examples show all four groups of prepositions. (Chapter 3 deals with the basics of case.)

>> Accusative preposition **durch: Mein Hund Bello läuft gern durch den Wald.** *(My dog Bello likes to run through the woods.)* The prepositional phrase is **durch den Wald** *(through the woods)*. **Der Wald** in accusative case is **den Wald.**

>> Dative preposition **mit: Ich laufe gern mit ihm (Bello).** *(I like to run with him.)* The phrase is **mit ihm** *(with him)*. **Ihm** is the dative case form of the personal pronoun **er.**

>> Genitive preposition **während: Während des Winters bleiben Bello und ich oft zu Hause.** *(During the winter, Bello and I often stay at home.)* The phrase is **während des Winters** *(during the winter)*. Because **während** is a genitive preposition, **der Winter** in nominative case changes to **des Winters** in genitive case.

>> Accusative/dative preposition **auf: Meistens liege ich allein auf der Couch, aber manchmal springt Bello auf die Couch.** *(I usually lie on the couch alone, but sometimes he jumps onto the couch.)* **Auf der Couch** *(on the couch)* is dative case; **auf die Couch** *(onto the couch)* is accusative case. The first denotes place, and the second describes movement.

Check out the section "Accusative, Dative, and Genitive Cases: How the Rest of the Phrase Shapes Up" for a complete discussion of case and why case is important when using prepositions.

Understanding what it all means

Meaning is another key to success with German prepositions. Know that the rules of mathematics don't apply here; the prepositions and their English counterparts aren't always equal. The preposition **in** looks like the English preposition *in*. Indeed, you can use it the same way in both languages: **Wie viele Fernseher haben Sie in Ihrem Haus?** *(How many TVs do you have in your house?)* But it can also mean *into* or *to*. Another preposition, **bei**, sounds like *by* but has a variety of meanings, including *at, near,* and *with:* **Bei mir gibt es keine Glotzen** *(There aren't any idiot boxes at my place).*

 WARNING Prepositions crop up in places you'd never suspect, and they take on new meaning in combinations with other words that can be surprising. It may be easy to assume there's a parallel in meaning between some German prepositions that resemble English prepositions, either in spelling or pronunciation, or both. You need to be very careful, because one preposition may have several different meanings. Often, these meanings don't parallel the way the preposition is used in English.

 TIP Know one or two common phrases or words that combine with each preposition to get a feeling for the various meanings a preposition may have. The trick to taming these beasties is remembering them in commonly used phrases, fixed idioms, or standard prepositional phrases — not all alone and naked.

Accusative, Dative, and Genitive Cases: How the Rest of the Phrase Shapes Up

When you use prepositions in your German, you want to use them correctly, right? If so (and I hope you said yes), this section is key. It explains the role that cases play in using prepositions. So exactly what is case? *Case* is like a marker — a tag or an ID for a word. It shows the word's role in relationship to other words in the sentence. There are three groups of prepositions, organized by the case that they need to form phrases. These three cases are accusative, dative, and genitive. Having said that, by far the most frequently used group of prepositions is yet another group, namely those that use both accusative and dative cases (fondly called the two-way prepositions). For that reason, I deal with them in a separate section later in this chapter.

 REMEMBER As you go through this section, keep in mind that prepositions pop up everywhere in German (and English for that matter). It's definitely worth your while to be patient and master the cases one by one. In addition, keep in mind that the context of the phrase influences the meaning of the preposition. **Nach,** for example, can mean three things in English: *after, past,* or *to.* Yet **nach dem Weg fragen** *(to ask for directions)* doesn't even translate using one of those three prepositions.

No finger-pointing: Accusative prepositions

Accusative prepositions express movement, opposition to something, and acts of excluding or receiving. The small band of accusative prepositions includes **bis, durch, für, gegen, ohne,** and **um.** These prepositions are strictly linked to the accusative case. Look at Table 13-1 for a list of these prepositions, their English equivalents, and a sample phrase or two.

Table 13-1   Accusative Prepositions

Preposition	English Equivalent(s)	Sample German Phrases	Equivalent English Phrases
bis	*till, until* (also: conjunction *until*)	**bis nächsten Sonntag**	*until next Sunday*
durch	*through, by*	**durch die Stadt (jemanden) durch einen Freund kennenlernen**	*through the city meet (someone) through a friend*
für	*for*	**für Sie** **für meine Freunde**	*for you* *for my friends*
gegen	*against, for*	**gegen die Regeln** **etwas gegen Kopfschmerzen nehmen**	*against the rules* *take something for a headache*
ohne	*without*	**ohne mich** **ohne Herrn Adler**	*without me* *without Herr Adler*
um	*around, for, at*	**um das Haus** **Ich bewerbe mich um die Stelle.**	*around the house* *I'm applying for the job.*

TIP

To form phrases with accusative prepositions, start with the preposition and add the information that the preposition is linking to the rest of the sentence: the preposition's object (noun) and any modifiers. If necessary, change the endings of any articles, pronouns, adjectives, and nouns following the preposition to the accusative case. The following outlines what needs to change:

>> Some definite articles change. The definite articles are easy because the only change is **der ⇨ den. Die** (feminine and plural) and **das** don't change. (See Chapter 3 for definite articles.)

>> The accusative prepositions build some contractions:

- **durch + das = durchs**

- **für + das = fürs**

- **um + das = ums**

In spoken, colloquial German, these contractions are very common.

>> Most of the pronouns change. The personal pronouns in accusative (direct-object) case are **mich** *(me),* **dich** *(you),* **ihn/sie/es** *(him/her/it),* **uns** *(us),* **euch** *(you),* **sie** *(them),* and **Sie** *(you).*

>> Adjectives may not undergo an ending change. (See Chapter 10 for adjectives.)

>> A few nouns undergo an ending change. (See Chapter 3 for more on nouns.)

Sammy das Stinktier sitzt ganz allein, ohne seine Freunde. *(Sammy the skunk is sitting all alone without his friends.)* The preposition **ohne** is followed by **seine Freunde;** both words have accusative plural endings.

Dann läuft er durch den Garten der Familie Finkenhuber. *(Then he runs through the Finkenhuber's garden.)* The preposition **durch** *(through* in this context) indicates movement. **Den Garten** is the masculine singular form of **der Garten** in the accusative case.

Sammy läuft um den Hund Bello und . . . psst! *(Sammy runs around Bello the dog and . . . psst!)* The preposition **um** *(around)* indicates movement. **Den Hund** is the masculine singular form of **der Hund** in the accusative case.

PRACTICE

In this exercise, use Table 13-1 to help you write the phrases in German. Some vocabulary is indicated in parentheses. Remember to change the articles, pronouns, adjectives, and nouns following the prepositions — if necessary.

Q. for you (singular, familiar) _____

A. **für dich**

1. around the garage (die Garage) _____

2. through the woods (der Wald) _____

3. for him _____

4. until tomorrow _____

5. against the law (das Gesetz) _____

6. for my boss (der Chef) _____

7. without me _____

8. take something for a stomachache (Bauchschmerzen)_____

9. around the village (das Dorf) _____

10. for us _____

11. until next Wednesday _____

12. without Mr. Holzhacker _____

13. through the city _____

Dative prepositions

Dative prepositions include some heavy hitters. Most dative prepositions express relationships of time (when), motion (where to), and location (where). Some have surprising variations in meaning. Eight are on the hit list: **aus, außer, bei, mit, nach, seit, von,** and **zu.** These particular prepositions have an exclusivity clause with the dative case. Table 13-2 shows the eight dative prepositions, their English equivalents, and some sample phrases for each.

Table 13-2 Dative Prepositions

Preposition	English Equivalent(s)	Sample German Phrases	Equivalent English Phrases
aus	*from, out of*	**aus den USA** **aus der Flasche**	*from the U.S.A.* *out of the bottle*
außer	*besides, except for*	**außer uns** **außer den Kindern**	*besides/except for us except for the children*
bei	*at* (a home of, a place of business), *near, with*	**bei Katharina** **bei der Straße** **Es ist anders bei mir**	*at Katherina's (place)* *near the street* *It's different with me.*
mit	*with, by* (means of transportation)	**Mit dem Hund** **mit dem Zug**	*with the dog* *by train*
nach	*after, past, to*	**nach einer Stunde** **Es ist fünf nach vier nach Paris** (no article for cities and countries in German)	*after an hour* *to Paris*
seit	*for, since*	**seit zwanzig Jahren** **seit dem Krieg**	*for 20 years since the war*
von	*by, from, of*	**von einem deutschen Maler** **ein Geschenk von dir** **am Ende vom Film**	*by a German artist* (created by someone) *a present from you* *at the end of the movie*
zu	**to** (with people and certain places)	**zur Universität** **Was gibt's zum Abendessen?**	*to the university* *What's for dinner?*

TIP

To form phrases with dative prepositions, start with the preposition and add the information that the preposition connects to the rest of the sentence (the object of the preposition and any articles or adverbs that modify it). Change the endings of any articles, pronouns, adjectives, and nouns following the prepositions — if necessary — to the dative case. The following list outlines what needs to change:

>> The definite articles change like this (see Chapter 3 for definite articles):

  der ⇨ dem

  die ⇨ der (feminine)

  das ⇨ dem

  die ⇨ den (plural)

Note: Not all prepositional phrases need an article (**dem, einen,** and so on) with the noun; these are generally fixed expressions such as clock times (**es ist Viertel nach acht** *[it's quarter past eight]*) or other types (**zu Hause** *[at home]* and **nach Hause** *[going home]*).

Zu Hause and **nach Hause** are two prepositional phrases that are often confused. **Zu Hause** means *at home.* It indicates location. **Nach Hause** means *going home.* It implies movement — motion in the direction of home.

> **Wo ist Birgit? Sie ist zu Hause.** *(Where's Birgit? She's at home.)*

> **Wohin geht Lars? Er geht nach Hause.** *(Where is Lars going? He's going home.)*

>> The contractions that dative prepositions build are

> **bei + dem = beim**

> **von + dem = vom**

> **zu + dem = zum**

> **zu + der = zur**

In spoken, colloquial German, these contractions are very common.

>> All the pronouns change. The personal pronouns in dative case are **mir** *(me)*, **dir** *(you,* **ihm/ ihr/ihm** *(him/her/it)*, **uns** *(us)*, **euch** *(you)*, **ihnen** *(them,* and **Ihnen** *(you)*. (See Chapter 3 for pronouns.)

>> Adjectives may not undergo an ending change. (See Chapter 10 for adjectives.)

>> A few nouns undergo an ending change. (See Chapter 3 for more on nouns.)

Essen wir heute Abend bei dir? *(Shall we have dinner at your place tonight?)* **Bei** is a true chameleon as far as variations in meanings goes. Here, take **bei**, add the dative pronoun **dir**, and presto! — **bei dir** = *at your place.*

Nein, ich möchte lieber zum Restaurant um die Ecke gehen. *(No, I'd rather go to the restaurant around the corner.)* The contraction of **zu + dem = zum.**

Luigis? Es ist seit einem Monat geschlossen. *(Luigi's? It's been closed for a month.)*

Wichtig ist nur, ich esse mit dir. *(It's only important that I eat with you.)*

This exercise is multiple-choice. Decide which of the three prepositions fits into the phrase or sentence, write it in the space, and then translate the sentence into English. Use Table 13-2 to help.

PRACTICE

Q. Was machen wir _____ diesem perfekten Tag? (a) seit (b) nach (c) zum

A. (b) **nach. Was machen wir** <u>nach</u> **diesem perfekten Tag?** *(What shall we do after this perfect day?)*

 Ich möchte allein _____ Strand gehen. (a) mit (b) bis (c) zu

_____

15 Ich möchte _____ dir sein. (a) zu (b) bei (c) aus

_____

16 _____ drei Jahren sagst du das. (a) mit (b) außer (c) seit

_____

17 Und _____ mir hast du noch eine Freundin. (a) außer (b) bei (c) zu

_____

18 Nein, _____ Lisa habe ich keine Beziehung. (a) zu (b) nach (c) mit

_____

19 _____ einer Stunde habe ich Kopfweh. (a) von (b) aus (c) seit

_____

20 Ich möchte _____ Hause gehen. (a) zu (b) bei (c) nach

_____

21 _____ mir ist es sehr gemütlich. (a) bei (b) nach (c) aus

_____

22 Warum? Es ist erst Viertel _____ neun. (a) von (b) nach (c) mit

_____

23 Ach, ich weiß, du kommst _____ einem anderen Planeten. (a) bei (b) von (c) mit

_____

24 Gut. Dann fliegen wir _____ deinem Planeten. (a) zu (b) nach (c) von

_____

25 _____ diesem Tag hört man . . . (a) von (b) mit (c) seit

_____

26 . . . nichts mehr _____ den beiden (the two [of them]). (a) zu (b) von (c) aus

_____

Genitive prepositions

The list of genitive prepositions is small, but these types are used almost as frequently as the others in this chapter. These particular prepositions describe duration of time, reasons for something, or opposition to something. Most of these expressions are equivalent to English expressions that include *of*: *instead of*, *because of*, and *inside* or *outside of*. The list includes **anstatt/statt, außerhalb, innerhalb, trotz, während,** and **wegen**. A few other genitive prepositions exist, but they're used less frequently.

REMEMBER

Especially in spoken German, but also in written German, it's common to use the dative personal pronouns with genitive prepositions, as in **wegen mir** *(because of me)* or **statt dir** *(instead of you)*. The list of genitive-type prepositions in Table 13-3 is short but powerful in expression and variations of usage. The table shows the six most common genitive prepositions, their English equivalents, and sample phrases.

Table 13-3   Genitive Prepositions

Preposition	English Equivalent(s)	Sample German Phrases	Equivalent English Phrases
(an)statt (no difference between **anstatt** and **statt**)	*instead of*	**(an)statt meines Autos**	*instead of my car*
außerhalb	*outside of*	**außerhalb des Hauses**	*outside of the house*
innerhalb	*inside of*	**innerhalb der Firma**	*within the company*
trotz	*in spite of, despite*	**trotz des Wetters** **trotz des Lärms**	*despite the weather* *in spite of the noise*
während	*during*	**während des Tages**	*during the day*
wegen	*because of, on account of*	**wegen der Kosten wegen mir**	*on account of the costs* *because of me*

TIP

To form genitive prepositional phrases, begin with the preposition and then add the information that the preposition links to the rest of the sentence. You need to change the endings of any articles, pronouns, adjectives, and nouns following the prepositions — if necessary — so that they're also in the genitive case. (See Chapter 3 for cases.)

Wegen der Hitze gehen wir nicht spazieren. *(We're not going for a walk because of the heat.)* **Die Hitze** in nominative case becomes **der Hitze** in genitive case.

Während des Winters bleiben wir meistens zu Hause. *(We usually stay at home during the winter.)* **Der Winter** in nominative case becomes **des Winters** in genitive case.

Note: In spoken German, some genitive prepositions — **anstatt/statt, trotz, wegen,** and **während** — are typically used with the dative case. This is especially true in the south and southwest German-speaking regions: **Bayern, Österreich, und die Schweiz** *(Bavaria, Austria, and Switzerland).* **Während** uses dative case less frequently in colloquial German than the other three. The meaning of these prepositions doesn't change when you use dative case.

In this exercise, fill in the spaces, using the prepositions in Table 13-3. Two tourists staying at a **Salzburger Pension** (*bed-and-breakfast*) are talking **während des Frühstücks** (*during breakfast*).

Q. _____ des Lärms ist diese Pension wunderbar, oder?

A. <u>Trotz</u> **des Lärms ist diese Pension wunderbar, oder?** (*Despite the noise, this pension is wonderful, isn't it?*)

27 Ja, _____ der Nacht habe ich sehr gut geschlafen.

28 Ich bin _____ fünf Minuten eingeschlafen.

29 Mmm. Heute trinke ich Kaffee _____ Tee.

30 Ich auch, aber _____ des Koffeins trinke ich nur eine Tasse.

31 Fahren wir heute _____ der Stadt? Ich möchte die Berge sehen.

32 Du, ich bin sehr müde. Heute bleibe ich _____ der vier Wänden meines Zimmers.

33 Wirklich? _____ des schönen Wetters?

34 Mach dir keine Sorgen _____ mir.

35 _____ des Nachmittags kann ich auf dem Balkon sitzen und relaxen.

Tackling Two-Way Prepositions: Accusative/Dative

The nine prepositions in this section are the types that can use either accusative or dative case, depending on meaning. The preposition in the accusative case describes movement, whereas the dative case describes position. Another way to tell them apart is by knowing that the preposition uses the accusative case to show a change of location, and it answers the question **wohin?** (*where to?*). The same preposition uses the dative case to refer to a location; the dative preposition answers the question **wo?** (*where?*).

English sometimes has two different prepositions that do the work of one German two-way preposition. Take *in* and *into*. *In* expresses where something is, and *into* refers to the movement from one place *into* the other. The German preposition **in** can use either accusative or dative case, depending on whether it expresses position (location) or movement (from one location to another).

TIP

To determine whether you need to use the preposition in accusative or dative case, visualize what you want to say. These prepositions indicate concrete spatial relationships, not intangible concepts, which makes it simple to imagine the difference between a cat lying *on* the table — **eine Katze liegt auf dem Tisch** (location = dative case) — and a cat jumping *onto* the table — **eine Katze springt auf den Tisch** (movement = accusative case).

Table 13-4 shows the two-way prepositions, their English equivalents, and a sample phrase for each with the English translation.

Table 13-4   Two-Way Prepositions

Preposition	English Equivalent(s)	Accusative Example	Dative Example
an	*at, on, to*	**Die Katze geht ans (an + das) Fenster.** *(The cat walks to the window.)*	**Die Katze sitzt am Fenster.** *(The cat is sitting at the window.)*
auf	*on, onto, to*	**Die Katze springt auf den Tisch.** *(The cat jumps onto the table.)*	**Die Katze steht auf dem Tisch.** *(The cat is standing on the table.)*
hinter	*behind, to*	**Die Katze geht hinter die Couch.** *(The cat is going behind the couch.)*	**Die Katze sitzt hinter der Couch.** *(The cat is sitting behind the couch.)*
in	*in, into, to*	**Die Katze läuft in die Küche.** *(The cat is running into the kitchen.)*	**Die Katze ist in der Küche.** *(The cat is in the kitchen.)*
neben	*beside,*	**Der Hund legt sich neben die Katze hin.** *(The dog lays itself down next to the cat.)*	**Die Katze liegt neben dem Hund.** *(The cat is lying next to the dog.)*
über	*above, over*	**Eine Maus läuft über den Teppich.** *(A mouse is running over the carpet.)*	**Eine Lampe hängt über dem Tisch.** *(A lamp is hanging over the table.)*
unter	*under,*	**Die Maus läuft unter den Teppich.** *(The mouse runs under the carpet.)*	**Der Teppich liegt unter dem Tisch.** *(The carpet is lying under the table.)*
vor	*in front of*	**Die Maus läuft vor die Katze.** *(The mouse is running in front of the cat.)*	**Der Hund sitzt vor dem Fernseher.** *(The dog is sitting in front of the TV.)*
zwischen	*between*	**Die Katze legt sich zwischen die Pfoten des Hundes.** *(The cat lies down between the dog's paws.)*	**Der Hund steht zwischen der Maus und der Katze.** *(The dog is standing between the mouse and the cat.)*

REMEMBER

There's no present continuous in German, so present tense *(the mouse runs)*, present continuous *(the mouse is running)*, or both may be logical translations.

To form phrases with accusative/dative prepositions, follow the guidelines I describe in the previous two sections for accusative prepositions and dative prepositions. Some two-way prepositions combine with articles to make contractions. These are mostly used in spoken, colloquial German:

>> **an** + **das** = **ans**

>> **an** + **dem** = **am**

>> **auf** + **das** = **aufs**

>> **in** + **das** = **ins**

>> **in** + **dem** = **im**

Other contractions that aren't as frequently used as contractions with **das** and **dem** include **hinters, hinterm, übers, überm, unters, unterm, vors,** and **vorm.**

The following examples clarify how to form and use these prepositions correctly:

Die Kinder sind im Bett. (The children are in bed.) The preposition **in** (here, it means *in*) uses dative case here to express location. Where are the children? In bed.

Die Kinder gehen ins Bett. *(The children are going to bed.)* The preposition **in** (here, it means *into*) uses accusative case to express movement. Where are the children going? To bed.

Ich wohne über einer Buchhandlung. (I live above a bookstore.) The preposition **über** *(over)* describes where it is. *Where* describes location; it takes the dative case.

Der Zeppelin fliegt über die Stadt. *(The zeppelin [blimp] is flying over the city.)* The preposition **über** *(over)* describes movement; it's in the accusative case.

PRACTICE

In this exercise, decide whether to insert the accusative or the dative prepositional phrase, and write it in the space provided.

Q. Ich schwimme gern _____. (im Meer/ins Meer)

A. Ich schwimme gern <u>im Meer</u>. *(I like to swim in the ocean.)* You swim in the water when you're already in it, so you need the dative prepositional phrase here.

36 Marco sitzt _____. (ans Fenster/am Fenster)

37 Alexandra arbeitet _____. (auf der Bank/auf die Bank)

38 Gehen wir _____? (ins Restaurant/im Restaurant)

39 Die Autos fahren schnell _____. (über der Brücke/über die Brücke)

40 Stellen Sie bitte ihre Schuhe _____. (unter den Sessel/unter dem Sessel)

41 Das Flugzeug fliegt _____. (zwischen die Bergen/zwischen den Bergen)

42 Ich wohne _____. (neben einer Kirche/neben eine Kirche)

43 Unsere Katze legt Mäuse _____. (vor der Tür/vor die Tür)

44 Komm doch _____. (im Bett/ins Bett)

45 Es gibt eine große Spinne *(spider)* _____. (in mein Wohnzimmer/in meinem Wohnzimmer)

46 Jetzt läuft sie _____. (hinter den Bücherschrank [*bookcase*]/hinter dem [hinterm] Bücherschrank)

Answers to "Your Preposition Primer" Practice Questions

1. **um die Garage.** No change necessary here. Only der changes to den in accusative.

2. **durch den Wald.** Der changes to den; der Wald is singular.

3. **für ihn. Ihn** is the accusative form of the personal pronoun **er** (he).

4. **bis morgen.**

5. **gegen das Gesetz.**

6. **für meinen Chef. Meinen** is the masculine, singular, accusative form of **mein**.

7. **ohne mich. Mich** is the accusative form of the personal pronoun **ich** (I).

8. **etwas gegen Bauchschmerzen nehmen.** You don't need the definite article here; you're talking about the pain in general.

9. **um das Dorf.** The contraction form of um + **das** is **ums**.

10. **für uns. Uns** (us) is the accusative form of the personal pronoun **wir** (we).

11. **bis nächsten Mittwoch.** Days of the week are masculine; the modifier **nächsten** is in the accusative case.

12. **ohne Herrn Holzhacker.** Remember the **n** at the end of **Herr**. **Herrn** is the accusative singular masculine form of **Herr**.

13. **durch die Stadt.**

14. **(c) zu. Ich möchte allein zum Strand gehen.** (*I'd like to go to the beach alone.*) The contraction zum is a combination of **zu** + **dem**.

15. **(b) bei. Ich möchte bei dir sein.** (*I'd like to be with you/at your place.*) **Bei dir se**in indicates where; it's the location. With **zu dir,** you'd need **gehen** (go to your place).

16. **(c) seit. Seit drei Jahren sagst du das.** (*You've been saying that for three years.*) In German, the present tense is used with **seit**.

17. **(a) außer. Und außer mir hast du noch eine Freundin.** (*And besides me, you have another girlfriend.*) Notice the word order. The verb hast is in second position after **außer mir**; the subject **du** (you) follows the verb.

18. **(c) mit. Nein, mit Lisa habe ich keine Beziehung.** (*No, I don't have a relationship with Lisa.*)

19. **(c) seit. Seit einer Stunde habe ich Kopfweh.** (*I've had a headache for an hour.*)

20. **(b) nach. Ich möchte nach Hause gehen.** (*I'd like to go home.*) **Nach Hause** implies movement, motion in the direction of home.

21. **(a) bei. Bei mir ist es sehr gemütlich.** (*It's very cozy at my place.*) **Bei mir** indicates where; it's the location.

22. **(b) nach. Warum? Es ist erst Viertel nach neun.** (*Why? It's only quarter past nine.*) No article is needed with this clock-time expression.

(23) **(b) von. Ach, ich weiß, du kommst von einem anderen Planeten.** (*Oh, I know. You come from another planet.*)

(24) **(a) zu. Gut. Dann fliegen wir zu deinem Planeten. (***Good. Then let's fly to your planet.***)

(25) **(c) seit. Seit diesem Tag hört man . . .** (*Since that day, one hears . . .*) **Man** can be translated as *one*, *you*, or *people*.

(26) **(b) von . . . nichts mehr von den beiden**. (*nothing more from the two [of them].*) Literally, **von den beiden** means *from the both*.

(27) **Ja, während der Nacht habe ich sehr gut geschlafen.** (*Yes, I slept very well during the night.*) The genitive case of **die (Nacht)** is **der.**

(28) **Ich bin innerhalb fünf Minuten eingeschlafen.** (*I fell asleep within five minutes.*) No article is necessary with this clock-time expression.

(29) **Mmm. Heute trinke ich Kaffee statt Tee.** (*Mmm. Today I'll have coffee instead of tea.*) No article needed here with **Tee.**

(30) **Ich auch, aber wegen des Koffeins trinke ich nur eine Tasse.** (*Me too, but because of the caffeine, I'll drink only one cup.*) Salzburg is world-famous for its "Kaffee Kultur," as is Vienna.

(31) **Fahren wir heute außerhalb der Stadt? Ich möchte die Berge sehen.** (*Shall we drive outside of the city today? I'd like to see the mountains.*)

(32) **Du, ich bin sehr müde. Heute bleibe ich innerhalb der vier Wänden meines Zimmers.** (*You know, I'm really tired. Today I'm staying within the four walls of my room.*)

(33) **Wirklich? Trotz des schönen Wetters?** (*Really? Despite the nice weather?*)

(34) **Mach dir keine Sorgen wegen mir.** (*Don't worry about me.*)

(35) **Während des Nachmittags kann ich auf dem Balkon sitzen und relaxen.** (*During the afternoon I can sit on the balcony and relax.*)

(36) **Marco sitzt am Fenster.** (*Marco is sitting at the window.*) **Wo?** (*Where's Marco? At the window.*) Dative case is used here.

(37) **Alexandra arbeitet nicht mehr auf der Bank.** (*Alexandra doesn't work at the bank anymore.*) The fixed expression for place of work is in dative case.

(38) **Gehen wir ins Restaurant?** (*Shall we go to a restaurant?*) **Wohin?** Movement indicates accusative case.

(39) **Die Autos fahren schnell über die Brücke.** (*The cars are driving fast over/across the bridge.*) Wohin? The cars are moving, so you need accusative case.

(40) **Stellen Sie bitte ihre Schuhe unter den Sessel.** (*Please put your shoes under the armchair.*) **Wohin?** Moving your shoes means you need the accusative.

(41) **Das Flugzeug fliegt zwischen die Berge.** (*The plane is flying between the mountains.*) Wohin? Flying is definitely movement: accusative case.

(42) **Ich wohne neben einer Kirche.** (*I live next to a church.*) **Wo?** (*Where do you live?*) Location means dative case.

43 **Unsere Katze legt Mäuse vor die Tür.** (*Our cat lays mice in front of the door.*) **Wohin?** (The mice are being placed in front of the door.)

44 **Komm doch ins Bett.** (*Please come to bed.*) **Wohin?** (*To bed.*) **Im Bett** would mean you're already in bed.

45 **Es gibt eine große Spinne in meinem Wohnzimmer.** (*There's a big spider in my living room.*) **Wo?** Location, so it's dative case.

46 **Jetzt läuft sie hinter den Bücherschrank.** (*Now it's running behind the bookcase.*) **Wohin?** Running is movement; that means accusative case.

4

Looking Back and Ahead: Talking about the Past and the Future

Chapter **14**

Conversing about the Past: Perfecting the Present Perfect

resent perfect in German is commonly described as the *conversational past* because — naturally — you use it in conversation. You also typically see present perfect in informal writing such as personal letters and emails. German uses the present perfect to talk about all actions or states in the past, finished or unfinished. English, on the other hand, tends to use the present perfect for actions that began in the past but have a link to the present.

The present perfect in German has two elements:

>> An auxiliary verb, also known as a *helping* verb. (English present perfect uses *have*.)

>> A past participle. (English examples are *gone, been,* and *known*.)

The two auxiliary verbs are **haben** (*to have*) and **sein** (*to be*). First, you conjugate the auxiliary in the present tense, and then you add the past participle of the verb (**gelebt** [*lived*]; **gewesen** [*been*]; **geschwommen** [*swum*]). Now comes the fun part: you kick the past participle to the end of the sentence or clause.

This chapter shows you how to form and use the present perfect in German and explains how the present perfect differs between German and English. You also get ample opportunities to practice the present perfect in German.

Forming the Present Perfect with Haben

The majority of verbs form the present perfect with the auxiliary verb **haben** (to have) plus the past participle of the verb you want to use. There are two main categories of verbs, classified by the way the past participle is formed. They're called *weak* and *strong* verbs. (Don't worry — you don't have to go to the gym to find the strong verbs!) Check out the next three sections for more information on weak and strong verbs.

To conjugate a verb in the present perfect with **haben**, you choose the simple present-tense form of haben: **ich habe, du hast, er/sie/es hat, wir haben, ihr habt, sie haben,** or **Sie haben.** Then you add the past participle of the verb. Check out the following example of **wohnen** (to live, reside) in the present perfect.

wohnen (to live)	
ich **habe gewohnt**	wir **haben gewohnt**
du **hast gewohnt**	ihr **habt gewohnt**
er/sie/es **hat gewohnt**	sie **haben gewohnt**
Sie **haben gewohnt**	

Here is the present perfect of **wohnen** in action:

Ich habe ein Jahr in Paris gewohnt. (I have lived/lived in Paris for a year.)

German word order follows specific rules. When you form a sentence with two verbs, the conjugated verb, (**haben** [to have], **sein** [to be], **werden** [will], **möchten** [would like], and so on) takes second position in the sentence, and you push the past participle to the end of the sentence. (See Chapter 1 for more info on word order.)

Forming the present perfect with regular weak verbs

Regular weak verbs are the largest group of verbs. To form the past participle, take the unchanged present-tense stem, which you form by taking off the **-en** from the infinitive of the verb, and then adding the **ge-** prefix and the ending **-t** or **-et**. You need the -et ending in the following cases:

>> For verbs whose stem ends in **-d** or **-t: heiraten** (to marry) becomes **geheiratet** (married), and **reden** (to talk, speak) becomes **geredet** (talked, spoken).

>> For some verbs whose stem ends in **-m** or **-n: regnen** (to rain) becomes **geregnet** (rained), and **atmen** (to breathe) becomes **geatmet** (breathed).

The verbs ending in **-ieren,** however, such as **interpretieren** *(to interpret),* which changes to **interpretiert** *(interpreted)* — don't add the prefix **ge-.**

So with the verb **arbeiten** *(to work),* you conjugate **haben** in the appropriate person and then add the past participle. To create the past participle, you chop off the ending **-en,** take the stem **arbeit,** and add **ge-** and **-et** like this: **ge-** + **arbeit b -et = gearbeitet.**

arbeiten *(to work)*	
ich **habe gearbeitet**	wir **haben gearbeitet**
du **hast gearbeitet**	ihr **habt gearbeitet**
er/sie/es **hat gearbeitet**	sie **haben gearbeitet**
Sie **haben gearbeitet**	

Here's how **arbeiten** would work in the present perfect tense:

> **Sie hat im Herbst bei der Filmgesellschaft gearbeitet.** *(She worked at the film company in the fall.)*

Table 14-1 shows some regular weak verbs with the German and English infinitives, followed by the German and English past participles.

Table 14-1   Past Participles of Regular Weak Verbs

Infinitive	Past Participle	Infinitive	Past Participle
arbeiten *(to work)*	**gearbeitet** *(worked)*	**lieben** *(to love)*	**geliebt** *(loved)*
drucken *(to print)*	**gedruckt** *(printed)*	**lernen** *(to learn)*	**gelernt** *(learned)*
führen *(to lead)*	**geführt** *(led)*	**machen** *(to make)*	**gemacht** *(made)*
hören *(to hear)*	**gehört** *(heard)*	**passen** *(to fit)*	**gepasst** *(fit)*
hoffen *(to hope)*	**gehofft** *(hoped)*	**regnen** *(to rain)*	**geregnet** *(rained)*
kaufen *(to buy)*	**gekauft** *(bought)*	**sagen** *(to say)*	**gesagt** *(said)*
kosten *(to cost)*	**gekostet** *(cost)*	**schenken** *(to give [a present])*	**geschenkt** *(given)*
kriegen *(to get)*	**gekriegt** *(gotten/got)*	**spielen** *(to play)*	**gespielt** *(played)*
lächeln *(to smile)*	**gelächelt** *(smiled)*	**surfen** *(to surf)*	**gesurft** *(surfed)*
leben *(to live)*	**gelebt** *(lived)*	**tanzen** *(to dance)*	**getanzt** *(danced)*

PRACTICE

Got the hang of creating the past participle? Fill in the blank with the corresponding correct answer. The first word is the infinitive. Next is the past participle.

Infinitive/Meaning   *Past Participle/Meaning*

Q. **fragen** *(to ask)* (_____)   _____

A. **fragen** *(to ask)*   **gefragt** *(asked)*

Infinitive/Meaning	Past Participle/Meaning

1 **brauchen** (to need) (_____) _____

2 **chatten** (to chat) (_____) _____

3 _____ (_____) **gefeiert** (celebrated)

4 **glauben** (to believe) (_____) _____

5 **jobben** (to do odd jobs) (_____) _____

6 _____ (_____) **gekocht** (cooked)

7 **schmecken** (to taste) (_____) _____

8 _____ (_____) **geschneit** (snowed)

9 **suchen** (to look for, search) (_____) _____

10 _____ (_____) **getötet** (killed)

11 **wohnen** (to live) (_____) _____

12 _____ (_____) **gezahlt** (paid)

PRACTICE

Try putting the verb **haben** and the past participle together to create the present perfect tense. (Don't worry — no boxing gloves are needed with those weakling verbs!) Refer to the previous section and Table 14-1 for help.

Q. Unser neues Auto _____ viel _____. (kosten)

A. Unser neues Auto <u>hat</u> viel <u>gekostet</u>. (Our new car cost a lot.)

13 Die Pommes frites mit Mayonnaise _____ sehr gut _____. (schmecken)

14 Warum _____ du gestern nicht _____? (arbeiten)

15 Wir _____ letzte Woche mit Nadal und Sampras Tennis _____. (spielen)

16 Mein Bruder _____ in der Schule Deutsch_____. (lernen)

17 Wann _____ du die Nachrichten _____? (hören)

18 Im Sommer _____ Johnny und Baby viel _____. (tanzen)

19 Die Eltern _____ nichts dazu _____. (sagen)

20 Wo _____ du den Laptop _____? (kaufen)

21 Es _____ nur einmal am Wochenende _____. (regnen)

22 Ich _____ meiner Freundin schöne Blumen zum Geburtstag _____. (schenken)

Forming the present perfect with irregular weak verbs

A very small number of weak verbs is irregular. What makes them irregular? They do have the prefix **ge-** and the ending **-t**, but they don't follow the same pattern as the regular weak verbs. The present-tense stem changes when you put it in the past participle. The good news is there aren't many of these rebels. The bad news: The only way to really identify them is to memorize these past participles, because they don't follow any recognizable pattern.

To form these irregular weak verbs in the present perfect, conjugate **haben** in the present tense and then add the past participle. Check out the following example with the verb **denken** (to think).

denken (to think)	
ich **habe gedacht**	wir **haben gedacht**
du **hast gedacht**	ihr **habt gedacht**
er/sie/es **hat gedacht**	sie **haben gedacht**
Sie **haben gedacht**	

Here's how **denken** would work in the present perfect tense:

> **Luka hat oft an seine Frau gedacht.** (Luka often thought about his wife.)

Table 14-2 shows irregular weak verbs with the German and English infinitives, followed by the German and English past participles.

Table 14-2   Past Participles of Irregular Weak Verbs

Infinitive	Past Participle
brennen (to burn)	**gebrannt** (burned)
bringen (to bring)	**gebracht** (brought)
denken (to think)	**gedacht** (thought)
kennen (to know a person)	**gekannt** (known a person)
nennen (to name, call)	**genannt** (named, called)
wissen (to know information)	**gewusst** (known information)

You can remember the past participles of the irregular weak verbs you use frequently by writing your own example sentences; then refer to them as needed.

Change the following sentences into the present perfect tense. Conjugate **haben** accordingly and add the appropriate past participle.

PRACTICE

Q. **Franz kennt ein sehr gutes Restaurant in Berlin.**

A. Franz <u>hat</u> ein sehr gutes Restaurant in Berlin <u>gekannt</u>. *(Franz knew a very good restaurant in Berlin.)*

 23 Das Holz brennt sehr schnell.

_____

 24 Wir bringen unsere Wanderschuhe *(hiking boots)*.

_____

 25 Ich weiß deine Emailadresse nicht. (Hint: **nicht** precedes the past participle.)

_____

 26 Der Verkäufer *(salesperson)* kennt die Produkte sehr gut.

_____

27 Die Kunden *(customers)* denken nur an den Preis.

_____

Forming the present perfect with strong verbs

With **strong verbs,** the past participle ends in **-en.** (The one exception is the verb **tun** *[to do]*; its past participle is **getan** *[done].*) In most strong verbs, the past participle begins with **ge-.** Many of these past participles can seem pesky at first. Why? They often have vowels and consonants that differ from those in the infinitive. I have good news, though: A lot of these verbs whose past participles go through such spelling contortions are high-frequency verbs. To form the present perfect with strong verbs, you conjugate **haben** in the appropriate person and then add the past participle.

trinken *(to drink)*	
ich **habe getrunken**	wir **haben getrunken**
du **hast getrunken**	ihr **habt getrunken**
er/sie/es **hat getrunken**	sie **haben getrunken**
Sie **haben getrunken**	

Here's how **trinken** would work in the present perfect tense:

Wir haben gestern viel Mineralwasser getrunken. (*We drank a lot of mineral water yesterday.*)

Table 14-3 shows some other strong verbs. I list the German verb with the English infinitive followed by the German past participle and its English translation.

Table 14-3   Past Participles of Strong Verbs

Infinitive	Past Participle	Infinitive	Past Participle
backen (*to bake*)	**gebacken** (*baked*)	**schreiben** (*to write*)	**geschrieben** (*written*)
beginnen (*to begin*)	**begonnen** (*begun*)	**singen** (*to sing*)	**gesungen** (*sung*)
essen (*to eat*)	**gegessen** (*eaten*)	**sitzen** (*to sit*)	**gesessen** (*sat*)
finden (*to find*)	**gefunden** (*found*)	**sprechen** (*to speak, talk*)	**gesprochen** (*spoken, talked*)
geben (*to give*)	**gegeben** (*given*)	**stehen** (*to stand*)	**gestanden** (*stood*)
halten (*to hold*)	**gehalten** (*held*)	**tragen** (*to wear*)	**getragen** (*worn*)
heißen (*to be called*)	**geheißen** (*been called*)	**treffen** (*to meet*)	**getroffen** (*met*)
helfen (*to help*)	**geholfen** (*helped*)	**trinken** (*to drink*)	**getrunken** (*drunk*)
lassen (*to leave, let*)	**gelassen** (*left, let*)	**tun** (*to do*)	**getan** (*done*)
lesen (*to read*)	**gelesen** (*read*)	**verlassen** (*to leave*)	**verlassen** (*leave*)
liegen (*to lie, be located*)	**gelegen** (*lain, been located*)	**verlieren** (*to lose*)	**verloren** (*lost*)
nehmen (*to take*)	**genommen** (*taken*)	**verstehen** (*to understand*)	**verstanden** (*understood*)
rufen (*to call*)	**gerufen** (*called*)	**waschen** (*to wash*)	**gewaschen** (*washed*)
schlafen (*to sleep*)	**geschlafen** (*slept*)	**ziehen** (*to pull*)	**gezogen** (*pulled*)

You can easily remember the meanings of many strong verbs because they're reasonably similar to the English verbs. Another plus: You can even find similar patterns to the English past participle forms. Take a look at these examples: **beginnen, begonnen** (*begin, begun*); **singen, gesungen** (*sing, sung*); and **trinken, getrunken** (*drink, drunk*).

Complete these sentences, putting the following verbs into present perfect tense. You can find these verbs in Table 14-3.

PRACTICE

Q. Wir _____ viele Freunde auf dem Fest _____. (treffen)

A. Wir <u>haben</u> viele Freunde auf dem Fest <u>getroffen</u>. (*We met a lot of friends at the party.*)

28 Der Fahrgast _____ die Fahrkarte aus dem Automat _____. (nehmen)

29 _____ du das Buch über den Skandal auf der Insel schon _____? (lesen)

30 Letztes Jahr _____ ich meine Kollegen in München _____. (treffen)

31 _____ du schon alle Emails _____? (schreiben)

32 Um wie viel Uhr _____ der Zug den Bahnhof _____? (verlassen)

33 Letzte Woche _____ ich mit Georg _____. (sprechen)

34 Ich habe kein Glück, ich _____ schon wieder in der Lotterie _____. (verlieren)

35 Der Hausmeister _____ meine schweren Koffer in die Wohnung _____. (tragen)

36 Oh, hallo, _____ du mich gerade _____? (rufen)

37 Mein Freund _____ hat mir bei den Aufgaben _____. (helfen)

38 Am Montag _____ die Ferien _____. (beginnen)

39 Zum Glück _____ Maria ihren Ring _____. (finden)

40 Du _____ noch nie Wildschwein _____? (essen)

41 Kein Mensch _____ sein Deutsch _____. (verstehen)

42 Die Lehrerin _____ mir das Buch _____. (geben)

43 _____ Sie besser auf der neuen Matratze _____? (schlafen)

44 Ich _____ einen Kuchen für meine Freundin _____. (backen)

45 Früher _____ wir viel mehr Bier _____. (trinken)

46 Oje! Ich _____ zu viel Salz in die Suppe _____. (tun)

Forming the Present Perfect with Sein

Some verbs form the present perfect with the auxiliary verb **sein** *(to be)* plus the past participle of the verb you want to use. All these verbs that use **sein** have two similarities:

>> They don't have a direct object, which means they're *intransitive*. The verb **laufen** *(to run)*, for example, is intransitive: **Wir sind schnell gelaufen** *(We ran fast)*. An example of a transitive verb (with a direct object) is **trinken** *(to drink)*, and it looks like this: **Ich habe eine Tasse Kaffee getrunken** *(I drank a cup of coffee)*. The subject *("I," in this case)* carried out a particular action *(drinking)*, and the direct object of that verb is *"a cup of coffee."*

>> They show a change in some condition — as with **werden** *(to become)* or some motion to or from a place — **kommen** *(to come)*.

Generally, you form the past participle with **ge-** + the stem from the infinitive + the ending **-en**. **Kommen** *(to come)* becomes **gekommen** *(come)*. But you also have the types of past participles that have gone through some spelling changes from the original infinitive form. **Gehen** *(to go, walk)* changes to **gegangen** *(gone, walked)*.

But of course, there are some rogues. The verbs **bleiben** (*to stay*) and **sein** (*to be*) don't meet the second criterion, but they still need **sein** to form the present perfect. Then you have yet another rogue: **rennen** (*to run, race*), which changes to **gerannt** (*run, raced*). It has a **-t** ending in the past participle.

To form the present perfect with **sein**, you first conjugate the present tense of the verb **sein** and then add the right past participle.

fahren *(to drive)*	
ich **bin gefahren**	wir **sind gefahren**
du **bist gefahren**	ihr **seid gefahren**
er/sie/es **ist gefahren**	sie **sind gefahren**
Sie **sind gefahren**	

Here's how **fahren** would work in the present perfect tense:

Bist du die ganze Nacht gefahren? *(Did you drive all night?)*

REMEMBER

Even in conversation, it's a lot more common to use the simple past of **sein** than the present perfect, as in **Wie war der Flug von Zürich nach San Francisco?** *(How was the flight from Zürich to San Francisco?)*. (For more information on how to form and use the simple past, check out Chapter 15.)

Look at Table 14-4, which shows a list of verbs that use **sein** in the present perfect. Some past participles have no stem change; others go through contortions to form the past participle, so you need to memorize them.

Table 14-4   Verbs Conjugated with Sein in the Present Perfect

Infinitive	Sein + Past Participle	Infinitive	Sein + Past Participle
bleiben *(to stay, remain)*	**ist geblieben** *(stayed, remained)*	**reiten** *(to ride [horseback])*	**ist geritten** *(ridden)*
fahren *(to drive)*	**ist gefahren** *(driven)*	**schwimmen** *(to swim)*	**ist geschwommen** *(swum)*
fallen *(to fall)*	**ist gefallen** *(fallen)*	**sein** *(to be)*	**ist gewesen** *(been)*
fliegen *(to fly)*	**ist geflogen** *(flown)*	**steigen** *(to climb)*	**ist gestiegen** *(climbed)*
fließen *(to flow, run)*	**ist geflossen** *(flowed, run)*	**sterben** *(to die)*	**ist gestorben** *(died)*
gehen *(to go, walk)*	**ist gegangen** *(gone, walked)*	**wachsen** *(to grow)*	**ist gewachsen** *(grown)*
kommen *(to come)*	**ist gekommen** *(come)*	**werden** *(to become)*	**ist geworden** *(became)*
laufen *(to run, walk)*	**ist gelaufen** *(run, walked)*		

PRACTICE

Now it's your turn. Put the verbs in present perfect tense in the following pairs of dialogues. Refer to the example for the conjugation of **sein** with the past participle of the verb **fahren**. You find the past participles you need in Table 14-4.

Q. Die Waldbrandgefahr _____ im letzten Sommer viel grösser _____. (werden)

A. Die Waldbrandgefahr <u>ist</u> im letzten Sommer viel grösser <u>geworden</u>. *(The forest fire danger became much greater last summer.)*

(47) Christian: _____ du heute Morgen _____? (reiten)

(48) Barbara: Nein, ich _____ im Park _____. (laufen)

(49) Udo: _____ er vom Dach _____? (fallen)

(50) Franz: Ja, und zwei Tage später _____ er leider _____. (sterben)

(51) Helena: _____ ihr im Winter in die Schweiz _____? (fahren)

(52) Ulla: Nein wir _____ zu Hause _____. (bleiben)

(53) Hannes: Wann _____ du zum Fest _____? (gehen)

(54) Janina: Ich weiß nicht. Ich glaube, ich _____ sehr spät nach Hause _____. (kommen)

(55) Horst: _____ du letzte Woche nach Florida _____. (fliegen)

(56) Karl: Ja, und bei der Ankunft _____ es sehr heiß _____. (sein)

(57) Luka: _____ Sie gestern auf den Hirschberg _____? (steigen)

(58) Andrea: Nein, gestern Nachmittag _____ es zu windig und kalt _____. (werden)

(59) Michaela: _____ deine Kinder gestern im Park _____? (sein)

(60) Jan: Nein, sie _____ im See_____. (schwimmen)

Eyeing the Present Perfect: German versus English

In the present perfect, German and English have some similarities and some differences. In both languages, you use the present perfect to talk about past activities, and both are used in conversation. Also, the construction looks similar, at least when you use the auxiliary verb **haben,** as in **Ich habe einen Kojoten gesehen** *(I have seen a coyote).*

DIFFERENCES

The differences in the present perfect come about when you want to add a time element, such as **gestern** *(yesterday):* **Gestern habe ich einen Kojoten gesehen** *(Yesterday I saw a coyote).* You use the present perfect in German, but in English, you use *saw* (the simple past). On the other hand, when you want to describe a past action that's still going on, you say something like **Seit einigen Jahren sehe ich Kojoten** *(I've been seeing coyotes for a few years).* Here, German uses the simple present, yet English uses the present perfect continuous. In this section, I provide you variations of these differences in verb-tense usage.

One for all: Representing three English tenses

Both English and German use the present perfect in conversation. The distinction here is that in German, you use it a lot more frequently in conversation and informal written language. Look at this example, which uses present perfect in German but simple past in English because *last night* is finished:

Was hast du gestern Abend im Fernsehen gesehen? *(What did you see on TV last night?)*

DIFFERENCES

German has only the one verb tense — the present perfect — to represent three tenses in English. Depending on what you want to say in German, the following forms are possible. Here are three acceptable translations of **Sie haben in Wien gelebt:**

» **Present perfect:** *They have lived in Vienna.* (Expresses that they may still live there.)

» **Simple past:** *They lived in Vienna.* (Says they no longer live there.)

» **Past continuous:** *They were living in Vienna.* (Talks about a relationship between two completed past actions. Usually, one action is longer than the other; the other past action may be described in a previous or subsequent sentence or in the same sentence.)

Look at the sentence *They were living in Vienna.* Because you don't even have past continuous in German (or any other continuous forms, for that matter), you use the present perfect as the pinch-hitter, like this: **Während des kalten Krieges haben sie in Wien gelebt** *(During the Cold War, they were living in Vienna).*

As soon as you understand how to form the present perfect, you'll find yourself using it very frequently to describe a great many situations in the past. In fact, unless you intend to pursue a career in German journalism or plan on writing the next great German novel, you won't have much use for the simple past or other past-tense verb forms.

Opting for the German present

Now look at two more German sentences and their literal and real English translations. You may be surprised (and relieved) that in German, you get by with simple present in some situations that call for using present perfect in English. Here's one more economizing step: You express both *since* and *for* with **seit** in German, as in these examples:

Seit wie lange warten Sie auf die U-Bahn? *(How long have you been waiting for the subway?* Literally: *Since how long wait you for the subway?)*

Wir stehen hier seit zehn Minuten. *(We've been standing here for ten minutes.* Literally: *We stand here for ten minutes.)*

Answers to "Conversing about the Past: Perfecting the Present Perfect" Practice Questions

1. **gebraucht** *(needed)*.

2. **gechattet** *(chatted)*.

3. **feiern** *(to celebrate)*.

4. **geglaubt** *(believed)*

5. **gejobbt** *(done odd jobs)*.

6. **kochen** *(to cook)*.

7. **geschmeckt** *(tasted)*.

8. **schneien** *(to snow)*.

9. **gesucht** *(looked for, searched)*.

10. **töten** *(to kill)*.

11. **gewohnt** *(lived)*.

12. **zahlen** *(to pay)*.

13. **Die Pommes frites mit Mayonnaise haben sehr gut geschmeckt.** *(The French fries with mayonnaise tasted very good.)* It may sound odd, but it's popular with some Germans.

14. **Warum hast du gestern nicht gearbeitet?** *(Why didn't you work yesterday?)*

15. **Wir haben gestern mit Nadal und Sampras Tennis gespielt.** *(We played tennis with Nadal yesterday.)*

16. **Mein Bruder hat in der Schule Deutsch gelernt.** *(My brother learned German in school.)* Assuming the brother is out of school, you'd use the simple past learned in English, yet it's present perfect in German.

17. **Wann hast du die Nachrichten gehört?** *(When did you hear the news?)* With the time element of when, you use simple past in English but present perfect in German.

18. **Im Sommer haben Johnny und Baby viel getanzt.** *(Johnny and Baby danced a lot in the summer.)* That summer's over.

19. **Die Eltern von Baby haben nichts dazu gesagt.** *(Baby's parents didn't say anything about it.)*

20. **Wo hast du den Laptop gekauft?** *(Where did you buy the laptop?)*

21. **Es hat nur einmal am Wochenende geregnet.** *(It rained only once on the weekend.)*

22. **Ich habe meiner Freundin schöne Blumen zum Geburtstag geschenkt.** *(I gave my girlfriend some pretty flowers on her birthday.)*

23. **Das Holz hat sehr schnell gebrannt.** *(The wood burned very fast.)*

24. **Wir haben unsere Wanderschuhe gebracht.** *(We have brought/brought our hiking boots.)*

25. **Ich habe deine Emailadresse nicht gewusst.** *(I didn't know your email address.)*

26. **Der Verkäufer hat die Produkte sehr gut gekannt.** *(The salesperson knew the products very well.)*

27. **Die Kunden haben nur an den Preis gedacht.** *(The customers thought only about the price.)*

28. **Der Fahrgast hat die Fahrkarte aus dem Automaten genommen.** *(The passenger took the ticket out of the machine.)*

29. **Hast du das Buch über den Skandal auf der Insel schon gelesen?** *(Have you read the book about the scandal on the island yet?)*

30. **Letztes Jahr habe ich meine Kollegen in München getroffen.** *(Last year I met my colleagues in Munich.)*

31. **Hast du schon alle Emails geschrieben?** *(Have you already written all the emails?)*

32. **Um wie viel Uhr hat der Zug den Bahnhof verlassen?** *(When did the train leave the station?)*

33. **Letzte Woche habe ich mit Georg gesprochen.** *(I talked with Georg last week.)*

34. **Ich habe kein Glück, ich habe schon wieder in der Lotterie verloren.** *(I have no luck; once again, I lost in the lottery.)*

35. **Der Hausmeister hat meine schweren Koffer in die Wohnung getragen.** *(The concierge/custodian carried my heavy suitcases into my apartment.)*

36. **Oh, hallo, hast du mich gerade gerufen?** *(Oh, hello, did you just call [for] me?)*

37. **Mein Freund hat mir bei den Aufgaben geholfen.** *(My friend helped me with the tasks/exercises.)*

38. **Am Montag haben die Ferien begonnen.** *(The [school] vacation began on Monday.)* **Ferien** is plural and often refers to school vacation. **Der Urlaub** is used to express vacation.

39. **Zum Glück hat Maria ihren Ring gefunden.** *(Luckily, Maria found her ring.)*

40. **Du hast noch nie Wildschwein gegessen?** *(You've never eaten wild boar [meat]?)*

41. **Kein Mensch hat sein Deutsch verstanden.** *(No one understood his German.)*

42. **Die Lehrerin hat mir das Buch gegeben.** *(The teacher gave me the book.)*

43. **Haben Sie auf der neuen Matratze besser geschlafen?** *(Did you sleep better with the new mattress?)*

44. **Ich habe einen Kuchen für meine Freundin gebacken.** *(I baked a cake for my [girl]friend.)*

45. **Früher haben wir viel mehr Bier getrunken.** *(We used to drink a lot more beer.)* **Früher** means *earlier*. There is no direct equivalent for *used to + verb*.

46. **Oje! Ich habe zu viel Salz in die Suppe getan.** *(Oh, dear! I put too much salt in the soup.)*

47. Christian: **Bist du heute Morgen geritten?** *(Did you go riding this morning?)*

48. Barbara: **Nein, ich bin im Park gelaufen.** *(No, I ran in the park.)*

(49) Udo: **Ist er vom Dach gefallen?** (*Did he fall off the roof?*)

(50) Franz: **Ja, und zwei Tage später ist er leider gestorben**. (*Yes, and unfortunately, he died two days later.*)

(51) Helena: **Seid ihr im Winter in die Schweiz gefahren?** (*Did you go to Switzerland in the winter?*)

(52) Ulla: **Nein wir sind zu Hause geblieben.** (*No, we stayed home.*)

(53) Hannes: **Wann bist du zum Fest gegangen?** (*When did you go to the party?*)

(54) Janina: **Ich weiß nicht. Ich glaube, ich bin sehr spät nach Hause gekommen.** (*I don't know. I think I came home very late.*)

(55) Horst: **Bist du letzte Woche nach Florida geflogen?** (*Did you fly to Florida last week?*)

(56) Karl: **Ja, und bei der Ankunft ist es sehr heiß gewesen.** (*Yes, and on [our] arrival, it was very hot.*)

(57) Luka: **Sind Sie gestern auf den Hirschberg gestiegen?** (*Did you climb up the Hirschberg yesterday?*) **Der Berg** means *the mountain.*

(58) Andrea: **Nein, gestern Nachmittag ist es zu windig und kalt geworden.** (*No, yesterday afternoon it got too windy and cold.*)

(59) Michaela: **Sind deine Kinder gestern im Park gewesen**? (*Were your children in the park yesterday?*)

(60) Jan: **Nein, sie sind im See geschwommen.** (*No, they were swimming in the lake.*)

Chapter **15**

Narrating the (Simple) Past: Fact and Fiction

Master storytellers and journalists both have an incredible knack for drawing their audience into a narrative. Storytellers lend a façade of reality to the wildest tales as they twist and turn, fold and unfold in front of rapt listeners (or readers), and well-written news reports of violence, natural disasters, and human prowess can also rivet the readers' attention. What these two types of narrators have in common is they have a command of the *simple past tense,* also referred to as the imperfect or the *narrative past.*

To describe any events or stories, you need verbs — and lots of them. In German, the verb tense of choice when narrating fact or fiction is the simple past tense, such as **er ging** *(he went),* **wir mussten** *(we had to),* or **sie sprachen** *(they spoke).* This chapter compares simple past tense with the other past tenses and helps improve your German by focusing on forming and using simple past tense.

TIP

To remember the difference in usage between the simple past and the present perfect in German, think of the simple past as the narrative past; you run across it more frequently in written German. Think of present perfect as the conversational past, the one that you hear in offices, cafes, and on the streets. (Check out Chapter 14 for more on present perfect.)

Conjugating the Simple Past

To talk or write formally about something that happened, you need to know how to conjugate verbs correctly in simple past tense. Luckily, the simple past verb form isn't too difficult to master. You just need to know that there are several types of endings according to which category the verb falls into:

>> Regular verbs, also called *weak verbs*

>> Irregular verbs, also known as *strong verbs*

>> Other irregular verbs such as **sein** and **haben**, and the modal verbs, also called *auxiliary* or *helping verbs*

Note: A fourth category of verbs, the separable-prefix verbs, includes verbs that have a prefix like **ab-** or a preposition like **mit-** in front of the verb; these verbs may be regular or irregular. The prefix is separated when you conjugate the verb, and it's generally placed at the end of the phrase. Two examples are **abfahren** *(to leave)* and **mitkommen** *(to come along)*. Chapter 8 deals with separable- and inseparable-prefix verbs.

DIFFERENCES The applications of the simple past are quite different when you compare German and English. The single most important aspect of the simple past in English is that it describes an action that's completed in the past, often with a reference to the past: *last month, in 2020,* or *when I was 13.* English uses the simple past in a great number of situations: to describe past events of both formal and informal (casual) nature, as well as for spoken and written language. German, on the other hand, tends to use the simple past in written language, especially newspapers, books, written texts, narrated stories, and even fairy tales. In German, the simple past is also a means of describing past events not connected to the present.

This section shows you how to conjugate different German verbs, including regular (weak) and irregular (strong), **haben** and **sein,** and modals. After you read this section, you'll know how to write about the past with eloquence and style. So, if you should choose to write a **Märchen** *(fairy tale)*, here's how you would begin: **Es war einmal . . .** *(Once upon a time . . .)*

Forming regular (weak) verbs in simple past

Regular verbs are the ones that don't have a stem change between the present tense and the simple past tense. The present tense stem of **wohnen**, for example, is **wohn-**, and the simple past stem is also **wohn-**. The endings make the difference between the two tenses.

Here's how to form the simple past of regular verbs:

1. Take the **-en** off the infinitive.

2. Add **-te**, which I refer to as the **-te** *tense marker.*

3. Add the additional endings (with the exception of the **ich** and **er/sie/es** forms, which have no ending other than **-te**). The endings are as follows: nothing, **-st**, nothing, **-n, -t, -n,** and **-n.**

Compare the present and the simple past of the verb **wohnen** *(to live)*. The present form is in parentheses after the simple past.

wohnen *(to live)* — **Simple past (present)**

ich wohn**te** (wohn**e**)	wir wohn**ten** (wohn**en**)
du wohn**test** (wohn**st**)	ihr wohn**tet** (wohn**t**)
er/sie/es wohn**te** (wohn**t**)	sie wohn**ten** (wohn**en**)
Sie wohn**ten** (wohn**en**)	

Here's the simple past tense of **wohnen** in action:

Die Familie **wohnte** in Dortmund. *(The family lived in Dortmund.)*

A second group of regular verbs are those with a stem ending in **-d** or **-t**. A small number of verbs with the stem ending in **-fn** or **-gn** also fall into this category, such as **öffnen** *(to open)* and **regnen** *(to rain)*. With these verbs, for the purpose of making them easier to pronounce, you put an additional **e** in front of the **-te** tense marker. Taking **arbeiten** *(to work)* as an example, you form the simple past like this: **ich arbeit** + **e** + **te** = **ich arbeitete**. Compare the present and the simple past:

arbeiten *(to work)* — **Simple past (present)**

ich arbeit**ete** (arbeit**e**)	wir arbeit**eten** (arbeit**en**)
du arbeit**etest** (arbeit**est**)	ihr arbeit**etet** (arbeit**et**)
er/sie/es arbeit**ete** (arbeit**et**)	sie arbeit**eten** (arbeit**en**)
Sie arbeit**eten** (arbeit**en**)	

Here's the simple past tense of **arbeiten** in action:

Die Handwerker **arbeiteten** sehr schnell. *(The craftsmen worked very fast.)*

Try out your grasp of forming regular verbs in the simple past tense. In this exercise, you see one of the persons (**ich, du, er/sie/es, wir, ihr, sie,** or **Sie**) and the German infinitive form. Fill in the simple past form you need to fit the person indicated.

Q. er _____ arbeiten *(to work)*

A. er <u>arbeitete</u>

1. wir _____
   (bezahlen)

2. ich _____
   (brauchen)

3. es _____
   (dauern)

4. Sie _____
   (fotografieren)

5. du _____ (hören)

6. sie *(she)* _____
   (kaufen)

7 es _____ (kosten)

13 wir _____ (reisen)

8 sie (they) _____ (lachen)

14 ihr _____ (sagen)

9 ihr _____ (lernen)

15 du _____ (tanzen)

16 sie (she) _____ (spielen)

10 ich _____ (machen)

17 Sie _____ (wandern)

11 Sie _____ (reden)

18 ich _____ (warten)

12 es _____ (regnen)

Forming irregular (strong) verbs in simple past

The verbs in this section are called *irregular* because unlike regular verbs, these verbs have a variety of vowel changes in the simple past form. The changes may simply be one vowel change, such as **i** to **a**; with the irregular verb **beginnen** *(to begin)*, the simple past stem is **begann** *(began)*. You need to memorize the simple past stem for each irregular verb to add the simple past endings to it. Fortunately, you encounter many of these verbs often, so you may already know the meaning and be familiar with the present tense form of several of them.

To conjugate irregular verbs in the simple past, note the following:

>> These verbs have no endings in **ich** and **er/sie/es** forms.

>> The other endings — those for **du, wir, ihr, sie,** and **Sie** — are the same as the present-tense endings. The endings are <nothing>, **-st,** <nothing>, **-en, -t,** and **-en.**

beginnen *(to begin)*

ich begann	wir begann**en**
du begann**st**	ihr begann**t**
er/sie/es begann	sie begann**en**
Sie begann**en**	

Here's the simple past tense of **beginnen** in action:

Er **begann** zu laufen. *(He began to run.)*

You're in luck again. Why? German has only a relatively small number of irregular (strong) verbs for you to worry about when conjugating the simple past tense.

Even better, these verbs are relatively easy because with many of them, you can draw on your knowledge of English irregular verbs to help you recognize the German cognates (words that are the same or very close in spelling and meaning in two languages). Table 15-1 lists verbs that are irregular in both English and German; they're cognates or at least verbs that begin with the same letter in English and German and mean nearly the same thing. A couple of verbs — **kommen** *(to come)* and **trinken** *(to drink)* — are different in spelling but quite similar in pronunciation. I give the **er/sie/es** form of the simple past in Table 15-1 because it doesn't have any endings.

Table 15-1   Simple Past of Irregular Verbs Resembling English Verbs

Infinitive	Simple Past (er/sie/es Form)	Infinitive	Simple Past (er/sie/es Form)
beginnen *(to begin)*	**begann** *(began)*	**lassen** *(to let, allow)*	**ließ** *(let, allowed)*
essen *(to eat)*	**aß** *(ate)*	**liegen** *(to lie [down])*	**lag** *(lay)*
fallen *(to fall)*	**fiel** *(fell)*	**reiten** *(to ride [a horse or bike])*	**ritt** *(rode)*
finden *(to find)*	**fand** *(found)*	**schwimmen** *(to swim)*	**schwamm** *(swam)*
fliegen *(to fly)*	**flog** *(flew)*	**sehen** *(to see)*	**sah** *(saw)*
geben *(to give)*	**gab** *(gave)*	**singen** *(to sing)*	**sang** *(sang)*
gehen *(to go)*	**ging** *(went)*	**sitzen** *(to sit)*	**saß** *(sat)*
halten *(to hold, stop)*	**hielt** *(held, stopped)*	**sprechen** *(to speak)*	**sprach** *(spoke)*
kommen *(to come)*	**kam** *(came)*	**trinken** *(to drink)*	**trank** *(drank)*

TIP

Many irregular verbs are very common verbs, so you can familiarize yourself with them by reading actively, which involves thinking beyond the gist of the text. How? By slowing your reading or by rereading a passage, you may notice how the verb stem is spelled differently from the present tense form. Try writing down the verbs as you come across them and figuring out the corresponding present tense; then you can familiarize yourself with the various spelling changes in the simple past.

PRACTICE

Before starting this exercise, go over Table 15-1 until you feel confident that you know the verb forms shown and the English meaning. Ready? Now fill in the missing words in this exercise. Many verbs have more than one space to be filled in, including the English meaning. No fair peeking.

Infinitive/Meaning		Simple Past (er/sie/es Form)

Q. beginnen *(to begin)* _____

A. beginnen *(to begin)* **begann**

19 essen (_____) _____

20 _____ *(to fall)* _____

21 _____ *(to find)* fand

22 fliegen *(to fly)* _____

23 geben (_____) _____

24 _____ *(to go)* ging

25 halten (_____) _____

26 kommen *(to come)* _____

27 _____ *(to let, allow)* _____

28 liegen (_____) _____

29 _____ *(to ride)* ritt

30 schwimmen *(to swim)* _____

Table 15-2 lists some irregular verbs that are irregular in both English and German, but they aren't cognates. What these verbs also have in common is that they're high-frequency verbs (verbs you encounter often in German). Try memorizing the infinitive and simple past forms together.

Table 15-2 Simple Past of Common Irregular Verbs (Noncognates)

Infinitive	Simple Past (er/sie/es Form)	Infinitive	Simple Past (er/sie/es Form)
fahren *(to drive)*	**fuhr** *(drove)*	**tragen** *(to wear, carry)*	**trug** *(wore, carried)*
fangen *(to catch)*	**fing** *(caught)*	**treffen** *(to meet)*	**traf** *(met)*
gewinnen *(to win)*	**gewann** *(won)*	**tun** *(to do)*	**tat** *(did)*
laufen *(to run)*	**lief** *(ran)*	**vergessen** *(to forget)*	**vergaß** *(forgot)*
lesen *(to read)*	**las** *(read)*	**verlieren** *(to lose)*	**verlor** *(lost)*
nehmen *(to take)*	**nahm** *(took)*	**verstehen** *(to understand)*	**verstand** *(understood)*
schneiden *(to cut)*	**schnitt** *(cut)*	**wachsen** *(to grow)*	**wuchs** *(grew)*
schreiben *(to write)*	**schrieb** *(wrote)*	**werden** *(to become)*	**wurde** *(became)*

TIP

At the same time you're saying each verb as a chant, demonstrate the action of the verb. With **treffen** (*to meet*), for example, outstretch your hand and pump it up and down as though you're shaking hands with the firefighter who just got your kitten out of a tree.

PRACTICE

In this exercise, you see the verbs from Table 15-3 with the simple past forms missing and around half of the English meanings left out. Try your memory, filling in the blanks without looking at the table.

Infinitive/Meaning	Simple Past (er/sie/es Form)
Q. fahren (*to drive*)	_____
A. fahren (*to drive*)	**fuhr**
31 fangen (*to catch*)	_____
32 gewinnen (_____)	_____
33 laufen (*to run*)	_____
34 lesen (_____)	_____
35 nehmen (_____)	_____
36 schneiden (*to cut*)	_____
37 schreiben (_____)	_____
38 tragen (*to wear, carry*)	_____
39 treffen (*to meet*)	_____
40 tun (_____)	_____
41 vergessen (_____)	_____
42 verlieren (*to lose*)	_____
43 verstehen (_____)	_____
44 wachsen (*to grow*)	_____

werden (_____) _____

46 werfen *(to throw)* _____

Forming haben and sein in simple past

When conjugating the two verbs **haben** *(to have)* and **sein** *(to be)*, you need to pay extra attention for two reasons:

» **Haben** and **sein** can function as auxiliary or helping verbs. Most verbs use the auxiliary verb **haben** to form the present perfect, but some irregular verbs use **sein**. (See Chapter 14 for more on present perfect.)

» Although German speakers usually use present perfect tense in conversations about the past (see Chapter 14), they use the simple past of **haben** and **sein** more frequently in conversation. (They also use the simple past of the modal verbs in conversation; check out the next section.)

You form the simple past of **haben** and **sein** with their respective stems, **hatte** and **war**. Similar to the irregular (strong) verbs, the **ich** and **er/sie/es** forms have no verb endings. Look at the two conjugations, with the verb endings in bold:

haben *(to have)*

ich hatte	wir hatt**en**
du hatt**est**	ihr hatt**et**
er/sie/es hatte	sie hatt**en**
Sie hatt**en**	

Check out an example of **haben** in the simple past:

Ich **hatte** viel Zeit. *(I had a lot of time.)*

sein *(to be)*

ich war	wir war**en**
du war**st**	ihr war**t**
er/sie/es war	sie war**en**
Sie war**en**	

And here's the simple past of **sein** in action:

Sie **waren** zu Hause. *(They were at home.)*

PRACTICE Last month, Helmut and Hannelore drove to Spain for **der Urlaub** *(the vacation)*. Hannelore wrote a diary while they were traveling. Read her diary, written in present tense; then fill in in the missing verbs in the German simple past. Some sentences have strong and weak verbs, but the majority contain **sein** and **haben**. *Note:* Spain is an extremely popular vacation spot for Germans and many other Europeans.

den 11. August

Wir sind in Madrid — endlich! Das Wetter ist absolut wunderbar, und wir haben ein Zimmer in einem sehr schönen Hotel. Wir gehen zum Prado Museum. Am 12. August fahren wir nach Córdoba.

den 13. August

Ich habe viel Glück am 13.! Wir sind in einer billigen, aber netten Pension in Córdoba in der Nähe von der Mezquita (die Moschee im Zentrum). Sie ist sehr, sehr groß! In der Moschee ist es kühler als in der Sonne.

den 14. August

Wir fahren nach Sevilla, aber zuerst bin ich drei Stunden allein. Ich gehe einkaufen. Die Geschäfte sind sehr interessant. Ich suche nach Lederartikeln, aber der Preis für eine Lederjacke ist zu hoch für mich. Der Euro macht alles sehr teuer.

den 15. August

Das Wetter ist schrecklich. Es gibt viel Regen, es ist kühl, und Helmut hat Kopfweh. Wir sind den ganzen Tag in Cafés, essen spanische Spezialitäten, und trinken Rioja.

den 17. August

Der Regen ist zu viel! Helmut hat keine Lust, in Sevilla zu bleiben. Also wir fahren nach Málaga.

den 18. August

Es ist herrlich! In Málaga ist es sonnig und heiß! Ich gehe schwimmen, und Helmut hat eine deutsche Zeitung. Das Leben ist perfekt!

11. August

Q. Wir _____ (sein) in Madrid — endlich!

A. Wir **waren** in Madrid — endlich! *(We were in Madrid — at last!)*

47 Das Wetter _____ (sein) absolut wunderbar . . .

48 . . . und wir _____ (haben) ein Zimmer in einem sehr schönen Hotel.

49 Am 12. August _____ (fahren) wir nach Córdoba.

13. August

50 Wir _____ (sein) in einer billigen, aber schönen Pension in Córdoba in der Nähe von der Mezquita (name of a famous **Moschee** [mosque]).

51 Sie _____ (sein) sehr, sehr groß!

14. August

52 Wir _____ (fahren) nach Sevilla.

15. August

53 Das Wetter _____ (sein) schrecklich (*awful*).

54 Wir _____ (sein) den ganzen Tag in Cafés.

17. August

55 Der Regen _____ (sein) zu viel! Helmut
_____ (haben) keine Lust, in Sevilla zu bleiben (*stay*).

56 Also _____ (fahren) wir nach Málaga.

18. August

57 Es _____ (sein) herrlich (*marvelous*)! In Málaga
_____ (sein) es sonnig und heiß!

58 Das Leben _____ (sein) perfekt!

Forming modals in simple past

The modal verbs are the small band of modifying or helping type verbs. (See Chapter 7 for in-depth treatment of the modal verbs.) These verbs modify another verb, although sometimes, they can stand alone. The list includes **dürfen** (*to be allowed to*), **können** (*can, to be able to*), **mögen** (*to like*), **müssen** (*to have to, must*), **sollen** (*to be supposed to, should*), and **wollen** (*to want to*). *Note:* Although **möchten** is included in this elite group in the present tense, it falls by the wayside because of its meaning (*would like to*) and joins forces with **mögen** in the simple past tense. Both have the meaning *liked to* in the simple past.

German speakers prefer to use the modal verbs in the simple past form when conversing or telling stories. The modal verbs are reasonably easy to remember in the simple-past form because they follow the same criteria:

>> The past stem changes have no umlaut.

>> You add the **-te** stem marker to the simple-past stem. The additional endings are as follows: <nothing>, **-st**, <nothing>, **-n, -t, -n,** and **-n.**

Look at Table 15-3, which shows modal verbs in simple past tense.

Table 15-3   Modal Verbs in Simple Past Tense

Infinitive	Past Stem	Tense Marker	Simple Past (ich, er/sie/es Form)	English Equivalent of Simple Past
dürfen	durf-	-te	durfte	*was allowed to*
können	konn-	-te	konnte	*was able to, could* (past-tense meaning)
mögen	moch	-te	mochte	*liked*
müssen	muss-	-te	musste	*had to*
sollen	soll-	-te	sollte	*was supposed to*
wollen	woll-	-te	wollte	*wanted to*

The following verb table shows the verb **können** conjugated, with the endings in bold, including the -**te** tense marker:

können *(to be able to, can)*

ich konn**te**	wir konn**ten**
du konn**test**	ihr konn**tet**
er/sie/es konn**te**	sie konn**ten**
Sie konn**ten**	

And here's the simple past of **können** in action:

Nach dem Skiurlaub <u>konnte</u> ich besser skifahren. *(I was able to ski better after the skiing vacation.)*

In the following exercise, some people are talking about a party they went to last week. A lot of things went differently from what was planned; in fact, the party was a comedy of errors. Refer to Table 15-3 and the preceding verb table. Write the correct form of the verb in parentheses.

PRACTICE

Q. Wir _____ nur einen halben Kuchen mitbringen. (können)

A. Wir konnten nur einen halben Kuchen mitbringen. (können) *(We were able to bring only half a cake.)*

59 Helena _____ früh nach Hause gehen. (müssen)

60 _____ du nicht mit deinem Cousin kommen? (wollen)

61 Marlene und Dieter _____ einen Salat machen. (sollen)

62 Ich _____ den Schweinebraten überhaupt nicht. (mögen)

63 Michael _____ seinen Hund nicht mitbringen. (dürfen)

64 Alex _____ gar nichts essen. (wollen)

65 Elisabeth _____ ein Kartoffelgericht mitbringen, (sollen) . . .

. . . aber sie _____ keine Zeit zu kochen. (haben)

Friedrich _____ keine alkoholische Getränke trinken. (dürfen) Warum?

Er _____ nach dem Fest Auto fahren. (müssen)

Contrasting Tenses

In addition to the simple past (<u>Ich sah</u> einen aktiven Vulkan [*I saw an active volcano*]), two verb tenses belong to the past-tense club:

>> The present perfect: <u>Ich habe</u> einen aktiven Vulkan <u>gesehen</u>. (*I have seen an active volcano.*)

>> The past perfect: <u>Ich hatte</u> einen aktiven Vulkan <u>gesehen</u>. (*I had seen an active volcano.*)

This trio is the mainstay for describing events in the past, in both English and German. But you can often get away with using the present perfect or even the simple past in describing events that may actually call for past perfect. In addition, past perfect isn't used very frequently in either German or English, so it takes a back seat, and that's a good way to remember when it's used — namely, to describe events that happened way before another past event. (Chapter 14 deals in depth with present perfect.)

The past perfect may not be very common, but before relegating the past perfect to oblivion, I want to contrast three past-tense verb forms: simple past, present perfect, and past perfect. Look at Table 15-4. You see how to form these past tenses, their applications (uses), and an example situation.

Table 15-4 German Usage of Past Tenses

Past Tense	How to Form	Use	Example Sentence/Translation/Explanation
Simple past (narrative past)	Use the simple past form of the verb	Used in formal, written language; preferred in spoken language in northern Germany; used with **haben**, **sein**, and modal verbs	Der Orkan **dauerte** insgesamt zwei Wochen. (*The hurricane lasted two weeks altogether.*) **Dauerte** is the simple past, third-person singular of **dauern** (*to last*).
Present perfect (conversational past)	Combine the present tense of **haben** or **sein** and a past participle of the verb	Used in casual, informal, spoken language when talking about the past; preferred in southern German-speaking regions	Gestern **haben** wir einen guten Film **gesehen**. (*Yesterday we saw a good movie.*) **Haben** is the present tense, first-person plural of **haben**; **gesehen** is the past participle of **sehen** (*to see*).
Past perfect	Combine the past of either **haben** or **sein** and a past participle of the verb	Used to describe a past event that happened before another past event, often with the two verbs in the same sentence	Nachdem sie schon zwei Stück Kuchen **gegessen hatte, nahm** sie noch ein Stück,. (*After she had already eaten two pieces of cake, she took another piece.*) **Hatte** is the simple past-tense, third-person singular of **haben**, and **gegessen** is the past participle of **essen** (*to eat*). **Nahm** is the simple past tense, third-person singular of **nehmen** (*to take*).

PRACTICE

Narratives often combine more than the simple past. Present perfect and past perfect also appear in the following true story about a young girl who **überlebte** (*survived*) **ein Flugzeugabsturz** (*a plane crash*). Write the simple-past form of the verb shown in parentheses. When you see the note for present perfect or past perfect, put that verb form in the two spaces provided. Table 15-4 will help you. Read the story before starting to get a sense of what happened.

Q. Wie _____ das Mädchen überleben? (können)

A. Wie <u>konnte</u> das Mädchen überleben? (*How was the girl able to survive?*)

Juliana Koepcke (69)_____ (leben) mit ihrer Mutter und ihrem Vater in Peru. Ihre Eltern (70) _____ (sein) Deutsche. Sie (71) _____ (arbeiten) im Museum of Natural History in Lima, Peru. Juliana (72)_____ (sein) ein sehr intelligentes Mädchen. Sie (73)_____ (können) Deutsch und Spanisch, und sie (74)_____ sehr viel über das Leben im Dschungel (74)_____ (lernen) (past perfect). Im Dezember 1971, (75) _____ (sein) sie auf einem Flug mit ihrer Mutter. Das Flugzeug (76) _____ (kommen) in einem Sturm und ist abgestürzt. Sie (77) _____ (stürzen) mit ihrem Sitz aus dem Flugzeug, und (78) _____ (landen) mit ihm in Ästen (*branches*) der Bäume (*trees*); so (79) _____ (überleben) sie das Desaster. Sie (80) _____ viele tote (*dead*) Personen am Boden (80) _____ (sehen) (present perfect). Leider (81) _____ (können) sie ihre Mutter nicht finden. Julia (82) _____ (sein) die einzige Person, die den Unfall überlebte (*survived*). Juliana (83) _____ (wandern) 11 Tage im Dschungel. Sie (84) _____ sehr wenig (84) _____ (essen) (present perfect), aber sie (85) _____ (können) das Wasser von einem Fluß trinken. Endlich (86) _____ (haben) sie Glück. Sie (87) _____ (finden) ein Camp im Dschungel, und die Männer dort (88) _____ ihr (88) _____ (helfen) (present perfect). Juliana (89) _____ (haben) zweimal Glück: sie (90) _____ (überleben) den Absturz und (91) _____ (treffen) die Männer in dem Camp.

Wenn sie Interesse an dieser Geschichte haben, können Sie die Autobiografie von Juliane Koepcke lesen: *Als ich vom Himmel fiel* (*When I Fell from the Sky*). Sie können auch den Dokumentarfilm *Wings of Hope* sehen. (1998, Regisseur: Werner Herzog)

Answers to "Narrating the (Simple) Past: Fact and Fiction" Practice Questions

1. **bezahlen** (*to pay*) wir **bezahlten.**
2. **brauchen** (*to need*) ich **brauchte.**
3. **dauern** (*to last, take [time]*) es **dauerte.**
4. **fotografieren** (*to take pictures*) Sie **fotografierten.**
5. **hören** (*to hear, listen to*) du **hörtest.**
6. **kaufen** (*to buy*) sie (*she*) **kaufte.**
7. **kosten** (*to cost*) es **kostete.**
8. **lachen** (*to laugh*) sie (*they*) **lachten.**
9. **lernen** (*to learn*) ihr **lerntet.**
10. **machen** (*to do, make*) ich **machte.**
11. **reden** (*to talk, speak*) Sie **redeten.**
12. **regnen** (*to rain*) es **regnete.**
13. **reisen** (*to travel*) wir **reisten.**
14. **sagen** (*to say*) ihr **sagtet.**
15. **tanzen** (*to dance*) du **tanztest.**
16. **spielen** (*to play [a game, cards]*) sie (*she*) **spielte.**
17. **wandern** (*to hike, wander*) Sie **wanderten.**
18. **warten** (*to wait*) ich **wartete.**
19. **essen** (*to eat*) **aß.**
20. **fallen** (*to fall*) **fiel.**
21. **finden** (*to find*) **fand.**
22. **fliegen** (*to fly*) **flog.**
23. **geben** (*to give*) **gab.**
24. **gehen** (*to go*) **ging.**
25. **halten** (*to hold, stop*) **hielt.**

26. **kommen** (*to come*) **kam.**

27. **lassen** (*to let, allow*) **ließ.**

28. **liegen** (*to lie [down]*) **lag.**

29. **reiten** (*to ride [a horse or bike]*) **ritt.**

30. **schwimmen** (*to swim*) **schwamm.**

31. **fangen** (*to catch*) **fing.**

32. **gewinnen** (*to win*) **gewann.**

33. **laufen** (*to run*) **lief.**

34. **lesen** (*to read*) **las.**

35. **nehmen** (*to take*) **nahm.**

36. **schneiden** (*to cut*) **schnitt.**

37. **schreiben** (*to write*) **schrieb.**

38. **tragen** (*to wear, carry*) **trug.**

39. **treffen** (*to meet*) **traf.**

40. **tun** (*to do*) **tat.**

41. **vergessen** (*to forget*) **vergaß.**

42. **verlieren** (*to lose*) **verlor.**

43. **verstehen** (*to understand*) **verstand.**

44. **wachsen** (*to grow*) **wuchs.**

45. **werden** (*to become*) **wurde.**

46. **werfen** (*to throw*) **warf.**

47. Das Wetter **war** absolut wunderbar . . . (*The weather was absolutely wonderful . . .*)

48. . . . und wir **hatten** ein Zimmer in einem sehr schönen Hotel. (*. . . and we had a room in a very pretty hotel.*)

49. Am 12. August **fuhren** wir nach Córdoba. (*On the 12th of August we drove to Córdoba.*)

50. Wir **waren** in einer billigen, aber schönen Pension in Córdoba in der Nähe von der Mezquita, eine Moschee. (*We were in an inexpensive but nice pension in Córdoba, near the Mezquita, a mosque.*) A **Pension** is similar to a bed and breakfast.

51. Sie **war** sehr, sehr groß! (*It was very, very big!*)

(52) Wir **fuhren** nach Sevilla, *(We drove to Sevilla.)*

(53) Das Wetter **war** schrecklich. *(The weather was awful [terrible].)*

(54) Wir **waren** den ganzen Tag in Cafés . . . *(We were in cafés the whole day . . .)*

(55) Der Regen **war** zu viel! Helmut **hatte** keine Lust, in Sevilla zu bleiben. *(The rain was too much! Helmut didn't feel like staying in Sevilla.)*

(56) Also **fuhren** wir nach Málaga. *(So we drove to Málaga.)*

(57) Es **war** herrlich! In Málaga **war** es sonnig und heiß! *(It was marvelous! It was sunny and hot in Málaga.)*

(58) Das Leben **war** perfekt! *(Life was perfect!)*

(59) Helena **musste** früh nach Hause gehen. *(Helena had to go home early.)*

(60) **Wolltest** du nicht mit deinem Cousin kommen? *(Didn't you want to come with your cousin?)*

(61) Marlene und Dieter **sollten** einen Salat machen. *(Marlene and Dieter were supposed to make a salad.)*

(62) Ich **mochte** den Schweinebraten überhaupt nicht. *(I didn't like the roast pork at all.)*

(63) Michael **durfte** seinen Hund nicht mitbringen. *(Michael wasn't allowed to bring his dog along.)*

(64) Alex **wollte** gar nichts essen. *(Alex didn't want to eat anything.)*

(65) Elisabeth **sollte** ein Kartoffelgericht mitbringen . . . *(Elisabeth was supposed to bring a potato dish)...*

(66) . . . aber sie **hatte** keine Zeit zu kochen. *(...but she had no time do cook/do any cooking.)*

(67) Friedrich **durfte** keine alkoholischen Getränke trinken. Warum? *(Friedrich wasn't allowed to drink any alcoholic drinks. Why?)*

(68) Er **musste** nach dem Fest Auto fahren. *(He had to drive [a car] after the party.)*

Juliana Koepcke (69) **lebte** mit ihrer Mutter und ihrem Vater in Peru. Ihre Eltern (70) **waren** Deutsche. Sie (71) **arbeiteten** im Museum of Natural History in Lima, Peru. Juliana (72) **war** ein sehr intelligentes Mädchen. Sie (73) **konnte** Deutsch und Spanisch, und sie (74) **hatte** sehr viel über das Leben im Dschungel (74) **gelernt**. Im Dezember 1971, (75) **war** sie auf einem Flug mit ihrer Mutter. Das Flugzeug (76) **kam** in einem Sturm und ist abgestürzt. Sie (77) **stürzte** mit ihrem Sitz aus dem Flugzeug, und (78) **landete** mit ihm in Ästen *(branches)* der Bäume *(trees)*; so (79) **überlebte** sie das Desaster. Sie (80) **hat** viele tote *(dead)* Personen am Boden (80) **gesehen**. Leider (81) **konnte** sie ihre Mutter nicht finden. Juliana (82) **war** die einzige Person, die den Unfall überlebte *(survived)*. Juliana (83) **wanderte** 11 Tage im Dschungel. Sie (84) **hat** sehr wenig (84) **gegessen**, aber sie (85) **konnte** das Wasser von einem Fluß trinken. Endlich (86) **hatte** sie Glück. Sie (87) **fand** ein Camp im Dschungel, und die Männer dort (88) **haben** ihr (88) **geholfen**. Juliana (89) **hatte** zweimal Glück: sie (90) **überlebte** den Absturz und (91) **traf** die Männer in dem Camp.

Wenn sie Interesse an dieser Geschichte haben, können Sie die Autobiografie von Juliana Koepcke lesen: **Als ich vom Himmel fiel** (*When I fell from the Sky*). Sie können auch den Dokumentarfilm *Wings of Hope* sehen. (1998, Regisseur: Werner Herzog)

Juliana Koepcke lived with her mother and father in Peru. Her parents were German. They worked at the Museum of Natural History in Lima, Peru. Juliana was a very intelligent girl. She could speak German and Spanish and she had learned a lot about living in the jungle. In December, 1971, she was on a flight with her mother. The plane came into a [thunder]storm and crashed. She plummeted/fell out of the plane in her seat, and landed with the seat in the tree branches; this was how she survived the disaster. She saw many dead bodies on the ground. Unfortunately, she couldn't find her mother. Juliana was the only person who survived the accident. Juliana wandered in the jungle for 11 days. She ate very little, but she was able to drink water from a river. At last she was lucky. She found a camp in the jungle, and the men there helped her. Juliana was lucky twice: she survived the crash, and she met the men in the camp.

If you are interested in this story, you can read the autobiography of Juliana Koepcke, **Als ich vom Himmel fiel** (*When I Fell from the Sky*). You can also see the documentary film *Wings of Hope*. (1998, German director: Werner Herzog)

Chapter **16**

Looking to the Future (And Avoiding It)

Whether you're the type to face the future head on, no holds barred, or you like to avoid the inevitable at all costs, this chapter has something for you. With all the complications of case endings and the three noun genders in German, at last the future pops up, simple and straightforward.

When you read the chapter title, unless you've been dusting off (and reading) English grammar books lately, you're likely to say that the future is one verb tense, the one associated with *will* + a verb (*I'll be home in five minutes*). Actually, English has several ways to express the future, although in German, you're on easy street. Why? In a great many situations, you can avoid using the future tense even while describing a future event. In fact, German uses the future verb tenses far less frequently than English does.

Before you travel into the future, though, the first stop is the German present tense. In the beginning of this chapter, you find out how versatile the German present tense is for situations in which English uses various future tenses. Later in the chapter, you jump on the future bus to take a short, smooth ride through the future, looking at how to form it and when to use the future tense. I also include the most frequently used time expressions associated with the future, as well as a short list of adverbs that typically combine with the future tense to express your attitude about a future event.

The Future Is Now: Using the Present Tense Instead

In general, you don't need to use the future in German when the context makes it clear that the action is describing something in future time. Imagine that you're standing on the subway platform, and the train is coming into the station at Marienplatz in Munich. You have six bags and a broken arm, and someone behind you says **Ich helfe Ihnen** (literally: *I help you*). In English, your helper would say *I'll help you*. This German volunteer isn't grammar-deficient; this person is an angel speaking perfectly idiomatic German.

DIFFERENCES

English has a total of four ways to express the future, as opposed to only two future tenses in German. In addition, future-tense usage in German is far less frequent than it is in English. Look at the following breakdown of how German and English express the future:

>> First is the present tense used for schedules, such as travel plans. This tense is the same in German: **Die Maschine startet um 7.40 Uhr** *(The plane leaves at 7:40 a.m.).*

>> Next is the *going to* future, *going to* + infinitive verb, as in *We're going to visit my cousins this weekend,* which doesn't exist in German. You usually use the German present.

>> English also uses the *present continuous* — *to be* + verb with *-ing* ending, as in *I'm taking the dog for a walk* — which is nonexistent in German. Generally, you can use present tense in German for these situations.

>> That leaves the *will* future verb form, which is equivalent to the German **werden** (*will*) + *infinitive verb* used to express the future. The usage is less frequent in German because present tense can punt for the *will* future in a great deal of cases. (Check out the last section of this chapter for more on using **werden** to express the future.)

This section more closely examines how German uses the present to express future actions.

Seeing when German present works perfectly

In English, you encounter all types of situations that require the future tense. But in German, you can state those same situations by simply using the present tense, especially when it's clear that you intend to express future time. (Chapter 5 deals solely with the present tense if you need a refresher.)

The following examples give you an overview of the range of situations in which German uses the present to express the future. In English, however, you generally use the future when you include an expression that refers to the future, such as *next week*.

Vielleicht kommt er morgen. *(Maybe he'll come tomorrow.)* **Morgen** *(tomorrow)* is an adverb of time that expresses the future.

Dieses Wochenende besuchen wir meine Kusinen. *(We're going to visit my cousins this weekend.)* **Dieses Wochenende** *(this weekend)* refers to the coming weekend; also, German has no equivalent to the English verb form *going to* + verb.

Die Kinder bleiben heute etwas länger am Strand. *(The children are staying a bit longer at the beach today.)* The reference to **heute** *(today)* in connection with **länger** *(longer)* indicates later today; also, German has no *-ing* verb equivalent.

Ich glaube/Ich denke, ich bleibe zu Hause. *(I think I'll stay home.)* German uses present tense here, but English expresses a spontaneous decision *(I think I'll . . .)* with the future.

Ich vergesse es nicht/Ich werde es nicht vergessen. *(I won't forget [it].)* In English, you use the future for a promise. (If you say *I don't forget,* it's a factual statement, not a promise.) In German, you have both options to make a promise.

Saying when: Using future time expressions with the present tense

When you talk about future events in English, you often include an expression of future time together with one of the future verb forms. Germans also use a wide range of future time expressions such as **heute Abend** *(this evening)* or **morgen früh** *(tomorrow morning)*. Here's good news for you: They frequently appear in combination with the present tense.

Take a look at a sampling of common time expressions:

>> **am Anfang der Woche** *(at the beginning of the week)*

>> **am Dienstag** *(on Tuesday)*

>> **diese Woche** *(this week)*

>> **diesen Monat** *(this month)*

>> **dieses Wochenende** *(this weekend)*

>> **heute** *(today)*

>> **heute Abend** *(this evening)*

>> **heute Morgen** *(this morning)*

>> **im Frühling** *(in the spring)*

>> **in vier Monaten** *(in four months)*

>> **in einer Stunde** *(in one/an hour)*

>> **morgen** *(tomorrow)*

>> **morgen früh** *(tomorrow morning)*

>> **morgen Nachmittag** *(tomorrow afternoon)*

>> **nächsten Dienstag** *(next Tuesday)*

>> **nächste Woche** *(next week)*

>> **übermorgen** *(the day after tomorrow)*

PRACTICE

The following sentences express future events with the present tense. Use the word bank to select the logical present tense verb for each sentence and write it in the space provided.

Q. Ich _____ am Freitag mit dem Fahrrad zur Arbeit.

A. Ich **fahre** am Freitag mit dem Fahrrad zur Arbeit. *(I'm riding my bike to work on Friday.)*

fahre	besuchen	bleibe	bleiben	bleibt
fahren	fährt	gehe	geht	kommen
läuft	mache	machen		

1. Monika _____ morgen nach Dänemark.

2. Wenn es am Wochenende regnet, _____ wir keine Ausflüge *(day trips/excursions)*.

3. Tom _____ bis morgen Abend zu Hause.

4. Alexandra _____ in drei Wochen in den Urlaub.

5. Achtung! Das Kind _____ auf die Straße!

6. Morgen _____ ich wahrscheinlich nicht zum Jazzkonzert.

   Warum nicht?

7. Ich _____ zu Hause und _____ mir ein schönes Abendessen.

8. Nächstes Jahr _____ wir nach Spanien.

   Wirklich?

9. Ja, Wir _____ eine Woche in Barcelona und . . .

10. . . . _____ die interessante Museen.

11. Vielleicht *(Maybe)* _____ wir nie zurück!

As you see in the preceding section, you can express future events in German simply by using a future time expression together with a verb in present tense, as in **Ich fliege nächste Woche nach Frankfurt** *(I'm flying to Frankfurt next week)*. When a sentence includes such information, German word order comes into play.

German word order is typically *time, manner,* and *place.* Look at the breakdown of the word order for a typical sentence:

1. Subject + active verb: **Ich fahre** (*I'm traveling*)

2. Time (when): **morgen Nachmittag** (*tomorrow afternoon*)

3. Manner (how): **mit dem Zug** (*by train*)

4. Place (where): **nach Hamburg** (*to Hamburg*)

Putting it all together, the sentence looks like this: **Ich fahre morgen Nachmittag mit dem Zug nach Hamburg** (*I'm taking the train to Hamburg tomorrow afternoon*).

When you're forming a sentence that has an expression of time, such as **am Mittwoch** (*on Wednesday*) or **morgen** (*tomorrow*), as well as an expression of manner and/or place, you may want to be very clear about when something is happening. In this case, simply place the time expression at the beginning of the sentence, followed by the verb and subject. Putting the time expression at the front of a sentence may also be easier if you have trouble remembering the correct word order for the trio *time, manner,* and *place.* That way, you've taken care of the time, and you have to remember only that manner is before place.

The following example sentences show when various activities take place. All four sentences are in present in German, but they express the future in four different ways in English. You may have more than one future-tense alternative for translating the sentences into English, but all are in present tense in German:

Ich fliege am Dienstag nach Graz. *(I'm flying to Graz on Tuesday.)*

Ich denke, ich arbeite dieses Wochenende zu Hause. *(I think I'll work at home this weekend.)*

Übermorgen habe ich einen Termin mit einem neuen Kunden. *(The day after tomorrow I have an appointment with a new customer.)* **Der Kunde** means the customer. **Übermorgen** is at the beginning, so the verb comes in second position, followed by the subject.

Heute Abend spreche ich mit dem chinesischen Lieferanten. *(This evening I'm going to speak with the Chinese supplier.)* **Der Lieferant** means the supplier. The time element is first, so the verb follows in second position, followed by the subject.

You work at an international company. Your German boss, Herr Fleischmann, calls you on Monday morning and wants to know your plans for the next three weeks. Using the calendar and some future time expressions, describe what you're doing on the days you've made notes of your activities. Try expressions other than dates (such as **am 20. Oktober**) whenever possible. Note that some examples cover more than one day.

Here's some useful vocabulary: **der Termin** (*the appointment*), **der Abgabetermin** (*the deadline*), **das Meeting** (*the meeting*), and **das Zoom-Meeting** (*the Zoom meeting*).

Note: German calendars begin the week with **Montag** (*Monday*).

Montag	Dienstag	Mittwoch	Donnerstag	Freitag	Samstag	Sonntag
Q. im Büro arbeiten 12. nach Köln fliegen (Abend)	13. in Köln Auto mieten (früh) 14. 2 Termine mit Kunden (Nachmittag) 15. Abend: mit dem Kollegen essen (Hotel-Restaurant)	16. nach Düsseldorf zur Messe (trade fair) fahren 17. nach Hause fliegen	18. Zoom-Meeting mit Herrn Fleischmann & Kollegen	19. Fleischmann den vollen Bericht e-mailen (Nachmittag)	20. bei der Familie	20. bei der Familie
21. Urlaub (vacation)	21. Urlaub	21. Urlaub	21. Urlaub	21. Urlaub	Halloween 	Allerheiligen (All Saints Day)
22. mit dem osterreichischen Lieferanten telefonieren				23. Nov. 6: wichtiger Abgabetermin!		

Q. Montag *(Monday)*: **im Büro arbeiten**

A. **Ich arbeite heute Morgen im Büro.** *(I'm working in the office this morning.)* You can use this standard word order or start with the time element if you find it easier: **Heute Morgen arbeite ich im Büro.** In the answer key, I use the standard word order.

12 _____

13 _____

14 _____

15 _____

16 _____

17 _____

18 _____

19 _____

20 _____

21 _____

22 _____

23 _____

Facing the Future with Werden

Sometimes, you need to use future tense in German. German speakers do indeed use the future to describe future events, either with or without a reference to time like **nächstes Jahr** (*next year*), although speakers of German prefer present tense when they're using a time expression in the same sentence.

REMEMBER

When you make no specific mention of when something will happen, you generally use **werden** to express the future. This section shows you how to conjugate the future tense and how to use it correctly in different circumstances.

Forming the future: Werden + infinitive verb

To form the future tense, you conjugate the auxiliary (helping) verb **werden** and add the infinitive form of the verb that you want to express in the future tense: **Ich werde bald nach Hause gehen** (*I'm going home soon*). In this context, **werden** means *going to* or *will*. Notice that the infinitive form, **gehen**, is at the end of the sentence.

werde gehen (*will go, going to go*)

ich **werde** gehen	wir **werden** gehen
du **wirst** gehen	ihr **werdet** gehen
er/sie/es **wird** gehen	sie **werden** gehen
Sie **werden** gehen	

Here's the future tense of **gehen** in action:

> Ich **werde** bald nach Hause gehen. (*I'm going [to go] home soon.*)

Werden is a sneaky verb; it has several meanings. In this section, it means *will* or *going to*. But when **werden** is the main verb, it means *to become* or *get*: **Wir werden immer älter** (*We're always becoming/getting older*).

WARNING

When English speakers see **will** in German, they tend to equate it with **werden**. Watch out, because *will* indicates the future only in English:

> **Ich will nach Hause gehen.** (*I want to go home.*) **Will** comes from **wollen**: *to want to*. It's a modal verb, which means that it modifies the main verb. (For more on modal verbs, see Chapter 7.)

> **Ich werde nach Hause gehen.** (*I will go/am going home.*)

Using the future: Assuming, hoping, and emphasizing intentions

German speakers use the future tense with **werden** in several situations to express future action. Table 16-1 shows future tense usage, an example sentence in German, and the English equivalent. Notice that the infinitive verb is at the end of the sentence.

Table 16-1   Future Using Werden

Usage of Future Tense	German Example Sentence	English Equivalent
Emphasizing intention that an event will take place in the future	Ich **werde** ein erholsames Wochenende zu Hause **verbringen.**	*I'm going to spend a restful weekend at home.*
Supposing, assuming, or hoping something will happen, expressed verbally	Ich hoffe, sie **wird** es nicht **vergessen.**	*I hope she won't forget [it].*
Supposing, assuming, or hoping something will happen, expressed with an adverb	Sie **wird** es wohl nicht **vergessen.**	*She probably won't forget [it].*
Giving strong advice or a stern warning	Du **wirst** jetzt ruhig **sein!**	*Be quiet!/You <u>will</u> be quiet!*
Indicating that an event will happen after another event stated in present tense	Joachim studiert sehr fleißig, und er **wird** später ein erfolgreicher Arzt **sein.**	*Joachim is studying very hard, and later he'll be a successful doctor.*

The people in the following exercise express their hopes, dreams, and intentions by using the future **werden**. Write the correct form of **werden** in the space provided.

PRACTICE

Q. Ich _____ Freitags nicht mehr arbeiten.

A. Ich <u>werde</u> Freitags nicht mehr arbeiten. *(I won't work anymore on Fridays.)*

24 Helga: Ich _____ eine große Familie haben . . .

25 . . . und ich hoffe, meine Kinder _____ im Garten spielen.

26 Eckbert: Meine Frau _____ arbeiten . . .

27 . . . und ich denke, ich _____ zu Hause bleiben.

28 Ulrike: Ich hoffe, in 10 Jahren _____ ich nicht mehr in der Stadt leben. Warum nicht?

29 Die Mietpreise (*rental prices*) _____ zu hoch sein.

30 In den nächsten Jahren _____ Herr und Frau Doldinger fleißig arbeiten. Und dann?

31 Sie _____ ein Restaurant eröffnen (*open [up]*).

32 Mein Bruder _____ auf einem Segelboot leben . . .

33 . . . Er _____ wenig Geld haben, aber er _____ glücklich sein.

Just as German speakers use the **werden** future to emphasize that something will happen in the future, they also use it to say that something will *not* happen. The two alternatives are **werden + nicht** (*will no /won't*) and **werden + kein** (*will not/won't*), depending on what you're negating.

There are clear differences in the usage of **kein** and **nicht.** (For further details on **kein** and **nicht**, go to Chapter 6.)

TIP

>> **Kein** negates a noun, as in **keine Zeit** *(no time)*. It has case and gender endings.

 Meine Freunde werden kein Geburtstagsfest für mich organisieren. *(My friends aren't going to organize a birthday party for me.)* **Kein** negates **Geburtstagsfest**; it replaces **ein. Kein** is in the accusative case.

>> **Nicht** generally negates a verb: **nicht gehen** *(to not go)*. It can also negate an adjective, like **nicht lustig** *(not funny)*, or an adverb, like **nicht pünktlich** *(not on time)*. **Nicht** has no case or gender endings.

 Ich werde nicht hier bleiben. *(I won't stay here.)* **Nicht** negates the information **hier bleiben.**

In the following exercise, respond to each prompt by writing a sentence saying that the events will or won't happen. To help you know whether to use **kein** or **nicht,** I underline the word or expression that you negate.

PRACTICE

Q. <u>reich</u> sein, wenn ich 70 Jahre alt bin.

 Ich _____

A. Ich <u>werde nicht</u> reich <u>sein</u>, wenn ich 70 Jahre alt bin. *(I won't be rich when I'm 70 years old.)* **Reich** is an adjective, so you need to use **nicht.** To express the same information in a positive sentence, leave out **nicht. Ich werde** reich **sein.** *(I will be rich.)*

34 <u>ein Haus</u> bauen

 Ich _____

35 in die Politik <u>gehen</u>

 Ich _____

36 mit meiner Familie nach Tehachapi <u>umziehen</u>

 Ich _____

37 reisen, wenn ich Zeit und Geld dazu habe

Ich _____

38 Haustiere (pets) haben

Ich _____

39 morgen zur Arbeit fahren

Ich _____

Answers to "Looking to the Future (And Avoiding It)" Practice Questions

1. Monika **fährt** morgen nach Dänemark. (*Monika is going to Denmark tomorrow.*)

2. Wenn es am Wochenende regnet, **machen** wir keine Ausflüge. (*If it rains on the weekend, we won't make any day trips/excursions.*)

3. Tom **bleibt** bis morgen Abend zu Hause. (*Tom is staying home until tomorrow evening.*)

4. Alexandra **geht** in drei Wochen in den Urlaub. (*Alexandra is going on vacation in three weeks.*)

5. Achtung! Das Kind **läuft** auf die Straße! (*Watch out! The child is running into the street!*)

6. Morgen **gehe** ich wahrscheinlich nicht zum Jazzkonzert. (*I probably won't to the jazz concert tomorrow.*)

   Warum nicht? (*Why not?*)

7. Ich **bleibe** zu Hause und **mache** mir ein schönes Abendessen. (*I'm going to stay home and make a nice dinner.*)

8. Nächstes Jahr **fahren** wir nach Spanien. (*Next year we're driving to Spain.*)

   Wirklich? (*Really?*)

9. Ja. Wir **bleiben** eine Woche in Barcelona und. . . (*Yes. We're going to stay/staying in Barcelona for a week and . . .*)

10. . . . **besuchen** die interessante Museen. (*. . .going to visit/visiting the interesting museums.*)

11. Vielleicht **kommen** wir nie zurück! (*Maybe we'll never come back!*)

12. Ich **fliege heute Abend nach Köln.** (*I'm going to fly/I'm flying to Cologne this evening.*)

13. Ich **miete morgen früh/am Dienstag früh ein Auto in Köln.** (*I'll rent a car in Cologne tomorrow morning/on Tuesday morning.*)

14. Ich **habe morgen Nachmittag/am Dienstagnachmittag zwei Termine mit Kunden.** (*I have two appointments with customers tomorrow afternoon/on Tuesday afternoon.*)

15. Ich **esse morgen Abend/am Dienstagabend mit dem Kollegen im Hotel-Restaurant.** (*I'm having dinner with the colleague in the hotel restaurant tomorrow evening/on Tuesday evening.*)

16. Ich **fahre übermorgen/am Mittwoch nach Düsseldorf zur Messe.** (*I'm driving to the trade fair in Düsseldorf the day after tomorrow/on Wednesday.*)

17. Ich **fliege übermorgen/am Mittwoch nach Hause.** (*I'm flying home the day after tomorrow/on Wednesday.*)

18. Ich **habe am Donnerstag ein Zoom-Meeting mit Ihnen (Herrn Fleischmann) und ihren Kollegen.** (*I have a Zoom meeting with you (Herr Fleischmann) and your colleagues on Thursday.*)

19. Ich **e-maile Ihnen am Freitagnachmittag den vollen Bericht.** (*I'll email you the whole report on Friday afternoon.*)

20. **Ich bin dieses Wochenende/am Wochenende bei meiner Familie.** *(I'll be with my family this weekend/on the weekend.)*

21. **Ich habe nächste Woche Urlaub.** *(I'll be/I'm going on vacation next week.)*

22. **Ich telefoniere am Anfang der ersten Woche im November mit dem österreichischen Lieferanten.** *(At the beginning of the first week of November, I'll call the Austrian supplier.)* In German, you telephone **mit** *(with)* someone.

23. **Ich habe am 6. November einen wichtigen Abgabetermin.** *(I have an important deadline on November 6.)*

24. Helga: Ich **werde** eine große Familie haben . . . *(I'll have a large family . . .)*

25. . . . und ich hoffe, meine Kinder **werden** im Garten spielen. *(. . . and I hope my children will play in the yard/garden.)*

26. Eckbert: Meine Frau **wird** arbeiten . . . *(My wife will work . . .)*

27. . . . und ich denke, ich **werde** zu Hause bleiben. *(. . . and I think I'll stay home.)*

28. Ulrike: Ich hoffe, in 10 Jahren **werde** ich nicht mehr in der Stadt leben. *(I hope I won't be living in the city in 10 years.)*

    Warum nicht? *(Why not?)*

29. Die Mietpreise **werden** zu hoch sein. *(Rental prices will be too high.)*

30. In den nächsten Jahren **werden** Herr und Frau Doldinger fleißig arbeiten. *(In the next years, Mr and Mrs Doldinger will work hard.)*

    Und dann? *(And then?)*

31. Sie **werden** ein Restaurant eröffnen. *(They'll open [up] a restaurant.)*

32. Mein Bruder **wird** auf einem Segelboot leben . . . *(My brother will be living on a sailboat . . .)*

33. . . . Er **wird** wenig Geld haben, aber er **wird** glücklich sein. *(. . . He won't have much money, but he'll be happy.)*

34. Ich **werde kein** Haus **bauen**/Ich **werde** ein Haus **bauen**. *(I won't/will build a house.)*

35. Ich **werde nicht** in die Politik gehen./Ich **werde** in die Politik **gehen**. *(I won't/will go into politics.)*

36. Ich **werde nicht** mit meiner Familie nicht nach Tehachapi **umziehen**./Ich **werde** mit meiner Familie nach Tehachapi **umziehen**. *(I won't/will move to Tehachapi with my family.)*

37. Ich **werde nicht reisen**, wenn ich genug Zeit und Geld habe./Ich **werde reisen**, wenn ich genug Zeit und Geld habe. *(I won't/will travel when I have enough time and money.)*

38. Ich werde **keine** Haustiere **haben**./Ich **werde** Haustiere **haben**. *(I won't/will have pets.)*

39. Ich **werde** morgen **nicht** zur Arbeit **fahren**./Ich **werde** morgen zur Arbeit **fahren**. *(I won't/will go to work tomorrow.)*

5

The Part of Tens

Chapter **17**

Ten Tips for Optimizing Your German

Studying a new language can seem daunting at times. You ask what you've gotten your-self into with all those cases, genders, moods, and tenses. No worries, though. In this chapter, I show you ten essential means of optimizing your German. Each tip contains practical guidelines on how to rapidly improve your command of the language. Just keep in mind that these tips offer you an edge *only when you follow through on them!* Try some or try them all; I know you'll reap the benefits.

Think Like a Native Speaker

What happens when you speak or write in your own language? The language flows out of your mouth or onto the page. Now think about what's going on in your mind when you start formu-lating a sentence in German. The process is slower, for one thing, and it's piecemeal. You're concerned about whether the noun is **der, die,** or **das;** you're juggling cases in your mind, and you're mapping out the word order.

TIP

To overcome all these time-consuming steps, do your level best to think like a native speaker. Here's how:

>> Start thinking in chunks of language. In other words, use the structures you already know in German, and apply them. Every language is filled with frequently used expressions, such as **Viel Spaß!** *(Have fun!)* and **das gefällt mir [nicht]** *(I like/don't like that)*. Some language comes in frequently used phrases, such as **zum Beispiel** *(for example)*, **ab und zu** *(once in a while)*, and **mehr oder weniger** *(more or less)*.

>> Look for compound words, such as **Umweltverschmutzung** *(environmental pollution)*, **der Autoschlüssel** *(the car key)*, **die Eselsbrücke** *(the memory aid* [literally: *the donkey bridge*]), or **das Fingerspitzengefühl** *(tactfulness* [literally: *the fingertip feeling*]).

Break Down Word Combinations

Although at first glance, a German text may seem to be filled with long, complicated words, go for the jugular: Break down those torturously long words, and figure out what each part means. Even short words may have two or more parts.

Nouns are notable for stringing words and word parts together; verbs are also culprits in this department. Take the verb **vorhaben;** it looks like the preposition **vor** *(in front of)* combined with **haben** *(to have)*. In English, it means *to plan something*. When you think about the literal meaning — *to have something in front* — you can often grasp the figurative meaning as well.

Use What You Know

If German is a mostly purebred language, English is a crafty mutt. Incorporated into English usage are elements of Latin, Greek, German, French, and even Danish. Why not dip into English, and use it in German? German hasn't been averse to using many words that English has borrowed. Both English and German have acquisitions from French (souvenir), Spanish (patio), Italian (ciao), and so on. *Cognates* — words that share an ancestor — include the chunk of Germanic-type words known to you in English but with some spelling differences. Be on the lookout for patterns, such as converting the **v** to *f* (as in **Vater** = *father*) or changing the **d** to *th* (as in **Bad** = *bath*).

WARNING

Check to make sure a word that *looks* like English has the same meaning in German. After all, **der Mist** isn't *a thick fog/fine rain;* it actually means *dung* in German!

Get Going on Grammar

After you dive into the Grand World of German Grammar, take things slow and easy. Don't panic. There's a whole lot of logic in German grammar. As you tread your way through, remember that the following elements are important in German grammar:

>> **Word order:** After you accept the rules of the game, you're all set to cut and paste the words you need to construct a grammatically decent sentence. Check out Chapter 2 for general info on word order.

>> **Case and gender:** You definitely need to know and accept these elements, not fight them. Try to master the ins and outs of one grammar aspect step by step. Consider a two-way preposition such as **in** (**ich gehe ins Hotel** versus **ich bin im Hotel**), which can be *I'm going in(to) the hotel* (movement = accusative) or *I'm in the hotel* (location = dative); then write down some examples you can use that show the difference between the two. Keep them handy for later use. (For more on prepositions, see Chapter 13.)

Read and Listen Actively

While you're reading or even listening to German, actively think about the grammar and word order. A word in context may show its gender, for example. As for verbs, notice the location of the verb parts in a sentence. For vocabulary acquisition, try lowbrow alternatives such as flashcards or highbrow gadgets like an electronic translator. The audio feature is helpful. Check out listening material for your car. Listen to podcasts and news in slow German. Watch German movies or documentaries.

TIP

One of the best ways to improve your German is to take advantage of all the German available to you on the Internet; just look for pages that use the .de option of your browser (in place of .com and other extensions).

Experiment with What Works Best

If there were ever an easy path to language fluency, the discoverer would make a million. Even so, no two people acquire a language in exactly the same way. You may not be the kind of person who learns to ski by going straight down the steepest slope the first day. You may need some gentle pointers about turning, braking, and knowing how to fall somewhat safely. Make it your mission to figure out what works best for you.

TIP

Mentally leaf through the list of any skills you've acquired successfully, even if they're unrelated to language, from assembling furniture to taking apart a car engine. Ask yourself how you did it. You may be the read-the-manual type, the trial-and-error type, or a blend of both. Now try experimenting. Get a dialogue, a text, or anything you want to use later. Try these three methods of gaining fluency:

>> **Seeing:** Draw sketches of significant German words. Don't stop at the obvious, such as nouns like **der Baum,** illustrated by a picture of a tree. Label a bunch of emojis with German adjectives that describe them. Indicate a verb such as **wandern** *(to hike)* with a stick figure walking up a mountain. (Don't forget the **Rucksack!**)

>> **Speaking and hearing:** Practice reading the material to yourself; then record your own voice, listen, and record again until you're reasonably satisfied with your results. Or read in a low voice, using a metronome or slow music for rhythm. Also, try singing some German songs, or chant phrases you need to use often.

>> **Doing:** Try reading out loud and walking slowly around your living room (but don't stumble over the dog). As you read through verbs, act out the motions. For **bezahlen** *(to pay)*, take an imaginary credit card out of your pocket. Use finger puppets to practice your own dialogues in situations such as shopping, making small talk, ordering in a restaurant, asking for directions, and so on.

Find what works and implement that technique for improving your German. Go ahead: Be a risk-taker! You've got plenty to gain from experimenting — drug-free!

Germanify Your Home

To get a firm understanding of German, why not Germanify your home? Whatever you do is bound to pay off down the line. Here are some ideas:

>> **Make sticky labels for furniture, appliances, objects, or even food items.** Concentrate on one room at a time, touching the objects and saying the names out loud.

>> **Describe daily chores and routines to yourself as you're doing them.** Write useful German phrases on a piece of paper and stick it on your bathroom mirror. Repeat the words while brushing your teeth (well, maybe while brushing your hair). Write shopping lists in German. Read supermarket flyers, mumbling the prices to yourself in German.

Integrate German into Your Routine

Face it: When you're serious about getting ahead with your German, you need time. But who has oodles of leftover hours each day? Try figuring out how to snatch some minutes from your regular routine and devote them to German. Spread out those time bites over a whole day and take your stuff with you on the road. If you're anything like the average somewhat-disorganized Tom, Dick, or Harriet, you're doing yourself a favor by organizing your time for German. Here are some ideas:

>> Listen to German podcasts while working out at the gym.

>> Tuck some good old-fashioned homemade flashcards in your pocket. I know a woman in upper-level management who used her cards whenever she was waiting for the elevator to arrive or a meeting to start.

Embrace the Culture

Your grasp of German is relevant only to the extent to which you're able to integrate language and culture. After all, language is intimately connected with the people who speak it. Broaden your horizons by finding out how German-speaking people think and act. Becoming aware of their hopes and dreams, and gaining insight into their way of life, is your path to a rich cultural heritage.

Set Goals and Reward Yourself

Set up a modest challenge for yourself by devoting one afternoon a month to pursuing your interest in German language and culture. Give yourself just rewards for your efforts. The idea here is looking at the bigger picture. Go online and plan a bicycling trip along the Danube next fall. Go to dinner at a German-style restaurant or try cooking some German specialties for your friends. Go all out: Change careers: Learn the beer-brewing trade at **Weihenstephaner Brauerei** in Bavaria. Enjoy even the smallest accomplishments you make. **Tschüss!** Oh, and **viel Spaß!**

Chapter **18**

Ten Pitfalls to Avoid in German

Everyone makes mistakes while learning a language — some big, some small, some horribly embarrassing, and some riotously funny. As you read this book, you don't have to worry much about making mistakes. But for someone sitting in a language class among peers or traveling in a far-off country, the fear of making a mistake can be strong enough to give a well-adjusted, normally curious person a deflated, get-me-out-of-this-muck type of mindset.

Doing the exercises in this book isn't a substitute for getting out there and talking and writing to as many people as possible — in German. But this book can help you come prepared. This chapter is aimed at helping you sidestep the biggest blunders you're likely to make in German. So never fear . . . help is on the way!

Attempting Word-for-Word Translations

Leave the translating to the translators. It's not your job. (If it were, you'd know instinctively to shy away from word-for-word translations!) The instant online translating tools will never be as accurate as the best simultaneous interpreters at the United Nations. Why not? Single words, let alone larger chunks of language, have many shades of meaning. When strung together in sentences, words can even mean something entirely different from the words as separate entities. So please don't try to win a Nobel Prize by analyzing German grammar or inventing mathematical equations consisting of German word A + German word B = English word AB.

TIP

Word-for-word translations may work, but then again, you may end up the laughingstock of your listeners or readership. Tell yourself not to succumb to the temptation of thinking that a word, expression, sentence structure, or grammar point — *anything at all* — in English is equivalent to something in German, or vice versa (unless you know for sure that it's a real *cognate* [a word with the same meaning in two languages]). **Butter** is what you put on your toast, but **Gift** is (ideally) *not* what you give someone on their birthday: **Gift** means *poison* in German!

Downplaying Gender and Case

By messing up the case and gender endings, you can come up with any number of very embarrassing results! Gender and case are the underpinnings of German grammar. Nouns, pronouns, adjectives, and prepositions are all influenced by gender and case, as well as number. Be sure you know what the three mean:

>> *Number* is whether a noun or a pronoun is singular or plural. Not even number is always the same in German and English; **die Schere** *(the scissors)*, for example, is singular in German.

>> *Gender* is the triumvirate of **der** *(masculine)*, **die** *(feminine)*, and **das** *(neuter)*, plus the other forms of **der, die,** and **das** that change spelling in various cases.

>> *Case* isn't related to brief-, suit-, or carrying case; rather, it's the essential tool for putting words together in a sentence to make sense. All four cases — nominative, accusative, dative, and genitive — are in the example sentence **Der Liebhaber gab dem Hund seiner Geliebten eine Leckerei** *(The lover gave his sweetheart's dog a treat)*:

- *Nominative:* **Der Liebhaber** *(The lover)*
- *Dative:* **gab dem Hund** *(gave [to] the dog)*
- *Genitive:* **seiner Geliebten** *([of] his sweetheart/his sweetheart's)*
- *Accusative:* **eine Leckerei.** *(a treat.)*

Wondering Which Word Order

In German, you may frequently get stumped on which word goes where. To avoid mistakes, make sure you know the basics of correct word order. Here's a quick overview of German's three main patterns:

>> **Standard:** The order is *subject + verb + other information*; the verb is in second position.

Bonnie hat viel Geld. *(Bonnie has a lot of money.)*

» *Verb in second position* is one essential mantra to remember. Look at the example. Substitute **ihr ältester Onkel, Zack Kohle aus Gelsenkirchen** (*her oldest uncle, Zack Kohle from Gelsenkirchen*) for **Bonnie**, and the word order would be the same: **Ihr ältester Onkel, Zack Kohle aus Gelsenkirchen, hat viel Geld**. Why? All the information about the uncle counts as one element — namely, the subject of the sentence.

» **Inverted:** The verb comes first, as in yes/no questions.

> **Hat Bonnie viel Geld?** (*Does Bonnie have a lot of money?*)

» **Subordinate clause:** The active verb (the conjugated part) comes at the end of a subordinate clause, preceded by the past participle (if present).

> **Bonnie hat viel Geld, weil sie eine Bank überfallen hat.** (*Bonnie has a lot of money because she robbed a bank.*) The conjugated verb **hat** is at the end of the sentence, preceded by **überfallen** (*robbed*), the past participle.

Think, Thought, Thunk: (Mis)handling Verbs

A sentence is made up of various parts of speech, such as nouns, verbs, and adjectives. The single most important part of speech of a sentence that communicates your ideas is the verb. Use the right verb to convey your thoughts, and people are likely to understand your message, even if other factors in your sentence — such as word endings, word order, and who knows what else — aren't quite up to snuff. So you select a verb. What next? You need to conjugate the verb correctly and know which verb tense to use; otherwise, people may stare at you as though you just landed from Mars.

You can rattle off **ich habe, du hast, er/sie/es hat** to your heart's content in the shower. But in a restaurant, you're communicating with the server about food, so you're probably better off combining verbs appropriately to order a meal: **Was würden Sie empfehlen?** (*What would you recommend?*)

(Mis)Placing Prepositions and Prefixes

Take on the task of tackling both groups of these tricksters: prefixes and prepositions. Prefixes are an important yet sometimes-overlooked part of German. They alter the meaning of the word they're attached to, and some prefixes in combination with certain verb tenses are unattached, so they have a quirky word order.

The preppy prepositions make great friends if you put in a fair amount of effort to find out which case you're dealing with. The bottom line: Never underestimate the power of a preposition. They're more influential in deciding the outcome of a noun or adjective's ending than you'd imagine at first. Also, some prepositions, such as **entlang**, are placed after the words they're linked to, as in **Gehen Sie die Straße entlang** (*Go along this street*).

Prepositions modify the information following them by using one of three cases: accusative, dative, or genitive. The words following the preposition have case endings corresponding to one of these three cases. **Mit** *(in, with)*, for example, always calls for the dative case. Check out the following sentence:

Ich fahre gern mit mein**em** alt**en** Kabriolet. *(I like to drive my old convertible [car].)* The case endings for the dative preposition **mit** are in bold.

Skipping Capitalization and Umlauts

Yield to the speed of lifestyles these days, and you're likely to wish that e. e. cummings had gotten his way and eradicated nearly all capitalization. Well, he didn't, and your otherwise-passable German can become confusing if you're sloppy about which words to capitalize.

Improper capitalization may just be the easiest blunder to remedy as soon as you realize how few ground rules there are. By now, you probably know to capitalize all nouns, as well as **Sie** (the formal address for *you*) and its sidekicks **Ihnen** and **Ihr**. The sticklers are the adjectives that function as nouns, such as nationalities and colors. You see nationalities and colors used as nouns and adjectives, but only the nouns are capitalized:

Ein Amerikaner (noun) f**uhr sein deutsches** (adjective) **Auto.** *(An American was driving his German car.)*

Er hatte die gelbe (adjective) **Ampel nicht gesehen, und fuhr bei Rot** (noun) **über die Ampel.** *(He didn't see the yellow light and drove through a red light.)* Although the *red* in *red light* is an adjective in English, it's a noun in German. How can that be? It's alone (**bei Rot**), without mentioning **Ampel**, so it's functioning as a noun.

Slipping on Super-Slick Sentences

Your engines are revved, and you're ready to **Deutsch sprechen oder schreiben** *(speak or write German)*, so you figure, why not make a nice long sentence instead of short, choppy baby sentences like *See Spot run?* Sure . . . if you know how to juggle a million grammar rules faster than the speed of your tongue or keyboard. How about slowing down? The goal of any language is communication, and a lean, clear sentence is more likely to get your point across. You're probably on thin ice grammatically speaking if your sentence runs longer than two lines — unless Goethe is your idol.

Being Informal on the Wrong Occasion

Being informal on the wrong occasion isn't a matter of wearing jeans to a country-club wedding; it's a matter of using **du** on the wrong occasion. You should show respect, distance, and decorum by addressing your listener or reader as **Sie** when appropriate. That last tidbit — *when* *appropriate* — is the kicker. In a nutshell, play it safe by using **Sie** to speak or write to everyone except relatives, children, friends, dogs, cats, and a talking horse.

Rejecting Review

Instead of hurrying with your writing, give it a quick read-through again. You can use a plethora of means to check your written language. Go for it. Try a different method for a week and decide what works best for you; maybe use all the methods you try. Here are some options that may be right for you:

>> Consult native speakers diplomatically (buy them lunch and ask for pointers on the market study you're preparing to implement).

>> Go to a bookstore that has the kind of coffee you like and peruse the German/English dictionaries . . . and your wallet. Then splurge. (I don't mean on the coffee.) Next, go online to compare dictionary resources there.

Giving Up

When you're working on mastering a new language or a new sport, you may reach a plateau where you get totally discouraged and want to throw in the towel. That's exactly the time to rally; run to the fridge; and grab a smoothie, energy drink, water, or whatever is going to enable you to get past that stumbling block — and beyond. When you hit that **Mauer aus Ziegelstein** *(brick wall)*, simply go around it. Feel good about what you already know. And, to close, I wish you **Viel Glück!** *(Good luck!)*

6

Appendixes

Appendix **A**
Verb Charts

In this appendix, I list the conjugations for various verbs in order of the subject pronouns, from first- to third-person singular, then from first- to third-person plural, and finally the formal second-person address: **ich, du, er/sie/es, wir, ihr, sie,** and **Sie.** For the imperative (used for suggestions and commands), the persons are **du, ihr, Sie.** You also find a list that contains the principal parts of high-frequency strong and irregular weak verbs.

Conjugating Verbs in Present and Simple Past Tenses

You conjugate verbs in the present and simple past by combining the appropriate stem and ending for that verb. I list the endings in Table A-1. The patterns are as follows:

>> **Present tense; simple past tense of weak regular verbs:** Start with the stem (infinitive minus **-en** ending); add the appropriate ending from Table A-1.

>> **Simple past tense of weak irregular verbs and strong verbs:** Begin with the simple past stem; add the appropriate ending from Table A-1.

Table A-1   Present-Tense and Simple-Past-Tense Verb Endings

Subject Pronoun	Present: Most Verbs	Present: Stem Ending in d, t, fn, gn	Simple Past: Weak Verbs (Regular and Irregular)	Simple Past: Weak Verbs, Stem Ending in d, t, fn, gn	Simple Past: Strong Verbs
ich	-e	-e	-te	-ete	-
du	-st	-est	-test	-etest	-st
er/sie/es	-t	-et	-te	-ete	-
wir	-en	-en	-ten	-eten	-en
ihr	-t	-et	-tet	-etet	-t
sie	-en	-en	-ten	-eten	-en
Sie	-en	-en	-ten	-eten	-en

Conjugating Verbs in the Present Perfect and Future

The following sections show you how to conjugate verbs so you can use them in your writing and speech.

Present perfect

To form the present perfect, you conjugate the present tense of the auxiliary **haben** (*to have*) or **sein** (*to be*); then add the past participle; for example, **ich habe gesehen** (*I have seen/saw*) and **ich bin gegangen** (*I have gone/went*).

For the past participle of most weak verbs, take the prefix **ge-**, add the infinitive stem (formed by dropping the **-en** from the infinitive), and add the ending **-t**. Example: **ge- + wohn- + -t = gewohnt** (*lived*). Verbs with the stem ending in **d, t, fn,** or **gn** add **-e** before the final **-t** ending. Example: **ge- + arbeit- + -et = gearbeitet** (*worked*).

Some verbs don't use the **ge-** prefix. Examples include verbs with the infinitive ending in **-ieren**, such as **informieren** (*to inform*) → **informiert** (*informed*) and **telefonieren** (*to telephone*) → *telefoniert* (*telephoned*). Some inseparable-prefix verbs that don't use the **ge-** prefix include **bekommen** (*to get*), **gehören** (*to belong to*), and **vergessen** (*to forget*).

The past participle of most strong verbs begins with the prefix **ge-** and ends in **-en**. Many past participles have stem vowel changes, and some have both vowel and consonant changes. For example, **sehen** (*to see*) ⇨ **gesehen** (*seen*) has no stem change; **finden** (*to find*) ⇨ **gefunden** (*found*) has a vowel change; and **sitzen** (*to sit*) ⇨ **gesessen** (*sat*) has both vowel and consonant changes. Table A-2, at the end of this chapter, shows the past participles for strong verbs.

The past participles of irregular verbs such as auxiliaries may have different endings. I show these endings separately in the corresponding charts in this appendix.

Future

For the future tense, conjugate the present tense of the auxiliary verb **werden** — **werde, wirst, wird, werden, werdet, werden, werden** — and add the infinitive form of the main verb. Example: **Ich werde fahren** (*I will go/drive*).

Weak Verbs

This section covers the various ways to handle weak verbs for different tenses.

Regular verbs (no stem change in the simple past)

wohnen (to live, reside)

Present Tense Stem: wohn-

Simple Past (1st/3rd-person singular): wohnte

Past Participle: gewohnt; **Auxiliary Verb:** haben

Present: wohn**e**, wohn**st**, wohn**t**, wohn**en**, wohn**t**, wohn**en**, wohn**en**

Simple Past: wohn**te**, wohn**test**, wohn**te**, wohn**ten**, wohn**tet**, wohn**ten**, wohn**ten**

Imperative: wohne, wohnt, wohnen Sie

Some other verbs like this are **brauchen** (*to need*), **feiern** (*to celebrate*), **glauben** (*to believe*), **hören** (*to hear*), **kaufen** (*to buy*), **lachen** (*to laugh*), **lernen** (*to learn*), **machen** (*to make, do*), **sagen** (*to say*), and **spielen** (*to play*).

Regular verbs (with stem ending in -d, -t, -fn or -gn)

arbeiten (to work)

Present Tense Stem: arbeit-

Simple Past (1st/3rd-person singular): arbeitete

Past Participle: gearbeitet; **Auxiliary Verb:** haben

Present: arbeit**e**, arbeit**est**, arbeit**et**, arbeit**en**, arbeit**et**, arbeit**en**, arbeit**en**

Simple Past: arbeit**ete**, arbeit**etest**, arbeit**ete**, arbeit**eten**, arbeit**etet**, arbeit**eten**, arbeit**eten**

Imperative: arbeite, arbeitet, arbeiten Sie

Some other verbs like this are **kosten** (*to cost*), **öffnen** (*to open*), **reden** (*to talk*), **regnen** (*to rain*), and **warten** (*to wait*).

Irregular weak verbs (stem change in the simple past)

denken (to think)

Present Tense Stem: denk-

Simple Past (1st/3rd-person singular): dachte

Past Participle: gedacht; **Auxiliary Verb:** haben

Present: denke, denkst, denkt, denken, denkt, denken, denken

Simple Past: dachte, dachtest, dachte, dachten, dachtet, dachten, dachten

Imperative: denke, denkt, denken Sie

Other verbs like this are listed in Table A-2, at the end of this chapter.

Strong Verbs

This section covers the various ways to handle strong verbs for different tenses.

Verbs with auxiliary haben

trinken (to drink)

Present Tense Stem: trink-

Simple Past (1st/3rd-person singular): trank

Past Participle: getrunken; **Auxiliary Verb:** haben

Present: trinke, trinkst, trinkt, trinken, trinkt, trinken, trinken

Simple Past: trank, trankst, trank, tranken, trankt, tranken, tranken

Imperative: trinke, trinkt, trinken Sie

Other verbs like this are listed in Table A-2.

Verbs with auxiliary sein

kommen (to come)

Present Tense Stem: komm-

Simple Past (1st/3rd-person singular): kam

Past Participle: gekommen; **Auxiliary Verb:** sein

Present: komme, kommst, kommt, kommen, kommt, kommen, kommen

Simple Past: kam, kam**st**, kam, kam**en**, kam**t**, kam**en**, kam**en**

Imperative: komme, kommt, kommen Sie

Other verbs like this are listed in Table A–2.

Verbs with present-tense vowel change in second- and third-person singular

lesen (to read)

Present Tense Stem: les-; **Present Tense Vowel Change:** liest

Simple Past (1st/3rd-person singular): las

Past Participle: gelesen; **Auxiliary Verb:** haben

Present: lese, **liest**, **liest**, les**en**, les**t**, les**en**, les**en**

Simple Past: las, las**est**, las, las**en**, las**t**, las**en**, las**en**

Imperative: lies, lest, lesen Sie

Other verbs like this are listed in Table A–2.

Separable-Prefix Verbs

Separable prefix have their own unique ways of forming tenses.

mitbringen (to bring along)

Present Tense Stem: bring- mit

Simple Past (1st/3rd-person singular): brachte mit

Past Participle: mitgebracht; **Auxiliary Verb:** haben

Present: mitbringe, mitbring**st**, mitbring**t**, mitbring**en**, mitbring**t**, mitbring**en**, mitbring**en**

Simple Past: brach**te** mit, brach**test** mit, brach**te** mit, brach**ten** mit, brach**tet** mit, brach**ten** mit, brach**ten** mit

Imperative: bringe mit, bringt mit, bringen Sie mit

Some other similar verbs are **anhaben** (*to wear*), **anrufen** (*to telephone*), **fernsehen** (*to watch TV*), and **vorhaben** (*to plan*).

Inseparable-Prefix Verbs (without Ge- Prefix in the Past Participle)

Inseparable prefix are also unique when it comes to forming tenses.

Verbs with a past participle ending in -t

bezahlen (to pay)

Present Tense Stem: bezahl-

Simple Past (1st/3rd-person singular): bezahlte

Past Participle: bezahlt; **Auxiliary Verb:** haben

Present: bezahle, bezahlst, bezahlt, bezahlen, bezahlt, bezahlen, bezahlen

Simple Past: bezahlte, bezahltest, bezahlte, bezahlten, bezahltet, bezahlten, bezahlten

Imperative: bezahle, bezahlt, bezahlen Sie

Some other verbs like this are **beantworten** (*to answer*), **besuchen** (*to visit*), **erklären** (*to explain*), **gehören** (*to belong to*), and **versuchen** (*to try*).

Verbs with a past participle ending in -en

gefallen (to like)

Present Tense Stem: gefall-

Present-Tense Vowel Change (in 2nd/3rd-person singular): gefäll-

Simple Past (1st/3rd-person singular): gefiel

Past Participle: gefallen; **Auxiliary Verb:** haben

Present: gefalle, gefällst, gefällt, gefallen, gefallt, gefallen, gefallen

Simple Past: gefiel, gefielst, gefiel, gefielen, gefielt, gefielen, gefielen

Imperative: gefalle, gefallt, gefallen Sie

Other verbs like this are listed in Table A-2, at the end of the chapter.

Auxiliary Verbs Haben, Sein, and Werden

The most common verbs in the German language — haben, sein, and werden — are also the strangest. Go figure.

haben (to have)

Present (and auxiliary for verbs using haben in present perfect): habe, hast, hat, haben, habt, haben, haben

Simple Past (1st/3rd-person singular): hatte

Past Participle: gehabt; **Auxiliary Verb:** haben

Simple Past: hatte, hattest, hatte, hatten, hattet, hatten, hatten

Imperative: habe, habt, haben Sie

sein (to be)

Present (and auxiliary for verbs using sein in present perfect): bin, bist, ist, sind, seid, sind, sind

Simple Past (1st/3rd-person singular): war

Past Participle: gewesen; **Auxiliary Verb:** sein

Simple Past: war, warst, war, waren, wart, waren, waren

Imperative: sei, seid, seien Sie

werden (to become, shall, will)

Present: werde, wirst, wird, werden, werdet, werden

Simple Past (1st/3rd-person singular): wurde

Past Participle: geworden; **Auxiliary Verb:** sein

Simple Past: wurde, wurdest, wurde, wurden, wurdet, wurden, wurden

Imperative: werde, werdet, werden Sie

Note: The present of **werden** is the auxiliary verb for forming the future tense.

Note: To express *would + [main verb]* for hypothetical statements, wishes, and to make polite requests, many verbs use: würde, würdest, würde, würden, würdet, würden, würden. Example: **Würden** Sie mir bitte **helfen**? (*Would you help me, please?*)

Modal Auxiliary Verbs

The modal verbs present some special challenges when forming tenses.

dürfen (to be allowed, may)

Present: darf, darfst, darf, dürfen, dürft, dürfen, dürfen

Simple Past (1st/3rd-person singular): durfte

Past Participle: gedurft; **Auxiliary Verb:** haben

Simple Past: durfte, durftest, durfte, durften, durftet, durften, durften

können (to be able to, can, to know how to do something)

Present: kann, kann**st**, kann, könn**en**, könn**t**, könn**en**, könn**en**

Simple Past (1st/3rd-person singular): konn**te**

Past Participle: gekonnt; **Auxiliary Verb:** haben

Simple Past: konn**te**, konn**test**, konn**te**, konn**ten**, konn**tet**, konn**ten**, konn**ten**

mögen (to like [to], want to)

Present: mag, mag**st**, mag, mög**en**, mög**t**, mög**en**, mög**en**

Simple Past (1st/3rd-person singular): moch**te**

Past Participle: gemocht; **Auxiliary Verb:** haben

Simple Past: moch**te**, moch**test**, moch**te**, moch**ten**, moch**tet**, moch**ten**, moch**ten**

Note: To express *would like [to]*, use **möchten:** möch**te**, möch**test**, möch**te**, möch**ten**, möch**tet**, möch**ten**, möch**ten**

müssen (to have to, must)

Present: muss, muss**t**, muss, müss**en**, müss**t**, müss**en**, müss**en**

Simple Past (1st/3rd-person singular): muss**te**

Past Participle: gemusst; **Auxiliary Verb:** haben

Simple Past: muss**te**, muss**test**, muss**te**, muss**ten**, muss**tet**, muss**ten**, muss**ten**

sollen (to be supposed to, should)

Present: soll, soll**st**, soll, soll**en**, soll**t**, soll**en**, soll**en**

Simple Past (1st/3rd-person singular): soll**te**

Past Participle: gesollt; **Auxiliary Verb:** haben

Simple Past: soll**te**, soll**test**, soll**te**, soll**ten**, soll**tet**, soll**ten**, soll**ten**

wollen (to want to)

Present: will, will**st**, will, woll**en**, woll**t**, woll**en**, woll**en**

Simple Past (1st/3rd-person singular): woll**te**

Past Participle: gewollt; **Auxiliary Verb:** haben

Simple Past: woll**te**, woll**test**, woll**te**, woll**ten**, woll**tet**, woll**ten**, woll**ten**

Principal Parts of Weak Verbs

Table A-2 contains high-frequency strong verbs, irregular weak verbs, modal auxiliaries, common separable-prefix verbs whose base verb is not listed, **haben** (*to have*), and **sein** (*to be*). The past participles that use the auxiliary **sein** are indicated; the others use **haben**.

Table A-2   Principal Parts of Strong and Irregular Weak Verbs

Infinitive	Stem Change (3rd-Person Singular Present)	Simple Past	Past Participle	English Meaning
anfangen	fängt an	fing an	angefangen	to start, begin
anrufen		rief an	angerufen	to telephone
beginnen		begann	begonnen	to begin
bekommen		bekam	bekommen	to get
bleiben		blieb	ist geblieben	to stay
brechen	bricht	brach	gebrochen	to break
bringen		brachte	gebracht	to bring
denken		dachte	gedacht	to think
dürfen	darf	durfte	gedurft	to be permitted to, may
einladen	lädt ein	lud ein	eingeladen	to invite
empfehlen	empfiehlt	empfahl	empfohlen	to recommend
entscheiden		entschied	entschieden	to decide
essen	isst	aß	gegessen	to eat
fahren	fährt	fuhr	ist gefahren	to go, drive, travel
fallen	fällt	fiel	ist gefallen	to fall
finden		fand	gefunden	to find
fliegen		flog	ist geflogen	to fly
geben	gibt	gab	gegeben	to give
gefallen	gefällt	gefiel	gefallen	to like
gehen		ging	ist gegangen	to go
gewinnen		gewann	gewonnen	to win
haben	hat	hatte	gehabt	to have
halten	hält	hielt	gehalten	to hold, stop
heißen		hieß	geheißen	to be called, named
helfen	hilft	half	geholfen	to help
kennen		kannte	gekannt	to know (person)
kommen		kam	ist gekommen	to come
können	kann	konnte	gekonnt	to be able to, can
lassen	lässt	ließ	gelassen	to let
laufen	läuft	lief	ist gelaufen	to run
lesen	liest	las	gelesen	to read
liegen		lag	gelegen	to lie (situated)
mögen	mag	mochte	gemocht	to like
müssen	muss	musste	gemusst	to have to, must
nehmen	nimmt	nahm	genommen	to take
schlafen	schläft	schlief	geschlafen	to sleep
schließen		schloss	geschlossen	to close
schreiben		schrieb	geschrieben	to write
schwimmen		schwamm	ist geschwommen	to swim

(continued)

Table A-2 *(continued)*

Infinitive	Stem Change (3rd-Person Singular Present)	Simple Past	Past Participle	English Meaning
sehen	sieht	sah	gesehen	to see
sein	ist	war	ist gewesen	to be
singen		sang	gesungen	to sing
sitzen		saß	gesessen	to sit
sollen	soll	sollte	gesollt	to be supposed to, should
sprechen	spricht	sprach	gesprochen	to speak
stehen		stand	gestanden	to stand
sterben	stirbt	starb	ist gestorben	to die
tragen	trägt	trug	getragen	to wear, carry
treffen	trifft	traf	getroffen	to meet
trinken		trank	getrunken	to drink
tun		tat	getan	to do
vergessen	vergisst	vergaß	vergessen	to forget
verlieren		verlor	verloren	to lose
verstehen		verstand	verstanden	to understand
waschen	wäscht	wusch	gewaschen	to wash
werden	wird	wurde	ist geworden	to become, will
wissen	weiß	wusste	gewusst	to know (fact)
wollen	will	wollte	gewollt	to want (to)

Appendix B
English-German Dictionary

Here's some of the German vocabulary used throughout this book, arranged alphabetically by the English translation, to help you when reading or listening to German.

a, an: **ein**
(to be) able to, can: **können**
after, to: **nach**
again: **wieder**
all: **alle**
to allow, let: **lassen**
(to be) allowed to: **dürfen**
also: **auch**
although: **obwohl**
always: **immer**
and: **und**
to answer: **antworten**
around, at: **um**

to ask: **fragen**
at: **an, auf, bei, um**
bad: **schlecht**
(to) be: **sein**
to be called, named: **heißen**
because: **da, denn, weil**
because of: **wegen**
to become, will: **werden**
to begin: **anfangen, beginnen**
before: **vor**
behind: **hinter**
between: **zwischen**
to bring: **bringen**

but: **aber, doch**
but rather: **sondern**
to buy: **kaufen**
by: **an, bei**
(to be) called, named: **heißen**
can: **können**
to carry: **tragen**
to come: **kommen**
to cost: **kosten**
to cut: **schneiden**
to dance: **tanzen**
to do: **tun, machen**
to drink: **trinken**
to drive: **fahren**
dry: **trocken**
during: **während**
to eat: **essen**
to enjoy: **gefallen**
except for: **außer**
to fall: **fallen**
few: **wenig(e)**
to find: **finden**
to fit: **passen**
to fly: **fliegen**
for: **für, seit** (time)
to forget: **vergessen**
from where: **woher**
from: **von, aus**
to get: **bekommen**
to give: **geben**
to give (a present): **schenken**
to go: **gehen, fahren**
good: **gut**
happy: **glücklich**
to have: **haben**
to have to, must: **müssen**
he: **er**
to hear: **hören**
to help: **helfen**
her: **sie, ihr**
here: **hier**

high: **hoch**
to hike: **wandern**
him: **ihn, ihm**
his: **sein**
to hold, stop: **halten**
to hope: **hoffen**
how: **wie**
how many: **wie viele**
how much: **wie viel**
I: **ich**
if, whether: **wenn**
if: **ob**
in: **in**
in case: **falls**
in order to: **um . . . zu . . .**
in spite of: **trotz**
inexpensive: **billig**
instead of: **statt**
it; its: **es, ihm; sein**
to know (fact): **wissen**
to know (be familiar with): **kennen**
last: **letzter**
to last: **dauern**
late: **spät**
to laugh: **lachen**
to learn: **lernen**
to let, allow: **lassen**
to like (to): **mögen**
to like, enjoy: **gefallen**
little (quantity): **wenig**
to live: **wohnen, leben**
to lose: **verlieren**
long: **lang**
lovely, gorgeous: **wunderschön**
to make, do: **machen**
may: **dürfen**
me: **mich, mir**
to meet: **treffen**
must: **müssen**
my: **mein**
(to be) named, called: **heißen**

near: **nah, in der Nähe von**
to need: **brauchen**
next: **nächster**
next to: **neben**
nice: **nett**
no: **nein**
not: **kein, nicht**
not only . . . but also: **nicht nur . . . sondern auch**
now: **jetzt**
of course: **gewiss, klar**
often: **oft**
old: **alt**
on: **auf, an**
only: **nur**
or: **oder**
our: **unser**
over: **über**
to pay: **bezahlen, zahlen**
perhaps: **vielleicht**
to play: **spielen**
polite: **höflich**
to put: **stellen, setzen**
to rain: **regnen**
to read: **lesen**
to recommend: **empfehlen**
to run: **laufen**
to say: **sagen**
to see: **sehen**
sensible: **vernünftig**
she, it, they: **sie**
to go shopping: **einkaufen**
should: **sollen**
since: **seit**
to sing: **singen**
to sit down: **setzen**
to sleep: **schlafen**
slow(ly): **langsam**
so; so that: **also; damit**
some, something: **etwas**
to speak: **sprechen**

to stand: **stehen, stellen**
to stay: **bleiben**
still: **noch**
to stop: **halten**
to study: **studieren**
such: **so**
sure: **sicher**
to swim: **schwimmen**
to take: **nehmen**
to talk: **reden, sprechen**
to telephone: **anrufen**
than: **als**
that: **dass**
the: **das** (n.)/**der** (m.)/**die** (f.)
their: **ihr**
them: **sie, ihnen**
then: **dann**
they: **sie**
to: **zu, nach**
to think: **denken**
this, that, these, those: **dies-**
through: **durch**
to throw: **werfen**
to: **zu, nach**
too; too many; too much: **zu; zu viele; zu viel**
to travel: **reisen**
to understand: **verstehen**
us: **uns**
to visit: **besuchen**
to wait: **warten**
to walk: **spazieren gehen**
to want (to): **wollen**
to wash: **waschen**
to watch TV: **fernsehen**
we: **wir**
to wear: **tragen**
wet: **nass**
what: **was**
what kind of: **was für**
when: **wann, wenn, als**

where: **wo**
where to: **wohin**
whether: **ob, falls**
which: **welch-**
who: **wer**
why: **warum**
will: **werden**
to win: **gewinnen**
with: **mit**
without: **ohne**
to work: **arbeiten**

would like to: **möchten**
to write: **schreiben**
yes: **ja**
you (impersonal), *one:* **man**
you (inf., pl.): **ihr, euch**
you (form.): **Sie, Ihnen**
you (inf., sing.): **du, dich, dir**
young: **jung**
your (form.): **Ihr**
your (inf., pl.): **euer**
your (inf., sing.): **dein**

Appendix **C**

German-English Dictionary

Here's some of the German vocabulary used throughout this book, arranged alphabetically by the German translation, to help you when reading or listening to German.

ab: *starting at, away, off*

aber: *but*

alle: *all*

als: *than, when*

also: *so, therefore*

an: *at, by, to*

anfangen: *to begin*

anrufen: *to telephone*

antworten: *to answer*

arbeiten: *to work*

auch: *also*

auf: *on*

aus: *from, out of*

außer: *except for*

beginnen: *to begin*

bei: *at, by, to, with*

bekommen: *to get*

besuchen: *to visit*

bezahlen: *to pay*

billig: *cheap, inexpensive*

bis: *by, until*

bleiben: *to stay*

brauchen: *to need*

bringen: *to bring*

da: *because*

damit: *so that*

dann: *then*

das (n.): *the*

dass: *that*

dauern: *to last*

dein (inf., sing.): *your*

denken: *to think*

denn: *for, because*
der (m.): *the*
dich (inf., sing., acc.): *you*
die (f.): *the*
dieser, diese, dieses: *this, that, these, those*
dir (inf., sing., dat.): *you*
doch: *but, nevertheless*
du (inf., sing.): *you*
durch: *through, by*
dürfen: *to be allowed to, may*
ein: *a, an*
einkaufen: *to go shopping*
empfehlen: *to recommend*
er: *he*
es: *it*
essen: *to eat*
etwas: *some, something, a little*
euch (inf., pl., acc./dat.): *you*
euer (inf., pl.): *your*
fahren: *to go, drive, travel*
fallen: *to fall*
falls: *if, whether, in case*
fernsehen: *to watch TV*
finden: *to find*
fliegen: *to fly*
fragen: *to ask*
für: *for*
geben: *to give*
gefallen: *to like, enjoy*
gehen: *to go*
gewinnen: *to win*
gewiss: *of course*
glücklich: *happy*
gut: *good*
haben: *to have*
halten: *to hold, stop*
heißen: *to be called, named*
helfen: *to help*
hier: *here*
hinter: *behind*

hoch: *high*
hoffen: *to hope*
höflich: *polite*
hören: *to hear*
ich: *I*
ihm: *him, it*
ihn: *him*
ihnen: *them*
Ihnen (form.): *you*
ihr: *you* (inf., pl.), *her, their*
Ihr (form.): *your*
immer: *always*
in: *in*
ja: *yes*
jetzt: *now*
jung: *young*
kaufen: *to buy*
kein: *no, not any*
kennen: *to know (be familiar with)*
klar: *of course*
kommen: *to come*
können: *to be able to, can*
kosten: *to cost*
lachen: *to laugh*
lang: *long*
langsam: *slow(ly)*
lassen: *to let, allow*
laufen: *to run*
leben: *to live*
lernen: *to learn*
lesen: *to read*
letzter: *last*
liegen: *to lie (down)*
machen: *to make, do*
man (impersonal): *you*
mein: *my*
mich: *me*
mir: *me*
mit: *with*
möchten: *would like to*
mögen: *to like (to)*

müssen: *to have to, must*
nach: *after, to*
nächster: *next*
nah: *near*
nass: *wet*
neben: *next to*
nehmen: *to take*
nein: *no*
nett: *nice*
nicht: *not*
nicht nur . . . sondern auch: *not only . . . but also*
noch: *still, yet*
nur: *only*
ob: *if, whether*
obwohl: *although*
oder: *or*
oft: *often*
ohne: *without*
passen: *to fit*
reden: *to talk*
regnen: *to rain*
reisen: *to travel*
sagen: *to say*
schenken: *to give (a present)*
schlafen: *to sleep*
schlecht: *bad*
schneiden: *to cut*
schreiben: *to write*
schwimmen: *to swim*
sehen: *to see*
sein: *to be*
sein: *his, its*
seit: *since, for*
setzen: *to sit down, to put*
sicher: *sure, certainly*
sie: *she, her, they, them*
Sie (form.): *you*
singen: *to sing*
so: *such, thus, so, as*
so . . . wie: *as . . . as*

sollen: *should*
sondern: *but rather*
spazieren gehen: *to walk*
spielen: *to play*
sprechen: *to speak, talk*
statt: *instead of*
stellen: *to put, stand*
studieren: *to study*
tanzen: *to dance*
tragen: *to wear, carry*
treffen: *to meet*
trinken: *to drink*
trocken: *dry*
trotz: *in spite of*
tun: *to do*
über: *over*
um: *around, at*
um . . . zu . . .: *in order to*
und: *and*
uns: *us*
unser: *our*
vergessen: *to forget*
verlieren: *to lose*
vernünftig: *sensible*
verstehen: *to understand*
vielleicht: *perhaps*
von: *from*
vor: *before, in front of*
während: *during*
wandern: *to hike*
wann: *when*
warten: *to wait*
warum: *why*
was: *what*
was für: *what kind of*
waschen: *to wash*
wegen: *because of*
weil: *because*
welcher, welche, welches: *which*
wenig: *little, few*
wenn: *if, when*

wer: *who*
werden: *to become, will*
werfen: *to throw*
wie: *how*
wie viel: *how much*
wie viele: *how many*
wieder: *again*
wir: *we*
wissen: *to know (fact)*
wo: *where*

woher: *from where*
wohin: *where to*
wohnen: *to live*
wollen: *to want (to)*
wunderschön: *lovely, gorgeous*
zahlen: *to pay*
zu: *to, at, too*
zu viel: *too much*
zu viele: *too many*
zwischen: *between*

Index

A

ab- prefix, 143
aber (but), 219
accusative case (acc.)
  about, 53
  adjective endings and, 184
  identifying common verb combinations in, 168–169
  kein (not), 112
  possessive adjective endings and first-person examples, 189
  preceded adjective and, 186
  reflexive pronouns in, 163
accusative prepositions, 232, 233–235
accusative/dative prepositions, 232, 240–242
active listening, 297
adding umlauts, in regular comparisons, 202–203
adjectives
  about, 175
  adverbs that modify, 210–211
  cognates, 176, 179–181
  collocations, 176, 181–183
  common endings for, 180
  comparing with adverbs, 197–215
  defined, 34
  describing appearance/personal traits, 176–178
  describing weather, 178–179
  forming endings on, 184–188
  helping, 183–188
  identifying unique adjective/adverb groups, 206–211
  opposites, 176–179
  participles that function as, 208–210
  possessive, 188–189
  practice questions, 176–183, 185–195
  regular, 198–203
  that act as nouns, 206–208

adverbs
  comparing with adjectives, 197–215
  defined, 34
  identifying unique adjective/adverb groups, 206–211
  participles that function as, 208–210
  regular, 198–203
  that modify adjectives, 210–211
-al ending, 180
als (as, when), 223
an (at, on, to), 241
an- prefix, 143
anfangen (to start, begin), 317
anrufen (to telephone), 317
-ant ending, 180
appearance, describing, 176–178
arbeiten (to work)
  about, 81
  forming in simple past tense, 265
  forming present perfect with, 251
  tense and, 311
articles
  defined, 34
  indefinite, 51
  missing, 51–52
auf (on, onto, to), 241
auf- prefix, 143
aus (from, out of), 236
aus- prefix, 143
außer (besides, except for), 236
außerhalb (outside of), 239
auxiliary verbs. *See* modal verbs

B

Bahnsteig (track), 17
be- prefix, 152
beginnen (to begin), 266–267, 317

irregular (weak) verbs. *See* weak verbs

-**isch** ending, 180

-**iv** ending, 180

K

kein (not), 111–114

kennen (to know [person]), 317

kennen- prefix, 144

kommen (to come)

about, 80, 317

tense and, 312–313

können (to be able to, can, to know how to do something)

about, 122, 125–127, 317

forming in simple past tense, 273

tense and, 316

L

Langsamer, bitte (More slowly, please), 12

lassen (to let), 317

laufen (to run), 317

lesen (to read)

about, 84, 317

tense and, 313

-**lich** ending, 180

liegen (to lie [situated]), 317

linking verbs, 54

los- prefix, 144

M

main verb, 123

male gender, 46

masculine gender, 46

meaning, finding through context, 36–37

miss- prefix, 153

missing articles, 51–52

mit (with, by), 236

mit- prefix, 144

mitbringen (to bring along), tense and, 313

möchten (would like to), 122, 129–130

modal verbs

about, 122–123

combining verbs with, 121–139

forming in simple past tense, 272–274

identifying, 122–123

tense and, 314–316

word order and, 123

mögen (to like [to], want to)

about, 122, 127–129, 317

tense and, 316

months, 22

müssen (must, to have to, need to)

about, 122, 131–132, 317

tense and, 316

N

nach (after, past, to), 236

nach- prefix, 144

narrative past. *See* simple past (narrative past) tense

native speakers, 295–296

near cognates, 71–72

neben (beside), 241

nehmen (to take), 84, 317

nein (no), 109

neuter gender, 46

nicht (not), 109–111

no, responding with, 109–114

nominative case (nom.)

about, 53, 54

adjective endings and, 184

kein (not), 112

possessive adjective endings and first-person examples, 189

preceded adjectives and, 186

reflexive pronouns in, 163

noun genders

about, 46

common, by subject, 47–48

About the Author

Wendy Foster grew up in Massachusetts. While studying in France, she traveled around Europe and became curious about the German language and culture. After graduating with a teaching certificate and a degree in French, she decided to return to Europe to study German. Her love of the Alps inspired her to live in Munich, where she spent 30 years. During that time, she studied German at the Language and Interpreting Institute in Munich, Germany, completed her MA in French at Middlebury College in Paris, and later learned Spanish in Spain. Her professional experience includes teaching German, French, and business English, as well as writing. Recently, she has been working from her home overlooking a spectacular salt marsh that constantly beckons her to go kayaking, walking, birdwatching, and swimming.

Dedication

This book is dedicated to the marsh; its wildlife; and the man I share it with, Phil.

Author's Acknowledgments

I must thank several people for their unwavering encouragement and support as I worked on this project. I thank my international friends Sandra Waller, Peter Hirschmann, Crista Zecher, and Udo Alter.

In addition, I would like to thank the editorial staff at Wiley for their insight, patience, and expertise, especially my project editor Paul Levesque, copy editor Keir Simpson, acquisitions editor Lindsay Lefevere, and technical editor Dr. Gerburg Garmann of the University of Indianapolis.

Publisher's Acknowledgments

Acquisitions Editor: Lindsay Lefevere

Senior Project Editor: Paul Levesque

Copy Editor: Keir Simpson

Tech Editor: Gerburg Garmann

Production Editor: Saikarthick Kumarasamy

Cover Image: © illpaxphotomatic/Shutterstock